Praise for Financial Pursuit *by Graydon G. Watters*

"The first edition of *Financial Pursuit* did what no other personal finance book had done effectively; Graydon showed that the aim of financial pursuit is not simply to make money but to make money with a view to improving the quality of your life. This new edition makes this point even more forcefully. It is packed with information, illustrations, charts, and quotes. It is visually pleasing and easy to read. With this new edition, Graydon firmly establishes *Financial Pursuit* as the 'King of the Hill' of investment books. No one who reads this book carefully can fail to achieve solid financial literacy. An impressive achievement. I strongly recommend this book."

—DR. CHUCK CHAKRAPANI,
Chairman, Investors Association of Canada,
Editor, Money Digest Magazine

"Canadians welcome education however the information must be clear, concise, and provide the investor with all aspects of investment strategies available. There is at last such a book called *Financial Pursuit*."

—G. GAIL KENNEDY, Author,
You're Worth It

"Graydon Watters has done a first-rate job of developing a program and support materials that anticipate and meet the retirement planning and savings needs of the average Canadian. This is a valuable and effective planning tool."

—JOHN MILNE, Executive Publisher,
Benefits Canada — Maclean Hunter

"Graydon Watters is the most dynamic, insightful, and just downright useful teacher of financial and lifestyle planning in Canada today. He has created the first total framework for planning our entire financial lifetime."

—DAN SULLIVAN, President,
The Strategic Coach

"*Financial Pursuit* and *Lifestyle Pursuit* are truly the dynamic duo of personal financial and retirement planning! The experience, insights, and energy embodied in these *Pursuits* combine to provide effective, user-friendly concepts and tools while inspiring and encouraging us to take control of our own financial destiny."

—JOHN MILLS,
Manager, Compensation and Benefits,
The Document Company — Xerox Canada

"Fundamentals are the keys to success. *Financial Pursuit* is clear, concise, and informative. Like a good mentor, the book will be a valuable aid in planning for a fulfilling retirement. Buy this book, but most importantly, use it!"

—JIM DOMANSKI, Vice-President,
Association of Mature Canadians—
Special Benefits Division

"My very sincere congratulations. An enormous, energetic, Canadian epistle—totally interesting and absorbing. Please order me four more copies and bill me. Again congratulations!!"

—ROBIN SOUTHGATE, Vice-President,
RBC Dominion Securities

"I am writing to you after reading your excellent book on personal finance, *Financial Pursuit*. May I congratulate you on the clarity as well as the quality of your presentation."

—TERENCE BUIE, President,
Dynamic Mutual Funds

"Your writing *Financial Pursuit* was a humanitarian act. A financially secure future is available to most Canadians. You have shown the way — a simple affordable way. I trust that people will wake up to the key — it's not how much you earn, but what you do with what you earn."

—TED HARRIS, Vice-President,
McLean Budden Limited

"I think the best thing about *Financial Pursuit* is that it truly represents the "Art of the Possible" no matter what stage you are at in your life. Your dreams can be transformed into reality if you are willing to adopt what you learn in this book."

—JEAN BUBBA, Pension Administrator,
Warner-Lambert Canada Inc.

"This is the best introduction and coverage of financial planning I have come across. Clear, concise, and to the point, it provides a common sense approach to the subject and should be the starting point for anyone wanting to retire with financial independence."

—VICTOR KLAAS, President,
Falcontec Investments

"Very readable yet logical and comprehensive. Full of practical advice and suggestions on finances and planning. A must-read for anyone concerned with their financial future."

—NORM WENTWORTH, National Manager,
Toyota Canada Inc.

"A remarkable achievement, this book integrates financial planning into life planning. Comprehensive, yet easy-to-read, Graydon's ideas will be of significant value to both the seasoned and the beginning investor. This is a book you will return to again and again. Reading it is a MUST."

—BRIAN J. DEERY, President,
Decision Assist Services, Inc.

"This is a formidable undertaking, lucid and comprehensive without excess detail. *Financial Pursuit* combines methodology with motivation."

—WILLIAM D. BRESSMER, Vice-President,
Leon Frazer & Associates Ltd.

"*Financial Pursuit* is an excellent complement to the more comprehensive *Lifestyle Pursuit*.....the most all encompassing program for pre-retirement planning I've come across and a definite "hit" in our company."

—JEFFREY SMITH,
Manager Profit Sharing & Stock Purchase,
Canadian Tire Corporation, Limited

"*Financial Pursuit* is outstanding — it provides an easy-to-follow plan for establishing a secure financial future, and the information is invaluable. I recommend it for anyone, of any age."

—ALISON BUCHANAN, Training Specialist,
MDS Health Group Limited

"It's worth spending the time to decide how to manage your money. *Financial Pursuit* allows you to do that in an easy to follow format. Well done!"

—DOUG MANSON,
Human Resources Officer,
Mutual Life of Canada

"Graydon — I did not read the original version of *Financial Pursuit*, nor have I had the honour of attending one of your workshops. But after seeing the table of contents, I want to order 20 copies for myself, my family, and our team of professionals here at ML Communications."

—MARY LOU GUTSCHER, President,
ML Communications Inc.

"*Financial Pursuit* brings to the average Canadian looking at retirement the financial and lifestyle know-how needed to make this exciting stage of life truly — the best of your life!"

—DAVID A. FRENCH, Chair,
Pension Investment Association
of Canada (PIAC)

"The first edition of *Financial Pursuit* set a new standard in simplifying, explaining, and systematizing complex financial planning issues. Once again, Graydon Watters offers a penetrating assessment — and a comprehensive game plan — that can benefit investors in all walks of life who are looking to build financial independence."

—PHIL CUNNINGHAM,
Senior Vice-President,
Mackenzie Financial Corporation

About the Author

GRAYDON G. WATTERS, *B. Comm., F.C.S.I., C.F.P.*, is the Founder and President of FKI Financial Knowledge Inc. He has devoted thirty-five years to the financial services industry, including a decade in banking and two decades in investment counselling. During this time he has assisted thousands of individuals with their investment decisions.

During the last several years Graydon Watters has pioneered the development of several exciting audio-visual presentations on financial and pre-retirement planning education. He wrote the best-selling book, *Financial Pursuit,* in 1988 for all age groups and developed a pre-retirement planning course, *Lifestyle Pursuit,* in 1990 for the 45 plus age group.

Graydon Watters facilitates numerous seminars and workshops every year; has been on radio and television; and has been quoted in many newspapers and financial publications. Testimonials to Graydon refer to his enthusiasm, commitment, dynamism, and innovative educational programs and systems. His seminars and workshops are tailored to suit the specific audience and he has lectured to corporate and professional audiences throughout North America.

FKI Financial Knowledge Inc. designs and delivers educational seminars and workshops for employers and their employees, as well as for professional associations. The main emphasis of their presentations is achieving financial security, a balanced lifestyle, and a retirement with dignity.

Graydon Watters and his associate facilitators are available for seminars and workshops. Please contact the following:

FKI Financial Knowledge Inc.
70 Nably Court
Scarborough, Ontario
M1B 2K9
Telephone: (416) 292-7020 Fax: (416) 292-2064

Financial Pursuit

Canada's working guide to personal wealth
How to retire with financial dignity

Graydon G. Watters

FKI

The author wishes to express thanks and appreciation to the following who granted permission to use their material:

1985 Commissioner's Individual Disability Table, Toronto, Ontario, for chart "Average Disability Which Lasts Over 90 Days," and "Number Disabled."

Andex Associates, Windsor, Ontario, for charts "Best Performing Assets," "Historical Risk/Reward Ratio — Long-term Normal Range of Results," and "Risk/Reward Ratio" from Andex Chart for Canadian Investors, 1994, by Anthony Di Meo and Dexter Robinson.

CPF Publishing Inc., Georgetown, Ontario, for chart "Asset Mix of Canadian Pension Funds."

Canada Trustco, London, Ontario, for chart modified entitled "Flow Chart of Executor's Duties and Responsibilities."

Jim Domanski, Vice-President Marketing, Association of Mature Canadians, Toronto, Ontario, for his work on Extended Health Care and Dental Insurance Options.

Health and Welfare Canada, Ottawa, Ontario, for statistics from their income security programs: Old Age Security, Guaranteed Income Supplement, and Canada Pension Plan.

The Investment Funds Institute of Canada, Toronto, Ontario, for historical data on chart "Projected Growth for Mutual Funds."

Jonathan Cape Ltd., London, England, for permission to quote from *Goldfinger* by Ian Fleming with acknowledgement to Glidrose Productions Ltd.

Realtors® Land Institute, Chicago, Illnois, for permission to quote from article "Procrastination."

Morgan Stanley & Co. Inc., New York, N.Y., for charts "The Composition of the World Markets," and "Times Change — So Should Your Investment Strategies."

Statistics Canada, Toronto, Ontario, for chart "The Consumer Price Index," "Your Life Expectancy," and "Individuals Per Tax Bracket."

Nicholas Stodin, Senior Financial Consultant, Toronto, Ontario, for his work on the Rate of Growth of Investable Capital (ROGI) and his contribution on income and life protection.

Jim Todd, C.A., R.F.P., Todd & Associates, Scarborough, Ontario, for his work and contribution on income tax planning.

The Toronto Stock Exchange, Toronto, Ontario, for charts on "How to Read Newspaper Listings," "You Can Participate in Business Expansion," "Toronto Stock Exchange Total Return Index," and "Toronto Stock Exchange — 14 Group Indices."

Leon Tuey Inc., Vancouver, British Columbia, for the quote from article "Important Market Factors."

Copy Editor: Susan Wallace-Cox
Design: Bold Graphic Communication Ltd.
Prepress and Film: Acuity Computer Services
Printed and bound in Toronto, Canada.

Canadian Cataloguing in Publication Data

Watters, Graydon G., 1943

    Financial pursuit: Canada's working guide to personal wealth: how to retire with financial dignity.

    2nd ed.

    Includes bibliographical references and index.

    ISBN 0-9693593-4-9

    1. Finance, Personal—Canada. 2. Retirement—Canada—Planning. 3. Retirement income—Canada.
I. FKI Financial Knowledge Inc.   II. Title.
HG179.W38 1994   332.024'01   C94-932237-7

Disclaimer

Every effort has been made to contact and acknowledge copyright holders of material used in this book. The author/publisher would welcome any further information pertaining to errors or omissions in order to make corrections in subsequent editions.

    The information contained herein has been obtained from sources which we believe reliable but we cannot guarantee its accuracy or completeness. This book is not and under no circumstances is to be construed as an offer to sell or the solicitation of an offer to buy any securities. This book is furnished on the basis and understanding that FKI Financial Knowledge Inc. is to be under no responsibility or liability whatsoever in respect thereof.

Contents

SEVEN

Territories of Financial Success 57

EIGHT

Investment Market Forces 69

NINE

Investment Planning 77

TEN

The Professional Financial Planner 87

List of Tables, Charts and Worksheets

THIRTEEN

Income and Life Protection

FOURTEEN

Income Tax Planning

FIFTEEN

Basic Steps in Retirement Planning

SIXTEEN

Your Sources of Retirement Income

SEVENTEEN

Registered Retirement Savings Plans

E I G H T E E N

RRSP Maturity Options

N I N E T E E N

Giving it Away—Estate Planning

T W E N T Y

Planning for the Opportunity of a Lifetime

A P P E N D I C E S

Acknowledgements

No one writes a book alone — it takes the enormous efforts of many people to ensure the book is a success. And what a success *Financial Pursuit* has been with sales of 25,000 copies which is excellent by Canadian standards!

The launch of the first edition of the book was due in part to the support of people like Stan Reid, my agent; Hilton Tudhope, my editor; and Jim O'Donnell, the past President of Mackenzie Financial Corporation, who ensured the book's success by purchasing and distributing numerous copies to members of the financial services community.

Countless hours have been spent preparing this revised second edition of *Financial Pursuit*. Many thanks to Rick Pearce for his guidance through the maze of the publishing world; to Michael Ortelli and Mario Zeskoski for their hours of creative design and computer time; and to Susan Wallace-Cox for her copy-editing skills and her positive attitude at all times.

Thanks to Jim Todd for his work on income tax planning; to Nick Stodin for the use of his "ROGI" model, and his assistance with the descriptions of insurance strategies; to Stephen Campbell and Steve Bernhut for several articles; to my network of coaches: Dan Sullivan, Hardie Collins, Stuart McKay, Victor Klaas, Mary Lou Gutscher and many other friends and colleagues for their knowledge and inspiration.

Thanks also to my team at FKI Financial Knowledge Inc. including my associates Jack Wright, Peter Ellis, Russell Todd, and Sheldon Denesiuk; and to all of our workshop facilitators; and a very special thank you to Penny Butt for her countless hours of word processing, reviewing, and reworking the manuscript.

And finally, my deepest thanks to my children Christina, Carolyn, and Matthew — you have all paid a substantial price called T-I-M-E, and to my wife and closest friend, Linda. God bless you all for your support, encouragement, and insight. May all your personal financial planning and retirement dreams come true.

G.G.W.

Preface

During the 1980s two or three days a week I commuted to Toronto by train. When I passed through Union Station I saw people lined up six deep at the lottery booths. In the concourse of my office building I saw the same thing. The lottery gambling habit was a $125–$150-a-month habit for one of the secretaries at my office. Imagine that kind of expenditure when the odds of losing Ontario's Lotto 649 are 13,999,999 in 14,000,000! Yet people go ahead and buy them anyway. I do admit to buying a lottery ticket now and then, but for some, it is their investment program—and a very poor one at that.

People who buy lottery tickets every week could earn the same amount a lottery pays by the time they retire if they would review their finances and begin a balanced investment program. Unfortunately, this option seldom crosses their minds. It has crossed yours, thank goodness.

Why is there such ignorance about investing? Why do Canadians know so little about the magic and power of compound interest? Why doesn't our educational system allow more time for teaching the practical application of basic mathematics to personal finances? One of the grave failures of our educational system is that there are few if any pre-college courses on money and the management of money. Post-college education is no better. Chartered banks, insurance and trust companies, and investment dealers have had over 100 years to educate the public. But like the schools, they have neglected this very important responsibility.

After three decades in the banking and investment industry and several years presenting seminars on personal financial planning to groups across the country, I took the matter to heart in 1988 and prepared *Financial Pursuit: Canada's Working Guide to Personal Wealth: How to Retire With Financial Dignity*.

This revised second edition of the "Working Guide" is your financial counsellor on paper. It contains all the techniques and advice you need to take control of your finances and start accumulating wealth. But knowing how dry and intimidating financial matters can appear, I have attempted to include, between the lines and on the lines, the factor that is so often absent from financial publications—encouragement. Success comes when you know you can achieve. So, I hope you find this book to be not only a valuable reference, but also a trusted "friend" as you work toward your financial freedom.

Graydon G. Watters
Toronto, September 1994

Introduction

Your health is your most important asset. If your health is failing, no amount of money in the world can give you comfort. Financial resources are your second most important asset through life, especially at retirement, because the amount of money you have dictates the lifestyle choices you can make.

There is not a great deal I can suggest to help your physical and mental health, other than to discuss proper diet, nutrition, and physical fitness programs. Much of your health is directly related to genetics, as well as the sum total of your cumulative life habits to date, and therefore regarding your health, I can really only hope that you are blessed with longevity.

Your financial future, however, is another matter. I can be instrumental in helping you develop a prescription for your future financial success and a retirement with financial dignity. Lottery tickets won't do it for you, Government can't do it for you, and your yearly earnings most certainly won't provide you with the cushion of financial security you will want when you reach retirement. The only certain way is to take the initiative yourself. Helping people take the right steps toward gaining financial control is my strength.

Every year you hear about hundreds of investment opportunities from friends, associates, and acquaintances. These "tips" are usually vague, out of context, questionable, and produce mixed results. The "Working Guide" will increase your investment knowledge so that you will make informed decisions that will enable you to accumulate wealth. It is a documented fact that in both Canada and the United States 9 out of 10 people do not acquire financial freedom by retirement age. They struggle daily to put food on the table and pay the rent. When you look at your long-term approach to finances, what leads you to believe you won't be one of the nine? Do you, in fact, have a long-term approach? You should, and you will need to. Without an active financial direction in your life, chances are you will join the ranks of the struggling.

Financial Pursuit can help you beat these disheartening odds. My job is to assist you in the decision-making process by helping you to establish priorities that will enable you to take the reins and begin to plan your future. In order to give you the knowledge and confidence to take control, this book addresses all aspects of financial planning that are necessary to face the various stages of your life: Personal Financial Planning, Insurance Planning, Income Tax Planning, Investment Planning, Retirement Planning, and Estate Planning.

It really isn't possible to talk about one area of the financial planning process without discussing the other areas because they are all interrelated. I will be directing you through the various exercises step-by-step so that you finish the "Working Guide" with the knowledge and ability to take control of your financial future and make it everything you want it to be.

The "Working Guide" will give you a detailed view of the personal financial planning process by supplying you with essential background information and tools to complete essential exercises. It will also show you how to develop the winning strategies you need to succeed in the face of the complex and ever-changing world of investment and finance.

In order to see your financial future realized, you will have to develop the following winning strategies:

- Pay yourself first (establish a savings program).
- Build a nest egg as early as possible during your working career.
- Learn that money makes money, and the money that money makes, makes more money.
- Be a self-starter and stay with your goals.
- Be enthusiastic about your goals and plans.
- Be aware of too much planning and very little action.
- Include your spouse in the decision-making process.
- Take prompt action.
- Exercise caution, but do not be overly cautious.
- Use self-discipline to achieve your goals.

In this book I will share a number of ideas with you about your true financial potential. I hope and trust they will inspire. Because your lifestyle today is probably exactly where you imagined it would be (though probably not what you hoped it would be), I will have done my job if I can leave you somewhat disturbed and uneasy about settling for your present financial position. Remember, 9 out of 10 people struggle through retirement. I hope to educate you in the world of finance, to convey to you the essential concepts of time, money and compounding (and how to use them for your benefit), and inspire you to put your knowledge into action by setting meaningful goals for yourself. In the words of the late Dr. Norman Vincent Peale, "Shoot for the moon, and even if you miss, you will still land up amongst the stars."

This is a book of seed ideas for your financial success and I believe it will lead you to take the necessary steps to that success. To that end I am pleased to share what I know. There will be many choices and obstacles to encounter during your financial planning journey. But remember, obstacles are what you see when you take your eyes off your goal.

Mark 9:23 in the Bible says, "All things are possible to him who believeth." Let me say at the outset that there will be no such thing as failure, just positive results if you have a positive mental attitude which is of paramount importance as you take control of your financial future. The responsibility to grow is yours, and I'm sure you will stretch yourself if you give the ideas contained here your best effort.

A Dollar in Perspective

*Ask both what you can do for your dollar
and what your dollar can do for you.*

Cost Versus Your Ability to Purchase

You may have heard the story of the woman who complained about the cost of a loaf of bread at $1.40. Here is what is involved in the price of that loaf:

- The farmer plows the soil, sows the seed, reaps and harvests the crop, and sends the harvest to the miller.
- The miller grinds the wheat to flour.
- The baker buys the flour and makes the bread.
- The bread is delivered by truck to the stores.
- The store stocks and sells the bread.

The point is not whether $1.40 is too much for a loaf of bread. It may be, but we can't change the price anyway. However, we can change our ability to purchase it. We *can* seem to make a dollar more than it is worth, because it is worth less and less every day.

What a Dollar Can Do For You

What is a dollar? We all know what a dollar is worth today in terms of what it will buy in goods or services. But what will our dollar buy in goods or services in 10 or 20 years if inflation averages 5% per year? (See Table 1-2) In just 20 years, the purchasing power of a dollar today would decline to just 0.38¢.

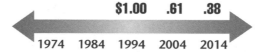

	$1.00	.61	.38	
1974	1984	1994	2004	2014

Look at what has happened to prices on these products during the last 30 years.

	1964	1994
Margarine (1 lb. / 454 g.)	$0.29	$1.85
Ground Beef (1 lb. / 454 g.)	$0.70	$1.99
Milk (1 litre)	$0.30	$1.37
Cotton Dress Shirt	$5.00	$40.00
Regular Leaded Gas (1 litre)	$0.08	$0.53
Passenger Car (North American average)	$4,000.00	$17,459.00

You can see what the ravages of inflation in our economy can do to the future purchasing power of the dollar. A dollar is

If you cannot make money on one dollar —if you do not coax one dollar to work hard for you, you won't know how to make money out of one hundred thousand dollars.

E.S. Kinnear

only worth a dollar at a specific point in time. In 10, 20, and 30 years from now, assuming the following base prices for 1994, what might these same products cost you if inflation were to average 5%? Use Table 1-3 to follow the calculations.

	1994	2004	2014	2024
Margarine (1 lb. / 454 g.)	$1.85	$3.01	$4.90	$7.99
Ground Beef (1 lb. / 454 g.)	$1.99	$3.24	$5.27	$8.60
Milk (1 litre)	$1.37	$2.23	$3.63	$5.92
Cotton Dress Shirt	$40.00	$65.20	$106.00	$172.80
Regular Leaded Gas (1 litre)	$0.53	$0.86	$1.40	$2.29
Passenger Car (North American Average)	$17,459.00	$28,458.00	$46,266.00	$75,422.00

Consumer prices have increased dramatically over the past few decades. This constant inflationary trend has already eaten away 70% of the dollar's value over the past 20 years. It is not unreasonable to assume that inflation will continue averaging somewhere between 4% and 6% over the long term. Will your earnings increase to match the factors affecting prices?

Canada's inflation rate history		
AVERAGE ANNUAL COMPOUND INFLATION RATES		
	Number of Years	**Inflation Rate**
1989-93	5	3.4%
1984-93	10	3.8%
1979-93	15	5.8%
1974-93	20	6.7%
1969-93	25	6.3%
1964-93	30	5.8%
1950-93	43	4.5%

How Much Money Can I Earn in My Lifetime?

Let's assume you are age 25 and have just started your working career. If you work for the next 40 years and your base salary today is $30,000, your total lifetime earnings will be $2,850,765, assuming your salary keeps pace with an inflation rate of 4%. If your salary were to keep pace with inflation at 6%, the total would amount to $4,642,859. (see Table 1-1)

These lifetime earning figures seem astronomical, but how much of those earnings will you save for a comfortable retirement? What you save is relative, based on inflation and the cost of goods and services. For example, the average price of a house in Toronto during the spring of 1994 was in excess of $200,000. What would that house cost over the next 40 years if inflation averaged 4% or 6%? (Use Table 1-3)

	Inflation at 4%	**Inflation at 6%**
1994	$200,000	$200,000
2004	$296,000	$358,000
2014	$438,000	$642,000
2024	$648,000	$1,148,000
2034	$960,000	$2,058,000

These figures are revelatory. You would have to earn millions of dollars per year in order to afford to own a home in the future.

Lifeline

To begin the financial planning process, it is important that you have an understanding of time. You see, time is your greatest ally. You have a lifeline between birth and death and you possess a bank of time which is yours to use in any manner you choose.

TABLE 1-1: LIFETIME EARNINGS POTENTIAL

Year	Age	Base Earnings $30,000 with 4% Annual Increase	Base Earnings $30,000 with 6% Annual Increase
1	25	$ 30,000	$ 30,000
2	26	31,200	31,800
3	27	32,448	33,708
4	28	33,746	35,730
5	29	35,096	37,874
6	30	36,500	40,147
7	31	37,960	42,556
8	32	39,478	45,109
9	33	41,057	47,815
10	34	42,699	50,684
11	35	44,407	53,725
12	36	46,184	56,949
13	37	48,031	60,366
14	38	49,952	63,988
15	39	51,950	67,827
16	40	54,028	71,897
17	41	56,189	76,211
18	42	58,437	80,783
19	43	60,774	85,630
20	44	63,205	90,768
21	45	65,734	96,214
22	46	68,363	101,987
23	47	71,098	108,106
24	48	73,941	114,592
25	49	76,899	121,468
26	50	79,975	128,756
27	51	83,174	136,481
28	52	86,501	144,670
29	53	89,961	153,351
30	54	93,560	162,552
31	55	97,302	172,305
32	56	101,194	182,643
33	57	105,242	193,602
34	58	109,451	205,218
35	59	113,829	217,531
36	60	118,383	230,583
37	61	123,118	244,418
38	62	128,043	259,083
39	63	133,164	274,628
40	64	138,491	291,105
Total Lifetime Earnings		**$2,850,765**	**$4,642,859**

> You cannot help men by doing for them what they could and should do for themselves.
> **Abraham Lincoln**

TABLE 1-2: COMPOUND DISCOUNT TABLE FOR $1

ANNUAL RATE OF RETURN

Year	1%	2%	3%	4%	5%	6%	7%	8%	9%	10%
1	0.99	0.98	0.97	0.96	0.95	0.94	0.93	0.93	0.92	0.91
2	0.98	0.96	0.94	0.92	0.91	0.89	0.87	0.86	0.84	0.83
3	0.97	0.94	0.92	0.89	0.86	0.84	0.82	0.79	0.77	0.75
4	0.96	0.92	0.89	0.85	0.82	0.79	0.76	0.74	0.71	0.68
5	0.95	0.91	0.86	0.82	0.78	0.75	0.71	0.68	0.65	0.62
6	0.94	0.89	0.84	0.79	0.75	0.70	0.67	0.63	0.60	0.56
7	0.93	0.87	0.81	0.76	0.71	0.67	0.62	0.58	0.55	0.51
8	0.92	0.85	0.79	0.73	0.68	0.63	0.58	0.54	0.50	0.47
9	0.91	0.84	0.77	0.70	0.64	0.59	0.54	0.50	0.46	0.42
10	0.91	0.82	0.74	0.68	0.61	0.56	0.51	0.46	0.42	0.39
11	0.90	0.80	0.72	0.65	0.58	0.53	0.48	0.43	0.39	0.35
12	0.89	0.79	0.70	0.62	0.56	0.50	0.44	0.40	0.36	0.32
13	0.88	0.77	0.68	0.60	0.53	0.47	0.41	0.37	0.33	0.29
14	0.87	0.76	0.66	0.58	0.51	0.44	0.39	0.34	0.30	0.26
15	0.86	0.74	0.64	0.56	0.48	0.42	0.36	0.32	0.27	0.24
16	0.85	0.73	0.62	0.53	0.46	0.39	0.34	0.29	0.25	0.22
17	0.84	0.71	0.61	0.51	0.44	0.37	0.32	0.27	0.23	0.20
18	0.84	0.70	0.59	0.49	0.42	0.35	0.30	0.25	0.21	0.18
19	0.83	0.69	0.57	0.47	0.40	0.33	0.28	0.23	0.19	0.16
20	0.82	0.67	0.55	0.46	0.38	0.31	0.26	0.21	0.18	0.15
21	0.81	0.66	0.54	0.44	0.36	0.29	0.24	0.20	0.16	0.14
22	0.80	0.65	0.52	0.42	0.34	0.28	0.23	0.18	0.15	0.12
23	0.80	0.63	0.51	0.41	0.33	0.26	0.21	0.17	0.14	0.11
24	0.79	0.62	0.49	0.39	0.31	0.25	0.20	0.16	0.13	0.10
25	0.78	0.61	0.48	0.38	0.30	0.23	0.18	0.15	0.12	0.09
30	0.74	0.55	0.41	0.31	0.23	0.17	0.13	0.10	0.08	0.06
35	0.71	0.50	0.36	0.25	0.18	0.13	0.09	0.07	0.05	0.04
40	0.67	0.45	0.31	0.21	0.14	0.10	0.07	0.05	0.03	0.02

ANNUAL RATE OF RETURN

Year	11%	12%	13%	14%	15%	16%	17%	18%	19%	20%
1	0.90	0.89	0.88	0.88	0.87	0.86	0.85	0.85	0.84	0.83
2	0.81	0.80	0.78	0.77	0.76	0.74	0.73	0.72	0.71	0.69
3	0.73	0.71	0.69	0.67	0.66	0.64	0.62	0.61	0.59	0.58
4	0.66	0.64	0.61	0.59	0.57	0.55	0.53	0.52	0.50	0.48
5	0.59	0.57	0.54	0.52	0.50	0.48	0.46	0.44	0.42	0.40
6	0.53	0.51	0.48	0.46	0.43	0.41	0.39	0.37	0.35	0.33
7	0.48	0.45	0.43	0.40	0.38	0.35	0.33	0.31	0.30	0.28
8	0.43	0.40	0.38	0.35	0.33	0.31	0.28	0.27	0.25	0.23
9	0.39	0.36	0.33	0.31	0.28	0.26	0.24	0.23	0.21	0.19
10	0.35	0.32	0.29	0.27	0.25	0.23	0.21	0.19	0.18	0.16
11	0.32	0.29	0.26	0.24	0.21	0.20	0.18	0.16	0.15	0.13
12	0.29	0.26	0.23	0.21	0.19	0.17	0.15	0.14	0.12	0.11
13	0.26	0.23	0.20	0.18	0.16	0.15	0.13	0.12	0.10	0.09
14	0.23	0.20	0.18	0.16	0.14	0.13	0.11	0.10	0.09	0.08
15	0.21	0.18	0.16	0.14	0.12	0.11	0.09	0.08	0.07	0.06
16	0.19	0.16	0.14	0.12	0.11	0.09	0.08	0.07	0.06	0.05
17	0.17	0.15	0.13	0.11	0.09	0.08	0.07	0.06	0.05	0.05
18	0.15	0.13	0.11	0.09	0.08	0.07	0.06	0.05	0.04	0.04
19	0.14	0.12	0.10	0.08	0.07	0.06	0.05	0.04	0.04	0.03
20	0.12	0.10	0.09	0.07	0.06	0.05	0.04	0.04	0.03	0.03
21	0.11	0.09	0.08	0.06	0.05	0.04	0.04	0.03	0.03	0.02
22	0.10	0.08	0.07	0.06	0.05	0.04	0.03	0.03	0.02	0.02
23	0.09	0.07	0.06	0.05	0.04	0.03	0.03	0.02	0.02	0.02
24	0.08	0.07	0.05	0.04	0.03	0.03	0.02	0.02	0.02	0.01
25	0.07	0.06	0.05	0.04	0.03	0.02	0.02	0.02	0.01	0.01
30	0.04	0.03	0.03	0.02	0.02	0.01	0.01	0.01	0.01	0.00
35	0.03	0.02	0.01	0.01	0.01	0.01	0.00	0.00	0.00	0.00
40	0.02	0.01	0.01	0.01	0.00	0.00	0.00	0.00	0.00	0.00

TABLE GUIDE

Under Annual Rate of Return column of 5% and End of Year 20 line, find 0.38 where column and line intersect.

TABLE 1-3: FUTURE VALUE OF $1, COMPOUNDED ANNUALLY BEGINNING OF YEAR

ANNUAL RATE OF RETURN

Year	1%	2%	3%	4%	5%	6%	7%	8%	9%	10%
1	1.01	1.02	1.03	1.04	1.05	1.06	1.07	1.08	1.09	1.10
2	1.02	1.04	1.06	1.08	1.10	1.12	1.14	1.17	1.19	1.21
3	1.03	1.06	1.09	1.12	1.16	1.19	1.23	1.26	1.30	1.33
4	1.04	1.08	1.13	1.17	1.22	1.26	1.31	1.36	1.41	1.46
5	1.05	1.10	1.16	1.22	1.28	1.34	1.40	1.47	1.54	1.61
6	1.06	1.13	1.19	1.27	1.34	1.42	1.50	1.59	1.68	1.77
7	1.07	1.15	1.23	1.32	1.41	1.50	1.61	1.71	1.83	1.95
8	1.08	1.17	1.27	1.37	1.48	1.59	1.72	1.85	1.99	2.14
9	1.09	1.20	1.30	1.42	1.55	1.69	1.84	2.00	2.17	2.36
10	1.10	1.22	1.34	1.48	1.63	1.79	1.97	2.16	2.37	2.59
11	1.12	1.24	1.38	1.54	1.71	1.90	2.10	2.33	2.58	2.85
12	1.13	1.27	1.43	1.60	1.80	2.01	2.25	2.52	2.81	3.14
13	1.14	1.29	1.47	1.67	1.89	2.13	2.41	2.72	3.07	3.45
14	1.15	1.32	1.51	1.73	1.98	2.26	2.58	2.94	3.34	3.80
15	1.16	1.35	1.56	1.80	2.08	2.40	2.76	3.17	3.64	4.18
16	1.17	1.37	1.60	1.87	2.18	2.54	2.95	3.43	3.97	4.59
17	1.18	1.40	1.65	1.95	2.29	2.69	3.16	3.70	4.33	5.05
18	1.20	1.43	1.70	2.03	2.41	2.85	3.38	4.00	4.72	5.56
19	1.21	1.46	1.75	2.11	2.53	3.03	3.62	4.32	5.14	6.12
20	1.22	1.49	1.81	2.19	2.65	3.21	3.87	4.66	5.60	6.73
21	1.23	1.52	1.86	2.28	2.79	3.40	4.14	5.03	6.11	7.40
22	1.24	1.55	1.92	2.37	2.93	3.60	4.43	5.44	6.66	8.14
23	1.26	1.58	1.97	2.46	3.07	3.82	4.74	5.87	7.26	8.95
24	1.27	1.61	2.03	2.56	3.23	4.05	5.07	6.34	7.91	9.85
25	1.28	1.64	2.09	2.67	3.39	4.29	5.43	6.85	8.62	10.83
30	1.35	1.81	2.43	3.24	4.32	5.74	7.61	10.06	13.27	17.45
35	1.42	2.00	2.81	3.95	5.52	7.69	10.68	14.79	20.41	28.10
40	1.49	2.21	3.26	4.80	7.04	10.29	14.97	21.72	31.41	45.26

ANNUAL RATE OF RETURN

Year	11%	12%	13%	14%	15%	16%	17%	18%	19%	20%
1	1.11	1.12	1.13	1.14	1.15	1.16	1.17	1.18	1.19	1.20
2	1.23	1.25	1.28	1.30	1.32	1.35	1.37	1.39	1.42	1.44
3	1.37	1.40	1.44	1.48	1.52	1.56	1.60	1.64	1.69	1.73
4	1.52	1.57	1.63	1.69	1.75	1.81	1.87	1.94	2.01	2.07
5	1.69	1.76	1.84	1.93	2.01	2.10	2.19	2.29	2.39	2.49
6	1.87	1.97	2.08	2.19	2.31	2.44	2.57	2.70	2.84	2.99
7	2.08	2.21	2.35	2.50	2.66	2.83	3.00	3.19	3.38	3.58
8	2.30	2.48	2.66	2.85	3.06	3.28	3.51	3.76	4.02	4.30
9	2.56	2.77	3.00	3.25	3.52	3.80	4.11	4.44	4.79	5.16
10	2.84	3.11	3.39	3.71	4.05	4.41	4.81	5.23	5.69	6.19
11	3.15	3.48	3.84	4.23	4.65	5.12	5.62	6.18	6.78	7.43
12	3.50	3.90	4.33	4.82	5.35	5.94	6.58	7.29	8.06	8.92
13	3.88	4.36	4.90	5.49	6.15	6.89	7.70	8.60	9.60	10.70
14	4.31	4.89	5.53	6.26	7.08	7.99	9.01	10.15	11.42	12.84
15	4.78	5.47	6.25	7.14	8.14	9.27	10.54	11.97	13.59	15.41
16	5.31	6.13	7.07	8.14	9.36	10.75	12.33	14.13	16.17	18.49
17	5.90	6.87	7.99	9.28	10.76	12.47	14.43	16.67	19.24	22.19
18	6.54	7.69	9.02	10.58	12.38	14.46	16.88	19.67	22.90	26.62
19	7.26	8.61	10.20	12.06	14.23	16.78	19.75	23.21	27.25	31.95
20	8.06	9.65	11.52	13.74	16.37	19.46	23.11	27.39	32.43	38.34
21	8.95	10.80	13.02	15.67	18.82	22.57	27.03	32.32	38.59	46.01
22	9.93	12.10	14.71	17.86	21.64	26.19	31.63	38.14	45.92	55.21
23	11.03	13.55	16.63	20.36	24.89	30.38	37.01	45.01	54.65	66.25
24	12.24	15.18	18.79	23.21	28.63	35.24	43.30	53.11	65.03	79.50
25	13.59	17.00	21.23	26.46	32.92	40.87	50.66	62.67	77.39	95.40
30	22.89	29.96	39.12	50.95	66.21	85.85	111.06	143.37	184.68	237.38
35	38.57	52.80	72.07	98.10	133.18	180.31	243.50	328.00	440.70	590.67
40	65.00	93.05	132.78	188.88	267.86	378.72	533.87	750.38	1051.67	1469.77

TABLE GUIDE

Under Annual Rate of Return column of 4% and End of Year 40 line, find 4.80 where column and line intersect. This is the future value of $1. Now multiply $200,000 cost of house today by 4.80 to obtain cost of house in 40 years. Result $960,000. Follow same process for inflation at 6%.

As you read this book, you may be in the early or latter stages of your working career. You are the best judge of where you are on your lifeline and the amount of time you have to reach your goals. It has often been said that the two things in life that are certain are death and taxes. Most of us live our lives believing that death is a long time away from the present—at some time in our mid-seventies if we're male and later seventies if we're female, according to actuarial statistics. Assuming you are an average male or female, you have an allotment of time to put to good use.

There are three types of time:

Past Time   It's dead, we can't recapture it, we can't have it back, and it has no value.

Future Time   It has not been born yet, we can't use it, it hasn't arrived, and it has no value until it arrives.

Present Time   It's arrived, it's the here and now, and it has value.

> The best time to buy stock is when you have the money.
>
> **John Templeton**

As you read this book, you are in present time. We all work and play in a contest with time and it is now, in the present, that you and I have a chance to communicate. In the next two chapters, I will provide you with an overview of financial planning and the power of compounding. As you acquire knowledge and new life skills in these early chapters, you will be prepared, by the time you get to Chapter 4, to make an honest assessment of what your personal finances are at present and what your financial planning potential is for the future. The major working papers to determine your net worth, cash flow, and lifetime earnings are found in Chapter 4. As you progress through Chapters 5 to 21, you will find the book acts as a gentle persuader to nudge you into taking control of your life. My mission is to provide you with the knowledge, skill, and appropriate tools for your financial pursuit. Your mission is to agree to stretch yourself and give this book your best effort so that all your dreams and aspirations for the future may come true.

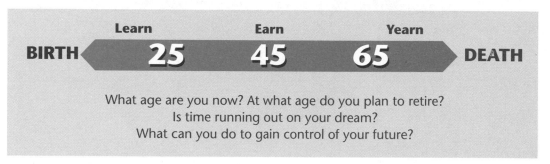

What age are you now? At what age do you plan to retire?
Is time running out on your dream?
What can you do to gain control of your future?

Personal Financial Planning: An Overview

Are you waiting for luck to solve your financial future?
The odds are against you. Whether you do it yourself
or hire a professional, you have to make financial plans
today if you want a comfortable tomorrow.

Financial planning is an ongoing process and although it is primarily designed to lead to a comfortable retirement, it is in fact as much concerned with the present as it is with the future.

I am often amazed at how hard people work to acquire money. I am even more amazed at how little they do with their money aside from spending it. What amazes me most, is how few people make their money earn more money so that they won't have to work their fingers to the bone until the day they die. It surprises me because financial freedom is easily attainable.

Financial freedom does mean planning and acting for the long term. If you are like most people, the future seems to be like a distant shore, too far off to see, and too far off to be concerned with. Occupied with the stresses and demands of the present and with making ends meet, you run as hard as you can to deal with what is urgent and routine. The future is a pleasant reverie, a daydream in which you spend warm, relaxing hours idly doing what you please. But how much time do you spend making sure that you can have your dream? Probably precious little.

Start now. Think about your financial fitness. Do you have a realistic plan for your financial independence? Complete the following quiz and find out.

> Lack of money is the
> root of all evil.
> **George Bernard Shaw**

WORKSHEET 2-1: YOUR FINANCIAL FITNESS CHECKUP

		Yes	No
1	Do you have a realistic plan for financial independence that will allow you to retire with financial dignity?	☐	☐
2	Have you established long-term financial goals and set specific objectives?	☐	☐
3	Is your cash flow under control—have you made room to pay yourself first in order to save for the future?	☐	☐
4	Have you taken appropriate action to shelter yourself from the ravages of inflation and deflation?	☐	☐

		Yes	No
5	Do you prepare monthly budgets and an annual net worth statement?	☐	☐
6	Are your investments arranged in a tax-effective manner?	☐	☐
7	Are you taking maximum advantage of tax-sheltered and tax-deferred investments such as RRSPs?	☐	☐
8	Are you maximizing your investment returns with dividend income and capital gains?	☐	☐
9	Are you taking advantage of income-splitting opportunities with your spouse?	☐	☐
10	Do you invest the family allowance cheque in your children's names?	☐	☐
11	Do you have a Registered Education Savings Plan (RESP) for your children?	☐	☐
12	Do you have liquid cash reserves to last six months in the event of an accident or disability?	☐	☐
13	Do you believe your investments are adequately diversified?	☐	☐
14	Have you reviewed your insurance program recently and are you getting the best value for your insurance dollar?	☐	☐
15	Do you have the maximum allowable income disability insurance?	☐	☐
16	Could your family live comfortably on your insurance proceeds in the event of your death?	☐	☐
17	Do you have an estate plan that will adequately ensure your family's financial future?	☐	☐
18	Have you reviewed your will during the last three years?	☐	☐
19	Are your retirement assets currently sufficient to allow you to retire when you wish?	☐	☐
20	Do you know how to evaluate a trusted personal investment advisor?	☐	☐
21	Do you know where you are now? Do you have a clear and concise picture of your present financial situation?	☐	☐
22	Do you know where you are going? Have you projected the probable consequences of your past decisions?	☐	☐
23	Do you know where you want to go? Have you clarified your goals for each stage of life, translating them into specific objectives and identifying present and future problem areas?	☐	☐
24	Do you know how you can get there? Do you have appropriate strategies to match your resources to your objectives?	☐	☐
25	Do you know who can help you? Have you identified and evaluated all of the alternative services and products available to you?	☐	☐

Well... Are You Financially Fit?

It can be a sobering thought to realize how little time you've spent planning your lifestyle goals. In the next few chapters, I will help you obtain concise answers to these questions. But for now, score the quiz you just took, giving yourself one point for each "No," and one point for each "Yes."

Score: Yes_____

No_____

From the score of "No" answers, if you have a total of:

5 Points or Less

You have excellent financial fitness and your main objective will be to fine-tune your strategies to stay fit.

6 to 15 Points

You have average financial fitness and your main objective will be to improve your program. You must capitalize on your strengths and learn some new techniques while considering other alternatives. You must also review the weaker areas and change those parts of your program.

16 to 25 Points

You have poor financial fitness. But don't despair, you are not alone. Only one person in 10 in Canada and the United States is financially fit. Read on—this book is for you.

The Passive Approach to Personal Finance

The Financial Fitness Checkup usually offers a sobering perspective that is difficult to look at objectively. So take a look at Susan and David Benson's situation and see if you have anything in common. (See Case Profile #1 below)

The Active Approach to Finances

Attaining your financial goals requires a powerful and flexible financial plan. But a financial plan does not spring into existence by itself. It begins with your effort, your resolve, your honesty—and a few winces along the way.

Case Profile ❶ David and Susan Benson

David Benson graduates from school and joins the work force. He establishes a bank account close to where he works. He meets Susan Clark through his fitness club and they are married within two years.

David and Susan work and save to buy their first home. They enlist the services of a real estate agent to make the purchase, a trust company for the mortgage, and a lawyer to complete the transaction. Jennifer is born 16 months after they buy their house, and David realizes he should have more insurance to supplement his small group policy at work. He purchases additional insurance from an agent.

Susan returns to work three years later and as a result, the couple builds surplus income. David wants to speculate on a hot tip he overhears in the cafeteria at work, so he establishes an account with a stockbroker to make the purchase.

David Benson's financial practice is not unique. He approaches his family's financial planning needs haphazardly. He *reacts* to the situation around him instead of following a structured plan, mapping common approaches to typical goals.

David is an example of the typical Canadian approach to financial fitness. He wants a home; he wants security for his family in the form of insurance; he wants an education fund to send his child to an institution of higher education; he wants to make sure that he can adequately provide for his retirement years; and he wants to draft a will to provide for his heirs. David's goals are specific and comprehensive. *His approach to them is not.*

Your financial plan results from the process of gathering, understanding, and managing your financial resources in order to use them more effectively to achieve your objectives. The plan is a detailed blueprint spelling out your specific goals and thoroughly documenting your financial strategies. With a financial plan, you have a structure, a way of knowing your money matters are organized, directed to maximum advantage, and providing you with as much future independence and security as our world will allow.

The key to financial planning is to start with a solid foundation, then construct your financial "house" in stages, planning each step along the way. Most people handle the basics in the lower part of the house, but few utilize the "windows of opportunities" to their maximum advantage. The potential is unlimited and I intend to take you through each step so that you can build your security dream house.

Learn the basics first. Chart 2-2 is a typical "financial planning for security" structure you can build on.

Starting the Financial Planning Process

Your initial financial plan is the starting point for what should become a routine process. Your plan ought to contain recommendations for improving your financial health by taking control of your cash flow (net income from all sources), and providing maximum utilization of your assets.

Financial planning is a dynamic, continuous process that must also take into account fluctuating economic, market, and social conditions, as well as your changing personal goals. It should be reviewed on a regular basis to reflect these changes and I recommend an annual review, or what I like to refer to as your annual "financial fire drill."

Reading books, articles, pamphlets, or attending seminars on the subject of

CHART 2-2:
FINANCIAL
PLANNING FOR
SECURITY

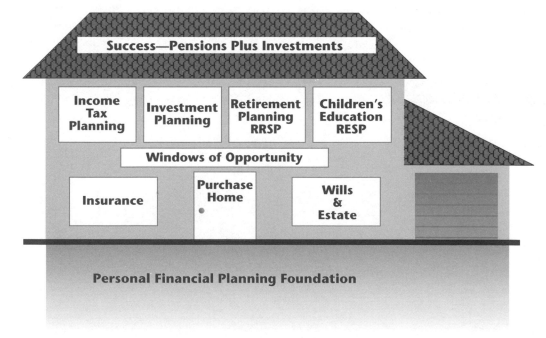

retirement planning are sufficient for some people's financial planning goals. These individuals approach their financial future as an ongoing do-it-yourself enterprise, with varying degrees of success. Others receive assistance at work. Financial planning has been dubbed "the employee benefit of the 1990s." From paid financial planning services for middle and upper management, to group workshops, planning seminars, and computer-generated plans for others in the organization, companies are becoming more aware of the value of financial planning to their employees.

Financial planning in the workplace is not available to the majority of working Canadians, however, and what is available is not as comprehensive as it might be. Canadians are increasingly taking a more comprehensive and direct approach themselves, looking outside the office to hone their skills and knowledge about financial and retirement planning; they are also supplementing their new skills with professional advice. It is a process that is bringing stability, promise, and excitement to many who did not recognize their own ability to take steps to secure their financial freedom.

People waste more time waiting for someone to take charge of their lives than they do in any other pursuit.
Gloria Steinem

The Power of Compounding

What you do with your existing assets and future cash flow will have a major effect on your retirement dreams. To make this money work for you, put it to work with the power of compounding.

The Money Magic of Compounding

One of the greatest gifts you could give your children (after you appreciate it yourself) is the information presented in Table 3-1 below. The table shows the relative effect of compounding on $100 invested each month at 10% and 15% annual rate of returns over 10–, 20–, 30–, and 40-year periods. If you take nothing else from this book, take the concept of compounding and share it with your son, daughter, niece, nephew, or any 25-year-old who is important in your life.

TABLE 3-1: $100 PER MONTH INVESTMENT AT 10% AND 15% COMPOUNDED ANNUALLY

Years	Amount Invested	At 10%	At 15%	Difference
10	$12,000	$21,036	$28,020	$6,984
20	24,000	75,600	141,372	65,772
30	36,000	217,128	599,952	382,824
40	48,000	584,220	2,455,140	1,870,920

When you invest $100 a month, the principal amounts to $12,000 after 10 years ($100 x 12 = $1,200 x 10 = $12,000). Compounded at 10%, the figure grows to $21,036, and at 15% it grows to $28,020.

Imagine the same investment compounding for 40 years. A total principal investment of $48,000 at 10% over 40 years will have grown to $584,220. At 15%, it becomes $2,455,140—more than four times the amount of growth for the additional five percentage points! That is the power of compounding.

What Is Compound Interest?

Compounding is the way in which money multiplies itself. Strictly speaking, compounding is how you measure the worth of your investment when you add the annual interest to it. So, every year the interest payment gets bigger and bigger because the amount the interest payments are made on has become larger and larger. For example, if you invest $100 at 7%, at the end of one year, you have your $100 plus $7 worth of interest. In year two, you have $107 to invest and at 7% you will make $7.49 in interest. At the beginning of year three, your total capital

I don't know what the Seven Wonders of the World are but I know what the Eighth Wonder is: Compound Interest.
Baron Rothschild

13

is now $114.49 and so on. This is how money makes more money.

Below is an example of the compounding process. Notice that the higher the interest rate and the longer the number of years to compound, the larger the future value of the investment. Look at Table 3-2 and see what a dollar can do for you if you invest one each year at various rates of return:

$1 invested each year for 10 years at 5% grows to $13.21.

$1 invested each year for 10 years at 10% grows to $17.53.

$1 invested each year for 10 years at 15% grows to $23.35.

You can see once again that after 10 years, you would have an extra $4.32 if you had made a return of 10% instead of 5%. And you would have an additional $10.14 if you invested at 15% instead of 5%. Watch what happens when you compound your $1 investment for 40 years at 5%, 10%, and 15%:

$1 invested each year for 40 years at 5% grows to $126.84.

$1 invested each year for 40 years at 10% grows to $486.85.

$1 invested each year for 40 years at 15% grows to $2,045.95.

TABLE 3-2: FUTURE VALUE OF $1, INVESTED AT THE BEGINNING OF EACH YEAR WITH INTEREST COMPOUNDED ANNUALLY

Year	ANNUAL RATE OF RETURN							
	3%	4%	5%	6%	7%	8%	9%	10%
1	1.03	1.04	1.05	1.06	1.07	1.08	1.09	1.10
2	2.09	2.12	2.15	2.18	2.21	2.25	2.28	2.31
3	3.18	3.25	3.31	3.37	3.44	3.51	3.57	3.64
4	4.31	4.42	4.53	4.64	4.75	4.87	4.98	5.11
5	5.47	5.63	5.80	5.98	6.15	6.34	6.52	6.72
6	6.66	6.90	7.14	7.39	7.65	7.92	8.20	8.49
7	7.89	8.21	8.55	8.90	9.26	9.64	10.03	10.44
8	9.16	9.58	10.03	10.49	10.98	11.49	12.02	12.58
9	10.46	11.01	11.58	12.18	12.82	13.49	14.19	14.94
10	11.81	12.49	13.21	13.97	14.78	15.65	16.56	17.53
11	13.19	14.03	14.92	15.87	16.89	17.98	19.14	20.38
12	14.62	15.63	16.71	17.88	19.14	20.50	21.95	23.52
13	16.09	17.29	18.60	20.02	21.55	23.21	25.02	26.97
14	17.60	19.02	20.58	22.28	24.13	26.15	28.36	30.77
15	19.16	20.82	22.66	24.67	26.89	29.32	32.00	34.95
16	20.76	22.70	24.84	27.21	29.84	32.75	35.97	39.54
17	22.41	24.65	27.13	29.91	33.00	36.45	40.30	44.60
18	24.12	26.67	29.54	32.76	36.38	40.45	45.02	50.16
19	25.87	28.78	32.07	35.79	40.00	44.76	50.16	56.27
20	27.68	30.97	34.72	38.99	43.87	49.42	55.76	63.00
21	29.54	33.25	37.51	42.39	48.01	54.46	61.87	70.40
22	31.45	35.62	40.43	46.00	52.44	59.89	68.53	78.54
23	33.43	38.08	43.50	49.82	57.18	65.76	75.79	87.50
24	35.46	40.65	46.73	53.86	62.25	72.11	83.70	97.35
25	37.55	43.31	50.11	58.16	67.68	78.95	92.32	108.18
30	49.00	58.33	69.76	83.80	101.07	122.35	148.58	180.94
35	62.28	76.60	94.84	118.12	147.91	186.10	235.12	298.13
40	77.66	98.83	126.84	164.05	213.61	279.78	368.29	486.85

After 40 years you would have an additional $360.01 if you were earning 10% instead of 5%. You would have an additional $1,919.11 if you were getting 15% instead of 5%, or an amount that was 16.1 times greater, by tripling your rate of return from 5% to 15%.

Compounding and Retirement Saving—When Should You Start?

Retirement planning should start the day you start work. There are no hard rules about how to save for retirement, but from the standpoint of retirement savings and compound interest, if you don't have a retirement savings plan today, start one yesterday!

As you have seen, the magic of compounding is always impressive but compounding works best when you start early—big results can come from a small investment. Unfortunately, very few young people give much thought to their retirement years. They are caught up with enjoying their youth and the acquisition of material possessions such as cars, stereos, TVs, and VCRs. That, in itself, is fine, if it is complemented by a disciplined savings program.

The fact remains that for young and old alike, the longer you delay the start of your savings program, the harder it will

You can only have two things in life— reasons or results. Reasons don't count.

TABLE 3-2: FUTURE VALUE OF $1, INVESTED AT THE BEGINNING OF EACH YEAR WITH INTEREST COMPOUNDED ANNUALLY (CONTINUED)

	ANNUAL RATE OF RETURN							
Year	11%	12%	13%	14%	15%	16%	17%	18%
1	1.11	1.12	1.13	1.14	1.15	1.16	1.17	1.18
2	2.34	2.37	2.41	2.44	2.47	2.51	2.54	2.57
3	3.71	3.78	3.85	3.92	3.99	4.07	4.14	4.22
4	5.23	5.35	5.48	5.61	5.74	5.88	6.01	6.15
5	6.91	7.12	7.32	7.54	7.75	7.98	8.21	8.44
6	8.78	9.09	9.40	9.73	10.07	10.41	10.77	11.14
7	10.86	11.30	11.76	12.23	12.73	13.24	13.77	14.33
8	13.16	13.78	14.42	15.09	15.79	16.52	17.28	18.09
9	15.72	16.55	17.42	18.34	19.30	20.32	21.39	22.52
10	18.56	19.65	20.81	22.04	23.35	24.73	26.20	27.76
11	21.71	23.13	24.65	26.27	28.00	29.85	31.82	33.93
12	25.21	27.03	28.98	31.09	33.35	35.79	38.40	41.22
13	29.09	31.39	33.88	36.58	39.50	42.67	46.10	49.82
14	33.41	36.28	39.42	42.84	46.58	50.66	55.11	59.97
15	38.19	41.75	45.67	49.98	54.72	59.93	65.65	71.94
16	43.50	47.88	52.74	58.12	64.08	70.67	77.98	86.07
17	49.40	54.75	60.73	67.39	74.84	83.14	92.41	102.74
18	55.94	62.44	69.75	77.97	87.21	97.60	109.28	122.41
19	63.20	71.05	79.95	90.02	101.44	114.38	129.03	145.63
20	71.27	80.70	91.47	103.77	117.81	133.84	152.14	173.02
21	80.21	91.50	104.49	119.44	136.63	156.41	179.17	205.34
22	90.15	103.60	119.20	137.30	158.28	182.60	210.80	243.49
23	101.17	117.16	135.83	157.66	183.17	212.98	247.81	288.49
24	113.41	132.33	154.62	180.87	211.79	248.21	291.10	341.60
25	127.00	149.33	175.85	207.33	244.71	289.09	341.76	404.27
30	220.91	270.29	331.32	406.74	499.96	615.16	757.50	933.32
35	379.16	483.46	617.75	790.67	1013.35	1300.03	1668.99	2143.65
40	645.83	859.14	1145.49	1529.91	2045.95	2738.48	3667.39	4972.59

be to acquire the nest egg you will want and deserve to have for your retirement years. When you are older, there is less time to make your money work. If you start contributions of $1,000 per year to an RRSP at age 50, and your rate of return is 10%, you will accumulate $34,950 by age 65. If you delay your $1,000 contribution for one year to age 51, your total accumulation amounts to $30,770, a lost opportunity of accumulating an additional $4,180.

Age	Amount	Years to 65	Rate of Return	Net Accumulation
50	$1,000	15	10%	$34,950
51	1,000	14	10%	30,770
				$4,180

Look at this same exercise for an individual age 25. If he or she delays the start of contributions for one year, the lost returns amount to $45,260.

Age	Amount	Years to 65	Rate of Return	Net Accumulation
25	$1,000	40	10%	$486,850
26	1,000	39	10%	441,590
				$45,260

This illustration was based on a contribution of $1,000. Consider how the figures in the illustration would change given higher RRSP contribution limits. Clearly, the opportunities for accumulating wealth are substantial.

Your Retirement Assets Should Be at Least $500,000

I feel that by age 65 everyone should have a liquid, or "spendable," estate worth at least $500,000. Examine Table 3-3 below.

We assume money, in this example, is compounding at 12% annually. To acquire your $500,000, starting at age 25, it would take $42 per month or one lump sum of $5,373. If you waited just 10 years to age 35, it would take $143 a month or one lump sum of $16,689 to reach $500,000. Delaying your investment program for 10 years has forced the ante up by more than three times.

Now look what happens if you wait to age 45. The cost soars from $42 a month at age 25, to $505—1200%! Finally, if you're like most people who put off retirement planning, or even thinking about retirement until you are 55 or more, it takes $2,174 per month or a $160,800 lump sum to accomplish that same $500,000 goal. Start retirement saving yesterday! Now you know why.

The Rule of 72: Doubling Your Money

The rule of 72 is a handy tool you can use to measure the growth of your investments. Simply divide the number 72 by the annual rate of return, and the resulting figure will always equal the number of years it takes for money to double.

TABLE 3-3: THE $500,000 RETIREMENT DREAM AT 12% COMPOUNDED ANNUALLY

Age	Monthly Contribution	(or)	Lump Sum Contribution	Years of Compounding	Rate of Return	Retirement Dream
25	$42	or	$5,373	40	12 %	$500,000
35	143	or	16,689	30	12 %	500,000
45	505	or	51,815	20	12 %	500,000
55	2,174	or	160,800	10	12 %	500,000

From Chart 3-4, you can see that if you were earning a 6% rate of return on a $1,000 investment, and you divide that rate into 72, your money would double in 12 years (72 ÷ 6 = 12). The time frame for the investment is 24 years, therefore the $1,000 will double twice during this period to a total of $4,000.

A return of 15% would double your money in 72 ÷ 15 = 4.8 years. With $1,000 invested over 24 years, your investment would double five times to a total of $32,000.

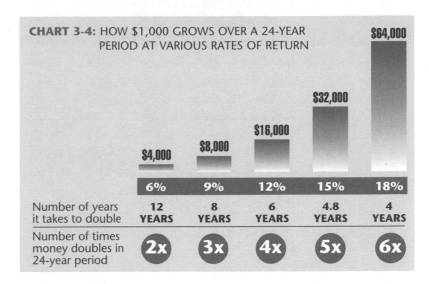

CHART 3-4: HOW $1,000 GROWS OVER A 24-YEAR PERIOD AT VARIOUS RATES OF RETURN

	6%	9%	12%	15%	18%
	$4,000	$8,000	$16,000	$32,000	$64,000
Number of years it takes to double	12 YEARS	8 YEARS	6 YEARS	4.8 YEARS	4 YEARS
Number of times money doubles in 24-year period	2x	3x	4x	5x	6x

The Future Value of a Compounded Dollar

Looking at Table 1-3 you will see that:

$1 invested for 10 years at 5% grows to $1.63.

$1 invested for 10 years at 10% grows to $2.59.

$1 invested for 10 years at 15% grows to $4.05.

After 10 years, you would have an additional $0.96 if you had a rate of return of 10% instead of 5%, and you would have an additional $2.42 if you invested at 15% instead of 5%. That difference itself is substantial. But look what happens if you invest that same $1 for 40 years at 5%, 10%, and 15% (Chart 1-3).

$1 invested for 40 years at 5% grows to $7.04.

$1 invested for 40 years at 10% grows to $45.26.

$1 invested for 40 years at 15% grows to $267.86.

Now you start to see the magic of compounding over a long period of time. At 5% for 40 years, $1 grows to $7.04, but at 10% for 40 years the same $1 grows to $45.26, almost 6.5 times greater by doubling the rate of return. At 15% for 40

years, $1 grows to $267.86. Astronomical! You tripled the rate from 5% to 15%, and the end result grew more than 38 times from $7.04 to $267.86.

Present value can be represented graphically. Recall that in compounding, the future value is directly related to the number of compounding periods and the interest rate. The greater the interest rate and/or the longer the time period, the larger the future value.

A Practical Application of Compounding: Education Plans

Planning ahead to ensure your child's higher education will make a significant difference in his or her ability to earn a comfortable income. It's also an excellent way to employ the magic of long-term compound interest.

Figures show that one year of schooling at a major Canadian university today can amount to more than $15,000 when food, lodging, and tuition are included. In 15 years it may rise to as much as $23,000, or nearly $100,000 for a four-year degree—all payable in after-tax dollars! These figures apply to community colleges and technical schools as well. How will you provide these large sums for one, two, or more children?

THE COST OF PROCRASTINATION

Ajit Sing
Age: 41
Invests $4000 / year at 12% for
30 years

Result:
$1,080,160

Amar Sharma
Age: 51
Invests $4000 / year at 12% for
20 years

Result:
$322,800

Case Profile ❷ Karen Fisher and Cheryl Gordon

Consider the example of two friends, Karen and Cheryl. Karen begins a Registered Retirement Savings Plan (RRSP) at age 19 when she starts work. For eight successive years she invests $2,000. Her investment grows at the rate of 10% per year. After the eighth year, Karen leaves work to become a homemaker and no further investments are made.

Cheryl does not begin her retirement savings contributions until she is 27 (the age at which Karen stopped her contributions). Cheryl invests $2,000 each year until age 65 at the same 10% growth each year.

You can see the incredible result in the table below. Karen, who contributed earlier with only eight contributions, ends up with more money than Cheryl, who made 39 contributions.

This is the power of compounding over time. The difference in the two investors' results is that Karen's compounding had an eight year head start. Those early years were worth more than the entire 39 later contributions made by Cheryl and left her free to follow the lifestyle she wanted without financial concerns. You might show this one to your kids!

Age	Annual Investment (Karen)	Year-End Value (Karen)	Annual Investment (Cheryl)	Year-End Value (Cheryl)
19	$2,000	$2,200	$0	$0
20	2,000	4,620	0	0
21	2,000	7,282	0	0
22	2,000	10,210	0	0
23	2,000	13,431	0	0
24	2,000	16,974	0	0
25	2,000	20,872	0	0
26	2,000	25,159	0	0
27	0	27,675	2,000	2,200
28	0	30,442	2,000	4,620
29	0	33,487	2,000	7,282
30	0	36,835	2,000	10,210
31	0	40,519	2,000	13,431
32	0	44,571	2,000	16,974
33	0	49,028	2,000	20,872
34	0	53,931	2,000	25,159
35	0	59,324	2,000	29,875
36	0	65,256	2,000	35,062
37	0	71,782	2,000	40,769
38	0	78,960	2,000	47,045
39	0	86,856	2,000	53,950
40	0	95,541	2,000	61,545
41	0	105,095	2,000	69,899
42	0	115,605	2,000	79,089
43	0	127,165	2,000	89,198
44	0	139,882	2,000	100,318
45	0	153,870	2,000	112,550
46	0	169,257	2,000	126,005
47	0	186,183	2,000	140,805
48	0	204,801	2,000	157,086
49	0	225,281	2,000	174,995
50	0	247,809	2,000	194,694
51	0	272,590	2,000	216,364
52	0	299,849	2,000	240,200
53	0	329,834	2,000	266,420
54	0	362,818	2,000	295,262
55	0	399,100	2,000	326,988
56	0	439,010	2,000	361,887
57	0	482,910	2,000	400,276
58	0	531,202	2,000	442,503
59	0	584,322	2,000	488,953
60	0	642,754	2,000	540,049
61	0	707,029	2,000	596,254
62	0	777,732	2,000	658,079
63	0	855,505	2,000	726,087
64	0	941,056	2,000	800,896
65	0	1,035,161	2,000	883,185
Less Total Invested		**16,000**		**78,000**
		$1,019,161		**$805,185**

KAREN FISHER Money Grew **64 fold**

CHERYL GORDON Money Grew **10 fold**

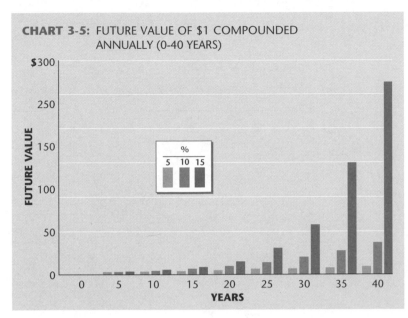

CHART 3-5: FUTURE VALUE OF $1 COMPOUNDED ANNUALLY (0-40 YEARS)

more money, what money is worth today is less than what it will be worth tomorrow. In other words, today's value is a *discount* of its tomorrow's value. With discounting, the present value of a future sum is *inversely* related to the interest rate and the number of time periods. The greater the interest rate and/or the longer the time period, the lower the present value.

The best way is with a Registered Education Savings Plan (RESP). An RESP is a government-approved plan developed to help parents save money for their children's post-secondary education. It is what amounts to a tax-sheltered savings account, one of the few tax shelters still available to Canadians. Interest earned on your savings compounds free of tax in your RESP.

Assume your child will require $80,000 for four years of university ($20,000 x 4 years) 10 years from now. What amount of capital would be required today to reach your target? There are two parts to this calculation:

1. Calculate the present value of an annuity due.
2. Calculate the present value of a lump sum in the future.

This calculation is what accountants call the "present value of an annuity due," or today's value of an amount of money some time in the future. Put another way, present value is the amount of money you must invest today at an assumed interest rate in order to accumulate a given amount of money some time in the future. Since money always earns

From Table 3-6 you can calculate the present value of $1 per year due at the end of each year. For example, $20,000 per year for four years requires capital of $70,920 invested at 5%; that is, $70,920 invested at 5% and removing $20,000 per year leaves $0.00 at the end of four years. The next step is to calculate the present value of the $70,920 required for the four years of education which will begin 10 years from now.

From Table 1-2 you can calculate the present value for this example.

$1 discounted for 10 years at 5% has a present value of $0.61.
$1 discounted for 10 years at 10% has a present value of $0.39.
$1 discounted for 10 years at 15% has a present value of $0.25.

The education funds required in 10 years, assuming a 5% rate of return, would have a present value of ($0.61 x $70,920 = $43,261). If you assume a higher rate of return on capital of 10% for 10 years, you would require today ($0.39 x $70,920 = $27,659) to meet your goal of $80,000 for education.

TABLE 3-6: THE PRESENT VALUE OF AN ANNUITY DUE—THE PRESENT VALUE OF $1 PER YEAR DUE AT THE END OF EACH YEAR

Table Guide

If you wanted to receive $1 per year for 4 years, how much would you have to invest today so that the $1 per year from that investment would leave $0.00 at the end of 4 years? Under Rate of Return column of 5% and End of Year 4 line, find 3.546 where column and line intersect. Therefore $3.546 invested today at 5% would provide an annuity of $1 per year or a total of $4 over 4 years.

Example

What sum would have to be invested at 5% to provide $20,000 per year for 4 years? Under Rate of Return column of 5% and End of Year 4 line, find 3.546 where column and line intersect. Now multiply $20,000 x 3.546 to obtain $70,920. Therefore $70,920 invested today at 5% would provide an annuity of $20,000 per year or a total of $80,000 over 4 years.

Year	ANNUAL RATE OF RETURN							
	5%	6%	7%	8%	9%	10%	11%	12%
1	0.952	0.943	0.935	0.926	0.917	0.909	0.901	0.893
2	1.859	1.833	1.808	1.783	1.759	1.736	1.713	1.690
3	2.723	2.673	2.624	2.577	2.531	2.487	2.444	2.402
4	3.546	3.465	3.387	3.312	3.240	3.170	3.102	3.037
5	4.329	4.212	4.100	3.993	3.890	3.791	3.696	3.605
6	5.076	4.917	4.767	4.623	4.486	4.355	4.231	4.111
7	5.786	5.582	5.389	5.206	5.033	4.868	4.712	4.564
8	6.463	6.210	5.971	5.747	5.535	5.335	5.146	4.968
9	7.108	6.802	6.515	6.247	5.995	5.759	5.537	5.328
10	7.722	7.360	7.024	6.710	6.418	6.145	5.889	5.650
11	8.306	7.887	7.499	7.139	6.805	6.495	6.207	5.938
12	8.863	8.384	7.943	7.536	7.161	6.814	6.492	6.194
13	9.394	8.853	8.358	7.904	7.487	7.103	6.750	6.424
14	9.899	9.295	8.745	8.244	7.786	7.367	6.982	6.628
15	10.380	9.712	9.108	8.559	8.061	7.606	7.191	6.811
16	10.838	10.106	9.447	8.851	8.313	7.824	7.379	6.974
17	11.274	10.477	9.763	9.122	8.544	8.022	7.549	7.120
18	11.690	10.828	10.059	9.372	8.756	8.201	7.702	7.250
19	12.085	11.158	10.336	9.604	8.950	8.365	7.839	7.366
20	12.462	11.470	10.594	9.818	9.129	8.514	7.963	7.469
21	12.821	11.764	10.836	10.017	9.292	8.649	8.075	7.562
22	13.163	12.042	11.061	10.201	9.442	8.772	8.176	7.645
23	13.489	12.303	11.272	10.371	9.580	8.883	8.266	7.718
24	13.799	12.550	11.469	10.529	9.707	8.985	8.348	7.784
25	14.094	12.783	11.654	10.675	9.823	9.077	8.422	7.843
26	14.375	13.003	11.826	10.810	9.929	9.161	8.488	7.896
27	14.643	13.211	11.987	10.935	10.027	9.237	8.548	7.943
28	14.898	13.406	12.137	11.051	10.116	9.307	8.602	7.984
29	15.141	13.591	12.278	11.158	10.198	9.370	8.650	8.022
30	15.372	13.765	12.409	11.258	10.274	9.427	8.694	8.055
31	15.593	13.929	12.532	11.350	10.343	9.479	8.733	8.085
32	15.803	14.084	12.647	11.435	10.406	9.526	8.769	8.112
33	16.003	14.230	12.754	11.514	10.464	9.569	8.801	8.135
34	16.193	14.368	12.854	11.587	10.518	9.609	8.829	8.157
35	16.374	14.498	12.948	11.655	10.567	9.644	8.855	8.176

The Honest Assessment

Make an honest assessment of where your finances stand right now. The quizzes and exercises in this chapter will give you the facts and figures to start structuring your own financial plan.

The Elements of Cash Flow

"Where does my money come from?" The answer seems obvious when you earn a regular pay cheque. But there are additional sources of income you benefit from that are not as readily apparent. These "pockets" of money may not be large compared to your regular earnings, but they are important. They have the potential to grow over the years and contribute significantly to your retirement funds.

Your income is called your *cash flow*. Whether the term is used in reference to a multi-national corporate giant or an individual wage earner, cash flow is the lifeblood of your financial system. Money is like a liquid that flows in as income and out as expenditures. The money flow may be positive (more comes in than goes out), or it may be negative (like many people, more goes out than comes in). The overall direction of your flow is called *net cash flow*. Positive net cash flow is ideal. The secret to your successful wealth accumulation over the years is to "pay yourself first" by turning a portion of your cash flow into capital.

Some of your personal cash flow may come from assets such as rental proper-

ties; some may be from investments that ultimately feed back into the system and add to the level of stored income already there.

There are many ways that cash flow can increase: you receive a raise in salary or perhaps a windfall inheritance, or some other boost in personal income; expenses go down when your child enters the workforce and becomes self-sufficient; you pay off your mortgage; you find ways to minimize your income taxes. We will look at many of these methods of increased cash flow in the coming chapters. They are numerous and it is encouraging to know they are there because these seemingly unimportant details regarding personal cash flow can make a great difference in the long-run in the amount of money you accumulate for retirement.

Determining Your Net Cash Flow

The value of accurately gauging your cash flow is that once you know where you stand, your actions can effectively control your financial future. Many seemingly unimportant details can make a great deal of difference in your cash flow. Capturing a portion of your cash flow and investing

O money,
money, money
I am not necessarily
one of those
Who think thee holy.
But I often stop
to wonder
How thee canst go
out so fast
When thou comest
in so slowly.
Ogden Nash

it prudently for maximum long-term growth is what developing a sound financial plan is all about.

To determine your net cash flow, estimate your annual income from all sources, then subtract your expected total payments of all kinds over the next 12 months. The result is your net annual cash flow. This figure represents the money you can save or invest.

WORKSHEET 4-1: ESTIMATED ANNUAL INCOME

Category	Item	ANNUAL AMOUNT		
		You	Spouse	Joint
Employment	Gross Pay	$ _____	$ _____	$ _____
	Bonus	_____	_____	_____
	Commissions	_____	_____	_____
	Other _____	_____	_____	_____
Self-Employment	Net Professional Income	_____	_____	_____
	Net Business Income	_____	_____	_____
	Other _____	_____	_____	_____
Child Tax Benefit	Child Support	_____	_____	_____
Trusts		_____	_____	_____
Pensions	Canada Pension Plan,	_____	_____	_____
	Old Age Security,	_____	_____	_____
	Guaranteed Income Supplement	_____	_____	_____
Annuities		_____	_____	_____
Registered Retirement Income Fund		_____	_____	_____
Life Income Fund		_____	_____	_____
RRSPs	(Cash Out)	_____	_____	_____
Investments	Bank Accounts	_____	_____	_____
	Guaranteed Investment Certificates, Notes, etc.	_____	_____	_____
	Canada Savings Bonds Regular	_____	_____	_____
	Money Market Funds	_____	_____	_____
	Loans Owned	_____	_____	_____
	Mortgages	_____	_____	_____
	Bonds, Debentures	_____	_____	_____
	Other Interest Income	_____	_____	_____
	Net Rental Income	_____	_____	_____
	Preferred Shares	_____	_____	_____
	Common Shares	_____	_____	_____
	Equity Funds	_____	_____	_____
	Business Interests	_____	_____	_____
	Limited Partnerships	_____	_____	_____
	Other _____	_____	_____	_____
Capital Gains	Withdrawal Plans	_____	_____	_____
	Other _____	_____	_____	_____
Gifts Received		_____	_____	_____
TOTAL ESTIMATED ANNUAL INCOME		$ _____	$ _____	$ _____

WORKSHEET 4-2: ESTIMATED ANNUAL EXPENSES

Category	Item	ANNUAL AMOUNT		
		You	**Spouse**	**Joint**
Home	Mortgage/Rent	$ _____	$ _____	$ _____
	Property Tax	_____	_____	_____
	Repairs	_____	_____	_____
	Renovations	_____	_____	_____
	Decorating	_____	_____	_____
	Gas	_____	_____	_____
	Electric	_____	_____	_____
	Water	_____	_____	_____
	Phone	_____	_____	_____
	Cable	_____	_____	_____
	Domestic Help	_____	_____	_____
	Insurance	_____	_____	_____
	Other _____	_____	_____	_____
Food	Groceries	_____	_____	_____
	Meals Out	_____	_____	_____
	Pet Food	_____	_____	_____
Health	Provincial Health Insurance	_____	_____	_____
	Additional Health Insurance	_____	_____	_____
	Disability Insurance	_____	_____	_____
	Medications	_____	_____	_____
	Pharmaceuticals	_____	_____	_____
	Dentist	_____	_____	_____
	Optical	_____	_____	_____
	Veterinarian	_____	_____	_____
Transportation	Payments	_____	_____	_____
	Insurance	_____	_____	_____
	Maintenance	_____	_____	_____
	Fuel	_____	_____	_____
	Parking	_____	_____	_____
	Public Transit	_____	_____	_____
Personal Items	Clothing	_____	_____	_____
	Footwear	_____	_____	_____
	Hair	_____	_____	_____
	Cosmetics	_____	_____	_____
	Allowances	_____	_____	_____
	Babysitters	_____	_____	_____
	Day Care	_____	_____	_____
	Dry Cleaning	_____	_____	_____
	"Mad Money"	_____	_____	_____
	Other _____	_____	_____	_____
Activities	Entertainment	_____	_____	_____
	Vacation, Trips	_____	_____	_____
	Education	_____	_____	_____
	Leisure	_____	_____	_____
	Hobbies, Crafts, etc.	_____	_____	_____
	Health/Fitness	_____	_____	_____
	Social Clubs	_____	_____	_____

Continued on page 24

WORKSHEET 4-2: ESTIMATED ANNUAL EXPENSES (CONTINUED)

Category	Item	You	Spouse	Joint
		ANNUAL AMOUNT		
	Memberships	$ _____	$ _____	$ _____
	Presents/Gifts	_____	_____	_____
	Special Occasions	_____	_____	_____
	Other _____	_____	_____	_____
Insurance	Group Life Insurance	_____	_____	_____
	Other Insurance	_____	_____	_____
	Unemployment Insurance	_____	_____	_____
Other Expenses	Accountant	_____	_____	_____
	Legal	_____	_____	_____
	Charitable Donations	_____	_____	_____
	Financial Planner	_____	_____	_____
	Loan Interest	_____	_____	_____
	Miscellaneous	_____	_____	_____
Income Tax	From Pay	_____	_____	_____
	Due at Tax Time (or Refund)	(_____)	(_____)	(_____)
Savings	Investments	_____	_____	_____
	Pension Plan (Company)	_____	_____	_____
	RRSP	_____	_____	_____
	Debt Reduction	_____	_____	_____
	Other _____	_____	_____	_____
TOTAL ESTIMATED ANNUAL EXPENSES		$ _____	$ _____	$ _____

WORKSHEET 4-3: STATEMENT OF NET ANNUAL CASH FLOW

		You	Spouse	Joint
		ANNUAL AMOUNT		
	Total Estimated Income	$ _____	$ _____	$ _____
minus	Total Estimated Expenses	$ _____	$ _____	$ _____
equals	**NET DISCRETIONARY CASH FLOW**	$ _____	$ _____	$ _____

Determining Your Net Worth

Your first objective was to determine your cash flow and see where you could find additional income for investment. Now you should look at what your net worth is. Your reservoir of money includes the dollar value of your property, cash value of your life insurance, investments, and so on, as you will see from the Calculation of Assets on page 25. When these assets are measured against your liabilities, the difference between them is called your personal net worth. While completing the following two worksheets, you will probably find your spouse's assistance to be valuable as you validate the estimates of your particular assets or liabilities.

WORKSHEET 4-4: CALCULATION OF ASSETS

As at (Date) _____

Category	Item	CURRENT VALUE		
		You	**Spouse**	**Joint**
Liquid Assets	Cash, Chequing & Savings Accounts	$ _____	$ _____	$ _____
	Treasury Bills, Term Deposits, CSBs	_____	_____	_____
	Life Insurance (Cash Value)	_____	_____	_____
	Other _____	_____	_____	_____
	Total Liquid Assets	$ _____	$ _____	$ _____
Investment Assets	Loans or Notes Receivable	$ _____	$ _____	$ _____
	Bonds	_____	_____	_____
	Common Shares	_____	_____	_____
	Preferred Shares	_____	_____	_____
	Mutual Funds, Common Stocks	_____	_____	_____
	Real Estate (Income Property)	_____	_____	_____
	Tax Incentive & Foreign Investments	_____	_____	_____
	Business Assets	_____	_____	_____
	Annuities	_____	_____	_____
	Retirement Plans (RRSP, RPP, Deferred Profit Sharing Plan)	_____	_____	_____
	Other _____	_____	_____	_____
	Total Investment Assets	$ _____	$ _____	$ _____
Personal Assets	Principal Residence	$ _____	$ _____	$ _____
	Recreational Property	_____	_____	_____
	Household Furnishings	_____	_____	_____
	Electronic Equipment	_____	_____	_____
	Jewellery, Art, Antiques, Coins	_____	_____	_____
	Autos, Boats, RVs	_____	_____	_____
	Expected Tax Refunds	_____	_____	_____
	Other _____	_____	_____	_____
	Total Personal Assets	$ _____	$ _____	$ _____
Direct Investments	Business Interests	$ _____	$ _____	$ _____
	Limited Partnerships	_____	_____	_____
	Other _____	_____	_____	_____
	Total Direct Investments	$ _____	$ _____	$ _____
TOTAL ASSETS		$ _____	$ _____	$ _____

WORKSHEET 4-5: CALCULATION OF LIABILITIES

Category	Item	You	Spouse	Joint
		CURRENT VALUE		
		You	**Spouse**	**Joint**
Current Liabilities	Personal & Installment Loans	$ _____	$ _____	$ _____
	Credit Cards	_____	_____	_____
	Accrued Income Tax Payable	_____	_____	_____
	Life Insurance Loans	_____	_____	_____
	Other _____	_____	_____	_____
	Total Current Liabilities	$ _____	$ _____	$ _____
Long-term Liabilities	Loans to Purchase Investments	$ _____	$ _____	$ _____
	Loans to Purchase Personal Assets	_____	_____	_____
	Mortgage—Principal Residence	_____	_____	_____
	Mortgage—Recreational Property	_____	_____	_____
	Other _____	_____	_____	_____
	Total Long-term Liabilities	$ _____	$ _____	$ _____
	TOTAL LIABILITIES	$ _____	$ _____	$ _____

WORKSHEET 4-6: STATEMENT OF NET WORTH

		You	Spouse	Joint
	Total Assets	$ _____	$ _____	$ _____
minus	**Total Liabilities**	$ _____	$ _____	$ _____
equals	**NET WORTH**	$ _____	$ _____	$ _____

The Finer Details of Net Worth and Cash Flow

What you can't communicate runs your life.

The Net Worth and Cash Flow Statements you have completed are two of the cornerstones of a good financial plan. There are additional financial statements and measurement statistics you can use as well to review your financial position. These include:

- Analysis of assets by expected yield, liquidity, diversification, and risk
- Analysis of liabilities by interest rate, repayment options, and tax deductibility
- Analysis of expenses by category of use and regularity
- Net cash flow projections for future years
- Projection of future financial position
- Income tax analysis
- Disability income analysis
- Survivor income analysis
- Estate analysis
- Retirement income analysis
- Projection of various other *What if?* scenarios

Most of you will not require the type of in-depth review suggested above. It is, however, an important part of a complete analysis of personal finances. These analyses, usually processed on computer, are typical services provided by professional financial planners. Some people can calculate these numbers on their own, but for most people, a professional financial planner is the logical person to assist you with a comprehensive review of your financial strategies. As you work through this book, remember there is help along the way. The professional financial planner is the ace up your sleeve.

Lifetime Earnings Potential

Almost everyone, at some time, will prepare a net worth statement and a cash flow statement if only for their banker when they are borrowing money. But have you ever given serious thought to what you have earned over the years and what your future earnings potential is? Access to a computer to make the calculations would be the ideal, but you may want to complete this chart on your own as Robin and June Douglas have done.

Case Profile ❸ Robin and June Douglas

Robin Douglas is 53 years old. He started working when he was 19, over 34 years ago. Robin remembers starting his working career at about $1,500 per year. He has worked for Bell Telecom Inc. throughout those years and now earns $44,000 as a personnel officer with his company. He and his wife June, a homemaker, have two grown children who now earn their own living. Until the last few years, it has been difficult for Robin and June to save very much money, but they have paid off their mortgage, and their bank savings accounts are reserved for emergencies. As well, Robin has a company pension plan, group insurance coverage, some term insurance of his own, and a disability insurance policy. He has also been putting money into a retirement savings plan for June. The Douglas's net worth statement is as follows:

Assets		Liabilities	
Liquid Assets	$ 15,000	Current Liabilities	$5,000
Investment Assets	15,000	Long-term Liabilities	0
Personal Assets	190,000		
TOTAL ASSETS	$220,000	TOTAL LIABILITIES	$5,000
		Total Net Worth	$215,000

Robin and June completed Worksheet 4-7 in the following manner: they estimated Robin's lifetime earnings to date at approximately $475,000 and entered that as his base earnings at age 52 last year. Robin's current salary at age 53 is $44,000 and he anticipates annual increases averaging 7% per year.

Their current chequing and savings accounts total $15,000, less their current liabilities of $5,000, which they have decided to pay off. That will leave them with net savings of $10,000—emergency money that they intend to leave in a savings account earning 6% interest. Robin has some investments currently worth $15,000 in mutual funds which have been earning approximately a 20% rate of return each year for the last five years. To be cautious, he assumes these investments will earn an average of 15% for the foreseeable future.

Robin plans to retire at age 63. He believes he can save 15% of his earnings during the next 11 years, and he intends to split this by putting 30% of those savings into his bank savings account and the balance toward his investments each year. A sample of the calculations is shown on page 28. (Use Table 1-3)

When Robin and June finished filling out Worksheet 4-7, they found that Robin's lifetime earnings would amount to $1,169,477. That seemed like a lot of money and they became very excited about "saving off the top" of Robin's salary for their retirement years. By "paying themselves first" they found their savings could grow to $63,421 and their investments could grow to $249,411, for a total retirement capital pool of $312,832.

The Douglas's could keep all of this money if it were tax sheltered in a registered savings plan, otherwise some of this compounded growth and income would be taxed away. I'll have more to say about the effect of taxes in a later chapter.

WORKSHEET 4-7: ROBIN AND JUNE DOUGLAS'S LIFETIME EARNINGS AND RETIREMENT CAPITAL

Prepared by: Robin Douglas - July 27, 1994

Compound No. of Years	Age	Earnings 7%	"Pay Yourself First" Savings 15%	Available for Savings 30%	Rate of Return 6%	Available for Investing 70%	Rate of Return 15%
12	Base Year	$475,000		$10,000	$20,100	$15,000	$80,250
11	53	44,000	$6,600	1,980	3,762	4,620	21,483
10	54	47,080	7,062	2,119	3,793	4,943	20,019
9	55	50,379	7,556	2,267	3,831	5,289	18,617
8	56	53,902	8,085	2,426	3,857	5,659	17,317
7	57	57,675	8,651	2,595	3,893	6,056	16,109
6	58	61,712	9,257	2,777	3,943	6,480	14,967
5	59	66,032	9,905	2,972	3,982	6,933	13,935
4	60	70,654	10,958	3,179	4,006	7,419	12,983
3	61	75,600	11,340	3,402	4,048	7,938	12,066
2	62	80,892	12,134	3,640	4,077	8,494	11,212
1	63	86,554	12,983	3,895	4,129	9,088	10,451
		$1,169,477			$63,421		$249,411

WORKSHEET GUIDE

❶ The Douglas's have current savings of $10,000 which will be invested for 12 years at 6% until Robin's retirement. Under Annual Rate of Return column of 6% and End of Year 12 line in Table 1-3, find 2.01 where column and line intersect. Now multiply $10,000 savings by factor 2.01 to obtain result of $20,100.

❷ Similarly, the Douglas's have current investments of $15,000 which will be invested for 12 years at 15%. Under Annual Rate of Return column of 15% and End of Year 12 line, find 5.35 where column and line intersect. Now multiply $15,000 investment by factor of 5.35 to obtain result of $80,250. Note how the Douglas's have entered these figures on the Base Year line of Worksheet 4-7.

❸ Robin currently earns $44,000 and anticipates saving 15% of his earnings each year. Multiply salary of $44,000 by 15%. Result: $6,600, of which 30% or $1,980 is for savings at 6%, and 70% or

$4,620 is for investments at 15%. Find the appropriate factors for 11 years in Table 1-3 to obtain the future value of these savings and investments.

❹ Robin currently earns $44,000 and anticipates salary increases of 7% each year. Multiply salary of $44,000 times 7%. Result: $3,080. Add $3,080 to $44,000 to give next year's salary of $47,080. From this, Robin will save 15% or $7,062, which will be distributed 30% or $2,119 for savings and 70% or $4,943 for investments.

Base Year Funds Available	Rate of Return	Factor (Table 1-3)	Result
❶ **Current Savings:** of $10,000 for 12 Years	6%	2.01	$20,100
❷ **Current Investment** of $15,000 for 12 Years	15%	5.35	$80,250
❸ **At Age 53** will save 15% of $44,000 = $6,600			
30% or $1,980 for savings for 11 Years	6%	1.90	$ 3,762
70% or $4,620 for investments for 11 Years	15%	4.65	$21,483
❹ **At Age 54** will save 15% of $47,080 = $7,062			
30% or $2,119 for savings for 10 Years	6%	1.79	$ 3,793
70% or $4,943 for investments for 10 Years	15%	4.05	$20,019
and so on...			

Determining Your Lifetime Earnings

Now it's your turn to calculate your past career earnings and your future earnings potential in Worksheet 4-8. Tables 4-9 and 4-10 will provide some insight as to where you stand today. It may be difficult to remember your earnings, especially if you already have worked 20 or 30 years. In this case, work with your total savings to date, and calculate your future savings and investment potential.

This exercise to determine your lifetime earnings requires many calculations. It is not essential to complete it at this stage, but it is included for those who wish to pursue their projected worth in greater detail. You may want to read the whole book before completing this exercise. You should also be aware that there are many computer programs that can do these calculations for you.

The focus of this exercise is to help you determine:

- Your past total earnings
- Your future earnings potential
- Your present savings and investment assets
- Your future savings and investment assets
- Your compounded retirement capital
- Your ability to retire with financial dignity.

As you can see, a fortune flows through most people's hands during their working lifetime. It is absolutely essential that you understand what I like to call the "dollar mechanics and magical benefits of compounding." You may not be able to change the amount of money you earn, but by employing the strategies and techniques suggested in this book, you can significantly enhance your purchasing power. Don't worry about how much you earn; worry about what you are doing with what you earn and, above all, be sure to set goals and objectives.

Setting Goals

As you go about establishing your goals, it is important to state each goal specifically. Make sure you include the following guidelines:

- Be absolutely honest with yourself. In the final analysis, it is your own desires, not those of others, that will dictate what you achieve.
- Be passionate about your goals. If you don't embrace your goals with a passion, the desire to achieve them will fade.
- Don't lose your perspective. Goals are not carved in stone; they can be changed, modified, or removed as your life circumstances change.

Establishing goals clarifies and establishes direction. Listed in Worksheet 4-11 are a number of common personal financial goals that you may wish to consider. Rank the importance of each goal to you personally on a scale of 1 (low) to 5 (high). If you have additional financial goals, write them in at the bottom of the list and rank them as well.

Are you accomplishing your goals? What *can* you do about them? What *will* you do about them? Look back and list your five most important goals. Use Worksheet 4-12 to obtain maximum results for each goal.

Formalizing Your Goals

Every goal you have should be put in writing. Putting pen to paper is the first serious step of commitment to your goal. The exercise defines it for you.

When listing your goals, employ the following guidelines:
- Make your statement short and concise (seven words or less).

If you worry about what might be, and wonder what might have been, you will ignore what is.

Dr. Robert Anthony

Don't Procrastinate— Graduate!

Financial Pursuit

WORKSHEET 4-8: YOUR LIFETIME EARNINGS AND RETIREMENT CAPITAL

Prepared by: _____

Compound No. of Years	Age	Earnings	"Pay Yourself First" Savings	Available for Savings	Rate of Return	Available for Investing	Rate of Return
	Base Year						

TABLE GUIDE

If necessary, make a longer copy of this table.

• Calculate your past career earnings, current age, anticipated retirement age, and the number of years until retirement, and enter on the first line. (Base year)

• List your current savings and anticipated rate of return.

• List your current investments and anticipated rate of return.

• List your current earnings and your expected future earnings increases. Use your past average earnings increases as a guideline, or a rate based on future inflation, such as 5%, if you don't know what your future earnings prospects are.

• Determine how much you can save "off the top" of your earnings by "paying yourself first."

• Divide your savings and investments and anticipate what rates of return you will earn on each.

• Use Table 1-3 for your calculations to determine factors for the future worth of $1 compounded annually.

30

TABLE 4-9: HOW MUCH HAVE YOU EARNED IN YOUR LIFETIME SO FAR?

(Based on starting work at age 25 and working to age 65)

| Age | Years of Work | MONTHLY INCOME | | | | Monthly Cheques Spent | Monthly Cheques Left |
		$2,000	$2,500	$3,000	$4,000		
26	1	$24,000	$30,000	$36,000	$48,000	12	480
27	2	48,000	60,000	72,000	96,000	24	468
28	3	72,000	90,000	108,000	144,000	36	456
29	4	96,000	120,000	144,000	192,000	48	444
30	5	120,000	150,000	180,000	240,000	60	432
31	6	144,000	180,000	216,000	288,000	72	420
32	7	168,000	210,000	252,000	336,000	84	408
33	8	192,000	240,000	288,000	384,000	96	396
34	9	216,000	270,000	324,000	432,000	108	384
35	10	240,000	300,000	360,000	480,000	120	372
36	11	264,000	330,000	396,000	528,000	132	360
37	12	288,000	360,000	432,000	576,000	144	348
38	13	312,000	390,000	468,000	624,000	156	336
39	14	336,000	420,000	504,000	672,000	168	324
40	15	360,000	450,000	540,000	720,000	180	312
41	16	384,000	480,000	576,000	768,000	192	300
42	17	408,000	510,000	612,000	816,000	204	288
43	18	432,000	540,000	648,000	864,000	216	276
44	19	456,000	570,000	684,000	912,000	228	264
45	20	480,000	600,000	720,000	960,000	240	252
46	21	504,000	630,000	756,000	1,008,000	252	240
47	22	528,000	660,000	792,000	1,056,000	264	228
48	23	552,000	690,000	828,000	1,104,000	276	216
49	24	576,000	720,000	864,000	1,152,000	288	204
50	25	600,000	750,000	900,000	1,200,000	300	192
51	26	624,000	780,000	936,000	1,248,000	312	180
52	27	648,000	810,000	972,000	1,296,000	324	168
53	28	672,000	840,000	1,008,000	1,344,000	336	156
54	29	696,000	870,000	1,044,000	1,392,000	348	144
55	30	720,000	900,000	1,080,000	1,440,000	360	132
56	31	744,000	930,000	1,116,000	1,488,000	372	120
57	32	768,000	960,000	1,152,000	1,536,000	384	108
58	33	792,000	990,000	1,188,000	1,584,000	396	96
59	34	816,000	1,020,000	1,224,000	1,632,000	408	84
60	35	840,000	1,050,000	1,260,000	1,680,000	420	72
61	36	864,000	1,080,000	1,296,000	1,728,000	432	60
62	37	888,000	1,110,000	1,332,000	1,776,000	444	48
63	38	912,000	1,140,000	1,368,000	1,824,000	456	36
64	39	936,000	1,170,000	1,404,000	1,872,000	468	24
65	40	960,000	1,200,000	1,440,000	1,920,000	480	12

TABLE 4-10: WHAT WILL YOU EARN BETWEEN NOW AND AGE 65?

	MONTHLY INCOME				
Age	$1,000	$2,000	$3,000	$4,000	$5,000
21	$540,000	$1,080,000	$1,620,000	$2,160,000	$2,700,000
22	528,000	1,056,000	1,584,000	2,112,000	2,640,000
23	516,000	1,032,000	1,548,000	2,064,000	2,580,000
24	504,000	1,008,000	1,512,000	2,016,000	2,520,000
25	492,000	984,000	1,476,000	1,968,000	2,460,000
26	480,000	960,000	1,440,000	1,920,000	2,400,000
27	468,000	936,000	1,404,000	1,872,000	2,340,000
28	456,000	912,000	1,368,000	1,824,000	2,280,000
29	444,000	888,000	1,332,000	1,776,000	2,220,000
30	432,000	864,000	1,296,000	1,728,000	2,160,000
31	420,000	840,000	1,260,000	1,680,000	2,100,000
32	408,000	816,000	1,224,000	1,632,000	2,040,000
33	396,000	792,000	1,188,000	1,584,000	1,980,000
34	384,000	768,000	1,152,000	1,536,000	1,920,000
35	372,000	744,000	1,116,000	1,488,000	1,860,000
36	360,000	720,000	1,080,000	1,440,000	1,800,000
37	348,000	696,000	1,044,000	1,392,000	1,740,000
38	336,000	672,000	1,008,000	1,344,000	1,680,000
39	324,000	648,000	972,000	1,296,000	1,620,000
40	312,000	624,000	936,000	1,248,000	1,560,000
41	300,000	600,000	900,000	1,200,000	1,500,000
42	288,000	576,000	864,000	1,152,000	1,440,000
43	276,000	552,000	828,000	1,104,000	1,380,000
44	264,000	528,000	792,000	1,056,000	1,320,000
45	252,000	504,000	756,000	1,008,000	1,260,000
46	240,000	480,000	720,000	960,000	1,200,000
47	228,000	456,000	684,000	912,000	1,140,000
48	216,000	432,000	648,000	864,000	1,080,000
49	204,000	408,000	612,000	816,000	1,020,000
50	192,000	384,000	576,000	768,000	960,000
51	180,000	360,000	540,000	720,000	900,000
52	168,000	336,000	504,000	672,000	840,000
53	156,000	312,000	468,000	624,000	780,000
54	144,000	288,000	432,000	576,000	720,000
55	132,000	264,000	396,000	528,000	660,000
56	120,000	240,000	360,000	480,000	600,000
57	108,000	216,000	324,000	432,000	540,000
58	96,000	192,000	288,000	384,000	480,000
59	84,000	168,000	252,000	336,000	420,000
60	72,000	144,000	216,000	288,000	360,000
61	60,000	120,000	180,000	240,000	300,000
62	48,000	96,000	144,000	192,000	240,000
63	36,000	72,000	108,000	144,000	180,000
64	24,000	48,000	72,000	96,000	120,000
65	12,000	24,000	36,000	48,000	60,000

- Make your goals realistic, so they can be achieved.
- Your goals should be challenging, so that you must strive to achieve them.
- Allow goals to overlap with other goals.
- Visualize your goals, imagining the experience of achieving your goal.

Setting Objectives

Objectives are measurable actions taken to accomplish goals. Now that you have defined your goals, develop a plan to put the process in motion by setting objectives. Objectives generate the urgency needed for inspiration. Set your objectives by specifying:

- What you will do
- When you will do it
- How much you will do to achieve the goal

The objective you establish will provide effective solutions for reaching your goal so long as the objective is:

- Specific
- Measurable
- Attainable within a limited time
- Identified with an actual result

You do have a purpose for everything you want in life. You have a purpose for your career, a purpose for your marriage, a purpose for your lifestyle goals, and a purpose for your monetary and retirement goals. You would not invest yourself in any of them if you did not. Look again and you will see that each purpose incorporates goals. You use your goal to focus energy on attaining your primary purpose.

Success is knowing you have done the best you can with what you have. You can apply this statement to every single aspect of your life.

WORKSHEET 4-11: YOUR PERSONAL FINANCIAL GOALS WORKSHEET

| | IMPORTANCE | | | | |
| | Low | | Medium | | High |
GOAL	1	2	3	4	5
Maintain my standard of living	☐	☐	☐	☐	☐
Improve my standard of living	☐	☐	☐	☐	☐
Choose a less expensive lifestyle	☐	☐	☐	☐	☐
Remain in my current career	☐	☐	☐	☐	☐
Change my career	☐	☐	☐	☐	☐
Change my business interests	☐	☐	☐	☐	☐
Plan a major holiday or sabbatical year	☐	☐	☐	☐	☐
Buy or upgrade residence	☐	☐	☐	☐	☐
Buy vacation property	☐	☐	☐	☐	☐
Buy expensive items: car, boat, RV	☐	☐	☐	☐	☐
Maintain a disciplined savings program	☐	☐	☐	☐	☐
Maintain a disciplined investment program	☐	☐	☐	☐	☐
Maintain charitable donations	☐	☐	☐	☐	☐
Maintain education funds for my children	☐	☐	☐	☐	☐
Maintain my estate for my spouse	☐	☐	☐	☐	☐

WORKSHEET 4-11: YOUR PERSONAL FINANCIAL GOALS WORKSHEET

	IMPORTANCE				
	Low		Medium		High
GOAL	1	2	3	4	5
Maintain my estate for my children	☐	☐	☐	☐	☐
Maintain adequate disability insurance	☐	☐	☐	☐	☐
Achieve financial independence at age _____	☐	☐	☐	☐	☐
Retire at normal age of _____	☐	☐	☐	☐	☐
Partially retire at age _____	☐	☐	☐	☐	☐
Retire early at age _____	☐	☐	☐	☐	☐
Other _____	☐	☐	☐	☐	☐
Other _____	☐	☐	☐	☐	☐
Other _____	☐	☐	☐	☐	☐
Other _____	☐	☐	☐	☐	☐

WORKSHEET 4-12: YOUR PERSONAL GOAL AND PLAN OF ACTION

Goal: (7 words or less)

_____

_____

Detailed Description of Goal:

_____

_____

_____

_____

Benefits From Goal:

_____

_____

_____

Objectives and Action Steps:	**Today's Date**	**Target Date**	**Completion Date**

Result:

_____

_____

_____

_____

Budgeting—Paying Yourself First

Most people look at their expenses and find nothing left for savings. You may be like these people—you don't have a structured plan for saving. The reason you don't is because you don't include yourself as one of your expenses! If you want to start saving wisely, it will mean looking at your budget in a new way.

Your personal budget includes four major costs: housing, food, transportation, and clothing. Beyond these four costs, we have all other monthly bills. Add yourself to the list. Learn to develop a "healthy selfishness" about your money by placing you and your family first.

Monthly Budget	$

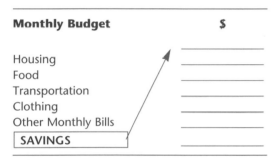

Housing	_____
Food	_____
Transportation	_____
Clothing	_____
Other Monthly Bills	_____
SAVINGS	_____

"Pay Yourself First" bring your planned savings to the top of the list.

Bring your regular savings plan to the top of the list and determine the amount you can save each month, whether it's 5%, 10%, or 15% of your gross income. Put a figure in at the very top of the list for savings. Then you can look after your hous-

ing, food, transportation, clothing, and remaining bills. "Pay yourself first" is the first premise in beginning a financial plan.

Earlier in this chapter you calculated your estimated annual income and expenses. Compare your budget to the following government chart based on the typical spending patterns of a Canadian family in 1986. Note that this chart does not include a category for saving and investing.

The Consumer Price Index (CPI) is based on total spending patterns. A successful budgeting program includes both savings and investing to allow you to pay yourself first. Using the Consumer Price Index chart as a guideline, plot your family's expenses and compare your results with the CPI. This will require you to do some grouping of your expenses. The easiest way is to:

- "Pay Yourself First"—determine how much you can set aside for saving and investing.
- Determine your four major costs: housing, food, transportation, and clothing.
- Group the remainder under other monthly bills.

The purpose of this exercise is to see how far apart your figures are for your four major expenses compared to the CPI figures. A good part of your saving and investing success will be derived from the figures listed in your "other monthly bills" category.

> The primary payment during your working career should be made to yourself to ensure adequate financial reserves for your retirement.
>
> **Graydon Watters**

TABLE 4-13: THE CONSUMER PRICE INDEX

Based on 1986 spending patterns

	%
Housing	36.3
Food	18.1
Transportation	18.3
Clothing	8.7
Recreation, Reading and Education	8.8
Tobacco and Alcohol	5.6
Health and Personal Care	4.2
TOTAL	100.0

WORKSHEET 4-14: YOUR PERSONAL FAMILY EXPENSES

	Expense	%	CPI 1986 AVG.	% Variance from CPI
Savings	_____	_____	– – –	– – –
Housing	_____	_____	36.3	_____
Food	_____	_____	18.1	_____
Transportation	_____	_____	18.3	_____
Clothing	_____	_____	8.7	_____
Other Monthly Bills	_____	_____	18.6	_____
TOTAL		100.0	100.0	_____

Helpful Hints for Successful Budgeting

The shortest recorded period of time lies between the minute you put some money away for a rainy day and the unexpected arrival of rain.

Jane Bryant Quinn

You have learned by now that successful financial planning is really managing objectives to attain your goals. If your goal is "I want to be rich," then establish a game plan to attain your goal. One of the first steps is to set up a budget. Your first decision will be to save money, and you will therefore have to find ways to cut back on some of your expenses. In the end, you will reach your goal, but right now you are just at the beginning. Follow these recommendations:

- Discuss your family's goals and objectives openly. Each person in your household must share a commitment to the plan.

- Determine how much it will cost and what sacrifices will have to be made in order to make your goals a reality.

- Pay yourself first! I have already discussed the importance of this method of budgeting, whereby you determine what you can save by cutting back on other expenses and non-essential items.

- Make sure your budget is flexible, rather than precise. Allow for a degree of error. Don't strap yourself to the point where you lose interest in your original goal.

- Allow for the unexpected in your plans. Situations change and emergencies come up. Don't allow these happenings to cause you to lose sight of your original goal.

- Make sure the budget is compatible with your personality and habits. No one knows you better than you know yourself. So plan accordingly, in line with your strengths and weaknesses.

- You have to know where your money is going, so you must develop a record-keeping system that is easy to follow. An accordion file is an excellent way of categorizing your expenses into groups such as food, clothing, housing, etc. It would also help to break down your expenses into fixed expenses, variable expenses, short-term expenses, and long-term expenses.

- Beware of buying things on impulse, and do not buy too much on credit. Pay off your charge cards monthly, whenever possible.

- Keep your borrowing to a minimum and, if you do need to borrow, make sure your loan interest is tax deductible.

- Give each person who shares a commitment to the plan an allowance for personal needs and expenditures. You can't earmark every single cent in your budget for savings and expenses or you will lose enthusiasm.

- Be sure to have a monthly and an annual "financial fire drill" to compare your actual experience to your budget objectives:
  - What parts of my budget are working well?
  - What do I need to change?
  - How can I improve the return on my savings?

Remember,

"All the money in the world is no use to a man or his country if he spends it as fast as he makes it. All he has left is his bills and the reputation for being a fool."

Rudyard Kipling

Money and a Positive Mental Attitude

The philosopher Lao Tzu said, "The journey of a thousand miles begins with a single step." You've already taken that step. The right attitude will keep you going towards your goal.

Why Many Personal Investment Programs Fail

The four greatest reasons investment programs fail are income taxes, inflation, procrastination, and *you*. By "you" I mean the inability of most people to adopt a winning mental attitude about money. We will bypass the discussion of taxes and inflation here. These are largely out of our direct control and I will discuss them later in the book in their more appropriate contexts.

Procrastination and mental attitude *are* under your control. They are personal factors that influence all your financial decisions and plans.

Procrastination

In matters of personal finance, procrastination reveals its true character—self-sabotage. The longer you wait to put money to work for yourself, the more money you will require when you eventually need it. Retirement income is seldom a concern when you are young. A house, car, travel, and perhaps a boat or cottage, enjoy higher positions of financial priority. Too often people reach age 55 or 60 and realize the paycheques will stop coming in a few years, and they have not adequately planned to meet their future expenses.

The realization is frightening, disarming, and in most cases, irreversible. Make time work for you, look at it as something under your control, something tangible. Time is your greatest ally. Below is an article by an unknown author entitled the "Bank of Time," which I came across many years ago.

If you had a bank that credited your account each morning with $86,400 and you were not allowed to keep any cash in your account overnight (in other words, the bank would cancel any part of the money you had not spent), what would you do? You would naturally draw out every cent. Well, you have such a bank and its name is "time." Every morning it credits you with 86,400 seconds. Every night it rules off as lost whatever time you have failed to invest to good purpose. You cannot carry over any balance and you are not allowed any overdraft. Each day, it opens a new account with you. Each night it burns the record of the day. If you fail to use the day's deposits, the loss is yours. There is no going back, and there is no drawing against tomorrow. We must live in the present so as to maximize our Health, Happiness, and Success!

> The worst bankrupt in the world is the man who has lost his enthusiasm. Let a man lose everything else in the world but his enthusiasm and he will come through again to success.
>
> **H.W. Arnold**

You have the opportunity to change the direction of your financial life and to develop meaningful interests for your retirement years. The process doesn't begin tomorrow. It begins *now*.

Mental Attitude

Much has been written about positive mental attitude. Hundreds of books and courses and a host of inspirational seminars offer encouragement that will help you recharge your batteries. I conduct many financial planning retirement seminars with motivational content, and I also attend seminars and workshops to recharge my own batteries. I encourage a positive mental attitude wherever I go and I start with myself.

A decade ago I decided to write this book. During that time, there were periods when the excitement of the project waned, and I lost sight of my original goal in the shuffle of my business, career, family, and recreational activities. I began to worry, but I found that worry was a greater hindrance than the work involved in completing the book. Before long, I acknowledged that it was time to regenerate my goal. A positive mental attitude was the key. I completed the book with an "I Can" attitude.

You can attain your financial planning goals the same way. You are in control of

your destiny and you will make the decisions that affect your life and your finances. *You* are where the buck stops — and the dollars begin.

Attitude Is a Scientific Process

Maintaining a positive mental attitude in the face of today's world is not easy. Our environment supports negativity. Most of what we read and watch in newspapers and on television is filled with negative input—natural disasters, fire, rape, murder, famine, war, international tension, lawsuits, divorce, and more. If the majority of your input is negative, the output will be as well, because the mind processes thoughts like a computer. We are bombarded by negative information because negativity sells, but sells what? Remember:

A Bad Attitude Produces Bad Results.
A Fair Attitude Produces Fair Results.
A Good Attitude Produces Good Results.

Success breeds success; failure breeds failure. Let's examine success, the result of a positive "I Can" attitude.

An "I Can" attitude sets a positive cycle in motion. Your faith and belief system programs the mental attitude of a winner. You do what you have to do to succeed. You can be successful; you can have

> Exercise your right
> to take action
> and leave the talking
> to others.
> **Graydon Watters**

CHART 5-1:

THE LAWS OF
ATTITUDE

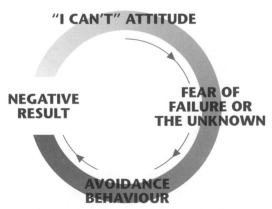

positive results. This leads you to take great leaps forward, which in turn, breeds still more positive results. Developing a positive mental attitude can carry you beyond the vicious circle of negativity to the victory circle. It is easy to write about and more difficult to put into practice, but it is inevitably more rewarding.

Winners Never Quit
Quitters Never Win

Some Considerations on Happiness

Does positive mental attitude lead to happiness? I will leave that up to your own experience. Happiness is everyone's goal, something to build. But in your search for happiness and success, don't overlook your own backyard. The foolish man seeks happiness in the distance; the wise man grows it under his feet. Happiness is like a kiss— in order to get any good out of it, you have to give it to someone else!

Zig Ziglar, in his book, *Steps To The Top*, shares his considerations on happiness: "I believe a person needs time to enjoy life. No matter how busy you are, you still have time to be one of two things: happy or unhappy. When you got up this morning, you might not have realized it, but you chose to be happy or unhappy."

Carol Burnett recently received a collection of poems from some children. One girl named Patricia wrote, "Happiness is to snuggle up in bed under all the blankets on a cold night. Happiness is just being happy."

Canadian author June Callwood relates that historian Will Durant looked for happiness in travel and found weariness; in wealth and found discord and worry; in his writing and was only fatigued. One day he saw a woman waiting in a car with a sleeping child in her arms. A man descended from a train and came over and gently kissed the woman and then the baby, very softly, so as not to waken him. The family drove away, leaving Durant with a humble realization: every normal function of life holds some delight.

The Train of Life—Engineering Your Direction

If positive mental attitude leads to success, attitude is scientific, and happiness is ever-present just waiting to be recognized, then consider your "Train of Life." Are you running it, or is it running you?

Can the caboose pull the train? **No.**
Can the freight car pull the train? **No.**
Can the engine pull the train? **Yes!**

The unalterable fact is that only the engine can pull the train. Unfortunately,

> Action may not always bring happiness; but there is no happiness without action.
>
> **Disraeli**

CHART 5-2: THE TRAIN OF LIFE

CIRCUMSTANCES · FAITH · FEELINGS · FACT

based on accepted circumstances, most people have everything caboose-backwards and their train runs backward. Going forward means putting yourself at the controls in the engine and engineering positive direction about where your life is going. It works like this:

- You awake feeling full of life; it's great to be alive, which leads to:
- Feeling good about yourself, which creates a positive experience, which leads to:
- Taking positive actions and doing the right things, which leads to:
- A positive result, for what you sincerely seek, you will find.

Success—from Concept to Action

Success comes when you put yourself on the line. Positive mental attitude is the key. The concept is simple, and I know that if you have read this book so far, you have already shown the tenacity it takes to look at yourself honestly and take a step in the right direction. Procrastination has no rightful place in your life from this day forward. I enjoy this poem written by Herbert Kauffman many decades ago, entitled "Victory."

You are the man who used to boast
That you'd achieve the uttermost,
Some day.

You merely wished a show,
To demonstrate how much you know
And prove the distance you can go ...

Another year we've just passed through,
What new ideas came to you?
How many big things did you do?

Time...left twelve fresh months in your care
How many of them did you share
With opportunity and dare

Again where you so often missed?
We do not find you on the list
of Makers Good.

Explain the fact!
Ah no, 'twas not the chance you lacked!
As usual—you failed to act!

The time to start planning for a comfortable retirement is now. Yesterday is gone. Tomorrow is a result of what we think and do today. Start now!

The longer you wait—
the steeper the climb

Courage is like a muscle: we strengthen it with use.

Ruth Gordon

The ABCs of Saving Versus Investing

When you save, you are only a loaner—lending money to a bank, a trust company, or the Government, and receiving low interest income. But when you invest, you are an owner—participating in free enterprise by buying ownership in a company. Canada built its future with investment. How will you build yours?

Savings Builds Character

Many years ago I came across an inspirational message written by H.A. McNeely, Executive Vice-President of the Tampa Savings and Loan Association in Florida, entitled "Walking Tall."

Your savings, believe it or not, affect the way you stand, the way you walk, the tone of your voice. In short, your physical well-being and confidence.

A man without savings is always running. He must. He must take the first job offered, or nearly so. He sits nervously on life's chairs because any small emergency throws him into the hands of others.

Without savings, a man must be too grateful. Gratitude is a fine thing in its place. But a constant state of gratitude is a horrible place in which to live.

A man with savings can walk tall. He may appraise opportunities in a relaxed way, have time for judicious estimates and not be rushed by economic necessity.

A man with savings can afford to resign from his job, if his principles so dictate.

And for this reason he'll never need to do so. A man who can afford to quit is much more useful to his company, and therefore more promotable. He can afford to give his company the benefit of his most candid judgments.

A man always concerned about necessities, such as food and rent, can't afford to think in long-range career terms. He must dart to the most immediate opportunity for ready cash. Without savings, he will spend a lifetime of darting, dodging.

A man with savings can afford the wonderful privilege of being generous in family or neighbourhood emergencies. He can take a level stare into the eyes of any man—friend, stranger, or enemy. It shapes his personality and character.

The ability to save has nothing to do with the size of income. Many high-income people,who spend it all, are on a tread-mill darting through life like minnows.

If you don't need money for college, a home, or retirement, then save for self-confidence.The state of your savings does have a lot to do with how tall you walk.

> Money makes money. And the money that money makes makes more money.
>
> **Benjamin Franklin**

I have yet to hear a better description of savings. Its glowing tribute to the man with savings would apply to all people who are sending money ahead for future delivery.

Savings Defined

Savings is the process of taking a certain percentage of your after-tax income and placing it in a bank or trust account in what I call a "loanership" fashion. Now, what is "loanership"? You *lend* your money to a bank or trust company and they, in return, pay you interest on your deposit. The bank then uses your money for their purposes, such as lending money to people who want to buy cars and household appliances, and to businesses for their operations.

Using a bank or trust company is the easy way to save, but it has a major drawback. The rate of return you receive is typically low when compared to other types of investment vehicles. As a saver (loaner), it is very difficult to build real wealth for the future. Yet without savings, you would have no money in the first place to put to work in more productive ways.

Types of Savings

Most people are familiar with the traditional savings vehicles offered by banks, trusts, credit unions, and other savings companies. It is not uncommon for most of us to have a chequing account for our day-to-day budgeting needs, as well as one or more savings accounts where we deposit money for some future need or purchase.

There are many variations on chequing and savings accounts. A straight chequing account pays no interest, but provides statements and returns your cancelled cheques. A chequing/savings account, which allows cheque-writing privileges in addition to savings at a reduced rate of interest, is another popular variation.

The premium savings account, on the other hand, usually offers a higher rate of interest for a minimum balance; in some accounts, the higher the balance, the higher the rate of interest earned. Try to find one with a daily interest feature; this means that the bank calculates the interest you've earned on your minimum balance each day and credits it to your account monthly. Premium savings accounts usually do not have chequing privileges; you withdraw funds in person.

Foreign currency savings accounts (such as United States dollars) may also be available. Check with your bank about the chequing and savings options that are available to you.

Savings provide a degree of comfort and the confidence of knowing you can meet any emergency. But, as you examine the various options set out here, remember that simple savings does not build real wealth.

When Saving Becomes Investing

Investing is putting your savings to work by the purchase of a security or other property with the expectation of a greater rate of return than you would earn by saving.

The first ingredient you need for any investment program is capital, which is simply another word for savings. Capital generally is acquired by employing a gradual accumulation program over a period of years. It can also come from an inheritance or a sudden windfall. But, for most people, disciplined savings usually provides the capital for investment.

The remainder of this chapter contains many details and technical terms. Don't despair, and don't feel you have to learn all the information before you can enjoy success. I will introduce many different tools to help you through the process.

It's good to have money, and the things money can buy, but it's good, too, to check up once in a while, and be sure you haven't lost the things money can't buy.

George Horace Lorimer

"Loanership" Securities

For our purposes in this book, savings has been defined as money you would lend to a bank or trust company. Once you take that money out of the savings account, I will consider that you are investing for higher returns. The following securities will generate higher returns than savings (see Chart 6-1) without adding appreciable risk to your capital.

Canada Savings Bonds (CSBs)

As the name implies, *CSBs* are a savings vehicle. They can be bought each year from late October until early November; the exact timing is up to the Minister of Finance. These bonds are a direct obligation of the Government of Canada and therefore the interest and principal are fully guaranteed. The bonds are purchased at par (100 cents on the dollar) and they do not fluctuate in price; they are always worth what you paid for them.

A popular method of purchasing *Canada Savings Bonds* is through payroll deduction. You acquire the bonds over the course of a year through regular deductions from your paycheque, then take delivery of the bonds the following November. Many people use this relatively painless method of saving because it satisfies the "If you don't see it, you won't feel it" attitude.

Canada Treasury Bills (T-Bills)

These short-term investments are another direct obligation of the Government of Canada. *T-Bills* are issued every Friday by the Bank of Canada. They have various maturities to a maximum of one year and are bought at a discount from par value. "At a discount" means you buy them for less than their face value and they mature at par. The difference is your interest.

T-Bills are traded in multiples of $1,000 and usually are subject to a minimum purchase of $5,000–$10,000. They are regularly traded by banks, brokers, corporations, and other investors with large amounts of money to lend for short periods.

The government also borrows money to finance its obligations over longer periods of time. Bonds guaranteed by the Government of Canada are available for terms of one to 30 years. More about these later.

Term Deposits (TDs) and Guaranteed Investment Certificates (GICs)

Term deposits are issued by banks and trust companies, usually in minimum amounts of $500. These are popular investments that generally offer higher interest than CSBs or T-bills on their one-year rates. TDs can be issued for terms under one year.

GICs are usually issued for terms of one to five years. Be sure to check the terms of a GIC before you commit your funds. Most stipulate that your money is locked in for the duration of the term and can only be withdrawn after paying a stiff penalty. If you require flexibility, shop around.

Monthly Income Receipts (MIRs)

Monthly Income Receipts are designed to provide monthly income, security, liquidity, and an attractive rate of interest. The receipts offer you a pooled investment in bonds, debentures, and treasury bills. The major benefits of this savings vehicle include steady monthly income and investment in securities that are backed by the Government of Canada and the provinces.

Savings and Deposit Insurance

For the purposes of this book and ease of explanation, I consider the vehicles discussed so far to be savings vehicles. You have loaned your money to the issuer. The underlying principal or capital is

There are two things to aim for in life:

❶

Get what you want

❷

Make sure you enjoy it.

Only those with lots of wisdom achieve the second.

issued to you at par value, or based on par value; your original capital is always worth 100 cents on the dollar at maturity.

These vehicles are all relatively risk-free and are backed either by the issuing bank or trust company, or by the Government of Canada or the provinces. You should always ensure, when applicable, that the issuing institution is a member of the Canadian Deposit Insurance Corporation (CDIC), a government agency that guarantees your principal to a maximum of $60,000 per account.

Savings Rate Comparisons

It is important to understand that in a savings, or loaning, environment, the rate of return can vary substantially on any given day. For example, on May 13, 1994, a typical trust company premium savings account rate was 1.5%. A 60-day term deposit with a bank was 5.5% and a Government of Canada treasury bill with an investment dealer was 6.5% for 91 days. The difference between these rates shows you how important it is to shop around.

Similarly, on May 13, 1994, there was a vast difference in savings rates. A major chartered bank offered the following rates:

- **Premium savings account**
  Minimum balance $1,000 ....1.00%
- **Investment savings account**
  Minimum balance $5,000 ....2.35%
- **Term deposit**
  Min.. $5,000 / 60-day term 5.50%
- **T-Bill**
  Under $100,000 / 91-day term.....6.75%

A major trust company offered these rates:

- **Premium savings account**
  Regular rate no minimum 0.50%
- **Savings account super rate**
  Minimum balance $25,000 ....4.25%
- **Super T-Bill**
  $60,000 to $100,000 ....5.35%
- **Guaranteed investment certificate**
  Three–year term 6.50%
- **Guaranteed investment certificate**
  Five–year term.............................7.25%

A major investment dealer offered the following rates:

- **Daily interest on account balance**
  under $25,000 ....3.75%
- **Daily interest on account balance**
  over $25,000 ....4.75%
- **Canada T-Bills**
  $10,000 to $50,000 ....6.50%
- **Canada T-Bills**
  Over $100,000 ....7.00%

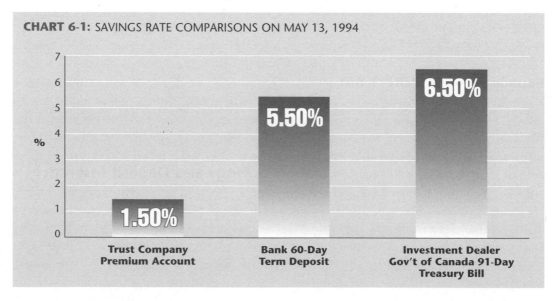

CHART 6-1: SAVINGS RATE COMPARISONS ON MAY 13, 1994

1.50% — Trust Company Premium Account
5.50% — Bank 60-Day Term Deposit
6.50% — Investment Dealer Gov't of Canada 91-Day Treasury Bill

As a point of comparison, note that Canada Savings Bonds issued November of 1993 yielded 4.25%. Effective August 1, 1994, the rate of interest on all outstanding CSBs was increased to 6.50% for the three–month period ending October 31, 1994.

"Loanership" Securities That Can Change in Value

When the value of a security can fluctuate according to the forces of the investment markets, there is increased risk to the capital if there is a chance that it may have to be sold prior to its stated maturity date. Wherever there is more risk, investors want a higher return. You may not think of a mortgage as risky, but there is certainly more risk in one than putting your money in a chartered bank.

Mortgages

Mortgage investments are usually made directly between the investor and the owner of a property, sometimes with the assistance of a mortgage broker. Be sure of the quality of the mortgage and whether it's a first, second, or third mortgage. Each additional mortgage on a property increases the degree of risk because each has less claim on the house in the event of default.

Direct investment in individual mortgages can be plagued by collection problems, and can be difficult to sell if interest rates are not moving in your favour. Periodic repayment of small amounts of principal may reduce the total yield because you may not be able to reinvest small amounts at the same rate as the mortgage rate. *Mortgage mutual funds* and *mortgage-backed securities* can alleviate these problems.

NHA Mortgage-Backed Securities (MBSs)

These are high quality securities, similar to government bonds, that provide higher yields than other savings options by investing in first mortgages on residential properties.

An MBS offers you a pool of mortgages insured by Canada Mortgage and Housing Corporation (CMHC), a Canadian government agency. The bank, trust company, or investment dealer that acts as the issuer of MBSs ensures that all the mortgage payments are made and distributes the proceeds to the holders of units in the pool.

The major features of mortgage-backed securities include:

- Attractive rate of return
- Monthly payments of principal and interest
- Guaranteed on-time payment each month
- Insured mortgages
- Liquidity
- No one-on-one personal mortgage management.

Bonds and Debentures

Bonds and *debentures* are issued by governments (both Federal and Provincial), municipalities, school boards, and other public bodies, to provide operating funds over and above those supplied by tax and other revenue.

Corporations also issue bonds, often secured by a mortgage on specific assets, and debentures, which may or may not be secured by specific assets. The proceeds from the sale of these securities are issued to finance business needs such as a new plant or equipment.

When you buy a bond, you are, once again, loaning your money to the issuer of the bond. Bonds and debentures are usually issued in maturities of from 2 to 30 years, and interest is generally paid semi-annually.

Bonds are traded in a market that is made up of banks, trust companies,

You are the product of what you choose for your life situation. You do have the capacity to make healthy choices for yourself by changing your attitude to one of creative aliveness.
Abraham Maslow

investment dealers, and other large corporate and individual investors.

The price at which the bond will trade depends on the quality of the issue, current interest rates, the maturity date, the number of bonds available for trading (the liquidity) of the issue, and other factors. In addition, bonds may carry certain privileges such as optional maturity dates that may have an influence on their prices.

The most important consideration when trading bonds is the outlook for interest rates. Bond prices and yields trade on an inverse relationship; that is, when interest rates go down, bond prices go up. The reason for this is simple: when interest rates drop, those bonds with a coupon (interest) rate higher than the rates currently available in the market become more attractive. Investors are willing to pay more to have their money earn a higher rate of interest. Figures A, B, and C demonstrate the effect of rates on bond prices.

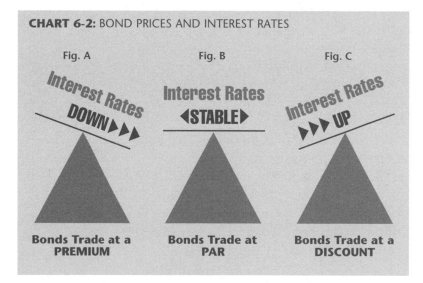

CHART 6-2: BOND PRICES AND INTEREST RATES

Fig. A — Interest Rates DOWN ▶▶▶ — Bonds Trade at a PREMIUM

Fig. B — Interest Rates ◀STABLE▶ — Bonds Trade at PAR

Fig. C — Interest Rates ▶▶▶ UP — Bonds Trade at a DISCOUNT

Strip Coupons

You may have heard of *Sentinels, Tigers, Cougars,* and other such coupons. These are all variations of a security called the *stripped coupon bond.* With this kind of investment, a dealer takes a high-quality Government of Canada or provincial government bond and separates the coupons from the principal amount. They then take those coupons, which come due every six months, and offer them to investors in separate parcels.

The reasons for stripping coupons from the principal of a bond are fairly obvious. "Strips," as they are called, are a simple way of buying a flow of income by discounting its future value to today's value.

The principal portion, or *residual,* serves the kind of investor who doesn't want or need current income but who would prefer to see his or her money grow over the long term. Residuals are sold at what is called the "deep discount"—at a small fraction of what they will be worth at maturity.

In the example below, the coupon maturity date of April 1, 2000, reflects a coupon that will be paid at that time. (This example was an actual offering, back in 1984, 16 years from maturity.) You would have paid $12.64 per $100, or a total of $884.80 to get back $7,000 when the coupon matured April 1, 2000. That $884.80 compared to what you get back ($7,000), on April 1, 2000, works out to an average annual yield of 14%.

Residuals are best held in a tax-exempt plan such as an RRSP, Registered Retirement Income Fund (RRIF), or a Registered Education Savings Plan (RESP). Within these plans, the interest compounds without any tax complications. In a taxable account, the accrued return must be reported as income at least every three years, even though you will not receive the income until maturity.

Convertible Debentures

You will recall that a *debenture* is like a bond, but is usually secured only by the company's promise to pay regular interest and return your principal at maturity. A convertible debenture allows you to convert your debenture into a specified number of the issuing company's common shares. As the common shares rise in price, the convertible debenture follows, often well above what would be expected given the interest rate it pays.

These unique debentures are often referred to as a "two-way" security. The privilege of converting into the company's common shares provides capital appreciation potential if the company performs well. You also get higher fixed income than you would get from the dividend on the common shares.

There are three terms to consider if you are thinking about the purchase of a *convertible debenture*:

- *Convertible Term*
  The number of years that the debenture remains convertible
- *Term to Maturity*
  The number of years until the bond matures at par
- *Term to Redemption*
  The number of years until the company may redeem the issue at their option

Convertibles often trade at a premium to the underlying common stock. The premium takes into account such things as the number of shares into which the debenture can be converted (convertible ratio), the level and trend of the stock price, and the coupon rate of the debenture.

The formula for calculating premium is:

% Premium=

$$\left[\frac{(\text{Debenture Price} \div \text{Convertible Ratio})}{\text{Common Price}} - 1 \right] \times 100$$

"Ownership" Securities

When you own part of a business, you share in all those things that go into a living, breathing operation: employees,

unions, markets, customers, competitors, technologies, and so on. That means you get to share in the good times and the bad times. True, there is risk involved, but the rewards of equity ownership can be great.

What Is Equity?

The term *equity* comes from the total value of a corporation beyond any debts it may owe, those debts being the ownership interest of a company held by its common and preferred shareholders. The word equity or shares is synonymous with the common and preferred stocks held by these shareholders. You will find that I often refer to common and preferred stocks as equity or shares.

Preferred Shares

Preferred shares are part of the equity or ownership of a corporation and are usually issued with a stated par value. They enjoy a prior claim on assets of the corporation to common shares in the event of breakup.

The dividends on preferreds rank ahead of the common, but after all creditors. Dividends are usually at a fixed rate, with the exception of variable-rate preferreds, and are usually paid quarterly. If a company has some short-term cash flow problems and can't pay their dividends for a period of time, they might resort to the cumulative feature on the preferred share whereby the company will pay back all past dividends when their cash flow improves.

Preferred shares should play a very important part of your overall portfolio structure. The most recent Canadian tax proposals make dividend income more attractive than interest income or capital gains. However, if you are going to participate in preferred shares, it is imperative that you understand their unique characteristics and privileges.

The secret of success is constancy of purpose.
Disraeli

Preferred Share Characteristics

- *High Dividend Yield*

  Preferred shares carry much higher dividend yields than common shares and, unlike common shares, the dividend is fixed at a certain rate unless it is a variable-rate preferred.

- *Better Protection of Capital*

  Preferred shares rank ahead of common shares in their claim on the issuer's assets. In other words, your capital is safer.

- *Replacement for Savings*

  Preferred share investments provide a larger after-tax return than many interest-bearing vehicles, due in part to the dividend tax credit.

Types of Preferred Shares

- *Straight Preferreds*

  Provide long-term dividend income. Sometimes these will have a sinking fund or purchase fund to retire the issue over time, or there may be no maturity date at all.

- *Retractable Preferreds*

  Generally offer high income for a fixed term. Their retraction date is usually between five and ten years with an additional five or ten years to redemption. When you buy this type of preferred, consider your current yield, yield to retraction, and yield to redemption.

- *Variable Rate Preferreds*

  Have their dividend fixed to a stated formula, often prime bank rate. Be careful to consider the direction of interest rates when evaluating your purchase. These shares are designed to adapt to changes in interest rates—up *and* down!

- *U.S. Pay Preferreds*

  These preferreds trade and pay their dividends in U.S. funds, but still retain all tax privileges relative to the Canadian dividend tax credit. Many seniors prefer these issues, especially if they winter in the sunbelt areas, because they provide a steady source of U.S. funds.

- *Convertible Preferreds*

  Usually have lower income than a straight or retractable preferred, but offer a higher yield than the underlying common. Convertibles provide growth opportunities if the underlying common shares of the issuing company are rising. As mentioned above, you should consider the conversion premiums and conversion terms in order to decide whether the common or convertible preferred is better value.

  Convertible preferreds have a number of characteristics that should be considered before they are purchased. These include:

Extra Yield

The higher fixed yield on the preferred provides more income and downside protection than the common yield.

Premium

For this extra yield, you pay a premium:

$ Premium=

$$\frac{\text{Price of Preferred}}{\text{Number of Common}} - \text{Common Price}$$

% Premium=

$$\frac{\text{\$ Premium}}{\text{Common Price}} \times 100$$

Payback

This is the number of years it will take for the extra yield from the preferred shares to repay or "pay back" the current premium.

Payback (in years)=

$$\frac{\text{Premium}}{[\text{Yield (Preferred)} - \text{Yield (Common)}]}$$

Term

There are different concepts of term that the investor should consider:

1 Conversion Term—The number of years that the preferred remains convertible.

2 Term to Redemption—Straight Redemption: the number of years until the company may redeem the issue at their option.

Early Redemption: may occur if the common shares trade above a stated price level.

Preferred Yields

- *Current Yield*

  Current yield is your dividend, divided by market prices.

- *Yield-to-Retraction*

  Some preferreds have a retraction date at some point in the future, with a fixed retraction price. ("Retraction" means an early maturity date for repayment of your principal.) This type of yield is based on your dividend, divided by the price at retraction.

- *Yield-to-Redemption*

  Most preferreds have a redemption date at some point in the future with a fixed redemption price. This type of yield is based on your dividend, divided by the redemption price.

Preferred Share Quality and Privileges

- *Canadian Bond Rating Service (CBRS)*

  An independent evaluation of credit worthiness whereby the quality of an issuing company is measured and rated on a system of P1 (highest) to P5 (lowest).

- *Term-to-Retraction*

  The number of years until the company must return your principal investment. Exercisable at your option.

- *Term-to-Redemption*

  The number of years until the company can pay off your investment at its option.

- *Sinking Fund*

  A method whereby the company purchases a given percentage of the issue on an annual basis. This provides you with some degree of liquidity, knowing that the company must purchase shares each year.

- *Purchase Fund*

  A method whereby the company purchases a stated number of shares each year, but only below par value. This helps to support the market price of the shares.

Common Shares

Common shares represent the ownership of a corporation, subject to the rights of the preferred shares. They usually give the stockholder or owner the right to vote on the selection of management and directors, and entitle the holder to a proportionate, but unspecified, claim on the profits. A part of the earnings is often paid out as dividends, subject to the discretion of the company's Board of Directors. The remainder may be reinvested in the corporation's business or held as retained earnings.

Dividends are not fixed at a set rate like preferreds, and if the company pays a dividend, they are usually paid quarterly. Common shares represent the permanent capital subscribed to the company. They are known as variable income investments and have the potential to grow in value, through earnings paid as dividends and earnings employed in capital growth and expansion. Depending on the conditions of the stock market and the outlook investors have for the company, these factors will usually enhance the value of the stock.

Voting and Non-Voting Shares

Common shares are sometimes divided into two classes, *voting* and *non-voting*. Usually, the non-voting share is granted some other privilege, such as a preferential dividend or a participating feature, or both. A company issues two classes of stock so that they can control the corporation with the voting shares and avoid the possibility of an unwanted takeover. By issuing non-voting shares they maintain access to new capital.

Par Value and No Par Value
Historically, all common shares were issued with a *par value*. During the last several decades, *no par value* stock has been the norm. This came about because there is usually very little relationship between the book value or asset value of the company and the par value of its stock.

Since most corporations today trade at some multiple above their book value, no par value is a more accurate description of the company's stock. The primary feature of a common share is its claim on the net earnings and assets of the company.

Preferred shares, you will recall, almost always have a par value, and their dividend rates are expressed as a percentage of their par value, or in dollars and cents per share.

Types of Common Shares
The 2,000 common stocks that trade on Canadian stock exchanges and over-the-counter markets generally fall into one of three categories:
- *Blue Chip or Investment Grade*
  You can expect relative stability and modest long-term growth, as well as regular (but not guaranteed) dividend income.
- *Growth Stocks or Investment Grade*
  You hope the prospects for growth will provide substantial intermediate and long-term capital gains. These companies may or may not pay dividends.
- *Speculative Stocks*
  Can offer you substantial success or dismal failure. This is the high risk area of the market that provides only a handful of winners, but trucks full of losers. Not for the faint of heart.

Mutual Funds

A *mutual fund* is just what it says—a pool of capital made up of money invested by individuals who want to achieve specific objectives such as long-term growth, current income, or safety of principal. Professional investment managers are hired by the fund to achieve its stated goals.

A mutual fund is the term commonly applied to an open-end investment company. These companies sell their treasury shares (or units) on a continuous (open) basis to the public and, in turn, invest the proceeds in a portfolio of securities in a way that will meet the advertised goals of the fund. They are obligated to redeem your units upon demand at the net asset value of all the investments being administered in the fund.

Open-end funds are bought and sold from the mutual fund manager through brokers, investment dealers, and financial planners.

Closed-End Investment Company

This type of company is similar to any other industrial company. It has a fixed capitalization, and once its authorized capital is issued, no further shares are usually offered. They also invest in a wide range of securities, but unlike the mutual fund, the *closed-end* company cannot redeem its own shares. Investors wishing to sell must do so at the prevailing price on the stock exchange where the units are listed.

Rights

This is a means of raising new capital for a corporation by offering existing shareholders the *right* to subscribe for additional shares. A company usually will issue one right for each common share you own and the subscription for new shares combines some multiple of the rights issued for each new share, for example, 5 rights plus cash = 1 new share.

The subscription price for the new share is set below the current market value of the company's shares, creating a value for the rights. You can dispose of your rights, or purchase additional rights on a stock exchange. Rights are usually issued for a period of three or four weeks, after which they become worthless.

Warrants

Warrants provide you with an opportunity to purchase shares in the underlying company at a fixed price for a fixed period of time, usually from one to several years. They are often attached as part of a preferred share, bond, or debenture financing as an inducement to help with the marketing of the issue.

Warrants are similar to rights in that they provide for the purchase of shares at a pre-determined price. Sometimes they have a two-tier fixed price such as one price for the first two years and a slightly higher price for the next two years. Some of the special features and selection consideration of warrants include:

Warrant Features
- Participation in the capital appreciation of the company's common shares.
- Increased leverage because of the generally smaller dollar consideration involved.

Considerations for Selection of Warrants
- As an investor, you must know what the outlook is for the company and its common shares.
- The exercise premium, the period expiry, and the leverage involved should be carefully analysed.

Derivatives — Options, Futures, Commodities

Every transaction in any marketplace has a buyer and a seller. In the marketplaces for *options*, *futures*, and *commodities*, the buyer is defined as a speculator—someone willing to take substantial risk in return for the opportunity for a large reward. My experience would suggest that very few speculators who are novices are successful using these tools. This is a game for the professionals!

The seller, on the other hand, is called the hedger—the person looking to avoid or reduce risk on an asset already owned. Options, futures, and commodities are very specialized, sophisticated tools that a hedger can utilize to enhance the return on a portfolio by locking in prices. As a rule, hedgers fare reasonably well in the long run because they assume a conservative position.

Sophisticated buyers and sellers and institutional investors have been using *derivatives* as they expand their portfolios to include foreign and global exposure. Derivatives are so-called because their value is derived from the value of the underlying security, stock index, or currency. The main reason investors use derivatives is to manage risk; often to hedge a portfolio weighted with foreign securities against fluctuating interest rates and currency exchange rates.

There is a numerous array of fancy names for these derivative products such as *TIPS*, *PINS*, *LEAPS*, and *PEACS*. Many of these derivatives are not suitable for the average investor; in fact even the professionals in the industry are few and far between when it comes to knowledge about derivatives, so shop carefully for investment advice.

Commodities are extremely risky as well because they involve very high leverage—the practice of putting up only a fraction of the value of the commodity for which you are contracting. This works very well when markets are going up; it also works against you just as quickly, when things are going down. Fortunes are won and lost overnight. Some individuals get in so deep, they lose everything — home, cottage and more. It *really* happens. Beware, Beware!

Precious Metals — Gold, Silver, and Platinum

These are what are known as inflation-hedge assets. Let's begin by looking at a chart of *gold* prices during the last 15 years. Generally, the *precious metals* move in unison. *Silver* and *platinum* would have enjoyed the same superior performance during the last major inflationary cycle.

Anyone who follows the market knows that the price of gold is extremely volatile. In recent years, gold has traded between Canadian $150 and $850 per ounce. The question is: How can something so volatile, so apparently unpredictable, something that pays no dividends and earns no interest, be part of a rationally-planned portfolio?

The answer is that while the *price* of gold may not be predictable, its behaviour certainly is. Gold outperforms all other investments during periods of economic and political uncertainty. That is why gold is not only a valid investment in its own right, but is also the only investment that can protect your portfolio against the extremes of either inflation or deflation.

According to John Ing, President of a Toronto investment firm and a precious metals analyst:

- The gold market reacts to economic, political, and social extremes wherever they may be happening around the world.
- Gold is a medium of exchange or barter that has been in use throughout history, and has always existed as a barometer of investor anxiety.
- Inflation and the supply/demand relationship between producers and consumers of gold are undoubtedly the most important considerations when thinking of gold as an investment.

There are, however, many other considerations involved with the gold market. Ian Fleming's book *Goldfinger,* showcasing the famed agent 007, James Bond, discusses the importance of the precious metal in terms of its defects:

The population of the world is increasing at a rate of 6,000 every hour. A small percentage of these people will become gold hoarders, people who are frightened of currencies, who like to bury some sovereigns in the garden or under the bed. Another percentage need gold fillings for their teeth. Others need gold rimmed

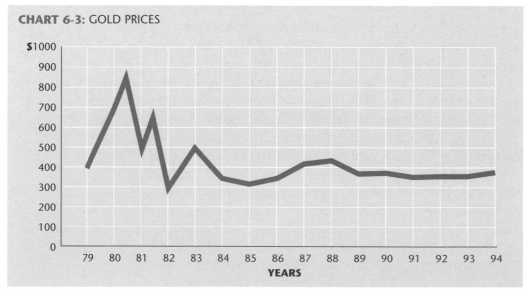

CHART 6-3: GOLD PRICES

(Y-axis: $1000, 900, 800, 700, 600, 500, 400, 300, 200, 100, 0)

YEARS (X-axis: 79 80 81 82 83 84 85 86 87 88 89 90 91 92 93 94)

spectacles, jewelry or engagement rings. All of these new people will be taking tons of gold off the market every year. New industries need gold wire, gold plating, amalgams of gold. Gold has extraordinary properties which have been put to new uses everyday. It is brilliant, malleable, ductile, almost unalterable, and more dense than any other common metal except platinum. There is no end to its uses. But is has two defects. It isn't hard enough. It wears out quickly, leaving itself on the linings of our pockets and in the sweat of our skins. Every year, the world's stock is invisibly reduced by friction. I said that gold has two defects. The other, and by far the major defect, is that it is the talisman of fear Fear, Mr. Bond, takes gold out of circulation, and hoards it against the evil day. In a period of history, when every tomorrow may be the evil day, it is fair enough to say that a fat proportion of the gold that is dug out of the one corner of the earth is at once buried in another corner.

Source: Excerpt from *Goldfinger* by Ian Fleming Glidrose Productions Ltd., publisher Jonathan Cape Ltd., London, England.

When you look at the chart, you can clearly see the effect on gold during the last inflationary spiral.

Antiques, Art, Rare Coins, and Stamps

These are also inflation hedge assets and they can provide a lot of enjoyment both as a hobby and an investment. The most serious drawback of these investments is their lack of liquidity, and the large difference between the bid (purchase price) and the offer (asking price).

The key to success with these investments is to simply enjoy them for what they are—and do your homework first! Know what you're buying.

Real Estate

The single largest investment you will probably ever make is in your home. And like most investments, real estate prices are subject to cycles, and people who allow their purchasing decisions to be ruled by their emotions usually buy at the wrong time and lose money. If you're planning to buy a dream home and want to make a purchasing decision that won't keep you up at nights with nightmares, you should learn how mortgages and the process of amortization work.

How Mortgages Work

A *mortgage* is a loan against which a house or property is pledged as collateral. Should you, the borrower (or mortgagor), fail to repay the loan on the agreed terms, then the lender (or mortgagee), is entitled to take possession of the house or property. The total sum borrowed for the mortgage is called the principal. Interest is paid on the principal to the mortgagee at an agreed rate for as long as the principal is outstanding.

House and property purchases require a downpayment and the conventional mortgage requires a downpayment of 25% of the appraised value of the house. It is possible to work with a smaller downpayment by using a high ratio mortgage, adding a second mortgage, taking out a personal loan, or obtaining a vendor take-back or balance-of-sale mortgage. Most often these features will cost you a premium to obtain.

The mortgage document describes in detail the rights and obligations of both parties to the agreement. The more important terms include amortization, which is the calculation of monthly payments necessary to pay off principal and interest over a period of time. Common amortization periods run from 20 to 30 years. Lenders set a term for the mort-

The best investment is land because they ain't making any more of it.
Will Rogers

53

gage, usually one to five years, at which time the mortgage must be paid or renegotiated even though the amortization may run for a 20- to 30-year period.

Payments on the mortgage are usually monthly and include both interest and a partial repayment of principal. This is known as a blended payment and quite often your taxes will be included in this payment as well, based on 1/12 of your annual tax bill on the property. Many mortgages include pre-payment options on the anniversary date of the mortgage, or allow you to prepay by increasing your monthly payments, or by making extra payments when it suits you. Let's take a closer look at mortgages, amortization, and downpayments.

Mortgages, Amortization, and Downpayments

A mortgage, for all intents and purposes, is the name given to the loan you take out to purchase your home. The *amortization* is simply the amount of time you will need to pay back the loan. If you spread your payments out over a long period of time, you will make small monthly payments, but end up paying an extraordinary total amount in the long run. Similarly, a short amortization period results in larger monthly payments, but a much smaller overall repayment.

Let's look at an example where interest rates on a mortgage of $75,000 are running 8% over 1 year, 8.50% over 2 years,

9.00% over 3 years, 9.50% over 4 years, and 10% over 5 years.

If you take out a 10-year amortization on a 1-year mortgage, your monthly payment is $909.96. If you take out a 30-year amortization, your monthly payment is reduced to $550.33. But saving $359.63 per month will cost you enormously in the long run. Take a calculator and work it out.

If, for example, you purchase a $100,000 house with a $25,000 downpayment, you are working again with a $75,000 mortgage. If the mortgage is at 10% based on a 5-year term and you choose a 10-year amortization, your monthly payment is $991.14. The monthly payment on a 30-year amortization, on the other hand, is $658.18.

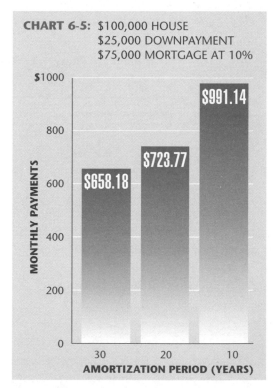

CHART 6-5: $100,000 HOUSE
$25,000 DOWNPAYMENT
$75,000 MORTGAGE AT 10%

Again, remember how long you will be paying that monthly amount. The monthly saving of $332.96 is deceptively attractive. The total cost of your home with a 10-year amortization on a mortgage of 10% is $118,937. The 30-year amortization results in a total cost of $236,945—more than two times the original cost of

TABLE 6-4: MORTGAGE RATES AND PAYMENTS ON $75,000

Term	1 Yr.	2 Yrs.	3 Yrs.	4 Yrs.	5 Yrs.
Interest Rate	8.0%	8.5%	9.0%	9.5%	10.0%
10-Year Amortization	909.96	929.90	950.07	970.49	991.14
20-Year Amortization	627.34	650.87	674.80	699.10	723.77
30-Year Amortization	550.33	576.69	603.47	630.65	658.18

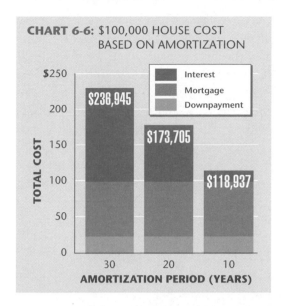

CHART 6-6: $100,000 HOUSE COST BASED ON AMORTIZATION

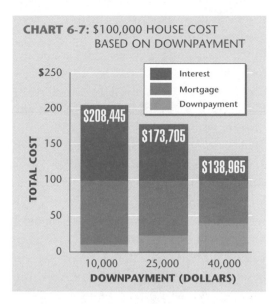

CHART 6-7: $100,000 HOUSE COST BASED ON DOWNPAYMENT

the house, and more than three times the cost of the $75,000 you borrowed as a mortgage to pay for it over time! Those monthly savings of a few hundred dollars turn out to be short-term gains, for a great deal of long-term pain in the pocketbook.

Now, let's look at purchasing a $100,000 house, amortized over a period of 20 years at a mortgage interest rate of 10%, with downpayments of $10,000, $25,000, and $40,000.

With a $10,000 downpayment and $90,000 mortgage, your purchase price over the 20 years totals $208,445. The $25,000 downpayment/$75,000 mortgage results in a total purchase price of $173,705. And with a $40,000 downpayment and $60,000 mortgage, your house will cost only $138,965.

The Ideal Home Purchase Plan

The ideal home purchase plan combines the maximum downpayment you can assemble, with the shortest amortization period you can afford.

This plan will mean some belt tightening such as going without some minor investments for a few years and putting off the purchase of a new car, furniture, and so on. You will have to do some careful planning around this decision,

but it will pay off. A sacrifice made in the early stages of paying for your house will mean a tremendous amount of savings to you in the long run—savings you can put into further investments for your retirement.

Reverse Mortgages

Reverse mortgages are a relatively new way to generate income from the equity in your home; the advantage is you don't have to sell your home. With a reverse mortgage, you put up all, or part, of the value of your home as security for a loan. Then you use the loan to buy an annuity. The annuity can be a lump sum payment, or a stream of periodic payments for life (paid monthly, quarterly, or annually). The payments are fixed and tax-free.

You are not required to pay back the principal on the loan and interest as long as you continue to occupy your home. Consequently, the outstanding loan amount grows, just as a conventional mortgage would grow if you never made payments.

The loan becomes due once both you and your spouse are dead or the last surviving spouse moves out. The house is then sold to pay back the outstanding loan. Alternatively, your children can take the house and pay off the loan as a conventional mortgage.

If your home appreciates in value more quickly than the rate at which the loan builds up, you or your estate can sell your home, pay off the loan, and pocket the difference. On the other side of the ledger, you or your spouse will be indebted if you sell the house at a price lower than the outstanding loan amount. There are, however, special provisions that protect you in case of prolonged medical absences or long vacations.

The above information covers the basics, but you should note that there are risks to reverse mortgages that should be carefully weighed. Under no circumstances should you enter into a reverse mortgage without the advice of a financial advisor and legal expert.

Making Money In Real Estate

Beyond your home and possibly a recreational property (the foundation of your assets), lies the world of income properties. As an investment, real estate more than any other investment, withstands the test of time, and many of the greatest fortunes this past century have been made in real estate.

For most people, however, there are significant obstacles associated with income property investments. The nature of the investment is rigid; it can take weeks or months to complete a purchase or sale. Added to these cash flow tensions are the extensive, practical, and legal responsibilities of being a landlord.

For most people, the obstacles are more than they can handle, and while I discourage no one from investing in real estate, you should be realistic. There are many "get rich quick" schemes out there, and numerous books to help you make your killing in real estate. Just don't shoot yourself in the foot.

The Hardy Can Take Heart

Volumes have been written specifically on options, futures, commodities, precious metals, art, rare coins, stamps, and real estate. It would be impossible to write about these subjects in any detail and still do them justice within the confines of this working textbook on financial planning.

For those of you who are interested in these risky ventures, who have the means to play the game, who have not a faint heart or weak stomach, and who are undaunted by my daunting, good luck—you'll be testing your mettle against some of the most sophisticated computer programs and professional investors in the world.

For those of you who remain, balanced, profitable investment strategies await you.

In any moment of decision the best thing you can do is the right thing, the next best thing is the wrong thing, and the worst thing you can do is nothing.

Theodore Roosevelt

Territories of Financial Success

You have to venture beyond the savings mentality if you want financial success. Invest in free enterprise—there is risk, but there is reward.

Free Enterprise—the Reward

During the last 20 years, inflation averaged 6.7%. On a lump sum of capital of $10,000, your prospects would have been very different had you been a saver rather than an investor. Consider the following examples (personal income tax rates on investment income notwithstanding):

- As a saver (loaner) receiving a rate of return of 6% for 20 years, your capital would have grown to $32,100.

- As an investor (owner) receiving a rate of return of 14% for 20 years, your capital would have grown to $137,400.

The difference of $105,300 is the additional reward the owner receives for taking the risks of investing in free enterprise.

The "real" long-term performance record of common shares (in other words, after inflation) far outstrips bonds, cash, and other low-growth assets. If you had invested $1 in common stocks in 1950, 44½ years later that investment would be

Money, which represents the prose of life, and which is hardly spoken of in parlors without an apology, is, in its effects and laws, as beautiful as roses.

Ralph Waldo Emerson

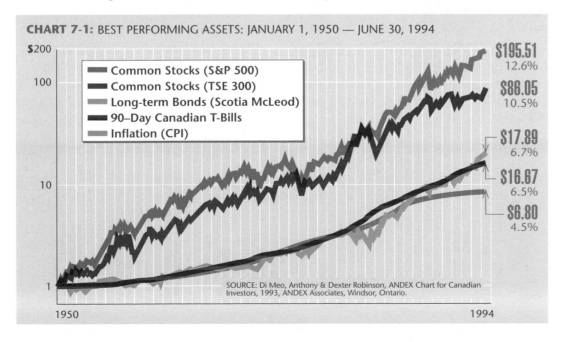

CHART 7-1: BEST PERFORMING ASSETS: JANUARY 1, 1950 — JUNE 30, 1994

Legend:
- Common Stocks (S&P 500)
- Common Stocks (TSE 300)
- Long-term Bonds (Scotia McLeod)
- 90–Day Canadian T-Bills
- Inflation (CPI)

$195.51 — 12.6%
$86.05 — 10.5%
$17.89 — 6.7%
$16.67 — 6.5%
$6.80 — 4.5%

SOURCE: Di Meo, Anthony & Dexter Robinson, ANDEX Chart for Canadian Investors, 1993, ANDEX Associates, Windsor, Ontario.

1950 — 1994

worth U.S. $195.51 or Canadian $86.05. If you had invested in bonds, your $1 would be worth $17.89. If you had invested in Treasury Bills, your $1 would have grown to only $16.67.

Common shares clearly offer substantial tax and performance advantages. I will discuss how to build the components of an investment portfolio in Chapter 10.

Are you going to be a loaner or an owner? As an owner, you invest. To invest, you pay yourself first by saving 5%, 10%, or 15% off the top of your gross income. But how will you choose to invest these savings?

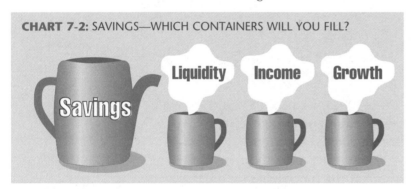

CHART 7-2: SAVINGS—WHICH CONTAINERS WILL YOU FILL?

The Canadian Investor

Over 75% of Canadian investments fall into the loaning category; this includes savings accounts, Term Deposits, GICs, and CSBs. It is estimated that 70% of RRSPs are deposited with banks or trust companies in a loaning format as well. The remaining 30% of RRSPs are invested in ownership assets.

I compiled data from several sources including the Toronto Stock Exchange which published a research study in 1993, entitled *1993 Shareownership Study*. Consider some of the statistical highlights:

- 4.2 million Canadians—21.5% of the adult population—own shares in either common or preferred stock of a publicly traded company.
- 4.7 million Canadians—23.9% of the adult population—own mutual funds invested in common or preferred stock.
- 5.6 million Canadians—28.5% of the adult population own other mutual funds invested in mortgage, bond, money market or real estate.
- The average age of shareholders is over 40.
- There has been a 65% increase in the level of share ownership since 1983.
- The ratio of male to female shareownership is about 2:1.
- The most substantial growth occurred in stock mutual funds. The level of stock mutual funds ownership increased 20 times since 1983.
- 80% of shareholders report that stock investments make up less than 20% of total individual assets.
- The primary reasons people say they do not invest is because of their lack of money and their lack of understanding about how the stock market works.

One of my primary reasons for writing this book is to address the lack of knowledge—and self-knowledge—that

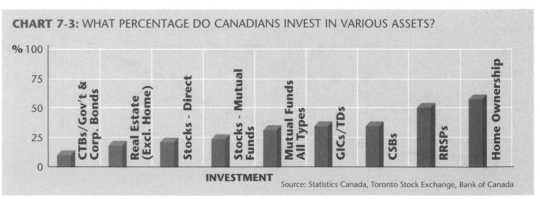

CHART 7-3: WHAT PERCENTAGE DO CANADIANS INVEST IN VARIOUS ASSETS?

Source: Statistics Canada, Toronto Stock Exchange, Bank of Canada

Canadians have about investing. Now is the time to start to learn!

Types of Risk

As we've seen in the previous chapter, investing in the free enterprise system by owning stocks hinges upon the concept of risk. But do not confuse risk with chance. Risk can be measured; chance cannot. Successful financial planning involves taking some measured degree of risk and, in general, as you increase your degree of risk, you increase your potential reward.

The types of risk are:

- *Interest Rate Risk*
  We've seen that as interest rates rise, the market value of fixed-return investments will, in most cases, decrease. This is interest rate risk. Since the relationship of price to interest rates is always *inverse,* we could think of falling rates as interest rate *opportunity*.

- *Market Risk*
  The uncertainty in future prices that arises from changes in investor attitudes or other unknown factors is market risk. This involves a change in market psychology that may cause a security's price to decline regardless of any fundamental changes affecting the company's earning power.

- *Purchasing Power (Inflation) Risk*
  This is a rise in prices that reduces the buying power of income and principal, or the chance that the value of your investment will deteriorate relative to a price index.

- *Financial Risk*
  A financial, or business, risk occurs when there is some doubt about whether you will be able to collect future returns from an investment due to poor management, unfavourable economic conditions, increased competition, or outdated technology.

- *Political Risk*
  Wage price controls, tax increases, changes in tariff and subsidy policies, government instability, nationalization of industry, dividend tax credits, and capital gains, are all political risks. All can easily depress investment values.

- *Liquidity Risk*
  Liquidity risk is the danger that you will not be able to sell your investment without significant delays or costly penalties.

Degrees of Risk

There is no such thing as a riskless investment. There are only degrees and types of risk. Fixed income investments such as CSBs, T-Bills, GICs, and bonds are subject to purchasing power risk as well as interest rate risk, both of which can be greater than the market risk involved in a well-balanced portfolio or a professionally managed equity fund.

Your degrees of risk can vary greatly. Many people think that by saving in a bank or trust company, by purchasing GICs, Term Deposits, or fixed income vehicles they are completely safe. In reality, you're actually "going broke safely" by losing ground to inflation on an after-tax basis. If you were earning 5% on a Term Deposit, and you were in a 40% tax bracket, you would have a net return of (5%–2%) = 3%. If inflation were at 4.2%, you could be losing 1.2% on your capital or purchasing power!

While there is no risk to your original capital in this example, you have no real gains; you have merely lost purchasing power. No gains, no headway! Contrast that to a ten-year record on a mutual fund. There are many professionally managed mutual funds that would have shown you a return in the order of 12-16% during the last ten years.

Life is either a daring adventure or nothing.
Helen Keller

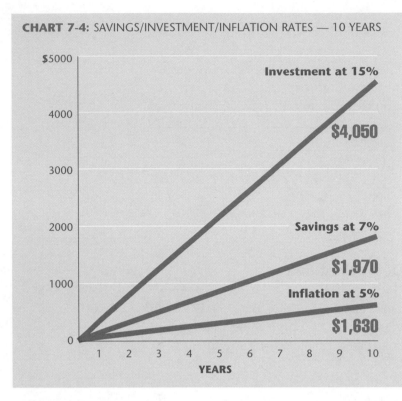

CHART 7-4: SAVINGS/INVESTMENT/INFLATION RATES — 10 YEARS

Assume inflation averaged 5%, your savings return averaged 7%, and your investment return averaged 15%. If you had invested $1,000 ten years ago, your results would look like Chart 7-4.

So, the question to ask yourself is: Where is the real risk? Have you been getting the rate of return you deserve? Look at Table 7-5.

What Is Your Financial Attitude?

To find out the answer to this question, you have to get to know yourself—financially. What kind of investor are you? What does your personal risk matrix look like? What is your financial attitude towards savings versus investing, and the risk/reward trade-off?

Complete the investment personality questionnaire and find out.

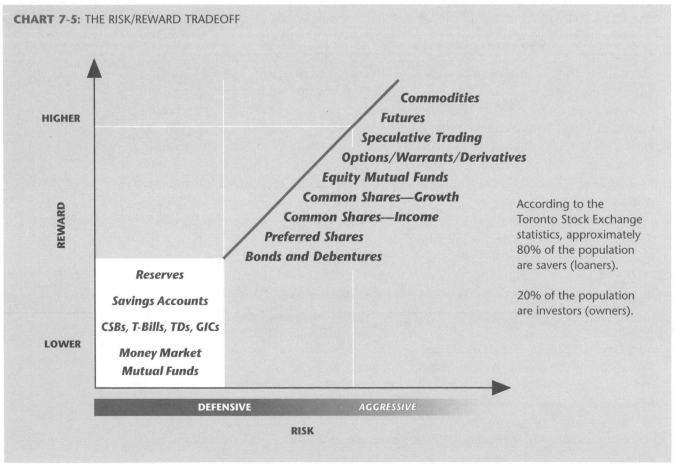

CHART 7-5: THE RISK/REWARD TRADEOFF

WORKSHEET 7-6: INVESTMENT PERSONALITY QUESTIONNAIRE

	STRONGLY AGREE			STRONGLY DISAGREE	
INSTRUCTIONS: *Statements 1 to 16 should be answered on the basis of how strongly you agree or disagree with each statement. Questions 17 to 25 measure risk tolerance based on which statements you choose.*	**A**	**B**	**C**	**D**	**E**
1 I want a guarantee of the income from my investments, even if I have to accept a lower yield.	☐	☐	☐	☐	☐
2 I can't afford any possible loss of capital regardless of the potential return.	☐	☐	☐	☐	☐
3 I want to be sure that I can sell my investments on short notice if necessary.	☐	☐	☐	☐	☐
4 I can't afford any significant loss of capital, but I want the best return I can get.	☐	☐	☐	☐	☐
5 I want to be sure I can get my money out of the market in case of recession or a stock market crash, even if I have to settle for a lower yield.	☐	☐	☐	☐	☐
6 I am satisfied with my yield from TDs, GICs, CSBs, CTBs, and bonds, so I would rather not invest in the volatile stock market.	☐	☐	☐	☐	☐
7 I don't feel capable of making investment decisions regarding common and preferred shares.	☐	☐	☐	☐	☐
8 I am concerned that my present savings structure will not provide the necessary income to offset the long-term effects of inflation.	☐	☐	☐	☐	☐
9 I require maximum income from my investments now and I'm not as concerned about the future.	☐	☐	☐	☐	☐
10 I have lots of income now so I want my investments to produce maximum income and growth for my retirement years.	☐	☐	☐	☐	☐
11 I want maximum capital growth potential for my retirement.	☐	☐	☐	☐	☐
12 I want a blend of safety, income, and growth right now and for my retirement years.	☐	☐	☐	☐	☐
13 I want the potential for capital growth, but I don't want to put all my eggs in one basket.	☐	☐	☐	☐	☐
14 Aggressive investors can earn higher returns and I am willing to accept the risk involved for those higher returns.	☐	☐	☐	☐	☐
15 My greatest concerns are inflation and taxes, therefore, I am willing to invest for maximum protection from these arch enemies.	☐	☐	☐	☐	☐
16 I am prepared to learn as much as I can about investments through financial books and publications and investment courses, so that I can make my own investment decisions and/or use professional help to attain my goals and objectives.	☐	☐	☐	☐	☐

	RISK TOLERANCE				
17 An investment you made six months ago turned sour and currently is showing a 30% decline. How would you respond? a) Do nothing and wait for a rebound? b) Sell and cut your losses? c) Buy more and dollar-cost-average your investment?	☐	☐	☐		
18 Given the following situations, which would you choose? a) $1,000 cash now b) A 50% chance of winning $3,000 c) A 20% chance of winning $10,000 d) A 10% chance of winning $25,000	☐	☐	☐	☐	☐
19 If you were faced with two potential gains, which would you choose? a) A 100% chance to win $2,000 b) An 80% chance to win $3,000	☐	☐			
20 If you were faced with two potential losses, which would you choose? a) A 100% chance to lose $2,000 b) An 80% chance to lose $3,000	☐	☐			

WORKSHEET 7-6: INVESTMENT PERSONALITY QUESTIONNAIRE (CONT.)

	RISK TOLERANCE				
	A	B	C	D	E

21 Which situation would you prefer? ☐ ☐
   a) Investments in money market vehicles, only to see that aggressive growth stocks appreciated by 40% during the year.
   b) Investments in aggressive growth stocks which appreciate very little during the year.

22 Which situation would you prefer? ☐ ☐
   a) Investment in money market vehicles that prevented you from losing 40% of your capital in a market correction.
   b) Investment in equities that double your money.

23 In an inflationary environment, hard assets such as precious metals, collectibles, and ☐ ☐ ☐ ☐
   real estate are expected to keep pace with inflation. You currently hold all of your assets in money market vehicles. Most market analysts and economists predict inflation will skyrocket next year. What would you do?
   a) Continue to hold your money market vehicles.
   b) Sell half of your money market vehicles and buy some hard assets.
   c) Sell all of your money market vehicles and buy hard assets.
   d) Sell all of your money market vehicles and buy hard assets and borrow additional money to buy more.

24. Based on a double-digit inflation forecast for the next several years and massive ☐ ☐ ☐ ☐ ☐
   government deficits how would you invest?
   a) Buy Canada Savings Bonds and Treasury Bills.
   b) Buy long-term GICs, TDs, and money market instruments.
   c) Buy long-term equity based mutual funds.
   d) Buy equities and real estate.
   e) Buy gold and precious metals.

25 You receive an inside tip from a close friend on a junior oil company that could ☐ ☐ ☐ ☐ ☐
   be a takeover candidate. if the deal goes through you could make a lot of money, but if it fails you could lose a substantial sum. How much stock would you buy?
   a) NONE
   b) $2,000
   c) $5,000
   d) $10,000
   e) $25,000

SCORING

Here are the points earned by each response:

1	A 1	B 2	C 3	D 4	E 5	**10**	A 5	B 4	C 3	D 2	E 1	**19**	A 1	B 5					
2	A 1	B 2	C 3	D 4	E 5	**11**	A 5	B 4	C 3	D 2	E 1	**20**	A 5	B 1					
3	A 1	B 2	C 3	D 4	E 5	**12**	A 5	B 4	C 3	D 2	E 1	**21**	A 1	B 5					
4	A 1	B 2	C 3	D 4	E 5	**13**	A 5	B 4	C 3	D 2	E 1	**22**	A 1	B 5					
5	A 1	B 2	C 3	D 4	E 5	**14**	A 5	B 4	C 3	D 2	E 1	**23**	A 1	B 2	C 3	D 5			
6	A 1	B 2	C 3	D 4	E 5	**15**	A 5	B 4	C 3	D 2	E 1	**24**	A 1	B 2	C 3	D 4	E 5		
7	A 1	B 2	C 3	D 4	E 5	**16**	A 5	B 4	C 3	D 2	E 1	**25**	A 1	B 2	C 3	D 4	E 5		
8	A 1	B 2	C 3	D 4	E 5	**17**	A 1	B 3	C 5										
9	A 1	B 2	C 3	D 4	E 5	**18**	A 1	B 3	C 4	D 5									

Total Score: _____

What kind of investment personality do you have? See the next page.

Your Investment Personality Score Results

25-50 points
Very Conservative (Risk-Avoider)
If you scored 50 or less points, you are likely a very conservative investor. Safety of capital is very important to you, so risk is something you prefer to minimize or even avoid altogether. Variability in your investments is not something you enjoy, and you are prepared to accept lower returns as a trade-off for being sure your capital is guaranteed. The types of products you favour are probably savings accounts and cash equivalents such as money market funds, T-Bills, CSBs, TDs, and GICs.

51-75 points
Conservative (Risk-Minimizer)
At 51 to 75 points, you are still quite conservative. Instead of totally avoiding risk, however, you are likely comfortable with a small bit of risk, but will try to minimize its effect. You favour the same products as the Very Conservative personality, but would also be comfortable with bonds and debentures, preferred shares, and some high-quality blue-chip common shares for income.

76-100 points
Growth-Oriented (Risk-Blender)
Between 76 and 100 points, you are a "risk-blender." You are less conservative than those who scored lower points, and you would like to see some growth in your portfolio. You will always have some conservative products in your portfolio. You will also want to have a good selection of common shares or mutual funds invested in stocks to achieve the desired growth in your investments. You might include a wide range of investment vehicles in your portfolio, including aggressive common stocks, foreign and global equity mutual funds, some convertible shares, warrants, and perhaps a tax-sheltered investment.

101-125 points
Speculative (Risk-Taker)
The highest scores on this questionnaire indicate that you are not only comfortable with risk, but also welcome it when you believe it will create the conditions for achieving the growth you seek. While your portfolio will have some cash and blue-chip stocks in it, you may lean towards more speculative common shares, options, futures, precious metals, certain higher-risk real estate investments, and special situations.

Your Investment Personality Profile gives you an indication of your comfort and tolerance levels with different types of investments, but will the financial vehicles associated with your "type" be the ones that will help you meet your retirement objectives? To help you answer this question, consider the Investment Pyramid of risks and rewards in Chapter 11; Charts 11-15, and 11-16.

Investment Personality Questionnaire Analysis

Your investment decisions are personal and will reflect your goals, needs, attitudes, and philosophy.

The 3 factors that will have the greatest impact on the amount of money you accumulate for retirement are:

1. How much money you save
2. How long your money is invested
3. What rate of return you earn on your investments

The **first** and most important step is to identify your goals: How much you'll need and when you'll need it.

The **second** step is to understand your comfort zone or tolerance for risk.

From Small Acorns, Giant Oak Trees Grow

We all have a fixed lifetime allotment. Look at the tree and try to visualize how your life might unfold during the balance of your lifetime.

Are you maximizing your true potential? Have you ever considered your investment habits? Complete the questionnaire in Worksheet 7-8 on investment habits and discover where you stand.

Let's take a closer look at your investment habits and gauge your potential results (See Chart 7-9).

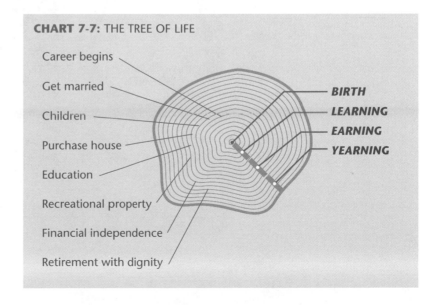

CHART 7-7: THE TREE OF LIFE

Career begins
Get married
Children
Purchase house
Education
Recreational property
Financial independence
Retirement with dignity

BIRTH
LEARNING
EARNING
YEARNING

WORKSHEET 7-8: YOUR INVESTMENT HABITS

Are you: a saver/loaner?   _____

an investor/owner?   _____

a speculator/trader?   _____

Do you know how your savings and investments are distributed?   _____

Do you know what investment returns you have been getting after you deduct taxes and inflation?   _____

Are your investments structured to protect you from the ravages of inflation?   _____

Do you know how much of your cash flow you must invest on a regular monthly basis to meet future goals?   _____

Do you know how much your investments must yield to reach these goals?   _____

Do you have a plan of action that will help you achieve your objectives?   _____

Does your net worth statement allow you to consider other investment alternatives?   _____

Do you feel you have enough balance and flexibility in your investments?   _____

Are you prepared to spend sufficient time keeping up with your investments through financial publications, newsletters, and courses?   _____

Would professional money management, such as carefully selected mutual funds, be a better alternative for your objectives, your training, and your temperament?   _____

CHART 7-9: SAVINGS VERSUS INVESTING GAUGE

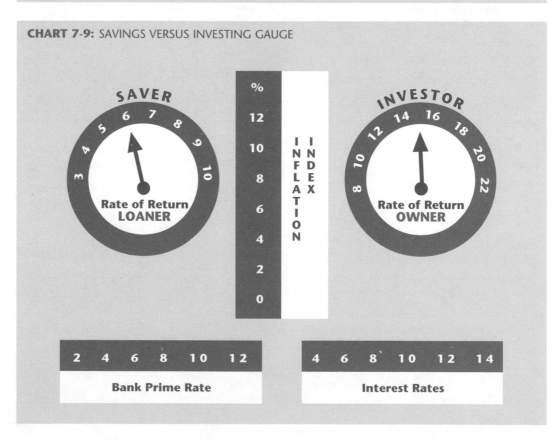

Are you a loaner averaging a 6% return or an owner averaging a 15% return? Are your investments structured to protect you from the ravages of inflation? Do your investments provide a real rate of return after taxes and inflation? Will changes in the bank prime rate or interest rates benefit or hinder your present investments?

Use this chart to establish what bank prime rate, interest rates, and the inflation rate are at present. Then compare your current rate of return on your investments to see how your results measure against these barometers.

Investors Often Make the Wrong Choices

Question number 19 in the Investment Personality Questionnaire asked: If you were faced with two potential gains, which would you choose?

a) A 100% chance to win $2,000

b) An 80% chance to win $3,000

Psychological studies have shown that most people would choose the guaranteed $2,000, even though the 80% chance to win $3,000 has a greater value, according to probability theory (80% of $3,000 = $2,400). If you consistently chose this second alternative, you would come out ahead over the long run. But most people have an aversion to risk and are bothered by the chance of losing, so they choose the sure thing.

In question number 20, however, (a 100% chance to lose $2,000 or an 80% chance to lose $3,000) the conservative stance of many people changes to one of taking risk. They are willing to gamble on the second alternative to avoid the sure loss of $2,000. Statistically, the second alternative would produce a greater loss (80% of $3,000 = $2,400) and, over time, you would lose more. This suggests that people fear losses even more than their aversion to taking risks.

In every investment decision, you will always have to consider these two questions in accordance with your personality profile:

a) What is the potential reward?

b) What is the risk?

Asset Allocation Profile

Now that you have completed the *Investment Personality Questionnaire*, you have a very good profile of yourself and your approach to investments. A financial advisor will need this type of investor profile in order to draft your personal asset allocation model. This is a very important step. It will give you a game plan to follow for the allocation of your assets.

An allocation strategy enables you to choose how you would like your assets diversified amongst several different types of investments. The percentages of your assets placed in the various investment categories is often more important than

TABLE 7-10: ASSET ALLOCATION AND INVESTMENT PORTFOLIO SELECTION

Step 1: *Asset Allocation*		Step 2: *Investment Selection*		
Savings	20%	Savings	Bank Account Savings	10%
			Trust Account Premium	10%
CSBs	10%	T-Bills or CSBs		10%
Preferred Shares	30%	Preferred Shares	Stock A	15%
			Stock B	15%
Mutual Funds	40%	Mutual Funds	Fund A	20%
			Fund B	12%
			Fund C	8%
	100%			100%

the individual investments you select for each category. Table 7-11 illustrates a vast array of investment types.

Let's suppose, from this list, a typical asset allocation is as follows:

Savings Accounts	10%
CSBs	10%
Convertible Debentures	20%
Common Shares, Income & Growth	50%
Precious Metals	10%
	100%

This illustration shows that during a deflationary market cycle, your bonds and stocks, representing 90% of your portfolio, could be doing very well, while your precious metals are lagging behind. Conversely, in an inflationary environment, all your investments could slow down somewhat, and the precious metals sector, representing just 10% of the portfolio, would provide excellent growth. That is why asset allocation is so important.

The asset allocation model can answer many questions that arise from the Investment Personality Questionnaire. For example: Will the portfolio provide real growth? Yes, it will! When we look at the example shown, we see that 80% of the assets are geared toward growth; convertible debentures 20%, common shares 50%, and precious metals 10%.

Assume the question was: Does the portfolio provide maximum safety and income? No, it does not! The portion of growth common shares and the precious metals do not meet the investor's qualifications.

Asset Allocation and Investment Portfolio Selection

Asset allocation is of paramount importance because it establishes a game plan or a road map for the investor, showing how to get from here to there.

The first step is to accurately determine the investor's comfort level regarding asset allocation for each type of investment. The second step involves the actual investment selections for each allocation.

Asset Allocation Model

Once you choose an allocation strategy, the details of any particular investment selection become secondary. Many investors will choose a cross-section of securities, while other investors will select a family of mutual funds that provide the ability to allocate and move freely between the various types of funds.

Table 7-11 measures your investment choices in terms of the safety, income, and growth potential each provides. From this table, you can also determine your risk/reward comfort zone for each asset allocation's ability to provide liquidity, currency, and inflation hedges.

Inflation and Compounding — Some Interesting Facts!

Inflation erodes wealth while compound returns builds it. Here are some interesting points that relate to inflation and compound returns:

- The last year in which there was a decline in the cost of living was 1953.
- The highest annual inflation rate in Canada's history was 12.5% in 1981.
- If the annual inflation rate is 6%, it would take about 12 years for the purchasing power of $1 to be cut in half.
- It would take nine years for $1 to double in value if invested at an annual rate of 8%.
- The average annual U.S. inflation rate from 1926 to 1993 was 3.1%.
- The average annual Canadian inflation rate in the 20-year period between 1971 and 1990 was 7.2%.

TABLE 7-11: ASSET ALLOCATION MODEL

Type of Investment	Safety of Capital	Liquidity	Current Income	Growth Potential	Currency Hedge	Inflation Hedge
Savings Accounts	Excellent	High	Very Low	None	None	Low
CTBs, CSBs	Excellent	High	Low	None	None	Low
GICs, TDs	Excellent	Limited	Low	None	None	Low
MIRs, MBSs	Excellent	Limited	Medium	None	None	Low
Bonds and Debentures	Very Good	Good	High	Some	Some	Low
Convertible Debentures	Very Good	Good	Medium	Good	Some	Medium
Mortgages	Very Good	Limited	High	None	Some	Low
Stripped Coupons	Excellent	Limited	High	Some	Some	Low
Preferred Shares	Very Good	Good	Medium	Some	Low	Low
Common Shares						
Income	Very Good	Good	Low-Med	Some	Low	Low
Growth	Good	Good	Low	Good	Low-Med	Medium
Speculative	Poor	Good	None	Variable	Low-Med	Variable
Mutual Equity Funds	Good	Good	Low	Very Good	Low-Med	Medium
Precious Metals	Fair	Good	None	Good	High	Med-High
Antiques	Fair	Limited	None	Good	Low	Low
Real Estate	Good	Limited	Medium	Good	Low-Med	Med-High

- The average annual inflation rate from January 1950 to June 1994 was 4.5%.

Risk/Reward Tradeoff

Let's summarize. Most people—roughly eight out of every ten people in the population—have never invested in a security. They are saving in banks, trusts, or credit unions and getting a low rate of return on their money.

What I am asking you to do is to increase your degree of risk just a little, to encompass some income securities and growth securities, all of which have defensive characteristics. You could invest in the more aggressive areas as well, if you choose. By encompassing some income and growth investments, you can really enhance your rate of return. As you increase your degree of risk, you can increase your degree of reward.

This is my central theme. You have to branch out beyond your saving mentality, your reserve scenario, and encompass common and preferred shares as part of your investment portfolio.

You can achieve this on your own if you have the time, training, talent, temperament, and adequate dollars. Or you can use professionally managed mutual funds to enable the compounding effect of time and money to go to work for you to help you acquire your retirement dream.

But before you make that commitment, let's look at one reason I'm suggesting a professional manager for your investments—the market itself.

Investment Market Forces

*Investing is an art, not a science.
Successful investors are people who
understand the cycles and psychology
of the investment marketplace.*

It Works in Theory, But Will It Work in Practice?

Much has been written about economic cycles and market psychology. Many theories have been developed by people who call themselves "fundamentalists" and "technicians." Don't believe that any one discipline or theory presents the full picture. Consider all the data available and choose the one that works best for you.

I have developed my own bias toward certain investment criteria during my careers in banking, investment, and education, and I have applied a lot of simple common sense.

In the first place, the price of anything can go up or down in response to one or more of three elements only:

• The demand for the product or service
• The supply of the product or service
• The value of the dollar

The first rule for investment success is based on the economic law of demand and supply:

• When demand increases, supply decreases and markets move up.
• When demand decreases, supply increases and markets move down.

With that introduction, let's look at what moves the market.

What Moves the Market?

The force of the market involves three key areas. The percentages are an estimate of the amount of influence each area has in moving the market in a given direction:

1. *Investor Psychology—50%*
   confidence, emotion—the "herd instinct"
2. *Technical—30%*
   economy, industry position, popularity, and fad
3. *Hard Facts—20%*
   earnings per share, dividends, return on investment, and selectivity.

In addition to the law of supply and demand, and the changing value of the dollar (important to foreign investors), you need to understand that the stock market is a continuous cycle of peaks and troughs, mostly influenced by investor psychology regarding the current market level in the cycle at any point in time.

Everything in life involves a cycle, beginning with life itself. The reproduction cycle passes from generation to

In Chinese, the word "crisis" is composed of two characters. The first— the symbol of danger; the second— opportunity.

> You must have an understanding of psychology to become a successful investor.
>
> **Graydon Watters**

generation. The four seasons, winter, spring, summer, and fall, are a cycle. Witness the changing of the tides influenced by the position of the moon and the earth as it revolves around the sun bringing us day and night. The stock market runs on cycles as well. There is a business cycle, an economic cycle, a presidential election cycle, a goods and services cycle, and a retail marketing cycle, to name a few. All of these cycles cause the stock market to fluctuate.

More zeal and energy, more fanatical hope, and more intense anguish have been extended over the past century in efforts to forecast the stock market than in almost any other single line of human action. Adam Smith, in *The Money Game*,

stated, "You have to know what time of market it is."

Investment markets go in cycles like all the other rhythms of life. There are four basic cyclic phases, according to Leon Tuey, one of Canada's top technical analysts. (Technical analysts predict stock prices by observing the patterns of price and volume. More about this later.)
- Bottom Accumulation Phase
- Top Distribution/Bull Phase
- Top Distribution/ Bear Phase
- Advanced Bear Phase Approaching Termination

Investor Psychology— the Gold Cycle

Let's look at a typical cycle. Picture the economic cycle that lasted four to five years, when gold was selling at $850 U.S. per ounce at the peak of the 1980 market.

At the top of that cycle, the gold market was in a state of absolute euphoria. The investor who bought at $600 had to believe that there was somebody to buy it from him or her at $800. The investor who bought at $800 had to believe somebody else would buy it at $1,000. At that time, they were talking about gold going to $1,500 to $2,000 per ounce or more.

You may recall the newspapers at that time—gold price performance was front-page news every single day. The media was talking about gold hitting a new high, setting new records. There were still wars, famine, drought, and all kinds of very significant things going on in the world, but that was all page 2 and page 3 news. At that time, this psychology of the crowd— this herd instinct—was reported, not just in every newspaper in Canada, but in every newspaper in every major city around the world with the same "gold hysteria news." There was absolute euphoria at the top. Gold would never stop going up.

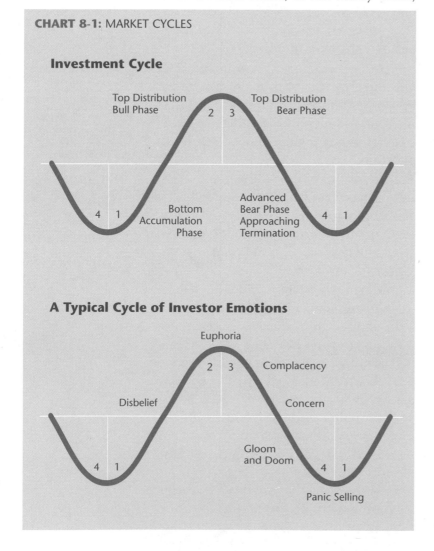

CHART 8-1: MARKET CYCLES

Investment Cycle

Top Distribution Bull Phase — 2 — 3 — Top Distribution Bear Phase

4 1 — Bottom Accumulation Phase — Advanced Bear Phase Approaching Termination — 4 1

A Typical Cycle of Investor Emotions

Euphoria

Disbelief — 2 — 3 — Complacency

Concern

4 1 — Gloom and Doom — 4 1

Panic Selling

CHART 8-2: THE GOLD CYCLE

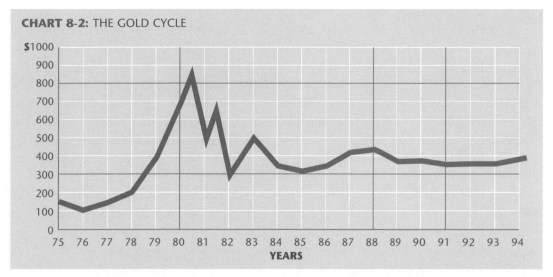

Then, inevitably, gold started to come down after many months of advances. Initially, it settled back to the $700 range. People became complacent with their investment, thinking it was bound to resume its upward trend at any moment. As gold fell to the $500–$550 range, concern began, particularly with those investors who had bought at or near the peak of $850 per ounce. Finally, as gold came down a little further into the $400 range, gloom and doom set in.

Gold eventually bottomed out just under $300. Panic selling started. People who had bought five years ago at $850 per ounce were giving gold away at $300 per ounce. Gold is currently changing hands at about $375 an ounce in the early stages of the next cycle.

If anyone has been through a cycle like that and bought gold at the peak, kept it for five years, and then sold at the bottom, what do you think happens when the next cycle begins? As gold starts in quadrant one, its long climb upwards in the next cycle to $400, $450, $500, $550 per ounce, people who have owned gold before, wonder in absolute disbelief. Why? Because they believe they are experts. They have been there before; they bought during the last cycle at $850 per ounce, and it went way down in price.

They are operating from past experience in absolute disbelief. What will happen as the momentum builds and gold, once again, becomes front-page news? Our investors will be back in the line-up on Bay Street just like the last time, waiting to buy gold at or near the cycle peak.

All you ever have to know about the market cycle is based on the simple economic rules of demand and supply. When you have more demand than supply, markets go up. When you have more supply than demand, markets go down. When the line-ups for gold eventually thinned out, there were no more buyers. Demand was exhausted. What had to happen? Gold had to decline in price. And it did.

Gold is at $375 per ounce today with no line-ups, no excessive demand or supply, and it represents much better value now that the line-ups are gone and the newspapers aren't carrying any front-page stories.

Gold should be viewed in terms of insurance. It might represent 2% to 10% of your portfolio as a hedge against inflation. John Ing, a renowned precious metals specialist, says, "Treat gold like fire insurance—something you hope you'll never need, but you're glad to have, just in case."

I don't know when the next major bull phase cycle will begin on gold, but I do know there will be another cycle. It could be every bit as great as the last cycle, and it could go through its previous high levels. History and markets always seem to surpass old highs, old levels. It may take one or two cycles to happen, but it *will* happen. Gold is currently in the bottom accumulation phase and it is only a matter of time before it moves into the top distribution bull phase.

Remember, however, there are many reasons why you shouldn't invest in a lot of gold. Gold investments do not earn interest or dividend income, in most cases. Some convertible preferred share vehicles, as well as a few precious metal funds, have a small return, but generally, gold is bought to hold for capital appreciation.

The Presidential Election Cycle

Let me elaborate on one more cycle, the presidential election cycle, and the effect it can have on the stock market. The presidential election cycle takes place every four years in the United States. Typically, year one in the cycle is very weak and years two, three, and four are much stronger.

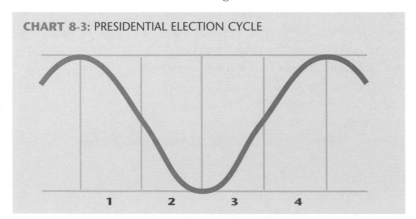

CHART 8-3: PRESIDENTIAL ELECTION CYCLE

1   2   3   4

Once a new president has been elected, he has a four-year mandate before he must face the voters again. This is the time when he tries to change things, at whatever cost to the market or economy, for long-term improvements in structure.

In year two of the presidential election cycle comes the mid-term elections, so presidents ease up on some of their programs. After all, they don't want to offend voters. As the cycle moves to year three and year four, the government is likely to stimulate the economy and to give the public many concessions; they want to be perceived as "good guys" in order to secure votes.

And so it is with the market cycle. The stimulus the president applied may not have been the best thing for the economy, but it definitely bought votes. The economy, however, reacted to the stimulus, and may have caused the stock market to reach new highs. The extreme of this condition will correct in the next cycle, probably year one of the presidential election cycle when, with a four-year mandate, the new president tightens up the system to get the economy back in good shape. The president does this because he doesn't have to face the voters for four more years!

Technical Analysis

Let's turn our attention to technical factors, which account for about 30% of what happens in the marketplace. Here, I want to show you a typical buy signal and a typical sell signal. You may find it interesting that the actions indicated by technical analysis are frequently opposite to what you might expect, given the reports of market conditions in the media.

Dow Theory Buy Signal

Now, a short course in technical analysis: Chart 8-4 illustrates a Dow Theory Buy Signal. In this case, a bear market forces the index from point 1 to point 2. This may last several months before the market sees a "secondary reaction" upwards to point 3. This takes from a few weeks to 2 or 3 months and consists of an advance,

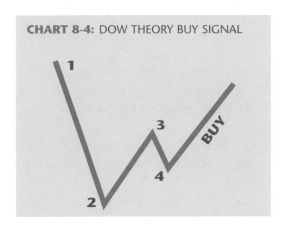

CHART 8-4: DOW THEORY BUY SIGNAL

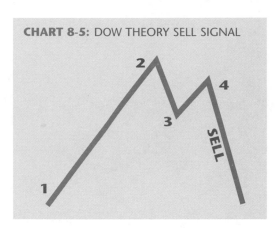

CHART 8-5: DOW THEORY SELL SIGNAL

usually in the range of 7% to 13%, of the value of the average as a whole.

Another way of viewing this is to consider it as an advance that will correct 1/3 to 1/2 of the previous decline. This is likely to work out to an advance of from 7% to 13% also.

From point 3, the market declines again, but only to point 4, slightly above point 2. Another advance develops from this point. It is at this stage that the Dow Theory Buy Signal can be produced. If, on the advance, the Dow Jones Industrial Average closes on any given day at a higher level than point 3, then, in Dow Theory terms, a new bull market has developed—provided the Transportation Average confirms this trend by forming a similar pattern.

There are minor trends lasting up to 20 days, intermediate trends of 20 weeks, and major trends that last 20 months or more. Charles Dow stated, "Once a major or primary trend is established, the stock market will tend to move in that direction for a considerable period of time, anywhere from six months to as much as three years." In terms of physics, what goes up must come down, and Sir Isaac Newton's laws of inertia stated that a body in motion tends to remain in motion in that direction until acted upon by some outside force.

If you would like to learn more about this fascinating form of investment research, there have been many books written about the subject. I feel the best is

Technical Analysis of Stock Trends by Robert Edwards and John McGee.

Dow Theory Sell Signal

Let's concentrate now on a sell signal originated by Charles Dow. Chart 8-5 will show you an example of a long upward trend in the market that might take place over 2 to 3 years from point 1 to point 2. A correction takes place from point 2 to point 3, and a subsequent rally takes us from point 3 to point 4.

Note that point 4 did not surpass point 2. The moment we reacted from point 4 and started back down through point 3, we had a clear-cut sell signal. Some technical analysts call this an "upside failure." In other words, there was not sufficient buying power to move the index to a new high point. Lower prices are almost always inevitable from such a chart formation.

Gold Sell Signal

Compare the sell signal on Chart 8-5 to gold. Look back on Chart 8-2 to 1978 as we moved into 1979. Gold started its momentous advance from the $250–$300 level and climbed aggressively to $850 per ounce by 1980. It subsequently corrected (declined) from $850 down to $500, rallied again towards $650–$675, and then started to fall again (see Chart 8-6).

Even if you had made a mistake and purchased gold at the peak in the $700–$850

CHART 8-6: A TYPICAL CYCLE—GOLD OVERLAP SELL SIGNAL

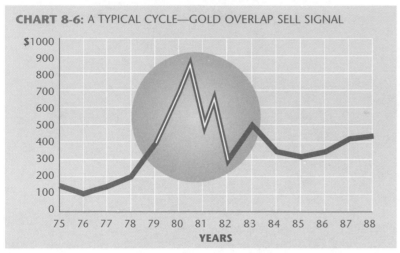

- **Tape Indicators**
  Measurements of various components of the market's actual price action, such as volume, breadth, advances/declines, highs/lows.
- **Sentiment Indicators**
  Measurements of investor optimism or pessimism, including insider buying or selling, large block trades, short sales, institutional cash balances unavailable for investment, and advisory letter sentiment.

Fundamental Analysis

Finally, we look at Fundamental Analysis, for which I gave a rating of about 20%. This overview of psychology (50%), technical analysis (30%), and fundamental analysis (20%), is the emphasis I place on the importance of these tools for determining the direction of the market. There are hundreds of evaluation techniques used by fundamental analysts. I will concentrate on just a few.

Yield

In Table 8-7, using Fundamental Analysis, we have an example of two stocks both trading at $20. Both earn $2 a share. In the case of company A, they pay out $1 in dividends. If you divide that $1 dividend by the market price of $20, it results in a yield of 5%. Company B, on the other hand, is also trading at $20 a share, but paying out a $0.20 dividend. If you divide the $20 market price into the $0.20 dividend, you come up with a yield of 1%.

If I asked which stock you would rather own, most people would pick stock A for

> Charts not only tell what was, they tell what is; and a trend from *was* to *is* (projected linearly into the will be) contains better percentages than clumsy guessing.
>
> **R.A. Levy**

range, and you had some basic technical analysis as part of your financial toolbox, you could have sold on the upside failure signal in the $600 range and saved yourself the anguish of the last decade while gold continued all the way down to $300.

In this scenario, you would have bought at the wrong time. You would have cut your loss to a few hundred dollars, but you would have been able to put your money to work in other areas of the market. You would be in a good position to take a serious look at gold in its next cyclical advance.

Other Technical Tools

In addition to studying chart formations—graphic patterns with odd names such as support/resistance levels, trendlines, flags, head-and-shoulders formations, and double-bottoms—there are many other tools a technical analyst can utilize.

- **Trends**
  Mathematical, computerized techniques for detecting developing market trends, including simple and exponential moving averages, bands, and oscillators.

TABLE 8-7: FUNDAMENTAL ANALYSIS

Stock	Market Price	Earnings Per Share	Dividend	Yield	Price-Earnings Multiple
A	$20.00	$2.00	$1.00	5%	10:1
B	$20.00	$2.00	$0.20	1%	10:1

the 5% yield. Think again. Stock A is probably a mature company like a bank, a trust, or a utility. Stock B is more likely a growth company holding much of its earnings back instead of paying out in the form of dividends. They direct earnings back into new plant and equipment for the future growth of the corporation. So, the investor in stock B might be in a more aggressive growth company. The investor here is more interested in higher returns through capital gains and future growth than in current dividends.

Price-Earnings Multiple

Note in Table 8-7 the price-earnings multiple. This multiple is calculated by dividing the earnings per share of $2 by the market price of $20. In both cases, these stocks are trading at 10 times earnings.

Historically, the average multiple for all stocks traded on the Dow Jones Index has hovered this century at approximately 14 times earnings. At times, they have been up higher, over 20 times, and in some of the more volatile sectors, as high as 25 to 30 times earnings on average. At other times, the multiples have declined to the 6 to 7 times range, as we experienced a few years ago. Price-earnings multiples are currently very high but are expected to decrease as corporate earnings increase.

In addition to the yield and price-earnings multiple, which are the two most popular ratios used by investors, there are a number of other ratios a fundamental analyst uses to determine a company's investment value. Each of the numbers produced in these calculations is compared to investing standards that are meaningful to the analyst in determining the relative values of the company being analysed:

Working Capital:
Current Assets ÷ Current Liabilities
Net Profit Margin:
Net Profit ÷ Net Sales **x** 100%

Return on Common Equity:
Net Profit – Preferred Dividends ÷ Common Equity **x** 100%
Return on Invested Capital:
Net Profit + Income Tax + Interest on Long-Term Debt ÷ Invested Capital **x** 100%
Equity Value of Common Shares:
Common Stock + Contributed Surplus + Retained Earnings ÷ Number of Common Shares Outstanding
Preferred Dividend Coverage:
Net Profit Available for Preferred Dividends ÷ Annual Preferred Dividend Requirements.

Many of the larger financial service firms, particularly those involved in the investment and administration of large pension fund accounts, employ economists who work in concert with the fundamental analysts to find new opportunities for profitable investment.

Econometric Models

Many economists develop predictive models of economic behaviour that are based on fundamental economic conditions such as inflation, interest rates, corporate profits, taxes, commodity prices, currency exchange rates, and government deficits.

Monetary Indicators

Economists also take measurements of credit availability for business expansion and consumer purchases. They assess current and future bank rate levels, prime rates, short and long-term lending rates, loan demand, and stock market margin levels.

Multiple Investment Disciplines

When you look at technical analysis, there are probably more than 100 different types of tools an analyst will use to measure marketplace performance. Similarly, a fundamentalist will look at numerous ratio analyses that pertain to a

> All things move in cycles, like the seasons: Times of abundance, when fortune smiles, alternate with times of scarcity, when our best efforts bear little fruit. The wise use such hard times for their own purposes, sowing seeds, waiting out the storm or dry spell, building foundations, preparing for opportunity when it comes.
>
> **Dan Millman**

company to make decisions about relative value of companies in the marketplace. A fundamentalist concentrates in his or her area and doesn't allow much room for the opinions of a technician.

A technician, on the other hand, thinks he or she has the best discipline and will not rely much on what the fundamentalists are doing. A technician will rely on charts and other data to make decisions about what represents good market performance value.

Let's look at one more tool that an analyst, or you, could use to analyse the market cycle of a particular commodity.

Copper Cycle

We've seen that all investments are affected by supply and demand. Take this chart on copper for instance. During the last 21 years, the London Metal Exchange average annual copper prices have oscillated between about U.S. $0.55 and $1.28. It appears that when copper inventories are low, copper prices rise quickly. When

inventories are rebuilt, there is too much supply, and prices decline to what seems to be a "floor price" of about U.S. $0.60.

Summary

The guiding principle in all your investment decisions should evolve around the fundamental law of supply and demand. When demand is high and supply is low, prices increase. Prices will decline when demand is low and supply is high. If you build this principle into your decision-making process every time you invest, you will have a very happy and rewarding investment experience.

We have looked at three major forces in the market—investor psychology, technical analysis, and fundamental analysis. There are literally hundreds of ratios, formulas, economic models, technical and historical data that are used to determine investment values. No one method or approach to investment analysis provides all the answers.

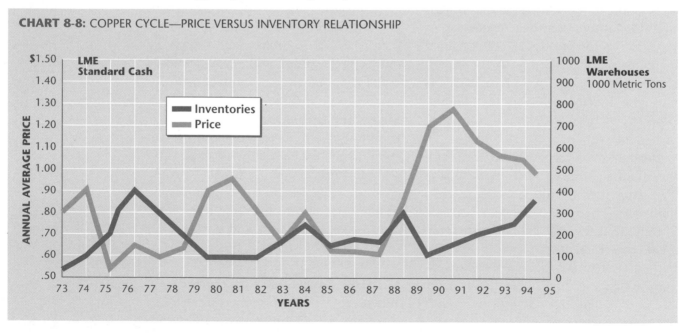

CHART 8-8: COPPER CYCLE—PRICE VERSUS INVENTORY RELATIONSHIP

Investment Planning

*There is no best investment. If there was, no
one would invest in anything else.
There is only best investing.*

Preparing to Invest

During the past half century, Canada has experienced inflation in 48 out of 50 years. During the last 40 years, we have had inflation every year. In most cases, you have to "own instead of loan" in order to accumulate wealth and retire with financial dignity.

Are you prepared to beat inflation? Ask yourself:

- How are my savings and investments distributed today?
- Am I a saver (loaner), an investor (owner), or both?
- Are my Canada Savings Bonds, Term Deposits, Guaranteed Investment Certificates, and other money market instruments protecting me from inflation?
- Does my net worth statement allow me to consider other investment alternatives?
- How much time am I prepared to spend on learning more about investments through reading financial publications, newsletters, and taking investment courses?
- Is professional money management a better alternative to suit my personal goals and objectives?

- How much can I invest today in a lump sum to begin my investment program?
- How much could I invest at regular intervals, for example, monthly or quarterly?

You know where you stand. You know the investment territory. You want to invest and it's time to start.

What Is the "Best" Investment?

Everyone you talk to knows the best investment, but no one agrees on the same answer. Is a size 9 shoe a "good" shoe? Only if it fits your foot. Is 10% a "good" return on investment? Only if it fits your objectives.

Suppose you need a 10% return on investment to get everything you want and the government issues Canada Savings Bonds paying 9% interest guaranteed for 20 years. Is this a good investment? Perhaps, but not for you: you cannot achieve your objective of a 10% growth rate—guaranteed!

On the other hand, if you know you need a 10% return, you care little which investment you have your money in as long as it earns 10% or more.

> In investing, the return you want should depend on whether you want to eat well or sleep well.
>
> **J. Kenfield Morley**

Don't Worry About Your Investment, Worry About Your Return

There is no "best" investment. One person's idea of a good investment may be another's idea of a gambling weekend in Las Vegas. What is more important is to identify the investment return you need in order to have everything you want, when you want it. That done, *any investment* that can give you at least that return is satisfactory—as long as it also allows you to sleep at night!

Suppose you need a 10% return on investment over the next year to be on target. A life insurance company has a 10% deferred annuity to offer, a trust company has a 10% GIC to offer, and Canada Savings Bonds come out at 10%. Is one 10% return better than another? Not really.

Outside of your personal preference and certain tax considerations, you actually shouldn't care whether you give your money to a trust company, life insurance company, or the government as long as the minimum requirement of 10% is achieved. No investment is better than another. *It depends on what that investment can do for you!*

The Investment Process

Investing is the process of putting money to work for the purpose of making more money. You can make more money through immediate income, or through the future profits of capital gains, or through a combination of these two factors. The planned combination you choose is called asset allocation, and the individual selections within each allocation are called an investment portfolio.

What is the right combination, or portfolio, for you? There are a number of factors to consider such as your age, temperament, tolerance for risk, dependents

and responsibility, education, financial resources, tax bracket, prospects for larger income, pension, annuity or a retirement income fund, and the element of time.

You may have the ability to discover your investment needs and objectives by analysing these factors on your own. Alternatively, a professional financial planner can prepare a portfolio for you that is in line with your specific needs and objectives so that each of these needs is satisfied in proper proportion.

But how do we determine the right mix of savings reserves versus growth investments?

Reserve/Growth Ratio

Look at the concept of the reserve/growth ratio in Table 9-1. In theory, if markets were going up, and you knew without doubt that markets were headed up, you would want to be fully invested in growth stocks. If you knew markets were headed down, you would want to be 100% in reserves, in cash, in 91-day T-Bills and Term Deposits—no risks at all.

In reality, you never know for sure what is going to happen with the market and the economy. In a rising market, therefore, you might have 30% in reserves and 70% invested. In a declining market, you might have 70% in reserves and 30% invested. You move between the 30% to 70% ratio within the reserve and growth sector, depending on what you think market conditions will be.

Many portfolio managers use sophisticated computer models to predict trends. When markets appear to be moving up, the professionals do the same thing as you, keeping reserves at 30% and working within the aggressive/defensive posture under growth 70% by varying the allocation of funds in various types of assets.

The strategies are varied and many. For one person in an up market, the

One of the most important functions of a financial plan is to identify the minimum performance you need in order to get what you want, when you want it.

Graydon Watters

TABLE 9-1: RESERVE/GROWTH RATIO

		Reserves	Growth
Theory	Markets go up		100%
	Markets go down	100%	
Reality	Markets go up	30%	70%
	Markets go down	70%	30%

		Reserves	Growth Defensive	Aggressive
Portfolio Managers				
	Markets go up	30%	30%	40%
	Markets go down	30%	60%	10%

reserve/growth split might be 30/30/40: 30% reserves, 30% defensive (conservative) investments, and 40% aggressive (risky) investments. Someone else might be 30/50/20. Conversely, in a down market, the reserve/growth split might be 30/60/10.

If you go less than 30% in either direction, you are no longer a conservative investor. In effect, you are limiting the growth opportunities to 70% of the portfolio by adjusting the aggressive/defensive mix according to what market circumstances dictate. In recent years, with the information age upon us and the sophistication of computers, investment theory relies more on aggressive/defensive switches, with less reliance on the actual mix of investments in the reserve. *It is better to own the wrong stock at the right time than the right stock at the wrong time.* There are many professional money managers who have used this approach successfully through every type of market condition.

Age Balance Indicator

Another way to look at the reserve/growth ratio is by the age balance indicator in Table 9-2. Take your age and call it a percentage figure (e.g. if you are 35, the percentage is 35%). Place that percentage in guaranteed reserves such as savings, GICs, TDs, and T-Bills, then put

the balance of your portfolio in investments for growth. Our 35-year-old would put 35% in reserves and 65% in investments. If you were age 65, you would have 65% in reserves and 35% in investments.

This indicator is a guideline or measuring tool used by many planners and consultants. It is another way of looking at how you can spread your investments between reserve and growth. I don't necessarily agree that you have to hold to those percentages. What is right for one person may not be right for the next.

TABLE 9-2: AGE BALANCE INDICATOR

Age	Reserves	Growth
35	35%	65%
50	50%	50%
65	65%	35%

Recommended Investment Mix for Various Age Groups

I often hear and read stories suggesting that you should concentrate on ownership assets when you are young, and loanership assets when you get older. These are sweeping generalizations, but it is clear that people need different kinds of investments at various stages in their lives. This is also called "asset allocation"—another way of indicating how you should spend your investment dollars.

Since there are no hard and fast rules to follow, I have allowed some room for flexibility in these asset classes. Every investor's circumstances are different.

These asset allocation and investment selection exercises are all designed to increase your personal wealth. By now

30% of your portfolio equity selections will account for 70% of your results; 70% of your portfolio equity selections will account for 30% of your results, due to mediocre performance, equities marking time, and small losses.

Graydon Watters

TABLE 9-3: RECOMMENDED INVESTMENT MIX FOR VARIOUS AGE GROUPS

Age	Liquidity Money Market, CSBs, CTBs, TDs, GICs	Income Bonds/Debentures, Preferreds, Income Common Shares, Mortgages	Growth Common Growth Shares, Convertible Preferreds, Base Metals, Options, Warrants	Inflation Hedge Precious Metals, Real Estate
21-30	30-40%	25-35%	25-40%	5-10%
31-40	10-20%	10-20%	60-75%	5-10%
41-50	5-15%	10-15%	70-85%	5-10%
51-65	5-15%	10-15%	60-75%	5-10%
65 +	15-25%	20-30%	30-50%	5-10%

you have realized there is no set method or formula to accomplish your investment strategies. However, a model developed by Nicholas Stodin, a well known financial planner in Canada, addresses the savings and investment process. The model is called Rate of Growth of Investable Capital.

Rate of Growth of Investable Capital (ROGI)

Stodin designed his strategy by looking at all the ways you can increase your wealth—all two ways!

1. Increasing your savings.
2. Increasing your return on investment.

ROGI Strategy Model

Capital	Goal
Savings	**Return on Investment**
Increase	Increase

Suppose you have $10,000 today and in one year's time you need to have $13,000. To reach that figure, your investable capital must be increased by $3,000 or 30%. Here is how the ROGI Strategy Model helps to make strategy design easy.

Suppose you could save $3,000 over the next 12 months. What do your investments have to earn? The following diagram shows that the return on your investment can be 0% and you still achieve your objective of $13,000 in one year's time. You can put your $10,000 under the mattress.

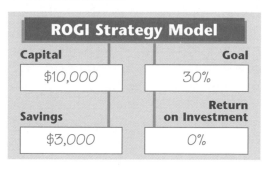

ROGI Strategy Model

Capital	Goal
$10,000	30%
Savings	**Return on Investment**
$3,000	0%

What if you invest your $10,000 at 30% for the next year? What will your savings have to be? $0. The $10,000 you invest at 30% grows to $13,000. You meet your objective without a penny saved.

ROGI Strategy Model

Capital	Goal
$10,000	30%
Savings	**Return on Investment**
0%	30% or $3,000

The above extremes illustrate how the model works. More typical is a situation where you save $1,500 and invest your capital at 10%. The diagram below shows that you would be $500 short of your target at the end of the first year. What is the solution?

ROGI Strategy Model	
Capital	**Goal**
$10,000	30%
Savings	**Return on Investment**
$1,500	10% or $1,000

There are only three ways to increase savings, and three ways to increase return on investment. You can increase your savings by:

1. Earning more
2. Spending less
3. Paying less income tax

And you can increase your return on investment by:

1. Taking more risk
2. Educating yourself to make better investment decisions
3. Hiring professional management

ROGI Strategy Model	
SAVINGS	**RETURN ON INVESTMENT**
Earn More	More Risk
Spend Less	Educate
Pay Less Tax	Hire a Professional

Imagine that you have hired a professional money manager. You want your manager to help you earn a minimum of 15% on your investment. If the money manager can do this, your savings of $1,500 together with the return on your capital will be enough to reach your

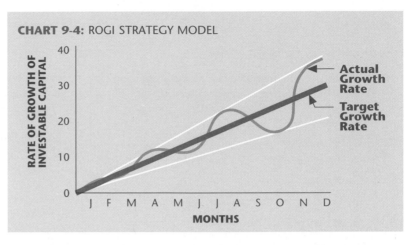

CHART 9-4: ROGI STRATEGY MODEL

Actual Growth Rate

Target Growth Rate

RATE OF GROWTH OF INVESTABLE CAPITAL

40 30 20 10 0

J F M A M J J A S O N D

MONTHS

target. What if you don't want to change your investments? Can you reduce your expenses by $500? If you can, that strategy will also reach your objective. Is one solution better than the other? No, they both get the job done.

Can you think of other ideas that will get the job done? You probably can, depending upon how creative you are.

The important thing is that no matter which strategy you select for yourself, you can determine whether your goal will be achieved in one year's time by looking at the total value of your investment.

Capital Versus Cash Flow— Determining Your Standard of Living

If you don't know what your financial destination is, how do you know when you have arrived? The purpose of designing a financial plan and using the ROGI Strategy Model is to create an after-tax indexed cash flow at a specific point in time to support a pre-determined standard of living. You have to decide the standard of living at which you want to live.

Your standard of living, however, does not equal the total amount you are worth. Many people confuse capital with cash flow. The following example illustrates the difference.

CHART GUIDE

It is important to realize that your investment returns will vary in the shorter term. The reason you review your financial plans regularly (for example by doing an annual financial fire drill) is to measure your actual performance against your targeted growth rate.

TABLE 9-5: ROGI STRATEGY EXAMPLES FOR SAVINGS AND INVESTING

STRATEGY EXAMPLES FOR SAVINGS

This side of the table highlights certain strategies within each of the three segments in the savings section of the ROGI model.

Earn more

- renegotiate compensation package
- change employers
- formal education for career advancement (night school, etc.)
- part-time activity in addition to current occupation
- consider employment for non-working spouse
- change career path within same organization (e.g. into sales)
- take personal growth courses to increase effectiveness
- any of above for working spouse

Spend less

- consolidate debts
- re-finance for better terms
- reduce luxury item expenditures
- install cash management program
- establish "forced" savings program
- review all expenditures (zero-based budgeting)
- reduce current standard of living
- use debt financing instead of capital expenditure
- defer capital expenditures

Pay less tax

- income splitting with spouse
- convert non-deductible interest to deductible interest
- convert interest income to dividend income
- convert interest income to capital gain
- contribute to RRSP
- consider use of registered education savings plan
- income split with children
- use of tax shelters to defer income
- re-arrange compensation package to reduce tax
- arrange capital cost allowance to offset taxable income
- office in home

STRATEGY EXAMPLES FOR INVESTING

This side of the table highlights certain strategies within the three segments in the investment section of the ROGI model.

Take more risk (to increase the investment return potential)

- increase interest income
  - use T-Bill accounts
  - use money market funds
  - use commercial paper
  - direct investment in first mortgages
  - direct investment in second and third mortgages
  - invest in pre-leased equipment
  - invest in longer-term bonds
- increase capital gain
  - invest larger percentage of assets in equities
  - leverage investment in equities
  - leverage investment in real estate
  - buy speculative stocks
  - invest directly in operating company
  - invest in start-up company

Educate oneself (to make better investment decisions)

- attend "free" seminars
- read investment-oriented books
- take courses in "how to invest"
- become expert on a particular type of investment
- question your financial advisors more thoroughly
- subscribe to specialty magazines and newsletters
- do more of the things you used to hire others to do (practise)

Hire professional management

- investment counsellors
- mutual funds
- discretionary accounts with stockbrokers
- limited partnerships
- management companies for direct real estate holdings

If I gave you $1 per month for the next year, that would be called cash flow. Suppose you would rather exchange the $1 per month for a single lump sum cheque today. Do you suppose I would give you $12? You would probably like that, but I would probably give you an amount less than $12. It's similar to paying off your car loan. The bank would not expect you to give them the balance of your car payments. They expect something less. I call that one lump sum cheque the *capital value.*

The capital value is an amount of money that, when invested, can produce the same monthly income. If today you traded your $1 per month cash flow (paid to you for 12 months), you would want $11.37. If you put the $11.37 in the bank at 10% interest, you could take out $1 every month for 12 months. After that, the account would have no balance in it. I say that the capital of $11.37 can produce a cash flow of $1 per month for 12 months, assuming a 10% rate of return.

Because your standard of living depends on how much money you receive every month, you must first determine how much you need (after-tax) to live the way you want to. You can then figure out how much capital is required to give you the investment income you need to supplement your earnings or pensions and maintain the standard of living you want.

One Standard of Living—Two Prices You Can Pay

Although you can determine your monthly cash flow, there are different prices you can pay for an identical cash flow, depending on the asset you decide to invest in. Suppose you want an annual income of $20,000, indexed to inflation, and you want to live only on the investment income. If you are a conservative investor, you need to invest about $400,000 today to provide that after-tax income, combining guaranteed investments and blue chip securities yielding between 9% and 10%.

On the other hand, if you choose investment real estate, you need only buy a property worth approximately $235,000 to produce the same $20,000 after-tax income. The difference exists because of the different ways of valuing a cash flow stream. An individual with $400,000 is equally as "wealthy" as the individual with $235,000 *because they both have the same standard of living.*

Securing Your Standard of Living—Unmasking Illusions of Wealth

People who think themselves well off generally do not seek advice. Some think that as long as they invest their money at a rate higher than inflation, they will enjoy a "real" increase in wealth. It isn't necessarily so. In fact, some financial planners ignore inflation, saying that inflation and investment return are relative. If inflation is 5% , GIC rates will be about 7% to 8%, producing a real return of 2% to 3%, but consider the following example:

	Rates of Return		
Investment return	6%	8%	13%
Inflation	3%	5%	10%
Real return	3%	3%	3%
Investment return less income tax @ 40%	2.4%	3.2%	5.2%
Return after tax and inflation	**.6%**	**–.2%**	**–2.2%**

You can see that even though the real return stays the same, the negative effect of income tax increases as inflation gets higher. All of us must plan to index our retirement income if we expect to maintain a constant standard of living during retirement. Tax planning and asset mix become increasingly important as inflation increases.

Your Investment Building Blocks— Products and Procedural Tools

When you implement your financial plan, you have two items at your disposal —products and procedural tools. Financial products include such things as Canada Savings Bonds, equities, real estate, and many, many more.

People often say, "I'd like to buy an RRSP (Registered Retirement Savings Plan)." You don't buy RRSPs. You buy an asset, and put it *in* an RRSP trust. An RRSP is a "thing," a procedural tool for holding an asset you put into it. A Canada Savings Bond put into an RRSP will not be taxed until it is taken out. If you don't put it into an RRSP, then the interest is taxable. Other procedural tools include corporations, educational trusts, limited partnerships, and so on.

Investment decisions are relatively easy, two-step events. You need to ask yourself: "Should I use a particular procedural tool and if so, which investment asset should I use within that procedural tool?" With those questions answered, you are on your way.

Implementing Your Investment Plan

If you don't do anything with your financial strategy, then you have wasted your time. There are three things you can do with financial advice once you receive it:

- Buy assets.
- Sell assets.
- Change title to assets.

Without a financial strategy, you cannot make effective savings and investment decisions. Without implementing

> We finally understand that the archetypal givens — earth, air, water — are the real currency of the future.
>
> **Faith Popcorn**

your plan, nothing can happen. Follow the ROGI Strategy Model process as illustrated in Chart 9-6 to create the investment or savings technique that is right for you.

The whole secret of wealth management is the design, implementation, and ongoing monitoring of financial strategies for the creation and preservation of personal wealth. Wealth management is the result of financial planning and the use of asset allocation strategies as well as investment selection techniques on your increased savings to give you a larger return on investment.

Financial Plan +
Implementation
=
$ucce$$

Why Financial Decision-Making Appears So Confusing

A study done in the late 1970s by the Stanford Research Institute showed that people generally make financial decisions in only one of three ways. The first way is called the *strategic approach* to financial decision-making. People who make financial decisions in this way have long-range goals.

Others make financial decisions using a *portfolio approach*. They look at everything they own, what they owe, and ask themselves, "Can I sleep at night with my decision?"

The third way of making financial decisions is called the *product/vendor approach*, based on the relationships people have with the sellers of the financial products or services, meaning that they may buy life insurance from their neighbour and stocks from their brother-in-law. Or their decision may be product-driven, meaning that they put their money in the bank "because every-

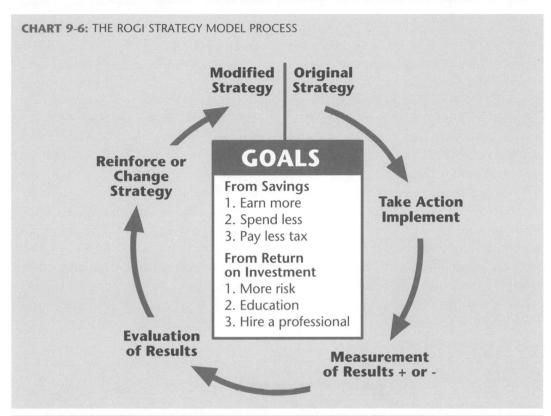

CHART 9-6: THE ROGI STRATEGY MODEL PROCESS

GOALS

From Savings
1. Earn more
2. Spend less
3. Pay less tax

From Return on Investment
1. More risk
2. Education
3. Hire a professional

Modified Strategy | Original Strategy

Reinforce or Change Strategy

Take Action Implement

Evaluation of Results

Measurement of Results + or -

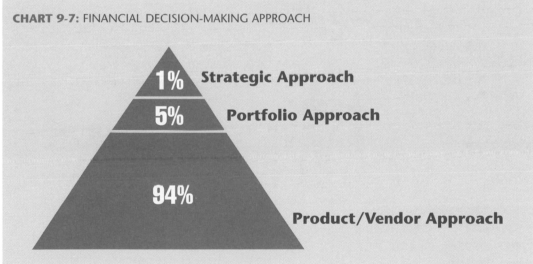

CHART 9-7: FINANCIAL DECISION-MAKING APPROACH

1% **Strategic Approach**

5% **Portfolio Approach**

94% **Product/Vendor Approach**

> The difference between a successful person and others is not a lack of strength, not a lack of knowledge, but rather in a lack of will.
>
> **Vince Lombardi**

body does." They buy insurance because "they know they should." I call this "herd instinct."

The most revealing fact of this study was that 94% of the population make their financial decisions by the product/vendor method. Do you fit in this category? If you do, be wary: you are not designing a *financial plan*; you are haphazardly assembling a *financial accident*.

Your 24 Financial Advisors

The Stanford Research Institute study also revealed that if you have an average family, you presently enjoy the service of about 24 different financial "advisors" (I use that term loosely), who sell 36 different products or services.

Start with your stockbroker, banker, accountant, and insurance agent. Add your car salesperson and real estate agent. Add to this growing list that "friend" who is always telling you what to do with your money. Include your remaining well-meaning, quasi-knowledgeable friends and their financial advice, and soon you reach a figure of approximately 24 financial advisors of one kind or another.

The problem is that these people come to you one at a time and they all want to direct all of your money one way, now. Says your banker, "I can solve all your problems, give me all your money." Declares your insurance agent, "Give me all your money, I can solve all your problems." Announces your stock-broker, "Your problems are solved, give me all your money."

You know in your gut you should be judiciously spreading your money around. Yet, no one tells you to do that. The Stanford study revealed that even though people use up to 24 different advisors, *they would really rather have 1 or 2 trusted advisors, but they really don't know who they should choose.*

Your cluster of investment opportunity requires constant monitoring and adjustment. Now that you are seriously considering how you will compose those investments into an investment portfolio, make sure it is in good hands, be they yours or an advisors.

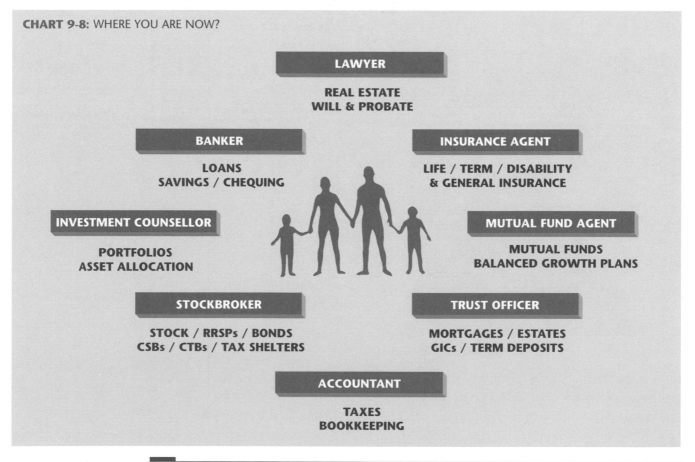

CHART 9-8: WHERE YOU ARE NOW?

LAWYER

REAL ESTATE
WILL & PROBATE

BANKER

LOANS
SAVINGS / CHEQUING

INSURANCE AGENT

LIFE / TERM / DISABILITY
& GENERAL INSURANCE

INVESTMENT COUNSELLOR

PORTFOLIOS
ASSET ALLOCATION

MUTUAL FUND AGENT

MUTUAL FUNDS
BALANCED GROWTH PLANS

STOCKBROKER

STOCK / RRSPs / BONDS
CSBs / CTBs / TAX SHELTERS

TRUST OFFICER

MORTGAGES / ESTATES
GICs / TERM DEPOSITS

ACCOUNTANT

TAXES
BOOKKEEPING

The Professional Financial Planner

If you need the help of a trustworthy financial advisor, get it. There are simple ways to ensure a wise choice.

What Is a Financial Planner?

A personal financial planner is a money counsellor in the truest sense. Depending on the specific role being performed at a given time, he or she may be called a financial planner, a financial advisor, an investment manager, or a money manager. A planner co-ordinates your financial goals and objectives into a coherent financial plan, and then works either alone or with your banker, lawyer, insurance agent, or broker, and you to implement the various elements in your plan.

Your financial planner should be part of a co-operative management approach to using the professional advisors in your life.

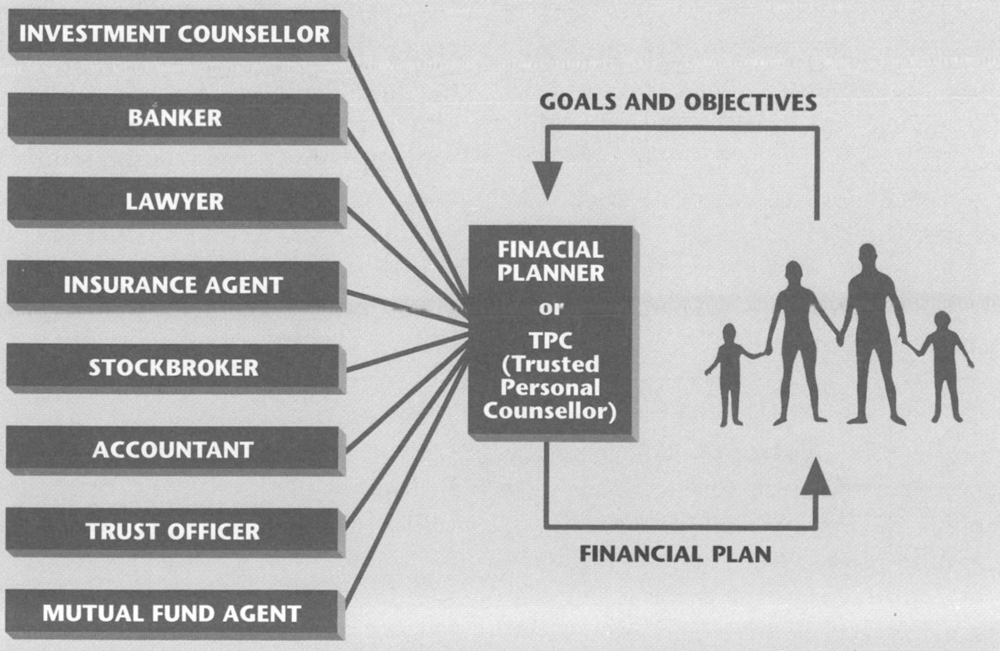

> Today we have a new kind of consumer emerging, who is better educated than in the past, more conscious of the need to be financially responsible at an earlier age, and inundated with more financial information, options, and decisions than at any other time. Competent financial planners are becoming a necessity in this information age.
>
> **Nicholas Stodin**

CHART 10-1: THE CO-OPERATIVE MANAGEMENT APPROACH

INVESTMENT COUNSELLOR

BANKER

LAWYER

INSURANCE AGENT

STOCKBROKER

ACCOUNTANT

TRUST OFFICER

MUTUAL FUND AGENT

GOALS AND OBJECTIVES

FINACIAL PLANNER or TPC (Trusted Personal Counsellor)

FINANCIAL PLAN

Who Are Professional Financial Planners?

Historically, there have been four pillars of finance in Canada—banks, trust companies, insurance companies, and investment dealers. As people like you continue to forge your own financial future, the old pillars must have increased flexibility to meet the demand. As a result, these institutions have begun vying for each other's business.

Banks want to get into the investment business. Trust companies want to perform more banking services. Investment dealers want to get in the banking business, and on it goes. Out of these crossing disciplines, the professional financial planner has emerged.

A financial planner may be a stockbroker, accountant, lawyer, insurance agent, or pension/benefit consultant. Most genuine financial planners were once associated with one of the above professions. In their role as financial planners, each tends to lean on the discipline from which they evolved. The financial planner is a generalist with broad financial training and experience in areas such as saving and investment strategies, income tax planning, accounting, preservation of wills and estates, and insurance and disability security, as well as the awareness of shifting tides in our economy, finance, and politics.

Do You Need a Financial Planner?

Only you can make that decision. By now, you will have a good idea of the advantages of owning versus loaning your capital, the importance of asset allocation, and how to design a portfolio blueprint. But that is not all that is required to reach your goal of investment success and retirement with financial dignity. There

> Nothing great was ever achieved without enthusiasm.
> **Emerson**

are pitfalls and opportunities at every corner and they are difficult to predict.

The Challenges You Face When You Go It Alone

According to Venita Van Caspel, one of North America's foremost financial planning authorities, if you manage your financial planning on your own, you need the following four ingredients known as the "3 Ts + M":
• Time
• Training
• Temperament +
• Money

These are the investment challenges you face. You must be able to master these in order to enjoy a successful investment experience.

Time

By *time* I mean time at the end of your day, after you have worked 8, 9, or 10 hours. When you come home, do you have time to sit down, pour over financial statements, and look at investment data? Do you have the time to read financial journals such as *Canadian Business, Forbes, Fortune, Business Week, The Financial Times*, or *The Financial Post*, to mention a few? Or would you rather spend three hours, maybe playing a game of tennis, spending some time with your spouse or family at home, or perhaps pursuing a hobby? This is not to discourage you, but to get you thinking honestly about your habits, schedule, interests, and the lifestyle you want.

Training

Do you have training in accounting, statistical analysis, marketing, or economics to help you with the overall analysis that is necessary for investment success? This training is essential for effective planning.

Look at your financial knowledge and consider the following fact. The message of the most recent Federal Budget, and all of the preceding budgets during the last decade, is that the Canadian Government can no longer afford to support all of the people in the manner to which they have become accustomed. There will be further tax increases and there will be further reductions in social programs. How will you adjust your plan to these events?

These are just some of the factors that might influence the overall effectiveness of your financial plan. Venita Van Caspel notes:

If you are a success in your chosen profession, you are no doubt devoting many hours to keeping thoroughly informed and to implementing that knowledge. This leaves little time for the very specialized and demanding area of financial planning. Therefore, to obtain the maximum performance of your investable dollars, you will need to search out and use the services of a dedicated, creative, knowledgeable, and caring money planner who is backed up by a team of professionals.

Temperament

Do you have the temperament to implement successful investment strategies? Every investment decision is made in a gray area. It is never black or white. By the time it is black or white, everyone has the same information and the same data and the real opportunity may have passed. Can you make effective decisions in the gray zone?

It is always tough to make a buy decision in the investment marketplace. It is even harder to decide to sell. Take the old proverb about the "Glass of Water." Do you see it half full or half empty? According to theory, the optimist sees it half full; the pessimist sees it half empty. In investing, how you see that glass depends on a lot of external criteria. Often the glass is definitely half full. Other times it is undeniably half empty. Know thyself.

Money

Finally, do you have enough money to invest? Do you have substantial dollars and enough capital to build a portfolio on your own with adequate diversification? If not, I suggest you go back to the earlier chapters of this book and get started on a capital accumulation program.

Do You Have What It Takes to Go It Alone?

Are you an investor that can adopt your own self-management style? Or should you opt for professional money management? Complete the following chart to see where you rank on a scale from 1 (low) to 5 (high).

WORKSHEET 10-2: SELF MANAGEMENT OR PROFESSIONAL MANAGEMENT?

	Low		Medium		High
Time	1	2	3	4	5
Training	1	2	3	4	5
Temperament	1	2	3	4	5
Money	1	2	3	4	5

Scoring

17-20
You've got what it takes. You know how to set goals and implement investment strategies to fulfill your needs and objectives.

12-16
You are well on your way. You know what your goals are, but you are not sure about implementing them on your own. You require the services of a stockbroker or a financial planner who understands your needs and objectives. Your investment strategies may take a self-managed approach with professional guidance from your stockbroker, or it may include professionally managed mutual funds.

4-11
You, along with 90% of investors, require professional money management. You need help in establishing your goals, and you require the assistance of a stockbroker, financial planner, or other professional counsellor to implement your plan for you. A combination of adequate reserves to match your selection of professionally managed mutual funds will allow you to accomplish your investment objectives, and provide you with financial independence in the future.

Two Investment Portfolios: Self-Managed and Professionally Managed

Two investors are involved in investment portfolio management, one using self-management, the other using professional money-management.

The Self-Managed Investment Portfolio

The first investor has a $100,000 portfolio, with 30% in the form of reserves and 70% in growth. The 70% growth sector is divided into seven equal parts with $10,000 in each of several different companies in various industries.

$100,000 Self-Managed Portfolio

Reserves	30%
Growth Equities	
Bank, Trust, or Financial	10%
Utility – Telephone	10%
Utility – Pipeline	10%
Industrial, Electronics, or High Tech.	10%
Cyclical – Mining, Oil, or Forest Products	10%
Merchandising or Retail	10%
Distilling, Food, or Beverage	10%
	100%

If just one of these investments starts to underperform the market, such as a real estate company or a natural resources company, performance starts to deteriorate. If two investments underperform the market, the investor will probably lose money.

There is a great deal of money to be made in stocks that rise in price due to cycles in the economy—if your timing is right. When timing is wrong, especially in the cyclicals, it can cost an awful lot of money and time in waiting for your investment to get back in step with the cycle.

Even a $100,000 self-managed investment portfolio can be affected enormously if one or two investments go sour. My message is simple: If you're going to invest on your own, make sure you know what you're doing and what factors affect your portfolio. For many Canadians who lack the management skills, a self-managed portfolio is rarely the way to a comfortable retirement.

The Professionally Managed Investment Portfolio

The second investor uses a professional management approach with the same $100,000 capital, 30% in reserves and 70% in growth. In this scenario, however, the growth sector is divided into three different equity funds—25% in Professionally-Managed Fund (PMF #1), 25% in PMF #2, and 20% in PMF #3.

$100,000 Professionally Managed Portfolio

Reserves	30%
Growth Equities	
PMF #1	25%
PMF #2	25%
PMF #3	20%
	100%

Each fund has 50 to 100 equity securities managed by a professional investment manager. It is not uncommon to find funds with over 100 securities. If one of the investment selections doesn't perform well (perhaps it was a cyclical stock as in the previous example), the investor is unlikely to be aware of it. His/her money is spread out over so many securities that the value of the investment units changes by a few pennies at most.

A professionally managed fund usually has more new money coming in all the time, so the money managers can buy more of an underperforming stock the fund may own already, thereby averaging down the original cost. Money managers can work their way out of just about any situation.

On the other hand, if the individual investor buys something at $20 and sees it drop to $15, he or she probably won't have the nerve or confidence to adjust the situation with dollar averaging. The investor who manages his or her own portfolio rarely has that fortitude or persistence. My experience has been that 9 out of 10 investors are afraid to send what they consider to be good money after bad. Yet, we know that these companies usually come back to their previous trading levels over time.

If you can master the four ingredients of *time, training, temperament,* and *money,* go it alone. If you can't, don't. Hire a professional.

"What Do I Want My Financial Planner to Be Like?"

If you decide to hire a professional planner, develop a relationship with one principal advisor, someone you can trust. Most investors would rather conduct their investing and financial planning with one person than with several. Although you will use various professionals for their specific expertise at times, you should have an overall advisor who knows how all the pieces of your financial life fit together. Deal with someone who understands your personal needs, who is not product-oriented, who is not commission-oriented, and who will provide service and follow-through.

Guidelines for Selecting a Financial Planner

Whoever your principal advisor may be, the key is to find a planner who possesses the traits and characteristics mentioned above and who makes you feel comfortable. The guidelines below should give you a framework to gauge that comfort level.

WORKSHEET 10-3: SELECTING A FINANCIAL PLANNER

Is the planner empathetic and compatible?

_____

_____

What is this person's educational qualifications and professional experience/credentials?

_____

_____

Is the planner financially bonded?

_____

_____

Is there a track record of past performance upon which you can base realistic expectations?

_____

_____

What types of clients does the planner serve? Will he/she provide you with a list of references?

_____

_____

Continued on next page

WORKSHEET 10-3: SELECTING A FINANCIAL PLANNER (CONTINUED)

What is the financial planning process he/she proposes to follow? Is it clearly presented to you, or mired in confusing language?

_____

_____

What type of report does this person prepare? Ask for a copy of a sample plan.

_____

_____

Does the planner have a particular area of client specialization? What aspects of your financial needs will not be covered?

_____

_____

What types of products does she/he recommend? Is the planner competent in all types of investments, insurance, tax advantaged vehicles and tax strategies, and estate planning?

_____

_____

Can the planner tap into a network of special professional services?

_____

_____

What role will the planner play in the implementation of the proposed financial plan?

_____

_____

How does this person charge for their services (Commission only? Fee only? Fee plus commission?) Are the fees and/or commissions fair and competitive? How do you know?

_____

_____

Does this planner exercise "due diligence" to fully assess all potential risks as well as rewards of each proposed investment?

_____

_____

What follow-up services does the planner offer after the initial plan is established?

_____

_____

Should the planner become unavailable, who will be assigned to work with your plan?

_____

_____

In the Office With Your Financial Planner

Most people think that creating a financial plan is complex. It isn't. Only three items of information are necessary:

1. What you own and what you owe
2. What you earn and what you spend
3. What standard of living you want when you retire

The financial planner first determines all of the above and then calculates what you must save and what your investments should earn over the next year to be on track. He or she then advises you on specific investments and savings plans. It's that simple.

A typical planning cycle looks like Chart 10-4 below.

Working With Your Financial Planner

Achieving financial success doesn't end with paying your money to a personal financial planner and foregoing any further responsibility. Once you have established a financial plan, you must be committed to it. The following checklist can help you keep on track.

1. Stay committed to your plan.
2. Communicate fully with your advisor.
3. Be honest with your advisor.
4. At the data-gathering stage, provide all the information you can, not bits and pieces, otherwise you may have to redo the plan.
5. Don't be afraid to ask questions if you don't understand.

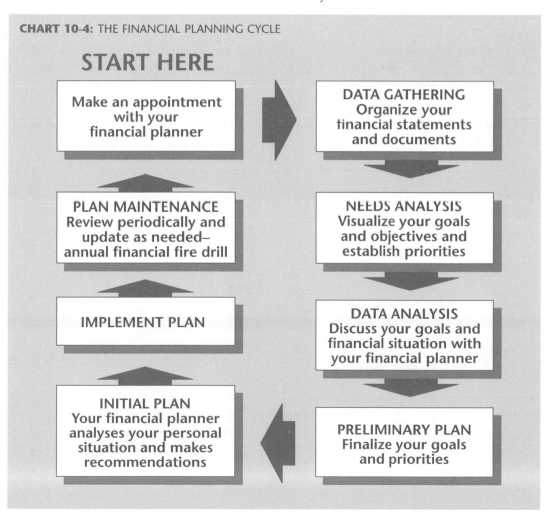

CHART 10-4: THE FINANCIAL PLANNING CYCLE

START HERE

Make an appointment with your financial planner

DATA GATHERING
Organize your financial statements and documents

PLAN MAINTENANCE
Review periodically and update as needed–annual financial fire drill

NEEDS ANALYSIS
Visualize your goals and objectives and establish priorities

IMPLEMENT PLAN

DATA ANALYSIS
Discuss your goals and financial situation with your financial planner

INITIAL PLAN
Your financial planner analyses your personal situation and makes recommendations

PRELIMINARY PLAN
Finalize your goals and priorities

6. At the preliminary and initial planning stages, discuss any parts of the plan that do not reflect your situation immediately.
7. As soon as you receive your financial plan, implement the recommendations right away.
8. Keep your advisor informed of any changes in your goals or financial status.
9. Be sure to have your annual "Financial Fire Drill."

Fees, Commissions, Your Financial Planner — and You

There are three ways to earn a living in the financial planning business: fee only, commission only, and fee plus commission. In the brokerage business, I see some products that have commission, some that don't. In the insurance industry, I see higher commissions on some types of products than others. In almost every scenario there is a commission or fee to contend with, and often, the fee or commission is hidden.

Many financial planners introduce their product area by giving you a financial plan that has no cost if you buy their product, but does if you don't. With accountants and lawyers, the meter is running, generally speaking, from the moment you sit down. You pay for their time and expertise. In addition to fees or commissions, many professional money managers charge annual administration and management fees.

In this era of de-regulation in the financial services industry in Canada, there is aggressive competition for the consumer dollar. There are discount brokerage operations with lower commissions and no service fees, and some banks and trust companies advertising No-Fee RRSP. When you look closely, you find that this usually applies to a fixed income

product with much lower potential returns in the long run. Most mutual funds offer a front-end commission option, or a back-end redemption charge on a decreasing time scale-out basis. The back-end charge can be applied to the original purchase price or the current market value at the time of redemption. In the latter case, if the fund performed well, you could find yourself paying a substantial commission. All of the major banks and trust companies and a number of independent companies offer a no-load family of mutual funds. Most often these companies charge only administration fees or set-up costs.

Another option the investor has is to deal with a discount broker. All of the major banks have a "no frills" discount brokerage division which is suitable only for investors who have the knowledge, training, and temperament to handle their own investment decisions. Different products also have close-out or termination charges. There are a multitude of other fee and commission variations.

Management Fees

If I buy a no-load mutual fund how does the fund manager get paid? It is important to understand that what we have discussed so far applies to the purchase or acquisition of a mutual fund and how the agent is remunerated.

As well, every mutual fund has a manager(s) or committee who makes all of the investment decisions pertaining to the fund. They must be compensated for their efforts and they are paid by charging a management fee, monthly, against the net asset value of the fund based on one-twelfth of a year. The management fee is determined by the type of asset under management. There is no free lunch. When you look closely and take into consideration all of the relevant factors, everyone is being paid somehow or some way. Follow the motto: "People get what they pay for." Worksheet 10-5 will give you an overview of the options available to you.

How Do Your Current Advisors Stack Up?

Now that you have an understanding of the guidelines to follow in the selection of a financial planner, how would you rate each of the many advisors you currently use? How well do they communicate with you; does the chemistry feel right? How would you rate their listening skills? Are they truly empathetic and responsive to your personal situation and needs? These are just a few of the questions you might want to ask yourself. You may find the exercise below valuable in measuring the strengths of your existing advisory relationships and in understanding where you may need professional assistance.

The Financial Planner and You — a One-to-One Relationship

After reading this chapter, you may decide that you would like a financial planner to help you. Or perhaps you discovered that you have what it takes to set your own financial planning course and to implement your own financial plan.

If you do choose to hire a professional, you will find that your relationship with him/her can be tremendously important. Your financial planner becomes an integral and intimate part of your life. It is a position of great trust, but if you choose your financial planner wisely, you will have a friend for life.

> Since the beginning of time, the most powerful influential and successful people have always been those with the greatest command of the written and spoken language.
> **Dan Sullivan**

WORKSHEET 10-5: ADVISOR RATING CHECKLIST

	Very Good	Good	Poor	Don't Have
Banker	☐	☐	☐	☐
Trust Officer	☐	☐	☐	☐
Accountant	☐	☐	☐	☐
Stockbroker	☐	☐	☐	☐
Lawyer	☐	☐	☐	☐
Insurance Agent (Life)	☐	☐	☐	☐
Insurance Agent (General)	☐	☐	☐	☐
Real Estate Broker	☐	☐	☐	☐
Financial Planner	☐	☐	☐	☐
Investment Counsellor	☐	☐	☐	☐
Mutual Funds Agent	☐	☐	☐	☐
Other	☐	☐	☐	☐
Other	☐	☐	☐	☐
Other	☐	☐	☐	☐

The Triangle of Finance

*Inflation and taxes trample profit.
You can "go broke safely" on interest
income, or you can outpace inflation by
adding strategic amounts of risk to the asset
mix in your investment portfolio*

The Triangle of Investment Objectives

Every sound financial plan should include four major strategies:

1. Preservation of capital
2. Accumulation of savings for investment
3. Conservation of savings/investment asset mix
4. Distribution of investments for adequate balance

These four goals group together in what I like to call a *Triangle of Investment Objectives* (see Chart 11-1). On the bottom, you have safety. Safety to most investors implies assurety of an income flow and instant liquidity. On the top, you have growth. There are two types of growth: defensive and aggressive. Picture yourself somewhere within the centre of this triangle.

I would like you to be aware of *not* being in any one point of the triangle. Picture yourself towards the centre of the triangle, participating with an asset allocation strategy that blends a mix of investments to meet your *liquidity, income,* and *growth* objectives.

Never invest your money in anything that eats or needs repairing.

Billy Rose

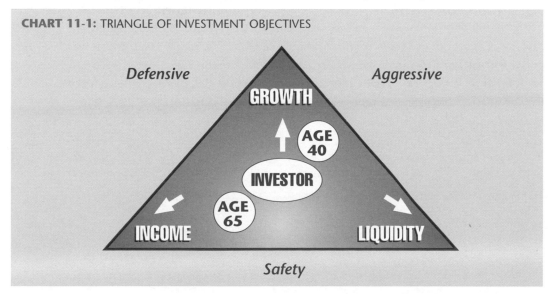

CHART 11-1: TRIANGLE OF INVESTMENT OBJECTIVES

Defensive   *Aggressive*

GROWTH

AGE 40

INVESTOR

AGE 65

INCOME   LIQUIDITY

Safety

For example, if you are one who has only Canada Savings Bonds in your portfolio, your emphasis is safety. You must understand this clearly. By cowering in the lower area of the triangle for safety, you forgo your opportunities in the upper area for growth. Try to balance your strategies. Get out of your restrictive safety net and start to participate with some growth in the defensive, and perhaps the aggressive, sectors of the triangle as well as in the income and liquidity sectors. Then you will have a mixture that gives you balanced performance.

If you are nearing retirement, or at retirement, you might be somewhere between income and liquidity in a defensive posture. If you are age 40, you may not be as concerned with liquidity and income because you have substantial earning power and many working years ahead. Your investing may be skewed more towards aggressive growth and therefore closer to the top right-hand area of the triangle.

Once again, regardless of your age, be sure you encompass all parts of the triangle in some degree. Remember the triangle as we look at the detailed development of your investment portfolio in this chapter.

Portfolio Construction

Just as an architect drafts construction plans for a house, an investor constructs an investment portfolio. Your mission is to design a portfolio mix tailored to fit your comfort zone. The eventual success of your portfolio depends on your asset mix and its tax implications. The asset mix you choose evolves from your three major investment objectives of liquidity, income, and growth. Three major asset classes; reserves, debt, and equity serve the investor very well in meeting the investment objectives. And each of these asset classes accommodate a particular investment suitable for our purpose of measuring risk/reward and return on investments. While there are a myriad of investments to choose from the three investments we will use are T-Bills, bonds, and stocks. (see Table 11-2)

> Because investing is an inexact science, it is better to be approximately right than precisely wrong.
>
> **George Hartman**

TABLE 11-2: MAJOR OBJECTIVE, ASSET CLASS, & INVESTMENT SELECTION

Major Objective	Asset Class	Investment Selection
Liquidity	Reserves	T-Bills
Income	Debt	Bonds
Growth	Equity	Stocks

Risk Versus Reward

Each of the investment selections provides a range of risks and rewards. Generally, the greater the risk, the greater the reward potential. We discussed risk versus reward at some length in Chapter seven. The major risks and rewards of the investment selections above are listed in Table 11-3. Now it's time to summarize all of the discussions we have had so far into

TABLE 11-3: ASSET CLASSES

Major Objective	Asset Class	Investment Selection	Major Risk	Major Reward
Liquidity	Reserves	T-Bills	Long-term Inflation	Liquidity
Income	Debt	Bonds	Mid-term Volatility/ Long-term Inflation	Fixed Maturity Value
Stocks	Growth	Equities	Short-term Volatility	Inflation Hedge

workable asset allocation solutions. To do so we will look at asset allocation modules, risk/rewards ratios, volatility, and portfolio weightings.

Asset Allocation Modules

Much work has been done compiling statistical data on the performance of stocks, bonds, T-Bills, and inflation over the past several decades. I would like to acknowledge four major sources I have drawn on to provide much of the data in this chapter:

- *Stocks, Bonds, Bills, and Inflation*, 1991 Yearbook, by Ibbotson Associates, Chicago is a wonderful source of long-term U.S. data covering 1926 to the present. I use the Ibbotson charts and acetates in our seminars and workshops.
- *Canadian Stocks, Bonds, Bills, and Inflation*, 1950–1987, by James E. Hatch and Robert W. White, published by The Research Foundation of the Institute of Chartered Financial Analysts. I had the pleasure of being taught by Professor Hatch in my fourth year of commerce at Sir George Williams University (Concordia University).
- *Risk is a Four Letter Word*, by George Hartman, published in 1994 by Stoddart Publishing Co. Limited, Toronto. This is absolutely one of the best books covering risk/reward and asset allocation strategies. Serious investors should consider purchasing a copy.
- *Andex Chart For Canadian Investors*, by Anthony Di Meo and Dexter Robinson, published by Andex Associates, Windsor, Ontario. If a picture is worth 1000 words Andex Associates have captured a history of the Canadian markets from 1950 to the present. The Andex charts are greatly appreciated by our workshop participants.

A study of the Andex Associates chart based on 43.5 years of historical data, –clearly illustrates the above average performance of equities versus T-Bills, Bonds, and GICs. However, the extreme highs and lows experienced by equities would have been nerve-racking for many investors and more than they could handle. Ask yourself how you would have coped during a year when your stocks were down 40%? For those who could stand the heat, they would have been well rewarded —equities ranked first in performance about 62% of the time. (See Table 11-4)

TABLE 11-4: RISK/REWARD RATIO

January 1, 1950 — June 30, 1993 *(Based on 510 Separate 1-Year Periods)*

Asset	High	Low	Average	Number of Times Asset Ranked 1st
T-Bills	19.5%	0.5%	6.7%	4.1%
Bonds	55.8%	–15.9%	7.4%	15.9%
GICs	17.5%	3.1%	8.1%	18.2%
Stocks (CDN)	86.9%	–39.2%	11.7%	26.1%
Stocks (US)	57.0%	–40.1%	13.8%	35.7%

Source: Di Meo, Anthony and Dexter Robinson, Andex Chart for Canadian Investors, 1993, Andex Associates, Windsor, Ontario.

Further analysis of this chart depicts the following:

- The most conservative investments, T-Bills, produced the lowest return at 6.7% on average, but they were always liquid.
- T-Bills were the least volatile, while equities were the most volatile, therefore, T-Bills are more suitable for portfolios with a shorter time frame and equities are a better fit for longer time frames.
- The major risk for T-Bills is long-term inflation; the major risk for equities is short-term volatility; the investor must therefore match their time frame with their investment personality.

Long-term Normal Range of Results

The relationships between the various asset class returns are derived from inflation, real interest rates, and risk premium.

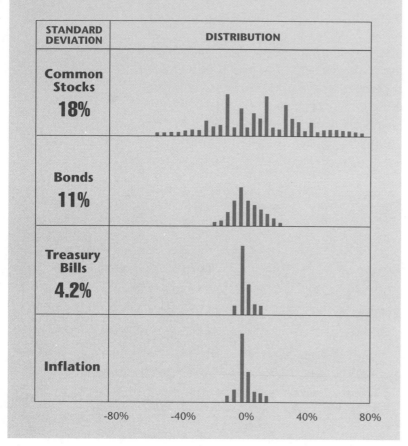

CHART 11-5: SUMMARY STATISTICS OF ANNUAL RETURNS—44.5 YEARS

STANDARD DEVIATION	DISTRIBUTION
Common Stocks **18%**	
Bonds **11%**	
Treasury Bills **4.2%**	
Inflation	

-80%   -40%   0%   40%   80%

example of annual returns is shown in Chart 11-5. There is a substantial variance between the highs and lows in this chart (standard deviation), however, the results are also distributed around the mean.

Standard Deviation

What do we mean by standard deviation? Ibbotson Associates states that it is simply the measure of the extent to which observations in the series differ from the arithmetic mean of the series. For a series of asset returns, the standard deviation is a measure of the volatility, or risk, of the asset. The standard deviation is a measure of the variation around an average or mean. In a normally distributed series, about two-thirds of the observations lie within one standard deviation of the arithmetic mean; about 95% of the observations, within two standard deviations; and more than 99% within three standard deviations.

As you can see standard deviation begins to get very technical. This is the bailiwick of actuaries and mathematicians. As well, all of our corporate clients' pension fund managers develop a series of core assumptions based on historical data to determine their investment strategies and asset mix. But how can we simplify this process for our purpose? Lets start by taking a look at Table 11-6.

T-Bills, have produced an annual compound return of 6.5% on average for 44.5 years with a volatility factor of 4.2%. This means that in any given year T-Bills have

We have learned that riskier assets such as common stocks will show a broad distribution of returns from very positive to very negative over a long period of time. Bonds offer a less risky distribution of returns and will produce a distribution of returns around the mean of the series. Treasury bills are the least risky and will produce a distribution of returns around the mean of the series to the right of zero return and rarely will show a negative return. An

TABLE 11-6: HISTORICAL RISK/REWARD RATIO—LONG-TERM NORMAL RANGE OF RESULTS

Asset	Compound Annual Return	Range Volatility	High	Low
Inflation	4.5%	+ or – 3.5%	8.0%	1.0%
T-Bills	6.5%	+ or – 4.2%	10.7%	2.3%
Bonds	6.7%	+ or – 11.0%	17.7%	–4.3%
Stocks	10.5%	+ or – 18.0%	28.5%	–7.5%

Source: Di Meo, Anthony and Dexter Robinson, Andex Chart for Canadian Investors, 1993, Andex Associates, Windsor, Ontario.

fluctuated between 2.3% (6.5% – 4.2%) and 10.7% (6.5% – 4.2%). Stocks during the same period produced an average annual return of 10.5% with a volatility factor of 18%. The yearly range for stocks has been from a low of –7.5% (10.5% – 18%) to a high of 28.5% (10.5% + 18%). We learned from Chart 11-5 that the annual returns could be very positive or negative in the extreme, but what Table 11-6 illustrates is a normal range of results. This is what Ibbotson Associates referred to as standard deviation—two-thirds of the time returns will be as you expect (normal range) and one-third of the time they will be outside of the normal range.

A Model For All Seasons

Investment returns have been expanding, especially during the last two decades. We have witnessed much greater extremes with inflation, deficits, interest rates, risk premiums, and investment returns. Therefore, if I were making projections for the next few decades I would adjust the anticipated long-term returns as follows:

TABLE 11-7: MODEL PORTFOLIO WEIGHTINGS

Investment	Compound Annual Return	Volatility
T-Bills	6%	+ or – 4%
Bonds	8%	+ or – 11%
Stocks	12%	+ or – 18%
Inflation	5%	+ or – 4%

It is apparent in all of our workshops that the participants, major focus is on which stock, bond, or security to buy or sell. Numerous studies, however, have proven that the return you expect to obtain is not determined by security selection, rather asset allocation will produce 90% of the result (see Chart 11-8). Conclusion: It's better to own the wrong investment in the right asset class than the right investment in the wrong asset class.

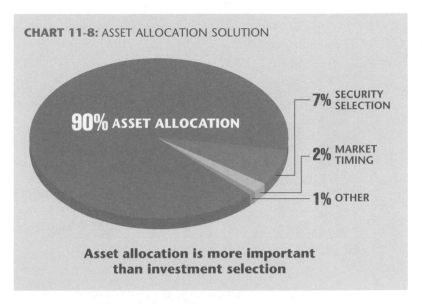

CHART 11-8: ASSET ALLOCATION SOLUTION

90% ASSET ALLOCATION

7% SECURITY SELECTION

2% MARKET TIMING

1% OTHER

Asset allocation is more important than investment selection

With this picture in mind let's look at four possible asset allocation solutions designed to match the investor profiles we discussed in Chapter seven.

The weighted portfolio returns range from 7.1% for a risk-avoider to 10.9% for a risk-taker. Which asset classes would you choose based on your investment personality? Before you answer this question let's

TABLE 11-9: TYPICAL PORTFOLIO WEIGHTINGS

Investor Type	Investment	% of Portfolio	X Expected Return	= Weighted Return
Risk Avoider (very conservative)	T-Bills	65%	6%	3.9%
	Bonds	25%	8%	2.0%
	Stocks	10%	12%	1.2%
	Total Weighted Return			**7.1%**
Risk Minimizer (conservative)	T-Bills	45%	6%	2.7%
	Bonds	30%	8%	2.4%
	Stocks	25%	12%	3.0%
	Total Weighted Return			**8.1%**
Risk-Blender (less conservative growth oriented)	T-Bills	15%	6%	.9%
	Bonds	30%	8%	2.4%
	Stocks	55%	12%	6.6%
	Total Weighted Return			**9.9%**
Risk-Taker (high risk growth speculator)	T-Bills	5%	6%	.3%
	Bonds	20%	8%	1.6%
	Stocks	75%	12%	9.0%
	Total Weighted Return			**10.9%**

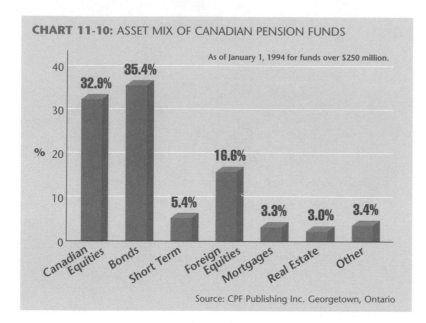

CHART 11-10: ASSET MIX OF CANADIAN PENSION FUNDS

As of January 1, 1994 for funds over $250 million.

Source: CPF Publishing Inc. Georgetown, Ontario

By now you have a good idea of your comfort zone and tolerance for risk. Its time to allocate your portfolio to the three asset classes in the Worksheet 11-11 below.

How Do We Measure Risk and Reward?

When we reviewed Model Portfolio Weightings in Table 11-7, we discussed the concept of volatility as it applies to each asset class. In order to understand the risk factor for a portfolio we measure the expected volatility times the percent of the portfolio in each asset class to obtain the weighted volatility for the portfolio. Let's return to the four risk scenarios we looked at for typical portfolio weightings. We do this exercise by repeating the process for each investor type by substituting expected volatility for expected return.

The weighted volatility returns vary greatly from the risk-avoider profile at 7.2% to the risk-taker profile at 15.9%. What this means is that a risk-avoider profile can expect a total weighted return of 7.1% with a volatility factor of 7.2%. We would therefore expect the returns to range between –.1% (7.1% – 7.2%) and 14.3% (7.1% + 7.2%). Two out of every three years this normal range will occur and one out of every

take a look at the Canadian Pension funds asset mix for funds over $250 million at January 1, 1994 in Chart 11-10.

This chart shows seven different asset classes. If we were to condense the seven asset classes to three, a typical pension fund would have the following asset mix and total weighted return.

Typical Pension Fund Weighting

Investor Type	Investment	% of Portfolio	X	Expected Return	=	Weighted Return
Risk Blender	T-Bills	5.4%	X	6%		.3%
	Bonds	38.7%	X	8%		3.1%
	Stocks	55.9%	X	12%		6.7%
	Total Weighted Return					**10.1%**

WORKSHEET 11-11: YOUR PORTFOLIO WEIGHTING

Investor Type	Investment	% of Portfolio	X	Expected Return	=	Weighted Return
_____	T-Bills	____%	X	6%		____%
	Bonds	____%	X	8%		____%
	Stocks	____%	X	12%		____%
	Total Weighted Return					____%

three years the volatility will be above or below this range.

The risk-taker weighted volatility returns were 15.9%. This means a person with this profile can expect a total weighted return of 10.9% with a volatility factor of 15.9%. We would expect returns to range from –5% (10.9% – 15.9%) to 26.8% (10.9% + 15.9).

Once again, in the Worksheet 11-13 below, it's your turn to bring forward the percentage you placed in each asset class in order to determine your portfolio's weighted volatility.

A Portfolio Blueprint

Most investors' portfolios consist of securities falling somewhere between low volatility and high volatility. Rarely does an investor actually compute all of the data as above. The vast majority of investors weigh the risk and reward of each investment selection in their minds. In practice, most investment decisions are made based on rough approximations measuring risk and reward. Generally, you should be conservative in the direction of your target.

While no two investors' needs and objectives are identical, a typical risk-blender might design a portfolio with a ratio of reserves 25%, debt 25%, and equities 50% structured as outlined in Table 11-14. Solomon Surti owns such a portfolio.

TABLE 11-12: TYPICAL PORTFOLIO VOLATILITIES

Investor Type	Investment	% of Portfolio	X	Expected Return	=	Weighted Return
Risk Avoider	T-Bills	65%		+ or – 4%		2.6%
(very conservative)	Bonds	25%		+ or – 11%		2.8%
	Stocks	10%		+ or – 18%		1.8%
	Total Weighted Volatility					**7.2%**
Risk Minimizer	T-Bills	45%		+ or – 4%		1.8%
(conservative)	Bonds	30%		+ or – 11%		3.3%
	Stocks	25%		+ or – 18%		4.5%
	Total Weighted Volatility					**9.6%**
Risk-Blender	T-Bills	15%		+ or – 4%		0.6%
(less conservative growth oriented)	Bonds	30%		+ or – 11%		3.3%
	Stocks	55%		+ or – 18%		9.9%
	Total Weighted Volatility					**13.8%**
Risk-Taker	T-Bills	5%		+ or – 4%		0.2%
(high risk growth speculator)	Bonds	20%		+ or – 11%		2.2%
	Stocks	75%		+ or – 18%		13.5%
	Total Weighted Volatility					**15.9%**

Typical Pension Fund Portfolio Volatility

Investor Type	Investment	% of Portfolio	X	Expected Return	=	Weighted Return
Risk Blender	T-Bills	5.4%		+ or – 4%		0.2%
	Bonds	38.7%		+ or – 11%		4.3%
	Stocks	55.9%		+ or – 18%		10.1%
	Total Weighted Volatility					14.6%

WORKSHEET 11-13: YOUR PORTFOLIO VOLATILITY

Investor Type	Investment	% of Portfolio	X	Expected Return	=	Weighted Return
_____	T-Bills	_____%	X	+ or – 4%		_____%
	Bonds	_____%	X	+ or – 11%		_____%
	Stocks	_____%	X	+ or – 18%		_____%
	Total Weighted Volatility					_____%

Case Profile ④ Solomon Surti

Solomon is 59 years old, and is three years away from mandatory retirement at age 62. Several years ago, his portfolio was 100% in reserves and debt (loanership). He had never owned a preferred or common stock. Solomon engaged the services of an investment advisor and as a result allocated 65% of his portfolio to equities. His portfolio is now worth $180,000 and has grown substantially during the last six years through dividend reinvestment and capital gains. Solomon uses flow-through shares and an RRSP as procedural tools for tax-deferral and tax savings strategies. He plans to convert his RRSP into a Registered Retirement Income Fund (RRIF) at some point in the future.

TABLE 11-14: PORTFOLIO BLUEPRINT—SOLOMON SURTI

		Value	**Distribution**
Reserves	Cash/Premium Savings Account	$45,000	25%
	Canada Savings Bonds		
	Canada Treasury Bills		
Debt	Guaranteed Investment Certificates	$18,000	10%
	Government and Corporate Bonds and Debentures maturing in 2-10 Years		
	Preferred Shares (Retractable and Convertible)	$27,000	15%
	Income Common Shares (Banks and Utilities)		
Equities	Common Stock		
	Growth: Manufacturing, Transportation, Broadcasting Publishing, Food and Beverage	$45,000	25%
	Aggressive Growth: Forest Products, Mining and Metals Oil and Gas, Real Estate, Precious Metals	$45,000	25%
	Total Portfolio	**$180,000**	**100%**

Investment Pyramid

As you build your portfolio, it helps to picture the investment structure in a pyramid and an inverse pyramid shape. (See Chart 11-15) The pyramid begins with your base—your safe reserves and income investments. The central body of your pyramid contains growth and income investments for capital gains and dividends. The peak of your pyramid includes aggressive growth stocks, primarily to generate capital gains. Naturally, as you increase your degree of risk, you increase your potential reward proportionately. The pyramid is inverted.

Building Your Investment Pyramid

As you build a portfolio (Chart 11-16), you start out with interest-sensitive vehicles such as savings deposits, Canada Savings Bonds, Canada Treasury Bills, Term Deposits, etc. This is the base of the pyramid, the solid foundation. Then add a layer of preferred shares, which are essentially income vehicles, then a layer of dividend-paying common shares for growth and income. Finally, add shares for aggressive growth, plus a capstone of assorted other security types such as gold, options, and futures if they meet your tolerance for risk.

You build your structure over time, depending on the risk/reward ratio you want to assume. You must construct your portfolio pyramid to fit your comfort zone. As you increase your degree of risk, you may lose some of your capital, but your minor losses will be more than offset by your increased reward potential in all but the most severe cases.

CHART 11-15: INVESTMENT PYRAMID—BALANCING YOUR INVESTMENT STRATEGY

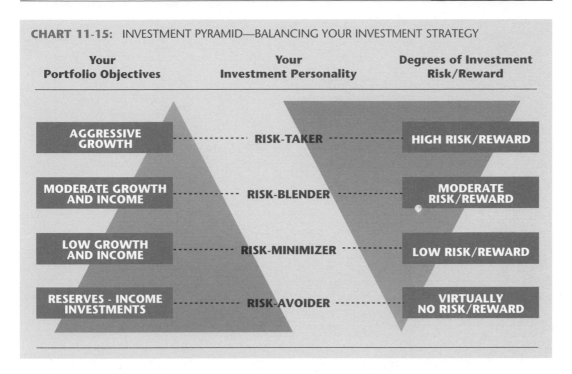

Your Portfolio Objectives	Your Investment Personality	Degrees of Investment Risk/Reward
AGGRESSIVE GROWTH	RISK-TAKER	HIGH RISK/REWARD
MODERATE GROWTH AND INCOME	RISK-BLENDER	MODERATE RISK/REWARD
LOW GROWTH AND INCOME	RISK-MINIMIZER	LOW RISK/REWARD
RESERVES - INCOME INVESTMENTS	RISK-AVOIDER	VIRTUALLY NO RISK/REWARD

CHART 11-16: INVESTMENT PYRAMID

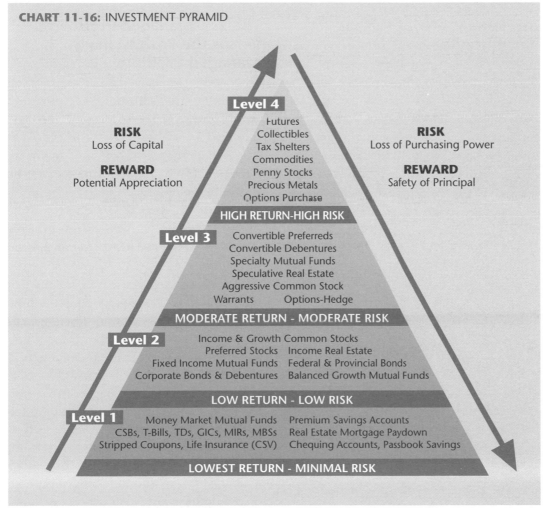

RISK
Loss of Capital

REWARD
Potential Appreciation

RISK
Loss of Purchasing Power

REWARD
Safety of Principal

Level 4
Futures
Collectibles
Tax Shelters
Commodities
Penny Stocks
Precious Metals
Options Purchase

HIGH RETURN-HIGH RISK

Level 3
Convertible Preferreds
Convertible Debentures
Specialty Mutual Funds
Speculative Real Estate
Aggressive Common Stock
Warrants   Options-Hedge

MODERATE RETURN - MODERATE RISK

Level 2
Income & Growth Common Stocks
Preferred Stocks   Income Real Estate
Fixed Income Mutual Funds   Federal & Provincial Bonds
Corporate Bonds & Debentures   Balanced Growth Mutual Funds

LOW RETURN - LOW RISK

Level 1
Money Market Mutual Funds   Premium Savings Accounts
CSBs, T-Bills, TDs, GICs, MIRs, MBSs   Real Estate Mortgage Paydown
Stripped Coupons, Life Insurance (CSV)   Chequing Accounts, Passbook Savings

LOWEST RETURN - MINIMAL RISK

All our dreams come true if we have the courage to pursue them.
Walt Disney

TABLE 11-17: INVESTMENT MIX AT VARIOUS TAX BRACKETS

Tax Bracket	Reserves	Income	Growth	Inflation Hedge	Procedural Tools
0- $29,590	Savings Accounts Money Market CSBs, CTBs, TDs, GICs	Bonds & Debentures Preferreds Mortgages	CV Preferred CV Debentures Balanced Mutual Funds	Gold	RRSP, LIF RRIF, LIRA Annuity RESP
$29,591- $59,180	All of the above	All of the above, plus Income Common	All of the above plus Growth Common, Base Metals, Growth Mutual Funds Cdn. & Global	Real Estate Precious Metals	All of the above plus Income Splitting
$59,181-	All of the above	All of the above	All of the above plus aggressive Growth, Junior Industrials	All of the above plus Currencies, Commodities, Specialty Mutual Funds	All of the above plus Tax Shelters, Flow-Though Shares, Limited Partnerships, Income Real Estate

Investment Mix at Various Tax Brackets

There are no hard and fast rules for selecting the appropriate securities by tax bracket, other than to suggest that, as your income increases, it is probably best to use more procedural tools for tax deferral and tax shelter. As a guideline, the lower your income, the more conservative your investment mix.

TABLE 11-18: SELF-MANAGED PORTFOLIO

Security	Cost Dec 31/83	Market Value Dec 31/93	Net Gain or Loss
Bank of Montreal	$13.75	$27.63	100.9%
BCE Inc.	$33.50	$46.25	38.1%
B.C. Telecom Inc.	$11.00	$25.38	130.7%
C.P. Ltd..	$16.75	$21.63	29.1%
Dylex Ltd.. APR.	$8.29	$1.49	(82.0%)
Imasco Ltd..	$17.62	$40.13	127.8%
MacMillan Bloedel	$9.83	$21.25	116.2%
Stelco Inc. Ser. A	$30.00	$8.75	(70.8%)
Portfolio Average			48.8%
T.S.E. Composite	2552.35	4321.43	69.3%

The Self-Managed Portfolio Versus the Professionally Managed Portfolio

Remember the self-managed portfolio and professionally managed portfolio scenario in Chapter 10? Let's look at the self-managed portfolio in more detail to track its performance of the individual elements.

Assume the year is 1983 and you are looking to invest in these securities. Now review the results 10 years later at the end of 1993.

Would you have chosen the top three or four performers, or might your portfolio have been saddled with some losers as well? If you had chosen all eight of these securities, the impressive gains on some stocks would have been offset by substantial losses on two stocks and lacklustre performance on some others. The result would have been an overall mediocre performance averaging 48.8%, about two-thirds the performance of the Toronto Stock Exchange Composite Index, which gained 69.3% during the 10-year period.

Undervalued securities don't generally stand up and wave at you. It requires a lot of time and effort and patience, and a steely constitution to find them. If this sounds like you, maybe it's time to think about a DRIP.

Dividend Reinvestment Plan

With solid evidence that stocks deliver the best long-term return of any investment instrument, a plan that offers investors a convenient, cost-effective way to increase their equity in a particular company is a welcome one indeed. It is all the more appealing in a time of rising equity prices—and dividend yields—such as the past few years. One such plan is a *Dividend Reinvestment Plan* (DRIP).

If you own shares in a company, a DRIP allows you to reinvest cash dividends from the preferred and common shares in additional shares without paying a brokerage commission. As well, some of those companies may also offer their shares at a slight discount to the market price. And as an added bonus, some companies even allow DRIP members to buy additional shares for cash.

Commission-free or cheaper purchases are not the only reasons to belong to a DRIP; rising dividend yield is another. Though the current dividend may be low—say 1% or 2% per cent—that particular company may have increased it steadily over the past years, so that the dividend rate has grown by as much as several hundred percent. When reinvested, dividends return dividends themselves; little dividends become big sums when compounded. For example, consider shares of BCE. If you had invested $1,000 in 1970 and withdrawn the dividends as you earned them, your investment would be worth $1,978 at June 30, 1994. However, had you reinvested all the dividends, your holding

would have increased to $5,675 by the end of 1993.

Approximately 80 publicly traded companies offer shareholders a DRIP. And of course, a DRIP is worthwhile only when a company pays a consistent dividend. At least 80 companies have paid a dividend every year for the past 25 years and 40 companies have paid

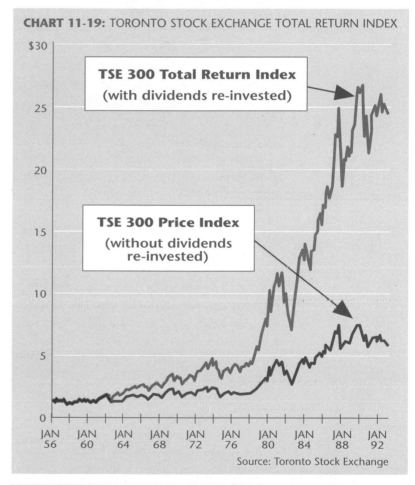

CHART 11-19: TORONTO STOCK EXCHANGE TOTAL RETURN INDEX

TSE 300 Total Return Index (with dividends re-invested)

TSE 300 Price Index (without dividends re-invested)

Source: Toronto Stock Exchange

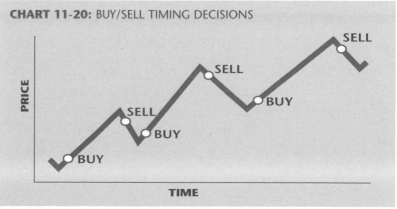

CHART 11-20: BUY/SELL TIMING DECISIONS

PRICE

TIME

BUY SELL BUY SELL BUY SELL

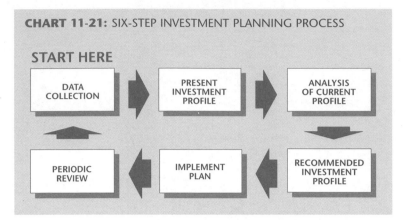

CHART 11-21: SIX-STEP INVESTMENT PLANNING PROCESS

START HERE

DATA COLLECTION → PRESENT INVESTMENT PROFILE → ANALYSIS OF CURRENT PROFILE

PERIODIC REVIEW ← IMPLEMENT PLAN ← RECOMMENDED INVESTMENT PROFILE

dividends for 50 years. Combined with a rising dividend yield and the benefit of the dividend tax credit, it makes a DRIP a valuable asset of every investment portfolio. As good as this seems it is not everyone's cup of tea. Managing an investment portfolio is a full time career and you probably already have one.

Professionally Managed Portfolio

For most investors, the answer is to entrust their investments to a professional stockbroker, mutual fund specialist, investment advisor, or financial planner, someone who is dedicated to the preservation and growth of their capital. For some people, however, this is not the answer.

Do *you* have what it takes to make buy and sell decisions at the appropriate time, or would a professional money manager be the solution for you?

To assist you with this decision, I have developed a questionnaire to allow you to construct your personal investment portfolio. Upon completion, you should have a pretty good idea of what is involved in portfolio construction and management, and which approach will

best work for you to achieve your goals of wealth accumulation and financial independence.

But first look at the six-step investment planning process (Chart 11-21) that you should complete either on your own or with the help of your investment advisor. Then, look at the role of the professional money manager and how to accurately evaluate her/his performance (Chart 11-22)

How to Select Your Investment Advisor

This is what you have been leading up to and here you are. But how do you choose the right advisor to help you accomplish your investment goals? Remember, next to your number one asset—your physical health, you are dealing with a very important asset—your financial health, and you cannot afford to make a major mistake.

Picture the selection process in the form of a baseball game:
- You want a pitcher (investment advisor) who can pitch a strong and fair game, or

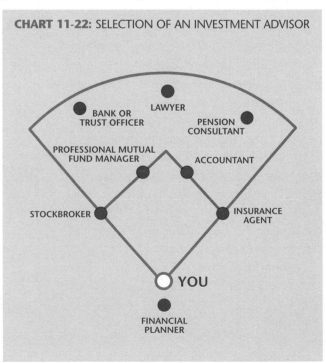

CHART 11-22: SELECTION OF AN INVESTMENT ADVISOR

BANK OR TRUST OFFICER

LAWYER

PENSION CONSULTANT

PROFESSIONAL MUTUAL FUND MANAGER

ACCOUNTANT

STOCKBROKER

INSURANCE AGENT

YOU

FINANCIAL PLANNER

you want a catcher (financial planner) who can direct your pitcher's aim.

- You are in the batter's box. You must decide your risk/reward tolerance. Do you want to be a long-ball hitter (the Big Payoff, the Pot of Gold at the end of the rainbow), or a consistent, on-base hitter (generating steady income and capital gains)? Very few home runs are hit in a game compared to singles, doubles, and triples.

If you were organizing your investment portfolio, estate plan, or tax plan, you would want to place your stockbroker, lawyer, or accountant on the pitcher's mound. We will cover these areas in upcoming chapters. For now, you should understand that the advisor position is a key role. You move players (change the positions of your financial professionals) to suit your needs. The key is to have an investment advisor or financial planner to call the game, surrounded by specialists to implement your goals.

Styles of Professional Money Management

Once you find an advisor you are comfortable with, try and determine his/her management style. There are many professional styles of money management. Every professional money manager employs at least one money management style and more often a combination. There are three types of market management personalities:

- Market timers
- Growth investors
- Value investors

Make sure your advisor's style and personality suit your personality and way of thinking.

- *Bottom-Up Style (Value Investor)*
  Seeks undervalued securities with little regard for overall economic and market

conditions. Selects stocks trading at a discount to book value and low price-earnings multiple, and is prepared to sit with the selected security for many years in order to recognize the stock's full potential.

- *Top-Down Style*
  (Group or Sector Rotator)
  Analyses the macro and micro economic trends and market forecasts, then selects attractive groups to participate in, with stocks that are the leaders and show the most promise in their industry.

- *Diversified Growth Style*
  Combines the bottom-up and the top-down styles to select a cross-section of securities poised for above-average growth over the intermediate to long-term. Selects stocks based on fundamentals with above average increases in cash flow, revenues, earnings per share, or market share.

- *Balanced Growth Style*
  (Asset Allocation)
  Combines the bottom-up and top-down styles and measures risk/reward by mathematical analyses of various classes of common shares, preferred shares, bonds and debentures, and a variety of money market assets in order to reduce risk. Uses fundamental analysis of economic growth, interest rates, and market analysis of securities.

- *Hedged Style*
  Can use any of the above approaches individually or together, including derivatives to enhance portfolio performance. A typical strategy that provides a less volatile performance is selling options on securities held in the portfolio. The premiums earned on the options provide steady income, but the hedged style also precludes the possibility of superior capital gains if the underlying stock is called away should the purchaser exercise the option.

Never buy a stock you can't illustrate with a crayon.
Peter Lynch

109

- *Market Timers*

  Technical analysis based on price trends for individual stocks or stock groups or market as a whole. Really good market timers are a rare breed and very hard to find.

  In addition to learning as much as you can about the manager's investment philosophy, strategy, and style, look for a verifiable long-term record of performance over one/three/five/ and ten years, encompassing both good and bad market periods.

How to Monitor the Performance of Your Money Manager

How can you measure the performance of your professional money manager?

I recommend using the investment industry's common performance criteria for a complete market cycle of approximately 4 to 4½ years. If your financial planner is performing well, his/her performance over the period of this market cycle will:

1. Exceed the Consumer Price Index by 3% to 5% compounded per year
2. Outperform the Toronto Stock Exchange Composite Index by 4% to 6% compounded per year
3. Perform in the top quartile amongst her/his peer group of managers
4. Outperform the Toronto Stock Exchange Composite Index during all down years.

WORKSHEET 11-23: HOW TO CONSTRUCT YOUR PERSONAL INVESTMENT PORTFOLIO

General Questionnaire

Is your portfolio currently structured to meet your needs and objectives within your risk tolerance level?

_____

_____

What is your balance between reserves, fixed income, growth, and aggressive growth?

_____

_____

Is your asset allocation and investment mix suitable for the current outlook on the market?

_____

_____

Are there too many or too few holdings relative to the capital asset size of your portfolio?

_____

_____

Do you have sufficient liquid reserves for unforeseeable needs and for future investment opportunities?

_____

_____

Are you taking maximum advantage of tax deferral and tax savings techniques, using procedural tools such as an RRSP?

_____

_____

Continued on next page

WORKSHEET 11-23: HOW TO CONSTRUCT YOUR PERSONAL INVESTMENT PORTFOLIO (CONTINUED)

Are your investments structured to take advantage of the Dividend Tax Credit and capital gains?

_____

_____

What is the general quality and liquidity of your portfolio?

_____

_____

What future cash flow is available for investing and what cash withdrawals may be required in the foreseeable future?

_____

_____

Reserves

Does your portfolio have adequate reserves in cash or cash equivalents to provide for emergency cash needs and future buying opportunities?

_____

_____

Should the term to maturity of your GICs and TDs be lengthened or shortened?

_____

_____

Are you holding too many reserves, therefore forsaking your opportunity to increase your return with income or growth securities?

_____

_____

Income Securities

Do you hold an appropriate percentage of income securities?

_____

_____

What is the average term to maturity of your bonds and debentures? Are they well staggered to provide you with good flexibility?

_____

_____

Are any of your holdings subject to retraction, redemption, extension, or conversion?

_____

_____

Are there trading or switching opportunities on your convertible, retractable, or extendible securities?

_____

_____

Have you considered the capital gains potential of buying deep discount bonds versus high coupon bonds?

_____

_____

Continued on next page

WORKSHEET 11-23: HOW TO CONSTRUCT YOUR PERSONAL INVESTMENT PORTFOLIO (CONTINUED)

Have you considered the taxable benefits of buying preferred shares with proceeds from your other fixed-income securities and some of your reserves?

_____

_____

Growth Securities

What is the general quality of your holdings and do they meet your risk/reward tolerance level?

_____

_____

Are the investments diversified by industry and country, in line with current market conditions?

_____

_____

Is there a reasonable balance between stable growth and aggressive or cyclical growth industries?

_____

_____

Have you considered whether to buy or sell off any odd lots, rights issues, warrants, or options you may be holding?

_____

_____

Are there any issues that offer better appreciation potential than the ones presently held in your portfolio?

_____

_____

Inflation-Hedge Assets

Are you holding any inflation hedge assets either inside or outside of your portfolio as insurance? Is the risk level tolerable for your comfort zone?

_____

_____

Have you considered holding some precious metal securities that can provide an attractive yield between market cycles?

_____

_____

What real estate holdings have you considered investing in besides your primary residence?

_____

_____

Have you considered owning stamps, coins, antiques, art, and other collectibles, both for your personal enjoyment and as a hedge against inflation?

_____

_____

Continued on next page

WORKSHEET 11-23: HOW TO CONSTRUCT YOUR PERSONAL INVESTMENT PORTFOLIO (CONTINUED)

Procedural Tools

Are you currently using RRSPs, RESPs, or RRIFs to defer tax?

_____

Are you employing income-splitting techniques with your spouse and other family members?

_____

_____

Have you considered using tax shelters such as flow-through shares and other limited partnerships?

_____

_____

Are you taking advantage of all tax concessions? Would the establishment of an incorporated business make sense for you?

_____

_____

Ten Primary Reasons Why People Fail, or the Ten Commandments for Investment Success

Now that you have had a chance to complete this questionnaire on how to construct your personal investment portfolio, let's look at why so many people fail to achieve positive investment results. I introduced these ideas in Chapter 5 in terms of attitude. Here we will look at these ideas in terms of their effect on your investment strategy.

In my opinion, the ten factors listed below are the most frequent causes of investment failure. The inverse of these factors constitute your touchstones for investment survival. Look at them positively and treat them as commandments. Apply the ones that pertain to you and work to master them all.

1. Public Enemy No. 1—Inflation

Too often we plan our financial future on the basis of a dollar value today. But that dollar, as we have seen, will be worth a lot less in terms of our future purchasing power.

The majority of people use fixed income products that provide a guarantee on their dollars rather than equity products that can provide conservation of their future purchasing power. Fixed income products such as CSBs, T-Bills, GICs, and TDs guarantee a return of your dollar plus interest, but they usually fail to provide a real rate of return to offset the equivalent buying power of the original dollars.

2. Public Enemy No. 2—Taxes

Many people fail to learn and apply our tax laws. You must learn how to make our tax system work for you. For example, an RRSP provides three types of tax benefits: immediate tax reduction, tax-free compounding, and tax deferral. This involves money you would otherwise pay to the government in taxes, which is set aside for your future use by deferring taxes to some future date that you would otherwise pay today.

3. Procrastination

The greatest deterrent to most people is procrastination. Many people wait for an opportune time to invest—the right time—but that right time never seems to arrive. After you acquire the many material goals in life such as the home, the car, the boat, and travel, suddenly you are age 55 or 60 and realize that your pay cheque is going to stop coming in a few years and you haven't adequately prepared for retirement.

When you are young, you seldom think of retirement; when you get older, it is often too late to put together the retirement income you need to live comfortably. There is no such thing as a future decision. There are only present decisions that affect the future. The longer you wait, the steeper the climb. Start now.

4. Attitude

Many people fail to win the money game because they have not developed a winning mental attitude with respect to money. Attitude affects not only money, but every aspect of your life. Everything in life operates according to the law of cause and effect. You must produce the causes; the effects will take care of themselves. Good attitude leads to good results. Fair attitude leads to only fair results.

5. Failure to Set Goals

If you aim at nothing, you are likely to get nothing. All successful people have a purpose: they believe in themselves! All successful people establish goals and define a specific financial target within a fixed period of time.

6. Protection Against the Loss of Earning Power

Disability statistics indicate that one person in seven aged 30 suffers a major disability lasting six months or longer prior to age 65. Many of these people are the breadwinners of the family unit. The potential devastation of such an event can easily be avoided by income disability insurance. The risks of being wiped out financially are just too great not to carry this insurance.

7. Protection Against Loss of Life

Most people buy, or more precisely are sold, the wrong type of insurance; this is often whole life insurance with a savings component provided at very low rates, instead of term insurance with an investment program.

The benefits of term insurance, with increased coverages for a growing family will, in most cases, far outweigh a whole life or universal life policy with much less coverage for the same premium.

8. Fear and Greed

These are the two greatest saboteurs of the investor, creating unacceptable risk tolerances by being too conservative or too aggressive. For the fearful investor, purchasing power plummets by investing too conservatively in a guaranteed, fixed income program. The greedy, on the other hand, take unacceptable risks and increase the probability of losing some or all of their capital.

9. Risk/Reward Tradeoff

Many investors make decisions based on emotion rather than logic. Each investment for consideration should measure 1) the risk involved, 2) the reward potential, and 3) the investor's risk/reward tolerance, in line with his/her comfort zone.

10. Honesty With Your Advisor

Deceiving your financial advisor won't help you. Develop a co-operative approach to financial planning with one key advisor. Be candid and honest about your affairs and your investment goals. Honesty always pays off in the long run.

To end this chapter, I would like to take aim at the failure factor that I see the most and shake my fists at the most—procrastination. Conquer procrastination and you will release the starting power you need to conquer anything.

Many years ago I uncovered a message on "Procrastination" written in the *Farm and Land Realtor* magazine, October, 1917. Enjoy it.

Procrastination

I hesitate to make a list
of all the countless deals I've missed;
Bonanzas that were in my grip–
I watched through my fingers slip;
The windfalls which I should have bought
Were lost because I over thought;
I thought of this, I thought of that,
I could have sworn I smelled a rat,
And while I thought things over twice
Another grabbed them at the price.

It seems I always hesitate,
Then make up my mind much too late.
A very cautious man am I
And that is why I never buy.

How Nassau and how Suffolk grew!
North Jersey! Staten Island, too!
When others culled those sprawling farms
And welcomed deals with open arms–

A corner here, ten acres there,
Compounding values year by year,
I chose to think and as I thought,
They bought the deals I should
have bought.

The golden chances I had then
Are lost and will not come again.
Today I cannot be enticed
For everything's so overpriced.
The deals of yesteryear are dead;
The market's soft–and so's my head.

Last night I had a fearful dream
I knew I wakened with a scream;
Some Indians approached my bed–
For trinkets on the barrelhead
(In dollar bill worth twenty-four
And nothing less and nothing more)
They'd sell Manhattan Isle to me,
The most I'd go was twenty-three.
The redmen scowled: "Not on a bet!"
And sold to Peter Minuit.
At times a teardrop drowns my eye
For deals I had, but did not buy;
And now life's saddest words I pen–
"If only I'd invested then!"

Source: Realtors ® Land Institute, Chicago, Illinois.

Mutual Funds

A mutual fund allows you to join with other investors to obtain diversification and professional management that is generally unavailable to you as an individual.

What Is a Mutual Fund?

A mutual fund is a pre-selected investment portfolio, chosen by a professional investment management firm and sold to the public as a single financial product in the form of units. A mutual fund allows you to join with other investors to secure advantages such as professional management and portfolio diversification that would not be generally available to you as an individual. Mutual funds are the answer for 90% of the investing population who lack the time and knowledge to make their own sound investment decisions in today's complex markets.

Who Invests in Mutual Funds?

Mutual fund sales have increased almost five-fold since 1990 and are fast becoming one of the more popular types of investments. Total assets were in excess of $132 billion in April, 1994.

Mutual fund investors are becoming more knowledgeable and individuals are starting to mix their funds for balanced performance. Statistics indicate that mutual fund investors are:

- Well educated—65% vs. 50% for individual shareholders
- Wealthiest—25% have portfolios worth more than $25,000 vs. 15% for individual shareholders
- Highest income—50% are from the highest income bracket vs. 33% for individual shareholders
- Most active—25% make more than six transactions per year vs. 10% for individual shareholders
- Institutional investors, including trusts, estates, insurance, pension funds, your employer's pension fund, and others.

Sophisticated as well as novice investors appreciate the advantages of mutual fund investment.

The Strategy Fund

Listed in Table 12-1 is the performance of 10 of Canada's top independent mutual equity funds summarized into a single fund, measured on a 1-, 3-, 5-, and 10-year basis, for the period ended March 31, 1994. The 10 top-performing RRSP-eligible funds each have assets exceeding $50 million under management and have been averaged to form what I call the "Strategy Fund."

Just as there is no perfect person or painting or poem, so there is no perfect investment. But the one that comes the closest for most people is the mutual fund.
Money magazine

117

I developed the concept of the Strategy Fund because it is unwise to even appear to recommend specific funds without knowing thoroughly an investor's circumstances. When your financial plan is complete, it will be much easier to determine which mutual funds are appropriate to satisfy your needs and objectives.

Returns such as are shown below are impressive and have been maintained by some fund managers for more than 25 years. Performance results can change from year to year, but there are many benefits to owning units in one or more mutual funds that make them the ideal type of investment for a wide range of investors.

TABLE 12-1: STRATEGY FUND—GROWTH FOR THE PERIOD ENDED MARCH 31, 1994			
1 Year	**3 Years**	**5 Years**	**10 Years**
28.6%	16.5%	10.9%	13.3%

Mutual Funds— The Major Benefits

There are many benefits to be derived from investing in mutual funds such as professional management, safety, liquidity, diversification, and the potential performance that a well-chosen fund can provide. The major benefits of mutual fund investments as follows:

Diversification

Funds provide you with a measure of safety by dividing your money into a wide cross-section of securities. This would be impossible to do on your own unless you had millions of dollars to invest. Instead of putting all of your eggs in a few baskets, you are able to enjoy the benefits of many baskets. Depending on their size, mutual funds generally hold anywhere from 30 to 300 different securities in many industries. A typical equity

mutual fund portfolio might be invested as shown in Chart 12-3.

Professional Money Management

Experienced professionals relieve you of the burden of day-to-day decisions required to manage an active portfolio. These individuals are fully conversant on all matters pertaining to investments and finance, and they have the resources and research facilities to provide top-notch results in the portfolios they manage.

Convenience and Simplicity

Units in mutual funds are easy to purchase, usually requiring as little as $500 to open an investment plan; additional contributions may be added whenever you choose. All the details of investing are handled by the fund administration.

You receive one contract from your investment fund for purchases or sales, income or capital gains, and tax reporting details, thus providing you with a complete and efficient accounting and record-keeping system.

Liquidity

Most investment dealers value their funds every day and your redemption price is based on the net asset value on the day you wish to redeem (sell) your units. By law, an investment fund must send you your money within seven days. You can also redeem partial amounts in most

TABLE 12-2: SAFETY BY DIVERSIFICATION				
Client A–Bank or Trust: Liquidity and Income				
$10,000	@	7%	for 20 years =	$38,700
Client B–Diversified: Mutual Funds				
$2,000	@	14%	for 20 years =	$27,480
$2,000	@	12%	for 20 years =	19,300
$2,000	@	10%	for 20 years =	13,460
$2,000	@	8%	for 20 years =	9,320
$2,000	@	6%	for 20 years =	6,420
				$75,980

CHART 12-3: PORTFOLIO DIVERSIFICATION OF INVESTMENT FUNDS

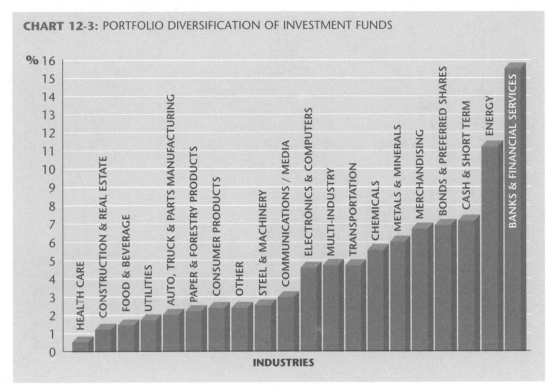

funds. Note that a few funds value on a weekly or monthly basis only.

Tax Advantages

These are discussed in detail in Chapter 14, but for now, take heart in the knowledge that dividend income and capital gains can be handled easily and efficiently. Over the years, this can amount to many thousands of dollars saved because in comparison, interest income is fully taxed.

Disclosure Statements

These are made by all mutual funds companies in their prospectus and must be issued by law. The investment policies and objectives are clearly stated as well as historical data on the fund.

Inflation

Inflation was discussed at length in Chapter 11. One of the best ways to avoid the erosion of purchasing power on your money is with the selection of an equity-based mutual fund with a good, long-term record of performance.

Lower Costs

Lower costs are available because most investors usually hold their mutual funds for longer periods of time. In self-managed investment portfolios, where investors tend to buy and sell individual stocks or bonds more often, commission charges on each transaction can lower the return significantly. Some mutual fund purchases incur a cost when purchased, and usually have no charge on redemption (sale). Most mutual funds are purchased with a deferred declining load option (the longer you own the fund, the less the cost). Other funds, called "no-load" funds, have no commission charges whatsoever.

Track Records

Track records of several hundred mutual funds are available to all investors. It is important to compare both short-term and long-term performance to obtain a true measure of a mutual fund's success record. 1-, 3-, 5-, and 10-year track records are published on a regular basis in most major newspapers including *The Globe &*

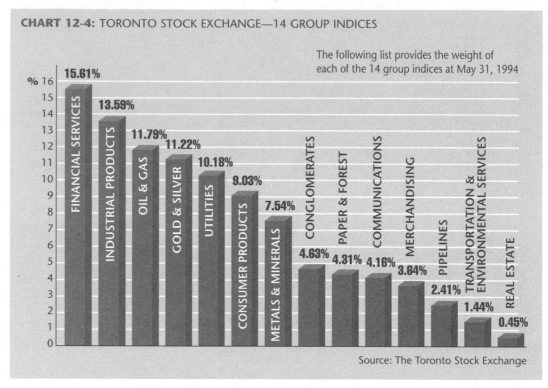

CHART 12-4: TORONTO STOCK EXCHANGE—14 GROUP INDICES

The following list provides the weight of each of the 14 group indices at May 31, 1994

- FINANCIAL SERVICES 15.61%
- INDUSTRIAL PRODUCTS 13.59%
- OIL & GAS 11.79%
- GOLD & SILVER 11.22%
- UTILITIES 10.18%
- CONSUMER PRODUCTS 9.03%
- METALS & MINERALS 7.54%
- CONGLOMERATES 4.63%
- PAPER & FOREST 4.31%
- COMMUNICATIONS 4.16%
- MERCHANDISING 3.64%
- PIPELINES 2.41%
- TRANSPORTATION & ENVIRONMENTAL SERVICES 1.44%
- REAL ESTATE 0.45%

Source: The Toronto Stock Exchange

Mail — Report on Business, Financial Times of Canada and *The Financial Post*, Canada's leading financial newspapers.

Reinvestment Privileges

These allow you to compound your original investment by reinvesting all dividends, interest, and capital gains distributions received, in more shares of the fund.

Exchange Privileges

These are offered by many mutual fund management companies that have a family of funds. They allow the investor the opportunity of exchanging one fund for another at a reduced cost or, in some cases, at no additional cost. Mutual funds are the only investment that permit such transactions.

Buy Term Insurance and Invest the Difference

This is discussed at length in Chapter 13. Mutual funds are the ideal alternative for most investors who want a disciplined,

regular, periodic, investment plan to complement their term insurance program.

Timing

Timing is no longer a crucial problem when investing in mutual funds on a regular basis, due to the benefits of dollar cost averaging (page 120). It removes the decision-making involved with the age-old question: "Is now the right time to invest?"

Purchasing Options

These include cash purchase, accumulation plans, systematic withdrawal plans, sheltered or unsheltered plans, and group plans, as well as the reinvestment privileges of interest, dividends, and capital gains.

Systematic Withdrawal Plans

These are excellent for investors who require a regular distribution such as a cheque a month to supplement their current needs. These plans can provide payments of income and capital gains or principal distributions.

Collateral

The use of mutual fund units as collateral for investment loans is readily acceptable by most major institutions due to the quality of the underlying mutual fund assets. These assets are liquid and easily redeemable.

Safekeeping

The custodian (bank or trust company) for the fund you select will hold the securities you purchase at no cost.

Ease of Estate Planning

There are five major benefits for which mutual funds simplify the settlement of an estate:

- Immediate valuation of the fund based on the net asset value at date of death
- Continuous professional money management while the estate is being settled
- More expeditious transfer of securities
- More equitable distribution to beneficiaries—it is much easier to divide units of a mutual fund than to divide a board lot of 100 shares of common stock among three beneficiaries
- Your immediate next of kin are given a choice as to whether they want to continue with the mutual fund holding, or to assume the task of managing their own portfolio.

All these benefits notwithstanding, the most important is the ease with which purchasers of mutual fund units can use the concept of dollar cost averaging.

Dollar Cost Averaging

Dollar cost averaging is the greatest tool at an investor's disposal for a long-term investment program. The concept of dollar cost averaging suggests that the best way to invest is by a systematic program of equal amounts over a reasonable period of time, particularly for RRSPs which require a periodic, long-term asset accumulation plan.

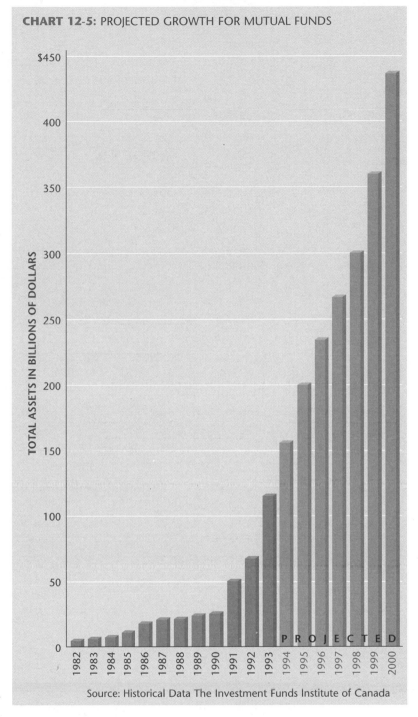

CHART 12-5: PROJECTED GROWTH FOR MUTUAL FUNDS

Source: Historical Data The Investment Funds Institute of Canada

This technique can be used for an individual stock acquisition over time, such as an employee stock purchase plan at regular intervals, or for a dividend reinvestment plan offered by many corporations. Dollar cost averaging is ideal for the individual who pursues an accumulation plan to purchase professionally managed mutual funds.

Imagine that you are investing $100 a month in a specific mutual fund. If the price per share of the fund is $10, that month's investment will buy you 10 shares.

Month 1	Investment :	$100
	Share Price:	$10
	Shares Bought:	10

Suppose that when your next month's installment is due, the shares drop to $6 each. That month you buy 16.6 shares.

Month 2	Investment:	$100
	Share Price:	$6
	Shares Bought:	16.666

Should the fund value increase to $9 per share in the third month, your $100 buys 11.1 shares.

Month 3	Investment:	$100
	Share Price:	$9
	Shares Bought:	11.111

Therefore, during the three month period you have bought a total of 37.78 shares for a cost of $300. At a current value of $9, your shares are worth almost $340, or over 13% more than you invested.

3 Month Summary	Cost:	$300
	Shares Bought:	37.777
	Current Price:	$9
	Value of Investment:	$340
	Increase:	13.333%

Even though the shares have dropped to $9 from $10, you are ahead in your accumulation program because you actually bought more shares at the lower price than at the higher price. If you had purchased all of the shares at the $10 price, your capital would actually decrease by 10%.

Dollar cost averaging takes the worry out of knowing when to invest by encouraging a steady pace over the long run. With dollar cost averaging, you gradually acquire a larger and larger block of shares, assuring that the most shares are bought when prices are lowest, because your money goes farther, and the least number of shares are bought when prices are highest. It is even possible to buy fractional shares so that you buy only what you can afford when you can afford it. That means smart conservation of financial energy.

Now that you understand dollar cost averaging, let's see how it works under three different sets of market conditions when applied to a mutual fund investment.
- Down and Up Market Cycle (A typical market scenario)
- Ever-Increasing Market Cycle (Unrealistic market scenario)
- Below and Return to Original Price Cycle (Very unlikely market scenario)

Down and Up Cycle

Suppose you invest $100 a month in a specific mutual fund. Your total contribution amounts to $1,200 per year. Over 10 years, your net investment is $12,000. With dollar cost averaging, you buy units at various prices, between a low of $3 and a high of $9 over the 10-year period (see Table 12-6). We assume the price of the units at the end of the tenth year is $10.

Over this 10-year period, you have accumulated 2206.189 units, with a price of $10 per unit at the tenth year, for a total value of $22,061.89. If you were to redeem your units, your profit would be $10,061.89, or a net increase of 83.8% ($10,061.89 ÷ $12,000 = 83.8%). Note that the average amount of your capital you had working over the 10 years would have been $6,000 ($1,200 in year one; $1,200 in year two; $1,200 in year three; etc). The return on your average capital invested would be 167.6% ($10,061.89 ÷ $6,000 = 167.6%).

Add to this example the dividend income you would have received, perhaps

Year	Average Unit Price	Units Purchased
0	$5.00	240.000
1	$3.00	400.000
2	$6.00	200.000
3	$4.00	300.000
4	$7.00	171.428
5	$5.00	240.000
6	$8.00	150.000
7	$6.00	200.000
8	$9.00	133.333
9	$7.00	171.428
10	**$10.00**	**2206.189**

TABLE 12-6: DOWN AND UP CYCLE—$1,200 PER YEAR FOR 10 YEARS

Year	Average Unit Price	Units Purchased
0	$5.00	240.000
1	$5.50	218.181
2	$6.00	200.000
3	$6.50	184.615
4	$7.00	171.428
5	$7.50	160.000
6	$8.00	150.000
7	$8.50	141.176
8	$9.00	133.333
9	$9.50	126.315
10	**$10.00**	**1725.048**

TABLE 12-7: EVER-INCREASING CYCLE—$1,200 PER YEAR FOR 10 YEARS

3% or 4% per year. While I did not include the dividend income in this example, it would have been possible to reinvest the dividends as well for even greater compounding.

In summary, the dollar cost averaging technique, on the average capital you were working with, provided a total return of 167.6% for the 10 years, or an average of 16.7% each year. With dividends included, it is possible to see how you would have achieved a total return of approximately 20% per year. Dollar cost averaging truly did take the worry out of the up and down market cycles experienced in this example.

This technique can be applied to individual stock selection or mutual funds. For greater diversification, I use a mutual fund example. This is an excellent tool to use with your self-directed RRSP or your company Group RRSP, if available.

Ever-Increasing Cycle

In this example, your total contributions are again $1,200 per year, and over 10 years, a net investment of $12,000. As you can see in Table 12-7, with dollar cost averaging, you buy units at various prices between $5 and $9.50 over the 10-year period, and we'll assume the price of the units at the end of the tenth year is $10.

Over this 10-year period, you have accumulated 1725.048 units, with a price of $10 per unit at the tenth year, for a total value of $17,250.48. If you were to redeem your units, your profit would be $5250.48 or a net increase of 43.8% ($5250.48 ÷ $12,000 = 43.8%). Once again note that the average amount of your capital you had working over the 10 years amounts to $6,000 ($1,200 in year one; $1,200 in year two; $1,200 in year three; etc). The return on your average capital invested would be 87.5% ($5250.48 ÷ $6,000 = 87.5%).

As in the previous example illustrating a "down and up market cycle," there would be the dividends of 3% to 4% per year to consider. You would have achieved a return of 11% to 12% per year for each of the 10 years you invested.

Of course, you realize by now the stock market never moves in a straight line, so this example would be a very unlikely real-life scenario.

Below and Return to Original Price Cycle

In this example (see Table 12-8), total contributions over the 10-year period total $12,000. With dollar cost averaging, you buy units starting at $5 all the way down to $1 and back up to $5, over the 10-year period.

During this time, you accumulate 5091.000 units with a price of $5 per unit at the tenth year for a total value of $25,455. If the units were redeemed, your profit would be $13,455, or a net increase of 112.1% ($13,455 ÷ $12,000 = 112.1%).

TABLE 12-8: BELOW AND RETURN TO ORIGINAL PRICE CYCLE— $1,200 PER YEAR FOR 10 YEARS

Year	Average Unit Price	Units Purchased
0	$5.00	240.000
1	$4.13	290.556
2	$3.25	369.230
3	$2.50	480.000
4	$1.75	685.714
5	$1.00	1200.00
6	$1.75	685.714
7	$2.50	480.000
8	$3.25	369.230
9	$4.13	290.556
10	$5.00	5091.000

Once again note that the average amount of your capital you had at work over the 10-year period was $6,000 and the return on your average capital invested would be 224.2% ($13,455 ÷ $6,000 = 224.2%). This would be an average of 22.4% per year and when dividends are included, averaging 3% to 4% per year, you would receive a return approximating 26% or 27% on an annual basis. It would be highly unlikely for the market to suffer as severe a loss over such a long period of time as we show in this example. However, the two key factors in this example are:

1. If the investor had sold the units during the first six years, he or she would have lost money
2. If the investor held the units for the 10-year period, a substantial return of 26% to 27% per year would have been earned even though the original price of $5 per share was never surpassed during the 10-year period.

This is the beauty of dollar cost averaging.

Institutional Investments in Mutual Funds

The most interesting development in mutual funds in the 1980s and 1990s is the dramatic increase in institutional mutual fund buyers. Rather than hire in-house professional money managers, it is easier for many smaller institutions to divide their trust money among several mutual funds instead of competing with them in the marketplace. Even institutions with their own money managers often invest a portion of their money with various mutual funds to obtain the balance and diversification they require.

Types of Funds and Investment Objectives

Fixed Income Fund

May include securities such as money market instruments, bonds and debentures, mortgages, and preferred shares that generate a high level of current income.

Money Market Fund

Invests in short-term instruments: 30-, 60-, 90-day notes, Canada Treasury Bills, and Government of Canada Bonds, maturing under one year. The rate of return will closely follow changes in the prime rate along with high security of capital.

Bond Fund

Invests primarily in bonds and debentures of Governments and high-quality corporations. The objective of this type of fund is to maximize short- to medium-term income plus capital gains from buying and selling bonds.

Mortgage Fund

Invests primarily in mortgages of residential, commercial, and industrial properties.

Preferred Income Fund

Invests in preferred shares. These funds provide monthly income, and are ideal for conservative and elderly investors. Because they invest in preferred shares, the fluctuations in the fund's principal are minimized. Being eligible for the dividend tax credit, preferred income funds provide a high after-tax yield.

Equity Fund

Invests in common shares for dividend income and capital gains. Their overall objective is to participate in the growth of the economy.

Growth Fund

Invests in common shares and convertible securities. Growth funds are very popular with RRSP investors. Their objective is to achieve a reliable record of long-term growth.

Balanced Fund

Invests in a variety of investments, including money market instruments, bonds, debentures, preferred and common shares. The objective of a balanced fund is to balance the risk/reward ratio, and to provide a mix of income, safety, and growth.

Choose Your Investments Carefully

Person is at work 7 hours per day, 35 hours per week. Money is at work 24 hours per day, 168 hours per week.

Money is at work almost 4.8 times greater than a person and money never takes a rest. As you grow older you have less and less energy to earn money from work; therefore you must create a wealth system to look after you at retirement by investing your money wisely 24 hours per day.

WORKSHEET 12-9: WHICH TYPES OF MUTUAL FUNDS MATCH YOUR OBJECTIVES?

Fund Type	Safety	Liquidity	Income	Growth	High Risk	My Personal Investment Needs
Money Market	✓	✓	✓			_____
T-Bill	✓	✓	✓			_____
Mortgage	P	P	✓			_____
Bond	P	✓	✓	P		_____
Strip Coupon	P	P	✓	P		_____
Real Estate	P	P	✓	P		_____
Global Bond	P	P	✓	P	P	_____
Preferred Income	P	P	✓	P		_____
Balanced (Diversified)	P	✓	✓	P		_____
Index			P	✓		_____
Ethical			P	✓		_____
Growth (CDN)			P	✓	P	_____
Growth (U.S.)			P	✓	P	_____
Aggressive Growth				✓	✓	_____
International				✓	✓	_____
Sector				✓	✓	_____
Specialty				✓	✓	_____
Precious Metal				✓	✓	_____

"P" denotes partial safety, liquidity, income, growth, or higher risk

Real Estate Fund
Invests in income-producing real estate. The objective is long-term growth through careful property selection, management, reinvestment of income, and capital gains from the sale of property.

Sector Fund
Invests in common shares of particular industries such as gold, oil and gas, precious metals, or high technology. These funds have a generally higher risk/reward ratio and provide diversification in a narrow segment of the market.

International Fund
Invests in securities in one or more foreign countries. The objective is to find the best companies in the most attractive industries in a given country, thereby providing the best market opportunities. Historically, these funds have provided excellent returns.

Ethical Fund
Invests only in companies that meet ethical or environmental standards as established by the fund manager.

CHART 12-10: TIMES CHANGE—SO SHOULD YOUR INVESTMENT STRATEGIES

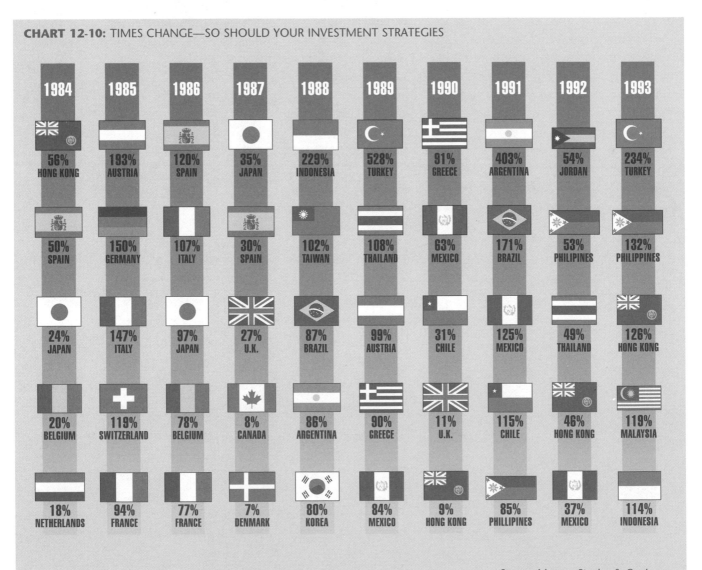

Source: Morgan Stanley & Co. Inc.

Global, International, and Foreign Funds

The global, international, and foreign group of funds led the performance parade during the last decade. The group includes three distinct types of funds:

- *Global Funds*

  Invest assets in securities of both foreign countries and their own.
- *International Funds*

  Invest assets in the securities of foreign countries, but not their own.
- *Foreign Funds*

  Invest in securities of one specific foreign country.

Foreign Markets

Sixteen stock markets make up the world market. Measured by the adopted standard of the U.S. dollar, their combined value totals almost $7 trillion (U.S.) (see Tables 12-11 and 12-12).

The U.S. and Japan dominate the world market, making up 62.6% of the total value. Canada ranks seventh in size representing only 2.3% of the world market. To put things in perspective, IBM is larger than the capitalization of the last nine countries on the list put together.

Investments made from abroad such as Japan or the U.S., into some of the smaller capitalized markets, can cause wild swings in price when they buy or sell. Therefore, these markets can be very volatile. Look for solid, long-term performance from these international and global funds and realize how important these markets could be to your portfolio.

Investing for yourself outside of Canada is very difficult to say the least, and all but impossible in some world markets due to non-residency laws. I feel that self-managed investing in the international market is suitable for only 10% of investors. You take on the added risk/reward of changing currency values when you invest abroad. However, the rewards can be great, and foreign investment can act as a hedge against currency fluctuations. I therefore feel that it is prudent to have some exposure to these markets if possible and professionally managed funds are the solution.

Beta and Variability = VOLATILITY

Beta is a measure of performance variability or risk, relative to the performance of the general market. It is a tool to help you predict the range of results you may receive. Betas are based on trading patterns measured by data analysed over an extended period of time, usually 60 or 120 months, and involve calculations used to measure the stability of a fund's rate of return in relation to the overall market situation or relative to other funds.

If an equity fund has a beta of 1.0, it is expected to equal the performance of the market. A fund with a beta of 1.15 is expected to have a rate of return 15% greater than the market when the market is rising, and 15% lower than the market when the market is in decline.

Many financial newspapers report monthly on mutual

TABLE 12-11: COMPOSITION OF THE WORLD MARKET BY 3 MAIN GEOGRAPHIC AREAS

As at March 31, 1994

	$U.S. Billions	%
North America	$2612	37.5
Pacific Basin	2356	33.9
Europe	1993	28.6
	$6961	100.0

Source: Morgan Stanley & Co. Inc.

TABLE 12-12: COMPOSITION OF THE WORLD MARKET BY 23 COUNTRIES

As at March 31, 1994

	$U.S. Billions	%
U.S.	$2436	35.0
Japan	1921	27.6
U.K.	698	10.0
Germany	278	4.0
France	267	3.8
Switzerland	210	3.0
Canada	164	2.3
Hong Kong	163	2.3
Netherlands	138	2.0
Australia	116	1.7
Italy	111	1.6
Malaysia	96	1.4
Spain	83	1.2
Sweden	66	0.9
Belgium	47	0.7
Singapore	45	0.7
Denmark	30	0.4
Finland	19	0.3
Austria	18	0.3
Norway	17	0.2
New Zealand	15	0.2
South Africa	12	0.2
Ireland	11	0.2
	$6961	100.0

Source: Morgan Stanley & Co. Inc.

fund performance statistics. They rank each fund in terms of volatility. If two funds both return an annual compound rate of 14% for five years, with one fund enjoying fairly consistent returns and the other fund encountering wide swings in arriving at the same result, the first fund is categorized as a low volatility fund, the second as a high volatility fund.

Working with volatility is another way to add measurable risk to the overall character of your portfolio. Low volatility funds offer narrower ranges of possible results than higher volatility funds. The funds you select should depend on your needs and objectives, the timing of the investment decision, as well as the anticipated holding period for the investment.

A Lesson on Volatility—What a Difference a Month Can Make!

After suffering about a 15% stock market correction during the second quarter of 1994, it is instructive to look back at the performance of the Strategy Fund using March 31, 1994 figures compared with June 30, 1994 figures.

While the 1-year average return has changed substantially, the 3-, 5-, and 10-year averages have not changed as much. This is the advantage of investing for the long-term.

In this comparison, what you are looking at are performance figures based on a high point in the cycle prior to the market correction, as well as the low point just after the correction. Over time you could expect returns that would be somewhere between these two extremes.

Leverage and Margin

One of the greatest investment tools at your disposal is the tactic of leverage. When you borrow money to invest, it is known as margin or leverage. Some of the greatest fortunes in history have been made using leverage. But some of the greatest misfortunes have also resulted from leverage.

During the crash of 1929, fortunes vanished in a matter of days. Many investors had borrowed up to 90% of the value of their stocks. When prices plummeted, they were unable to pay back their loans and they lost everything.

With margin limits today set at 50%, the potential for disaster is greatly reduced. Nevertheless, wisely used, leverage is one of your greatest investment tools. A typical leveraged position might look like Table 12-14.

In an unleveraged investment, the rate of return is 30% ($3,000 profit divided by the original capital of $10,000). The leveraged investment provides a 51% rate of return after the borrowed funds are repaid. Note that the loan interest is for purposes of earning investment income and therefore is a deduction for tax purposes; this increases the return even more.

Leverage, however, works both ways. For the unwary investor, leveraged losses can be devastating, as you will see from from Table 12-15.

In the unleveraged scenario, the investor lost 30% of capital ($3,000 loss divided by the original capital of $10,000). The leveraged loss was much greater at 69%. As in the leveraged positive scenario, a small amount of money is recaptured against the borrowed funds for investment purposes, due to tax law. This reduces the loss by a few percentage points, but it doesn't restore the ruins of a bad investment.

TABLE 12-13: STRATEGY FUND—GROWTH COMPARISONS

	1 Year	3 Years	5 Years	10 Years
Mar. 31, 1994	28.6%	16.5%	10.9%	13.3%
Jan. 30, 1994	2.6%	13.5%	8.2%	12.8%

TABLE 12-14: LEVERAGED VERSUS UNLEVERAGED INVESTMENTS—POSITIVE RESULT		
	Unleveraged	**Leveraged**
Your Capital	$10,000	$10,000
Borrowed from Stockbroker		10,000
Total Investments	10,000	20,000
Sale of Investments	13,000	26,000
Less Repayment of Borrowed Funds		(10,000)
Less Interest @ 9% for 1 Year		(900)
Net Proceeds	13,000	15,100
Return of Capital	10,000	10,000
Net Profit	$ 3,000	$ 5,100
Return on Investment	**30%**	**51%**

TABLE 12-15: LEVERAGED VERSUS UNLEVERAGED INVESTMENTS—NEGATIVE RESULT		
	Unleveraged	**Leveraged**
Your capital	$10,000	$10,000
Borrowed from stockbroker		10,000
Total Investments	10,000	20,000
Sale of Investments	7,000	14,000
Less repayment of borrowed funds		(10,000)
Less Interest @ 11% for one year		(900)
Net Proceeds	7,000	3,100
Return of Capital	10,000	10,000
Net Loss	($3,000)	($6,900)
Return on Investment	**(30%)**	**(69%)**

Leverage Can Reduce Risk—In Certain Situations

Assume an investor has a goal of a 12% return and is willing to assume risk on fixed income investments, but not on equities. There may be occasions when the use of leverage applied to fixed income investments such as bonds and debentures can help attain the target rate of 12% when current bond yields are only 10%. This can occur through a combination of borrowed funds at a lower cost than the current yield on bonds. It can also be advantageous to use leverage on a fixed income investment at a time when interest rates are declining and bond prices increasing.

Leverage and Real Estate

Virtually every real estate transaction is a leveraged transaction, whether it's the purchase of a residence or an income-producing property. After all, who do you know who can afford to buy a house for cash?

A typical house purchase may involve a cash down payment of 15% to 30%, with the balance paid over many years on a mortgage. The housing market has its ups and downs, but generally proves to be a good investment over time. Due to the fixed term and amortization of mortgages with set interest rate costs, very few people get caught in a leverage squeeze. In the early 1980s, however, when interest rates on mortgages reached 18%, it was a disastrous time for some people whose mortgages came up for renewal. When pressured, people usually find alternatives to selling their home. To most Canadians, once acquired, a house is almost sacred.

Leverage and Mutual Funds

This is the area where I start to have some concerns. Mutual funds are obviously the ideal investment for 90% of Canadian investors who do not have the time, knowledge, temperament, and capital to diversify on their own. What alarms me are overly enthusiastic sales people, guiding inexperienced investors to extensive and highly dangerous leveraging of mutual funds.

The Investment Funds Institute of Canada estimates that about 20% of all mutual fund purchases are leveraged. They are also aware that some purchasers have borrowed as much as 80% to 100% of their mutual fund purchase from banks and trusts, often using their home as collateral by raising money out of the equity. Unfortunately, these individuals don't truly understand the risks involved, and the sales person has not taken the time to explain. This is unlike the stockbroker's margin positions. The stockbroker is aware of the leverage status of every client's account.

Having stated my concerns, I am also aware that borrowing to invest at the appropriate time can build real wealth. The best rule to follow is — *caveat emptor* (let the buyer beware). *Know yourself and your ability to tolerate risk. Tread cautiously when it comes to the consideration of using leverage as a market tool.*

Protection For the Mutual Fund Investor

According to The Investment Funds Institute of Canada (IFIC) the following safeguards are in place to protect the investor:

- Assets are held by a custodian which must be a Canadian bank or trust company.
- Funds received from clients must be segregated from the dealer and sent to the mutual fund company promptly.
- The mutual fund manager is prohibited by law from using the fund assets in any other way than making investments for the benefit of the unit holders.
- Most provinces have established contingency funds against loss due to fraud or theft.
- Independent mutual fund dealers and institutions that sell mutual funds must post bonds as insurance against the loss of assets.

Mutual Fund Performance Statistics

In many of the earlier chapters, I illustrated the magic of time, money, and the effects of compounding at a 10% return versus a 15% return. My hope is that you would recognize the significant effect those 5 percentage points can have in the total assets accumulated over time.

Now, let's take a look at the "real world"—Canada. It is not uncommon on a 1-, 3-, 5-, and 10-year basis to have a number of Canadian mutual funds, from among the several hundred different funds available, that consistently return in the range of 13% to 16% over many years. In the U.S. and other markets, it is not uncommon to see some funds on those same time frames, especially the longer term of 5 and 10 years to be showing returns in the 16% to 20% range.

Returns can be greater in foreign economies than in our economy. International economies, in general, are not as resource-based, and therefore not as cyclical, as industries are in Canada. Nearly 50% of the stocks on the Toronto Stock Exchange are cyclical—mining and metals, oil and gas, forest products, fishing, as well as construction and real estate.

In the international markets, the industries are more balanced. Many companies in other countries have developed industries to a degree that is just not possible in Canada such as hospital care, pharmaceuticals, and major electronics.

For instance, if you wanted to buy a computer or electronic stock in Canada such as IBM, Digital, or Sony, you go to the U.S. or Japanese markets. The auto industry in Canada offers stock in General Motors and Ford, but they trade based on the events of the U.S. industry, where the parent companies are located.

In an RRSP you must allocate 80% of your funds in Canadian investments. When you are looking at "pure" investing outside of an RRSP, attempting to make headway in the market place, strive for global diversification.

The reason we enjoyed such high returns until recently, was due to higher than normal inflation and extremely high "real" interest rates. If we were to take a measurement of performance over two or three decades, the long-run returns would be substantially lower, perhaps in the 11% to 15% range for equity funds. They would, however, still be considered excellent returns compared to returns on fixed income vehicles through that time period with low inflation and extremely low interest rates. The differences in returns between fixed income vehicles and equities are always relative to the economic circumstances of the time.

Are Mutual Funds the Investment Solution for You?

The following Worksheet will help those of you who choose the professionally managed money approach to select a mutual fund. The first two questions determine your comfort zone with regard to investing. The format of the questions is a traffic light approach. Your answer should be an emphatic **Stop**, an enthusiastic **Go**, or a definite maybe—**Caution**. Place a ✔ under your chosen response.

WORKSHEET 12-16: ARE MUTUAL FUNDS THE SOLUTION FOR YOU?

	Stop	Caution	Go
I am comfortable with:			
High risk investments	☐	☐	☐
Moderate risk investments	☐	☐	☐
Low risk investments	☐	☐	☐
Risk-free investments	☐	☐	☐
What type of mutual funds best fit my investment needs and objectives, and will help me attain my financial goals?			
Money Market Fund	☐	☐	☐
T-Bill Fund	☐	☐	☐
Mortgage Fund	☐	☐	☐
Bond Fund	☐	☐	☐
Real Estate Fund	☐	☐	☐
Global Bond Fund	☐	☐	☐
Preferred Income Fund	☐	☐	☐
Balanced Fund	☐	☐	☐
Growth Fund (CDN)	☐	☐	☐
Growth Fund (U.S.)	☐	☐	☐
Aggressive Growth Fund	☐	☐	☐
International Fund	☐	☐	☐
Sector Fund	☐	☐	☐
Specialty Fund	☐	☐	☐

Continued on next page

WORKSHEET 12-16: ARE MUTUAL FUNDS THE SOLUTION FOR YOU? (CONTINUED)

What has the past performance of the fund been like on a 1-, 3-, 5-, and 10-year basis?

_____

_____

Who is the fund manager(s), and what is his/her track record?

_____

_____

Would the funds selected fit my risk/reward tolerance level?

_____

_____

Does the beta and variability level fit my investment profile?

_____

_____

What fees, commissions, and other charges are involved?

_____

_____

Are my funds flexible? Can I switch within a family of funds at little or no cost if my needs or objectives change?

_____

_____

How liquid is the fund? Is it valued daily, weekly, or monthly?

_____

_____

Most successful investors hold their funds through long periods of time, dollar averaging their costs, buying more units when prices are lower. Am I prepared to leave the money allocated for funds on a long-term basis through both bull and bear markets?

_____

_____

Will this fund's rate of return offset the ravages of inflation and income taxes?

_____

_____

Does my investment in these funds satisfy my need for convenience, simplicity, diversification, and no longer having to make timing decisions?

_____

_____

WRAP Accounts

One of the greatest growth areas in the U.S. this decade has been the packaged or managed product approach to investing known as WRAP accounts. Historically, the managed approach was through mutual funds, but now most investment dealers are establishing WRAP accounts to increase and maintain their market share.

Managed money provides fee based income for the manager and therefore an ability to stabilize income and reduce the cyclical nature of the industry. One of the key value determinants in the investment industry is based on assets under administration. Control of capital determines cash flow which in turn is the lifeblood of the corporation.

Generally, the investor must have an account valued at six figures ($100,000 and over) to be offered this service. Fees can range 3.5%, declining to lower levels the more money you have under management. For this fee the agent will make all buy and sell decisions, execute trades, provide custodial services, maintain record keeping and tax data, and provide monthly performance reports.

We live at such a hectic pace with so many things competing for our time that WRAP accounts are an ideal solution to our money management problems. As well most of us do not have the knowledge or temperament to make our own decisions. These facts bode well for the continued growth of both WRAP accounts and mutual funds in Canada for the foreseeable future.

How to Select a Professionally Managed Fund Manager

There are several things an investor should consider when selecting a money manager (See Chart 12-17):

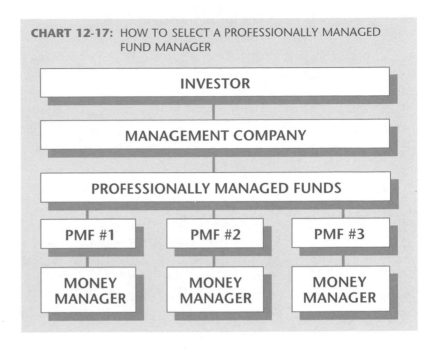

CHART 12-17: HOW TO SELECT A PROFESSIONALLY MANAGED FUND MANAGER

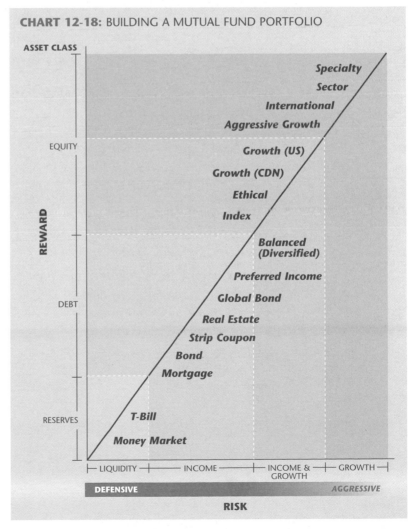

CHART 12-18: BUILDING A MUTUAL FUND PORTFOLIO

- The investor genrally chooses a management company based on past performance and proven management track record.
- Most management companies have a family of funds from which to choose. You select a fund that will fit your needs and objectives in concert with your tolerance.
- Each professionally managed mutual fund has a money manager(s) who is responsible for the day-to-day operation and overall performance of the fund.

It is important to know that a typical money manager is:

- compensated on performance
- paid a salary and usually a performance bonus
- not commission driven
- results oriented, since his or her job is on the line and investment decisions are reviewed usually on a monthly or quarterly basis
- a fulltime professional involved with investment selection.

Mutual Funds—a Summary

I would like to leave you with these thoughts:

"You can probably find a mutual fund that fits about any kind of investment you can think of..." **Washington Post**

"... mutual funds offer investors literally a smorgasbord of financial products that can appeal to almost everyone—from security conscious grandmothers to daredevil financiers." **Navy Times**

"For investors operating on a modest scale, mutual funds offer a combination of services impossible to obtain any other way." **Make Your Money Grow.** A Kiplinger-Changing Times Book

"For most investors, mutual funds still offer the only access to professional money management." **Money**

"If you lack the time or expertise to manage your own portfolio, or if your nest egg is small, consider a mutual fund." **Working Woman**

"...much less time-consuming and tricky than choosing your own investments. There are now funds for every purpose ... and within each group, there are several types to suit your own needs...." **Kiplinger Washington Letter**

"The advantages (of mutual funds) to investors are three-fold; a greater degree of diversification, a lessened degree of risk because of this diversity, and the services of some of the best money managers in the business at no extra cost." **Town and Country**

"...no matter what your financial goals, whether you're a novice or a seasoned investor, have a small sum or a bundle to invest, mutual funds may be your ideal investment." **Woman's Day**

"An investor without a personal money manager should probably be buying good mutual funds." Jane Bryant Quinn, Syndicated Columnist, **Newsweek**

> Diversification by asset allocation and equity investment selection are of paramount importance to the success of most wealth accumulation programs.
>
> **Graydon Watters**

Income and Life Protection

A family should carry 6 to 10 times their gross income in life insurance. Canadians, on average, carry only 3.2 times gross income. And most Canadians carry the wrong type of insurance.

Life Insurance— a Simple Concept

Put in its simplest form, life insurance is cash at death. You buy money to be delivered at some time in the future (i.e., on the insured's death). The idea of life insurance developed many years ago out of the concept of shared risk. When someone in a village died, that person's family was suddenly faced with hardships. Neighbours, family, and friends all pitched in to help in any way they could.

Eventually, villages began to expect that a certain number of their members would die each year. So they began to "pass the hat" before anyone actually died to create a village "pot of money" to help families of the deceased. Because no one knew exactly who would die next, everyone contributed to the pot. If they didn't contribute, they would not receive. The concept is the same today.

Let's use some numbers in the example of the village above. Suppose that the village has 100 people who live there. They expect two people to die each year. The village would like to make sure that each family that suffers a death receives $1,000 to help them through the difficult times.

Therefore, the pot should have $2,000 (2 deaths x $1,000 to each family) put in it every year. How much should each villager put into the pot every year? Take $2,000, divide it by 100 villagers. Answer: $20. That is, in its most basic form, how an insurance premium is calculated.

Life Expectancy Projections

How do people come to a projected figure of two deaths per year? They guess! But it is an educated guess. Extensive research is done on all aspects of human life expectancy. The study is today called *mortality*. These analyses are done by professionals called *actuaries*. You might consider these

TABLE 13-1: YOUR LIFE EXPECTANCY		
Based upon deaths occurring between 1985 and 1987—Statistics Canada		
Age	**Females**	**Males**
10	70.46	63.88
20	60.65	54.27
30	50.88	44.92
40	41.20	35.52
50	31.87	26.47
60	23.17	18.41
70	15.35	11.80
80	8.83	6.91

The whole or cash value life policy is certainly in its time one of the most cleverly designed financial products (from the insurance industry's viewpoint) of all times.

Chris Welles

135

people to be "odds-makers." Over the years, their life expectancy calculations have been very accurate. They know how many people are going to die in a year—they just can't tell you who it will be. Table 13-1 presents an example of the "odds."

What Happens to the Interest the Money in the Pot Earns?

Return to the village example for a moment. Each villager had to put $20 into the pot every year. If they could figure out when, during the year, those two people might die, they could invest the money in the pot and earn interest. This would mean that everyone might only have to put $18 into the pot because the pot would still have the necessary $2,000 when the interest is added. We now call this *investment experience.*

There is always money in the pot for those who pay, until the end of the period as set out. However, in reality many people quit their plans along the way and on occasion, if too many people leave there can be a financial loss suffered by the insurer.

Only one more thing happens at this point. Someone has to take care of the money. So each family puts in an extra dollar to pay for the investing and the record keeping. The total payment for each family is then $19. Today this is known as *overhead.*

Mortality, investment experience, and overhead are the three basic components of determining the cost of an individual life insurance policy.

Types of Life Insurance

Term Insurance

As you may already know, the older you get, the more life insurance costs. How much would you pay for $1,000 of life insurance the day before you died? Well, if the insurance company knew you were going to die, they would want you to pay $1,000, wouldn't they?

This type of pure insurance is called *term insurance.* In this case, it is 1-year term insurance because the price you pay (called the *premium)* is good for only one year. It increases the following year and every year after that. What do you suppose 5-year term insurance is? If you think it is insurance with a changing premium every 5 years, you are correct! After 5 years, the premium goes up because the probability of you dying has taken a small jump. In 10-year term insurance, you pay

Insurance Pot

[Insurance Pot diagram: two "INSURANCE POT" circles each with a "MANAGER" box and surrounding circles (families) with arrows pointing into the pot. Labels include "FAMILY", "Pay 2 Years", "Pay 25 Years", "Quits after 12 Years-No Cash Refund", "Pay 30 Years", "FAMILY".]

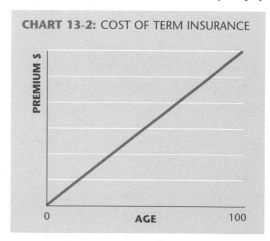

CHART 13-2: COST OF TERM INSURANCE

(Graph with vertical axis labeled PREMIUM $ and horizontal axis labeled AGE from 0 to 100, showing an upward sloping line.)

the same premium for 10 years before it increases, and so on.

Some people feel that *the older they get, the less insurance they need.* What these people would like is to pay the same premium every year and have their insurance decrease automatically. This kind of insurance is called *decreasing term insurance.* Most often, it is known as *mortgage insurance* because as the mortgage decreases, so does the insurance coverage.

Although the need for insurance may decrease each year, it is important to realize that the dollar value remaining on a decreasing term policy can erode substantially when there are high inflation rates in the economy. This factor coupled with the fact that a typical decreasing term policy declines by 8%–9% per year may well leave an individual under-insured in some instances. Decreasing term insurance is best used as coverage against specific short-term borrowings and at times when the economy is experiencing low inflation and low interest rates.

Term to Age 100

The basic term insurance plan is renewable annually which means you pay a premium for one year to obtain one year of insurance coverage. As previously discussed 5– and 10–year terms are the same except the premium stays level for the 5 or 10 years. Of course the older you are the greater the cost of insurance. Longer term contracts such as 20 year term, term to age 65 and term to age 100 are similar in that the premium stays level for the period specified. These longer term plans may offer options to convert to other life insurance or in the case of term to age 65, a renewal privilege at a higher premium.

Term to age 100 usually costs about two to four times more than 10–year term. One major benefit offered by some companies is a "reduced paid-up" option, which permits the owner to stop paying

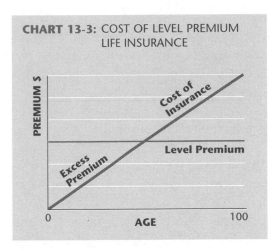

CHART 13-3: COST OF LEVEL PREMIUM LIFE INSURANCE

premiums after a long number of years and receive a new policy for perhaps half the original face value, fully paid for. This option provides higher coverages when really needed and lesser amounts when the client is older.

Term to 100 is less expensive than whole life insurance because it is pure insurance; there is no tacked-on savings plan attached to the policy.

Whole Life Insurance

Some people don't like the premium increasing every year, because the older they get, the less they can afford it—at the time they often need it most. The answer to this dilemma is the "average premium."

Chart 13-4 shows that in the early years, the premium is higher than the cost of term insurance and lower as you get older. This is called the *level premium method.* The kind of policies that use this method are generally called *whole life insurance.* If you cancel this kind of policy, you get back the extra money you gave the insurance company because you wanted level premiums. This money is called the *cash value.* This feature is often sold as a savings plan even though it isn't really designed to be a savings plan. The whole life policy pays out the death benefit which, in fact, includes part of the cash value or reserve. Part of the premium you pay on a whole life policy takes into consideration the fact that the risk to the insurance company decreases as the cash value portion increases. Therefore the company charges a smaller premium than they would otherwise have to charge if the death benefit were constant and did not include part of the cash value.

Universal Life

In the last few years, insurance companies have designed a savings plan that automatically pays your life insurance premiums for you. The insurance premiums are 1-year term insurance. (Remember, the price increases every year, but it is also the least expensive insurance.) You can put any amount into your savings plan whenever you like as long as there is enough to pay the monthly insurance premium. Most companies offer you a number of different investments which you can put your savings into. This kind of insurance is called *universal life*.

Whole life insurance has two components: one is the death benefit, or the insurance; the other is the cash value, or the savings. Over time the insurance component gradually reduces as the cash value increases. This cash value feature can provide a major advantage in your overall investment plan due to the elimination of so many other types of tax shelters. Why? Life insurance policies have two income categories: one is tax-exempt; the other is non-tax exempt. The exempt category is the key because it allows your cash reserves to grow tax-free, much like the savings in your RRSP. A universal life policy is funded with after-tax money placed in a deposit account. The deposit account earns a return based on the type of investment and it is this return on the investment that pays the premium on the insurance. This means the actual premiums that are withdrawn from the deposit account are pre-tax. The end result is that some very

sophisticated tax-sheltering possibilities can be obtained using whole life and universal life insurance for people with large amounts of cash at their disposal and who have topped up their RRSPs. Extreme caution and expert advice from your accountant, lawyer, and insurance agent is recommended before you proceed with any intricate insurance/investment plans.

A universal life policy is usually very flexible. It allows you to increase or decrease your insurance coverage, or change the type of investment your savings are deposited in. It also returns the savings portion in addition to the death benefit when you die (whole life policies usually return the life insurance amount, but keep the "savings.") Universal life can provide guarantees on every aspect of the policy: expenses, death benefit premiums, the deposits guaranteed never to rise, and the income on investments is guaranteed. Variations on this theme are also available for people who would like to invest in equities however this option of course could not be guaranteed.

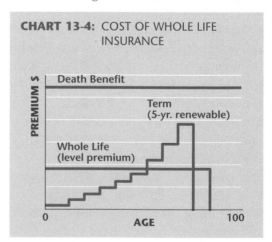

CHART 13-4: COST OF WHOLE LIFE INSURANCE

That covers all the major kinds of life insurance. You will find that the hundreds of different life insurance policies on the market today essentially are combinations and variations of these four types: *term, term to 100, whole life,* and *universal life*.

What Is a Life Insurance Dividend?

A life insurance dividend is not like an ordinary dividend. A life insurance dividend is "a return of an overpayment of premium." This kind of insurance policy is called a *participating policy*. This means that in addition to the normal premium, your insurance company asks you to give them an extra amount. If they do not need the extra amount, they give the money back.

This is not as silly as it may seem. If you do not give them this extra amount of premium, they still have to include an extra amount in their calculations as a "cushion" or "margin of error." After all, they are only making educated guesses about how many will die, what they (the insurance company) will earn on their investments, and what their overhead will be.

Between 90% and 97% of the profits from participating life insurance premium investments must be paid back to the policy owner. The largest companies are closer to 97%; this is an important factor when determining the lowest net cost of insurance.

A new option has been added to whole life participating policies. This type of policy is called an enhanced whole life policy. The *enhanced whole life policy*, instead of returning the dividend to you, offers you an opportunity to use the dividend to purchase term insurance with the excess premiums. This allows you to acquire large amounts of additional term insurance for low premiums. However, because the dividend amount is not guaranteed, you will not be able to accurately determine the amount of your coverage. Some companies, however, now guarantee this enhanced amount for life. As well, they permit you to use the dividends to purchase paid up life insurance

bonus amounts will substantially add to your coverage over time.

In a non-participating policy, if the insurance company guesses correctly, they do not return the cushion to you. They have guaranteed the death benefit to you. They are bound by law to have the money to pay the death benefit at all times.

How Much Life Insurance Do I Really Need?

That really depends upon your wishes. No insurance agent has the right answer. However, your agent can assist you by listening to your needs and plans for your family and can provide a needs analysis formula for life insurance, disability income, and retirement income. The question is: "How much money do you want your family to receive when you die?" Those people who don't care what happens to their families when they die don't need any. But if you feel any sense of responsibility for your dependents' well-being, you should have life insurance.

The first thing you probably want to happen after your death is to have all your debts paid off—your mortgage, car loans, personal loans, and so on. Some of these already may be life insured automatically. Check and see.

The largest amount of money is usually required to provide an investment income for your family. They won't need as much income to live on as when you were alive because they have no debts and because, sadly, they have lost you as a family member. Consider also whether your spouse will work or not after your death. The rule of thumb most people use is for income of 65% to 100% of your income depending on lifestyle.

You may also want to leave an amount of cash for things such as funeral costs,

Money may be the husk of many things but not the kernel. It brings you food, but not appetite; medicine but not faithfulness; days of joy, but not peace or happiness.

Henry Ibsen

education funding for your children, emergency money, charities, and other expenses.

Calculating your actual insurance needs is a relatively simple exercise:

1. Determine the cash needs of the family at the time of your death: debts, funeral expenses, education funding, etc.
2. Multiply your current income by a factor of 8 to 10 times to determine the gross amount of insurance you will need to provide the capital and income that will support the style of life to which your family has become accustomed. The amount will depend on how your family is going to invest those insurance proceeds, based on their ability to use money as an investor rather than as a saver.
3. Add the above together to calculate the total cash required.
4. Identify how much cash you already have—investments plus existing life insurance.
5. Identify any income your surviving spouse will receive from your employment, plus benefits from the Canada Pension Plan (CPP) as well as Survivors Benefits for dependent children.
6. Subtract your existing resources from your cash requirements to determine if you need to purchase more life insurance. If you do not have a shortage, then you will need no additional life insurance.

Life Insurance Need =

(Cash Needs + Income Needs) – Existing Capital

What Type of Life Insurance Should I Buy?

There is a place for every type of insurance product, depending upon individual circumstances. In my opinion, if you are like most Canadians, you should buy term insurance for a period of 20 to 25 years, during the time you are raising your family and require the maximum affordable protection.

In addition to your insurance program, you should establish an investment program. You will probably find that once you have completed your term insurance period at age 50 to 55, you do not even require insurance because of the investment income you have earned during your working years.

The major question you should ask yourself when purchasing insurance is "What is the total insurance coverage I need for my family and what is our cash flow?" Let's assume you determine that you need $300,000 for your estate coverage. The next step is to ask yourself the following questions:

• How much can I afford?
• How long am I willing to pay premiums for?
• Am I looking at a short-term or a long-term need?
• Do I prefer leasing (term insurance) or buying (whole life insurance)?
• Do I prefer a level premium concept or is an increasing premium concept acceptable?
• If I use the concept of buying term and investing the difference, will I actually have the discipline to invest the difference?

Table 13-5 illustrates a typical situation. A man is earning $40,000 a year. He has a wife and two children at home. He wants to be able to provide for them at the same $40,000 income level they have now. Multiplying his income by a factor of 10, he would need $400,000 of insurance, assuming the proceeds of the $400,000 were invested at 10%, to generate the required $40,000 annual income.

To buy a $400,000 whole life insurance non-smoking policy at age 40 costs about $765 per $100,000 coverage, or $3,060 in total. What person making $40,000 a year

TABLE 13-5: INSURANCE COSTS—$100,000 POLICY

Age	5-Yr.. Term Renewable	Whole Life with Enhancement	Invest Difference	Rate of Return 10%	Rate of Return 15%	Cash Surrender Value at age 65
40 - 45	$220	$765	$545	$24,617	$69,160	
46 - 50	$320	$765	$445	$12,482	$28,079	
51 - 55	$465	$765	$300	$5,226	$9,411	
56 - 60	$685	$765	$80	$864	$1,249	
61 - 65	—	$765	$765	$5,134	$5,930	
Total Premium Paid	**$8,450**	**$19,125**		**$48,323**	**$113,829**	**$34,450**

can afford to spend $3,060 on insurance? Most people cannot. However, if your family was able to earn a 15% return, you would only need $250,000 to $275,000 of insurance.

Most people who have whole life insurance have a policy for $25,000 and perhaps $5,000 to $10,000 on their spouse. If something happens, there is usually not enough money to enable the survivors to maintain the standard of living they enjoyed before. But there is a better way—term insurance.

Term insurance maximizes the protection of your assets and the protection of your family. It also offers you the opportunity to take the money you would have spent on extra premiums in whole life or universal life and to put that money to work for you, either in an RRSP or in an investment program, to build capital for your retirement years.

Compare the costs at age 40 of a 5–year renewable term policy with the average annual premium starting at $220; increasing to $320 at age 45; $465 at age 50; and $685 at age 55; with whole life at $765. Take the difference between whole life and term to age 60, and invest the difference at 10% and 15% for 25 years in a tax-sheltered RRSP.

Instead of buying the whole life policy, buy the 5-year renewable term policy for a period of 20 years and invest the difference for 25 years. By using this approach you can accumulate $48,323 invested at

10% by age 65. Invested at a 15% return for the same 25-year period, the amount grows to $113,829.

The theoretical examples portrayed here are based on insurance policies kept in force over long periods of time. Recent studies indicate that whole live policies are kept in force for 5 to 10 years and term insurance policies 7 to 12 years.

How Much Insurance Does My Money Buy?

In Chart 13-6, you can see how much or how little your insurance dollars will purchase, depending upon the type selected. When you purchase 5-year renewable term insurance, you get a great deal of coverage per dollar invested. Generally, 5–year renewable term insurance costs up to 70% less than whole life insurance.

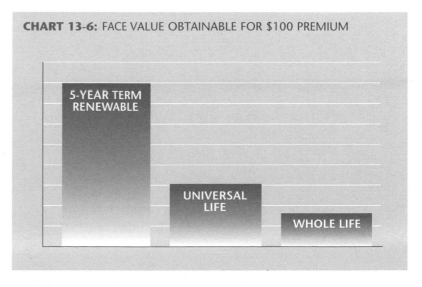

CHART 13-6: FACE VALUE OBTAINABLE FOR $100 PREMIUM

Disability Insurance

This type of insurance is designed to provide you with an income when you become disabled as a result of accident or sickness. The effect of a prolonged disability can be devastating if you have no way of replacing your loss of income from employment. In many cases, disability coverage is provided by your employer and is called *long-term disability coverage*. It pays you a percentage (60%–80%) of your normal income depending upon the terms of the group contract. This benefit is usually payable until you reach age 65.

Disability insurance is a very complex and specialized field. No one has difficulty agreeing on whether or not someone is dead in order to activate the benefit payments of a life insurance policy. Disability insurance, however, is frequently entangled in contentious legal definitions of what is and what is not a disability.

If you have this coverage at work, then you should find out the answers to the following questions:

- When do your benefits start after you have been disabled?
- What amount of benefit do you receive (dollars per month)?
- How long do the payments last?
- What kind of disabilities are excluded (alcoholism, nervous breakdown, etc.)?
- Do any other employee benefits alter as a result of your disability?

TABLE 13-7: AVERAGE DISABILITY WHICH LASTS OVER 90 DAYS

Age	Years	
25	2.3	
30	2.7	*Are you willing to take*
35	3.1	*the chance that your*
40	3.3	*income will not be*
45	3.4	*interrupted?*
50	3.3	
55	2.9	
60	1.9	

Source: 1985 Commissioner's Individual Disability Table

If you do not have disability benefits at work, or if you have not bought any coverage privately, consider the following information. The 1985 Commissioner's Individual Disability Table indicate the chances of at least one disability, lasting 90 days or more, before the age of 60. Of 1,000 men, the number disabled before 60 will be:

TABLE13-8: INDIVIDUAL DISABILITY TABLE

Age	Number Disabled
25	474 (4 out of 9)
30	446 (4 out of 9)
35	418 (2 out of 5)
40	389 (3 out of 8)
45	354 (1 out of 3)
50	309(3 out of 10)
55	245 (2 out of 9)
60	148 (1 out of 7)

Source: 1985 Commissioner's Individual Disability Table

Disability insurance is sold by many different life and casualty insurance agents. The RHU designation indicates that the individual is a specialist in the disability area. Although it is possible to find good agents without the RHU (Registered Health Underwriter) designation and lots of expertise, make sure you are dealing with a qualified professional. Credentials are extremely important. Make sure you confirm them.

Property/Casualty Insurance

Property/casualty insurance is used to protect people from financial losses. You might be more familiar with property/casualty insurance as automobile, home, and liability insurance.

You may suffer three types of property losses:

- Loss of property
- Loss of income from the use of property
- Additional expenses incurred due to the loss of property

You may also suffer a financial loss as a result of your actions towards another person or their property. This is covered with liability insurance. To be legally liable, your negligence must be proven. In other words, you must be proven guilty of carelessness resulting in damage to another person or their property.

In addition to liability insurance, the category called casualty insurance includes losses resulting from fire and theft. It is important to make sure you are insured for replacement cost on, for example, your house and contents. Review your policy annually to confirm that the amount of the policy adequately covers the increasing value of your home.

From Whom Should I Buy My Life Insurance?

Most people usually buy insurance from a friend or someone referred to them by a friend. That is fine, but remember three important things when you choose your agent:

1. The agent should have professional credentials such as a CLU (Chartered Life Underwriter) or equivalent experience of at least five years. Sometimes the agent does not have a CLU or the experience, but the company he/she represents does have the back-up support you need. The combination of a good legal department, tax specialists, and an insurance agent who believes in service after the sale and who has your best interests at heart can be your better choice.
2. Determine immediately if the agent can only sell the insurance products of one company, or if he/she has the freedom to shop the market on your behalf. One is not necessarily better than the other, but be aware before you begin working with the agent.
3. As in the other areas of financial planning you should review your insurance needs every two or three years.

Special Situations for Insurance Coverage

There are a number of instances where insurance products are necessary:

- *After-retirement insurance*
  After-retirement insurance can:
  a. offset a decrease in pension incomes
  b. pay income taxes with discounted dollars to preserve capital
  c. meet your estate planning objectives by offsetting taxes payable, thereby preserving capital for your beneficiaries.
- *Key-person insurance*
  Key-person insurance is a corporate measure taken to offset any loss that might be incurred in the event of the death of a valuable employee and to provide enough funds to hire another experienced person to perform the same duties as the deceased.
- *Business-loss insurance*
  Business-loss insurance for service industry personnel offsets the loss of income a business would suffer if its main operator became deceased. An example of this kind of loss is the value of a stockbroker's clientele with his/her services provided compared to the value of the business without those specific services.

What Insurance Does My Employer Offer?

Employers who provide life insurance do so on a group basis. The insurance is 1–year term and the premium is based upon the "average" age of all the employees. In this way, the younger employees are paying a slightly higher premium and the older employees are paying slightly less than their actual age would require. This premium is recalculated annually and may increase or decrease based upon what happens to the average age of the group. Many employers also offer insurance and other medical and dental health care as part of their benefits package. An extensive benefits program can cost an employer as much as one-third of the employee's income.

What Extended Health Care and Dental Insurance Options Are Available When I Leave My Employer?

The ongoing cost of continuing to provide benefits to retirees is placing an increasing financial burden on corporations. This is due to two main factors:

1. Employees are retiring younger due to right-sizing, right-aging, re-engineering, and a multitude of other early leave situations
2. Employees are living longer; in fact, they are adding one or more years to their lifespan every decade.

Therefore, more and more companies are backing away from providing post-employment benefits because of the burden that these future liabilities could place on the corporation.

For many self-employed, and employees working for companies who are not insured by their employers, their options for extended health and dental insurance needs have been provided by organizations such as Blue Cross, subject to medical approval. At retirement, many employees who did have an attractive benefits package find themselves with no further benefits coverage after they leave their employer. What options do these employees have? Read On!

Retirees Group Extended Health and Dental Benefits and the Association of Mature Canadians, Special Benefits Division (AMC)

Through our educational network at FKI Financial Knowledge Inc. we met Jim Domanski whom I'm indebted to for providing an overview of the services AMC

provides. The objective of the Association is to assist its members, through education, communication, and knowledge to deal with the emerging changes in health care needs, and to enrich their lifestyle and wellness in a socially and financially responsible way.

But more importantly, the association offers employees who will be retiring and will lose their group health and dental benefits, the opportunity to enroll in the Association's Retiree Extended Health and Dental Plan.

Without the protection of an extended health care and dental plan, a substantial portion of your pension and savings may be needed to pay for soaring medical and dental expenses that are not covered by your provincial health plan.

With increasing extended health care and dental benefits costs and government health care cost-shifting initiatives, individuals cannot afford to ignore the ever increasing burden of extended health care and dental costs. The provincial government reductions in health care funding could prompt individuals to rethink the benefits of an individual health plan for coverage such as extended health care, prescription drugs, and dental plans.

If you are over age 50, now you and your spouse have the opportunity to maintain your semi-private hospital accommodation, extended health care and dental coverage through the Retirees' Benefit Extension Program at a time when you may need them the most.

You are eligible to enroll in this program provided you do so within 90 days after your official retirement date, or when your present health and dental benefits terminate. There is a 10-day inspection period, so there are no risks in acquiring these benefits.

Some of the features and benefits of the plan are:

- No medical questionnaires or physical examinations required
- One rate for all ages
- Plan is effective the day your application is received
- Premiums do not automatically increase as you age
- Includes prescription drugs—even over age 65
- Provides dental coverage including crowns, dentures, and bridgework
- Includes semi-private hospital accommodation
- Includes eyeglasses and hearing aids.

We would like to believe that nothing will happen to us because we are healthy and have never been sick a day in our life. If you wait until you need the plan because of a medical problem or you now require ongoing medication and it is beyond the 90-days from when your group benefits ended, it is usually too late. The few carriers who provide a health and dental plan on an individual basis require a completed medical questionnaire prior to acceptance. Depending on the medication that you are now taking and/or depending on your medical condition when you apply for coverage, your application could be declined.

Think of this coverage as you would car insurance or fire insurance. If you do not have any type of car insurance or fire insurance and you were involved in an accident or you had a fire in your home, in all likelihood it would be very difficult, if not impossible, to obtain coverage since the incidents had already taken place. Health insurance is no different. It is too late to apply for coverage when your medical condition changes and you may require ongoing medication or other health care services.

The type of coverage available depends on the benefits you enjoyed through your employee group plan. If you had extended health care and/or dental benefits, you

Extended Health and Dental Benefits—What Choices Do I Have?

Choice #1 Apply for coverage through the Association (AMC) within the 90-days (No Medical Questionnaire Required.)

Choice #2 Elect not to enroll until you need the coverage. If it is beyond the 90-days, you are no longer eligible for coverage through the Association (AMC). If you can find another carrier that provides Health and Dental Benefits, you may be required to complete a medical questionnaire and your application may be declined depending on your medical condition.

Choice #3 Depending on your particular situation, your spouse may be employed at a company that provides coverage for their retirees and you may be eligible to receive benefits under your spouse's employer. Phone the Human Resources Department of your spouse to verify if retirees and their spouse are entitled to receive Health and Dental Benefits after retirement

may continue them under the AMC Program. With these plans, you are assured of the financial security that will help make your well-earned retirement a long and happy one.

Insurance Summary

Insurance plans should not be chosen on the basis of cost alone. Individual preferences and philosophical approach should be taken into consideration when choosing the appropriate coverage based on needs.

There is a place for every type of insurance product, depending upon the individual's circumstances. The overall conclusion, however, is that most people should use term insurance for a period of 20 to 25 years when they are raising a family and require maximum and affordable protection, and they should supplement this insurance program with an investment program. They may not even require insurance beyond the age of 50 to 55 if they have a well-thought-out investment plan that provides wealth accumulation through the majority of their earlier working years.

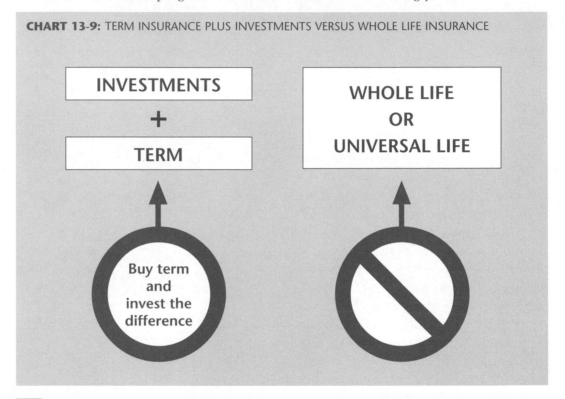

CHART 13-9: TERM INSURANCE PLUS INVESTMENTS VERSUS WHOLE LIFE INSURANCE

Income Tax Planning

*Some close their eyes to taxes, some plug their ears,
and some shut their mouths, but everyone pays
through the nose. The trick is to keep what is really
yours. You're about to learn how.*

Why a Tax on Income?

Our government provides us with many services. All require great expenditures of money. This money is raised primarily through taxation.

When the government spends more money than it brings in, it is said to have a deficit. But, unlike a business or an individual, if the government does not have enough money, it just prints up more paper dollars. This is one of the major causes of inflation. So, with things costing more and more each year, the government has to collect more dollars or print more money. It is a no-win situation–higher taxes or higher inflation.

A Tax on Inflation

In the early 1970s, the government introduced capital gains tax. This tax has sometimes been called a *tax on profits*. More accurately, it seems to be a tax on inflation.

Suppose you purchase something (technically called capital asset) for $1,000. If inflation has been 6% for a 12-year period, then the item you purchased is now worth $2,000 because of inflation.

If you then sell this property, your capital gain (profit) is $1,000. With capital gains tax, you must pay tax on three-quarters of this gain ($750)! This *tax on inflation* borders on *legal embezzlement*.

Two Methods of Taxation

There are two methods of levying income tax. The first is on one's ability to pay. The second is calculated on benefits received.

Our system today is called a *progressive* tax system. The more an individual earns, the larger percentage of income goes to paying income tax. In other words, the more you make, the more they take.

During the last decade the government has attempted to simplify the tax system. The government's intention is to bring more fairness, simplicity, consistency, and reliability to Canadian taxpayers.

Personal Tax Rates

The Canadian tax system has three basic tax brackets. Your applicable marginal tax rate increases as your taxable income increases through the tax brackets; your marginal tax rate is the rate of tax you pay on each additional dollar of income earned.

> The difference between the tax collector and the taxidermist: the taxidermist takes only your hide.
> **Anonymous**

TABLE 14-1: 1994 MARGINAL TAX RATES

Taxable Income	Federal Rate	Combined Federal Provincial Rate*	Combined Federal/Provincial Rate Including Surtaxes
$0 – $29,590	17%	27%	27%
$29,591 – $59,180	26%	41%	45%
$59,181 +	29%	46%	53%

*Assumes a provincial tax of 58% of the Federal rate.

The tax rates in 1994 show the combined federal tax rate for each bracket including surtaxes and a provincial rate of 58% of the amount of federal tax payable, based on an average of all provincial tax rates.

When you convert these three tax brackets to numbers of individuals, the results look like Chart 14-2.

Guess who carries the brunt of the tax load? The upper end of low-income earners and the middle-income group. This segment of the Canadian population accounts for 95% of the government's tax base from individuals. The difference in federal tax payable between the middle income (26% tax rate) and the upper income (29% tax rate) is only 3%. The difference in federal tax rates for a person earning $40,000 is only 3% less than for someone earning $400,000. And yet, who has the greater ability to pay?

Not only is this system failing to produce the revenue that the government needs, but someone earning $40,000 is paying almost the same percentage as someone earning $400,000!

The very rich can use tax planning techniques. Many of them pay little, if any, income tax. The new *alternative minimum tax,* however, makes it unlikely that anyone will be able to avoid paying income tax.

A number of influential people in the United States would seriously like to see the imposition of a "flat tax." This method says that everyone benefits equally from the services provided by the government and, therefore, everyone should pay the same for these services. This means that everyone would pay, for example, 20% of their income in income tax. At the same time, many of the tax deductions for the rich would be eliminated so that they too would pay their fair share.

This system would not penalize entrepreneurship and is seen as a fairer way to enable free enterprise to flourish. The Canadian Government seems to be moving in this same direction with its *"alternative minimum tax."* I look forward to the era of flat tax. The day we get it is the day Canada decides to genuinely support free enterprise.

CHART 14-2: INDIVIDUALS PER TAX BRACKET

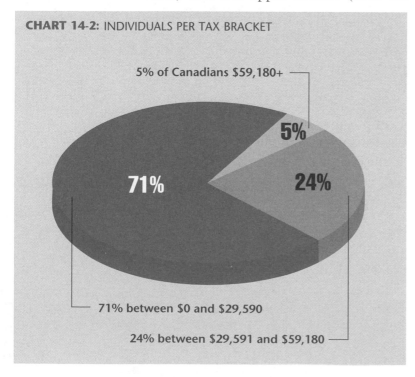

5% of Canadians $59,180+

5%

71%

24%

71% between $0 and $29,590

24% between $29,591 and $59,180

Calculation of Income Tax

There are four steps involved with the calculation of your personal income tax:

1. Calculate total income.
2. Make allowable deductions to arrive at taxable income.
3. Calculate the basic tax payable on taxable income.
4. Claim tax credits and calculate tax payable.

Calculating Income

There are four kinds of income:

1. Income from employment
2. Income from business
3. Income from property
4. Capital gains on the disposition of property

Certain types of income do not clearly fit into the specific sources of income in the Income Tax Act. These amounts are included in net income under specific provisions of the Act. Among the most important are:

1. Pension benefits
2. Retiring allowances
3. Death benefits
4. Unemployment benefits
5. Alimony and maintenance payments
6. Grants and allowances
7. Benefits from certain deferred compensation plans

It is not always an easy matter to determine which kind of income one has received. There are hundreds of pages in the Income Tax Act that address this very question, and there are many personal cases that provide direction to tax professionals. The kind of income you have determines what tax credits you are allowed to claim. The greater your tax credits, the less income tax you will pay.

There has been a major overhaul of the Canadian tax structure during the last decade. I am indebted to Jim Todd, C.A., R.F.P., a fee-based financial planner, for his assistance in this area. A note of caution should also be expressed: under no circumstances should you enter into sophisticated tax strategies without the advice of a professional tax advisor or a financial planner.

Deductions from Income

In order to maximize deductions, a description of those deductions should be considered. The only deductions from employment income are those specifically set out in the Income Tax Act. The most important of these deductions in arriving at net income are:

1. Salesperson's expenses
2. Travelling expenses
3. Dues and other expenses
4. Contributions to registered pension plans and RRSPs

Certain tax credits should also be taken into consideration in determining tax payable:

1. Personal credits
2. Charitable donations
3. Medical expenses
4. Educational fees
5. Pension income ($1,000 maximum)
6. CPP and UIC contribution

Consider This...

"The debt is so astonishingly enormous that it completely escapes the minds of most men. They merely sit back and whine for government to redistribute accumulated wealth to them. They lack even the originality or perhaps the honesty to ponder how, and by whom, that wealth was created. They never ask how it came to pass that even the welfare recipients of today, enjoy a standard of living which would have been undreamed of luxury by the upper classes of merely a century ago. What moral right do they have to this wealth? What moral right do they have to demand from the government creation of debt which shall destroy our social and economic system?" **Ayn Rand**

TABLE 14-3: FEDERAL PERSONAL TAX CREDITS — 1994

Basic personal amount	$1,098
Married (or equivalent) dependent ❶	$915
Dependants age 18 & over and mentally and physically infirm ❷	$269
Disability amount	$720
Age amount (65 & over) ❸	$592
Medical Expense over 3% of income or $1,614 whichever is less	17%

Child Tax Benefit

Basic Benefit Per Child	$1,020
Additional amount for third and subsequent children	$75
Additional "supplementary benefit" lesser of $500 and 8% of "adjusted net income" in excess of $3,750	
The supplementary benefit is reduced by 10% of parent's adjusted income in excess of $20,921 and eliminated at $25,921	
Additional amount for each child under 7 years of age	$213
This additional amount is reduced by one-quarter of child care expenses claimed for all children. This total is then reduced by 5% (2.5% in cases where there is only one qualified dependant) of adjusted earned income in excess of $25,921	

❶ Tax credit reduced if spouse's net income exceeds $539.

❷ Tax credit reduced if dependants net income exceeds $2,690.

❸ Tax credit reduced if income exceeds $25,921 and eliminated if income exceeds $49,134

Three Types of Investment Income — Interest, Dividends, and Capital Gains

There are three basic forms of investment income: interest, dividends, and capital gains. Each type of income is treated differently for tax purposes. Therefore, it is more important for the investor to focus on an investment's after-tax return rather than its pre-tax return.

TABLE 14-4: TAXATION OF INVESTMENT INCOME

Interest & Foreign Income	100% fully taxed
Dividends	25% gross up and 13.3% tax credit
Capital Gains	first 25% of gain tax-free; 75% taxable on the balance

Interest Income

Interest income does not receive any special tax treatment and is fully taxed. Since 1990, interest income must be reported annually in the year the interest is received or earned. Interest income on investments made prior to 1990 can be reported one of three ways—cash, accrual, or triennial accrual.

The cash method simply declares the interest in the year it is received.

The accrual method declares the interest be reported in the year it is deemed to be earned, if it has not been reported as received.

The triennial method requires that interest be declared every three years if it has not been reported as received (from

TABLE 14-5: INTEREST INCOME AFTER-TAX RETENTION PER $1,000

(Taxable Income Bracket)	$0 to $29,590	$29,591 to $59,180	$59,181 +
Interest Income	$1,000	$1,000	$1,000
Combined Tax	$274	$449	$532
Investor Keeps	**$726**	**$551**	**$468**

compounding investments such as CSBs, GICs, and stripped coupon bonds.)

Dividend Income

Investing in Canadian corporations often pays dividends. Collecting dividends from your investments is a small pleasure; however, it's made even smaller by the tax you must pay. While you can't avoid that reality, you can reduce the tax payable. Though the income cannot be tax exempt or deferred, it can be tax-preferred.

When you receive interest income from Canadian and foreign investments, and dividends from foreign corporations, you are taxed fully on that income, at your marginal tax rate. However, you'll get a relatively kinder, gentler treatment for dividends from Canadian corporations. That's because your tax on these dividends will be reduced by the federal dividend tax credit. The credit is offered to encourage you to invest in common and preferred shares of Canadian corporations.

To calculate the tax, increase or "gross up" your dividends by 25%. For example, if you receive $100 in dividends, the grossed-up amount will be $125. Net federal tax payable is calculated by using this grossed-up amount and deducting a tax credit of 16.66% of the actual dividend received or 13.33%t of the grossed-up dividend—from the grossed-up dividend. Provincial tax is then calculated on the net federal tax payable.

Since most of your financial decisions will depend on what an investment earns after tax, it may make buying stocks of a Canadian corporation preferable to other options.

Interest vs. Dividends— After-tax Returns

Astute investors never lose sight of the fact that it is their after-tax return on their investments that will determine their ultimate performance. And the fact is that taxpayers retain approximately 27% to 37% more from dividends than interest —

TABLE 14-6: DIVIDEND INCOME AFTER-TAX RETENTION PER $1,000

(Taxable Income Bracket)	$0 to $29,590	$29,591 to $59,180	$59,181 +
Dividend Income	$1,000	$1,000	$1,000
Gross-up (25%)	$250	$250	$250
	$1,250	$1,250	$1,250
Federal Tax	$212	$325	$362
Less Tax Credit	$167	$167	$167
Federal Tax	$45	$158	$195
Surtax	$2	$5	$16
Provincial Tax (60.5% of Federal)	$27	$110	$148
Combined Tax	$74	$273	$359
Investor Keeps	**$926**	**$727**	**$641**

$1 of dividends is equal, after-tax, to about $1.27 to $1.37 of interest. A sampling of some dividend yields and the interest equivalent required to produce the same after tax income is as follows:

Dividend Yield	X Ratio 1.32	Interest Equivalent
2.5%		3.3%
4.0%		5.3%
5.5%		7.3%
7.0%		9.2%

Capital Gains

Major changes were introduced in the February 22, 1994 budget affecting the future treatment of capital gains:

- elimination of the $100,000 lifetime capital gains exemption (LCGE) for gains accruing after February 22, 1994
- unrealized capital gains accruing prior to February 22, 1994, may be claimed by reporting their value based on February 22, 1994 values (valuation day) and filing an election with your 1994 personal income tax return
- the $500,000 LCGE for small business and farm property remains intact.

Claiming a Capital Gains Exemption

To claim the exemption for the eligible portion of the accrued gains, an individual will be required to file an election with his or her 1994 tax return. By filing an election for a property, the individual will be treated as having sold that property for proceeds equal to the amount designated by the individual. This amount may not be less than the adjusted cost base (ACB) of the property, nor exceed its fair market value on budget day.

The exempt portion of the gain realized by filing an election will be calculated in the same way it is under the existing rules. Three-quarters of the elected gain will be included in income and the portion qualifying for the exemption will be deductible in calculating the individual's taxable income.

A capital gain on the sale of an asset will occur if the asset is sold for a greater sum than its ACB. Similarly, a capital loss will occur if the asset is sold for less than its ACB.

In order to determine your taxable capital gain (loss) each asset that you sell (less costs associated with the sales) is taxable

Case Profile ⑤ Pauline Dvorak

Crystallizing a Gain

Budget Day — Pauline owns $50,000 in securities that have increased in value and originally cost $20,000. Pauline has not used any of her $100,000 exemption so she will crystal-lize her full value and she has no CNIL balance (see below)

When Pauline later sells a security her cost base will be the lessor of its value on Budget Day and her net proceeds (but not less than her original ACB)

Value of Pauline's securities	$50,000
Less adjusted cost base (ACB)	$20,000
Unrealized capital gain to be elected	$30,000
75% taxable portion	$22,500
Less capital gains exemption @75%	$22,500
Net taxable amount	$0

on 75% of the gain/loss. All assets sold during the year must be taken into account to determine your net capital gain or loss. It is important to know that a capital loss occurring in a year can only be offset against any capital gains occurring in the same year resulting in a net gain or loss for the year.

Net capital losses for a year can be carried back up to three years or carried forward indefinitely. Some investors attempt to create superficial losses to offset capital gains. To minimize this event occurring, the tax rules state that you may not report a loss if you repurchase the same asset 30 days prior to, or immediately after, the disposition of the investment. This rule applies to assets acquired by the spouse or a company controlled by the investor or the spouse.

Cumulative Net Investment Loss (CNIL)

Since 1988, access to the capital gain exemption has been further restricted by a set of rules known as CNIL. An investor's CNIL is the amount by which his/her investment expenses exceed investment income for the years after 1987. CNIL is calculated on a global or portfolio basis; not on an asset by asset basis. It has become mandatory for an investor to track both his/her cumulative investment income and investment expenses each year. For practical purposes, the CNIL only affects people who borrow heavily to invest, or invest in tax sheltered vehicles such as syndicated real estate partnerships.

TABLE 14-7: CAPITAL GAINS (BEFORE EXEMPTION) AFTER-TAX RETENTION PER $1,000			
(Taxable Income Bracket)	**$0 to $29,590**	**$29,591 to $59,180**	**$59,181 +**
Capital Gain	$1,000	$1,000	$1,000
Taxable Portion	$750	$750	$750
Combined Tax	$205	$337	$399
Investor Keeps	**$795**	**$663**	**$601**

Recap — Taxation of Investment Income

Sources of Interest Income

To recap, sources of interest income include Savings Accounts, Term Deposits, Mortgages, Canada Savings Bonds, Guaranteed Investment Certificates, Treasury Bills, and Government and Corporate Bonds.

Sources of Capital Gains

The sources of capital gains are not as common as those of interest income for most of us. Only 20% of the population work within this area. Most people are working strictly with interest income vehicles. Our main sources of capital gains come from common shares, convertible preferred shares and convertible debentures, precious metals,

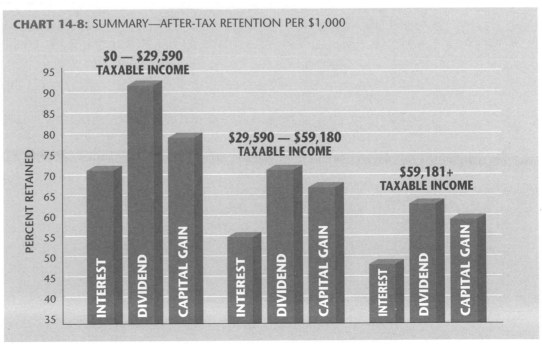

CHART 14-8: SUMMARY—AFTER-TAX RETENTION PER $1,000

options and commodities, real estate, and many other inflation-hedge assets.

Sources of Dividend Income

Our sources of dividend income stem from common shares and preferred shares. Under preferred shares there are five main types: straight, retractable, variable, convertible, and U.S. pay preferreds.

After Tax Per $1 Earned

For each $1 earned, dividend income is taxed least, followed by capital gains and interest income, assuming that you have used your capital gains exemption. Are your investments positioned to take advantage of these tax benefits?

Tax Planning

Tax planning revolves around two principles.
1. Minimize current tax payable.
2. Defer current taxes until a later date.

I must warn you of the way in which the tax department deals with individuals. Consider that our system of justice in Canada is based upon the concept that a person is innocent until proven guilty; this puts the onus on the accuser to find evidence and prove guilt. If there is any doubt of guilt, the accused is innocent.

The exact opposite is true in matters of income tax. *You are guilty until you can provide the indisputable evidence of your innocence.* You are required to keep accurate records. If you fail to produce your records, you lose.

Table 14-9 introduces the concept of taxflation. Here's how it works. At a 40% tax bracket at a 5% projected rate of inflation, you will have to earn 8.3% in a taxable investment just to maintain the purchasing power. Now fill in the figures for your own situation.

At my current _____% tax bracket and my projected rate of inflation _____% I will have to earn _____% in a taxable investment just to break even. Are any of my investments currently earning less than the break-even point?

Personal Tax Management Strategies and Tactics

There are three main ways to reduce your taxes:
1. ***Reduce Your Taxable Income***
   For example, you could borrow for investment and pay down your mortgage.
2. ***Reduce Your Effective Tax Rate***
   For example, adjust your portfolio so that you receive more dividend income than interest income; establish an education trust for your children or a spousal RRSP for income splitting.
3. ***Defer Taxable Income to Future Years***
   Unrealized capital gains defer taxes until the asset is sold. An RRSP defers taxes until retirement. In effect, you have an interest-free loan from the government.

Broken down into their specifics, these three approaches create over 100 different tax-reducing tactics, but that is the subject of another book. The three approaches do, however, produce two fundamental tax-saving strategies:
1. Your number one strategy should be to save and invest.
2. Your number two strategy should be to complement your number one strategy with tax savings and tax deferral strategies.

TABLE 14-9: TAXFLATION

Investment returns needed to maintain the purchasing power of your money

Tax Bracket	Projected Rate of Inflation %					
	4	5	6	7	8	9
25%	5.3	6.6	8.0	9.3	10.7	12.0
30%	5.7	7.1	8.6	10.1	11.4	12.9
35%	6.2	7.7	9.2	10.8	12.3	13.8
40%	6.6	8.3	10.0	11.7	13.3	15.0
45%	7.2	9.1	10.9	12.7	14.5	16.4
50%	8.0	10.0	12.0	14.0	16.0	18.0

The most important tax-reducing tactics derived from these two strategies are listed below.

- Establish bank accounts for your children and deposit Child Tax Benefits and any income they earn from part-time jobs such as babysitting, lawn care, snow shoveling, etc. in their names (or in trust) so that the interest income is taxable to them.
- Plan to have $1,000 pension income tax credit. Include spouse if applicable. Note that some pension income such as OAS and CPP doesn't qualify.
- Borrow for your investment asset purchases rather than personal assets so that your interest expenses are deductible.
- Principal residences in a family can be sold tax free. Only one principal residence per year is exempt from tax in a family but, subject to an individual's use of the $100,000 capital gains exemption limit, a portion of the gain on other properties before March, 1992 can be crystallized on his/her 1994 tax return.
- Set up a trust to transfer investment income (in an RESP) or capital gains to the much lower tax bracket of your children or grandchildren.
- Purchase prescribed annuities to maximize return and income flow.
- Establish dividend rather than interest income if it produces higher after-tax income with equivalent investment risk. If you are in a very high tax bracket, consider the purchase of discount bonds for a combination of interest income and capital gains.
- Plan to contribute the maximum per year to an RRSP.
- Spousal RRSPs are an excellent way of equalizing family income in retirement and lowering taxes.
- Medical and charitable donations may be claimed by either spouse and should be claimed by the spouse who will receive the greatest tax benefit. Any 12-month period ending in the year may be used to claim medical expenses; the calendar year is used for charitable donations. Medical expenses must exceed the lesser of 3% of net income or $1,614 for a 17% tax credit.
- If applicable, and when available, consider the use of oil and gas or mining flow-through shares, real estate, mutual funds, and other types of limited partnership tax shelters.
- Consider employing your children in your business.
- Choose a year-end for your new business, if applicable, such as January instead of December, to achieve the maximum deferral of income tax payable.

We'll look at a few of these in greater detail.

Registered Retirement Savings Plans (RRSPs)

If I were to pick one tactic above all others, it would be the immediate tax reduction, the tax deferred benefits, and the tax-free compounding of your money in an RRSP. This subject is a basic cornerstone of your financial and retirement plans. It deserves a full chapter of its own, and will be covered in depth in chapter 17.

Family Allowance—Something Old; Something New

The evolution of the federal government's family allowance or baby bonus program is a barometer of this country's and the government's changing attitude to social assistance. The program was first introduced by the Mackenzie King government in 1945. Its purpose was to encourage population growth and to help lower-income families. The program was also universal. The Mulroney government changed that in the 1980s by "clawing back" some or all

> Next to being shot at and missed, nothing is really quite as satisfying as an income tax refund.
>
> **F.J. Raymond**

of the payments from families whose highest income earner made more than $50,000. Effective 1993, it introduced a radical new plan, one based on need. Instead of benefiting everyone equally, family assistance now benefits lower and average-income families more than those with a higher income.

The new system replaces three programs: the existing family allowance benefits; the child credit which all parents could claim; and the refundable child tax credit for families of modest means. Under the new system eligible families will receive one monthly payment.

The basic allowance for each dependent child is now $1,020, with additional amounts for third and subsequent children and for children under age 17, up to a family net income of $25,921. Above that amount, the benefit is reduced by 2.5% for families with one child, and 5% for those with two or more. Single parents can still claim the equivalent to married credit. As well, low-income families are eligible for a new supplement up to $500. If you can, consider investing this allowance in your child's name to shelter future taxes away from you.

Registered Education Savings Plans (RESPs)

Registered Education Savings Plans are designed to provide funds to assist the student in financing post-secondary education. Income accumulates tax-free in the plan in the meantime and is taxed to the beneficiary when eventually withdrawn. Contributions are not deductible for tax purposes. RESP limits are currently set at $1,500 per year for each beneficiary to a maximum of $31,000.

Provision for your children's educational needs should begin long before the children reach college age. There are several excellent education plans available today to facilitate the need for educational savings.

The oldest are the scholarship trust plans—Canadian Scholarship Trust Foundation, and University Scholarships of Canada both of which invest funds in fixed-income instruments. While these plans may suit you if you're a conservative investor, you will still be taking a risk: what if your child decides not to go to university? Though you'll receive your initial capital back, you will lose the compounded interest. However, if you have more than one child, you can name them all as RESP beneficiaries; even if only one goes to university, he or she can withdraw all of the money in the RESP. Another kind of RESP invests in mutual funds. Though you may realize higher returns than with a fixed income RESP, you will still face the same penalty if your child decides not to go to university. You do however, have the flexibility to name other beneficiaries such as a niece, nephew, or any other person as a beneficiary of the plan.

A third kind of RESP is a self-directed plan. These RESPs are available from investment dealers and provide greater flexibility than traditional RESPs, while allowing you to control investment decisions and maintain access to your capital. Instead of stipulating an age of maturity, these plans allow up to 25 years from the date of the first deposit until the date of the final withdrawal of earned income. And, while the income earned by the plan must once again be used to finance post-secondary education, the designated beneficiary may be any age and may be changed at any time, for a fee. You can even name yourself, if you plan to further your own education in the future. If after 25 years no one uses the plan, the earnings must be donated to a post-secondary institution, which you designate on opening the plan.

> The only thing that hurts more than paying an income tax is not having to pay an income tax.
>
> **Thomas Robert Dewar**

Case Profile ⑥ Mr. & Mrs. David Anderson

Mr. and Mrs. Anderson are currently considering establishing a self-directed RESP for their two children. Presented is their future education

costs and the amount that could be accumulated in the RESP. Note that this example assumes a 5% rate of inflation.

Projected costs are based on the costs being paid in four annual payments starting 4 years from now in Susan's case and 10 years from now in Johnny's case.

	Susan	Johnny
Years Until University	4	10
Years of Study	4	4
Annual Cost Today	$10,500	$10,500
Projected University Costs	$55,009	$73,718
RESP Accumulation at Start of University		
Principal	$6,000	$15,000
Investment return @10%	$1,658	$11,297
	$7,658	$26,297

An investment in knowledge pays the best interest!
Benjamin Franklin

Because funds invested in a self-administered RESP aren't pooled with other plan-holders, the payout from this type of RESP depends entirely on your investment performance. The plan functions much the same as a self-directed RRSP. The choice of whether to invest in GICs, bonds, or publicly traded securities is yours, along with the degree of risk you wish to take.

An RESP allows the contributor to remove the principal at any time, but the investment return must be used for education.

Prescribed Annuities

People generally purchase annuities for one of the following reasons:
- to guarantee income flow
- to maximize income flow
- to lock in a rate of return
- to reduce money management responsibilities

There are two types of annuities—*term certain* or *life*. A term certain annuity is for a specified number of years, while a life annuity is payable for life, but may have a

minimum guaranteed payment period. You can buy a term certain or life annuity with the money from any source including a registered savings plan, such as a RRSP or RRIF. If you want to buy a prescribed annuity, however, you can use savings only from a non-registered source. But rather than a restriction, that is actually an advantage.

When you buy a prescribed annuity, your payments are deemed or prescribed to be a blend of interest and principal. Since you've already been taxed on the principal, you'll pay tax only on the interest portion. Moreover, the annual taxable portion will remain fixed as long as you receive payments.

As a result, a prescribed annuity allows you to pay less tax in the early years than on an interest-only investment such as a GIC. In fact, in this era of low interest rates, a prescribed annuity offers a greater return than any fixed-income investment. A prescribed annuity's certainty will also give you peace of mind—from trying to guess right on interest rates and from manag-

Case Profile ⑦ Gertrude Toye

Age:	70 years old.
Marginal Tax Rate:	43%
Funds to Invest:	$75,000 unregistered
Option 1:	Purchase 5-year GIC @7%, produces $5,250 annual income or $2,993 after-tax.
Option 2:	Purchase a prescribed annuity @8.5%, produces $8,200 annual income or $6,491 after-tax. Capital depleted.

> Life is not always a matter of holding good cards, but sometimes of playing a poor hand well.
>
> **Robert Louis Stevenson**

ing your investments in an increasingly sophisticated environment.

If you buy a prescribed annuity, consider using only a portion of your capital. The interest rate will be fixed, possibly at a (much) lower rate than may prevail five or ten years from now, and you'll be tying up capital that you will never be able to access again.

If the surrender of your capital at death is an issue and you want to preserve an estate for your heirs, then you'll want to buy a prescribed annuity and combine it with a life insurance policy. This is commonly known as a back-to-back annuity which consists of two separate policies; a single life annuity and a life insurance policy. At death your heirs would receive the funds from the insurance policy. Even with the added cost of the insurance policy, which can be funded with part of the additional after-tax cash flow from the prescribed annuity, you may be able to derive more income than from the GIC alternative, depending on your age, sex, and health at the time of purchase.

Income Splitting

There is a major inequity in the Canadian tax system. A one-income family is taxed much more heavily than if the same income had been received equally by husband and wife. You can reduce that inequity with income splitting. Income splitting diverts income or gains from assets to other family members who will pay less tax over the year because they earn significantly less than you and therefore belong to lower tax brackets.

Family income splitting has the potential to be one of your best personal tax saving strategies. It has gone largely unrecognized by most investors for its great tax saving potential because people mistakenly believe it to be a very complicated system.

Our tax system works on the basis of the more you earn, the more tax you pay. Since investment income is usually added to our other income, it is taxed at our highest marginal rate. By income splitting, you channel investment income through the lower marginal tax rate of your spouse or child, and take advantage of the personal tax credits available to each member of the family. Makes sense, doesn't it?

Attribution Rules

Attribution is a taxation principle which "attributes" income earned by a spouse or any child under 18 years of age, back to the individual who provided the funds in the first place. In other words, if a father gives the bulk of his fortune to his 12-year old son, he continues to be taxed on any investment income earned by those funds (even though the income would no longer be his) until the year in which the child turns 18 years of age. In the case of a transfer of assets to a spouse, this attribution continues as long as the parties remain married (or live common law).

Attribution applies to any transfer of property to a spouse or minor child only. It follows, of course, that one may therefore make a gift to any other person, including a child. Furthermore, since this system of taxation applies to Canadian residents only, a non-resident of Canada may make a gift to a minor child without attribution. This has been a favourite means of transferring property to a child (from a non-resident grandparent, for example).

Income Splitting with Children

Attribution rules do not apply to gifts made to family members 18 years of age and older, or to capital gains realized by children. To retain control of the availability of the income and assets gifted to the family member, however, you must establish a trust.

Income Splitting with a Spouse

Income splitting with your spouse is a very straightforward process. Begin by investing the employment earnings of the lower-income spouse. If the after-tax earnings of that spouse are kept separate and invested in his/her name, investment income will be taxed at their lower marginal rate. The earnings of the spouse with the higher marginal tax rate can then be used for the living requirements of the family.

Spousal RRSPs

Contribute to a spousal RRSP. When the funds are withdrawn from the spousal plan in the future, tax is payable by the spouse, except for spousal contributions in the current or preceding two years. There is an additional benefit: the spouse can take advantage of the $1,000 pension tax credit when the RRSP is matured.

Earn Income on Income

It is still beneficial to loan money to a spouse and generate income taxable in their hands. This works because under the rules "income earned on income" is not subject to attribution. The income earned on the original loan capital attributes back to the lending spouse, but this same income becomes the capital for reinvestment for the spouse who received the loan.

Case Profile ⑧ Becky and Issac Steinberg

Issac Steinberg loans $100,000 to his spouse Becky who then invests it at 10%. In the first year, all of the $10,000 income is taxable in the hands of Issac, but this same $10,000 becomes Becky's capital for re-investment. In the second year, income is earned on this $10,000 which is taxable to Becky, and so on. Over 10 years, and assuming Issac pays the tax liabilities incurred by Becky she will accumulate $159,375.

Year	Lender's Principal (Issac)	First Income Lender Taxed (Issac)	"Income on Income" Spouse Taxed (Becky)	Spouse's Principal (Becky)
1	$100,000	$10,000	$0	$10,000
2	100,000	10,000	1,000	21,000
3	100,000	10,000	2,100	33,100
4	100,000	10,000	3,310	46,410
5	100,000	10,000	4,641	61,051
6	100,000	10,000	6,105	77,156
7	100,000	10,000	7,716	94,872
8	100,000	10,000	9,487	114,359
9	100,000	10,000	11,436	135,795
10	100,000	10,000	13,580	**159,375**

The Effect of Income Tax on Wealth Accumulation

To estimate an after-tax rate of wealth accumulation, simply take the rate of return on a given investment and multiply it by the applicable tax rate. Next take the product and subtract it from the rate of return.

Case Profile ⑨ Robert Scanlon

Robert Scanlon can put $1,000 per year into an income fund, where he anticipates an interest return of 14% per annum. His annual income is currently $43,000, which puts him in the 45% tax bracket. He plans to invest $1,000 per year for the next 10 years and believes his tax bracket will remain the same. The 10-year compounded rate of return after applying a 45% tax rate, increases the $1,000 per year of invested capital to $15,326.

Rate of return 14% x tax rate 45% = 6.3%

Rate of return 14% – 6.3% = 7.7% after-tax rate of return

(From Table 3-2 under Annual Rate of Return column of 7% and End of Year 10 line, find 14.78 where column and line intersect = $14,780. Under Annual Rate of Return column of 8% and End of Year 10 line, find 15.65 where column and line intersect = $15,560. Extrapolate returns of 7% and 8% to find 7.7% $15,560 – $14,780 = $780 x .7 =$546 + $14,780 = **$15,326**)

TABLE 14-10: THE EFFECT OF INCOME TAX ON WEALTH ACCUMULATION

	10 Years	20 Years	30 Years	40 Years
Without Taxes				
$1,000 invested at 14% annually	$22,040	$103,770	$406,740	$1,529,910
With Taxes *				
$0 – $29,590 tax bracket = 27%				
$1,000 invested at 10.22% annually A.T.	$17,750	$64,730	$189,030	$517,935
$29,591 – $59,180 tax bracket = 45%				
$1,000 invested at 7.70% annually A.T.	$15,380	$47,680	$115,490	$257,880
$59,181+ tax bracket = 53%				
$1,000 invested at 6.58% annually A.T.	$14,440	$41,740	$93,380	$191,040

*Assumes combined Federal/Provincial rate, including surtaxes, shown in Table 14-1.

Table Guide

Investment return is 14%.

Individual earning $45,000 is taxable at 45%.

Therefore 14% x 45% = 6.3%.

Investment return 14% — 6.3% = 7.7% after-tax rate of wealth accumulation.

Dealing with Inflation

We have discussed three of the four greatest reasons why people fail in their investment programs: procrastination, lack of a winning attitude, and income taxes. Now it's time to take a hard look at the fourth reason, inflation.

The effect of income taxes on wealth accumulation is well known. But, when coupled with the ravages of inflation, many investors are left with little or no return. During the last few decades, most people have been losing 2% to 3% of their real purchasing power each year. But there are measures you can take to get back on top.

Put Inflation to Work For you

Inflation redistributes wealth. It hurts the elderly and those on fixed income, but it can help those who have financial resources and can harness its energy. In an inflationary environment such as the period of the early 1980s, you could have accumulated a lot of money if you had had sufficient capital.

You can be either the victim of inflation or its beneficiary. If you learn to substitute the word dilution every time you see the word inflation, you will come to have a better understanding of inflation.

If you are a saver placing your savings in a "guaranteed" position, you are a gambler, and if the past is any indication of the future, you are guaranteed to lose.

Think in terms of a total portfolio positioned efficiently at the proper time to beat inflation. Your portfolio must maximize your after-tax return, balanced against a level of risk that provides you with peace of mind.

Inflation—Victim or Beneficiary?

Venita Van Caspel, in her book *The Power of Money Dynamics,* looks at inflation two ways—you can be either a beneficiary or a victim of inflation.

Chart 14-11 depicts the scenario. The centre line of the chart shows inflation at 5%. The reason I pick 5% is because of the fact that over the last 15 years, inflation has averaged in excess of 6%. It's a little bit lower right now, in the 2% range, but over the last 43 years it has averaged 4.5%.

The Victims

Consider the difficult existence of retired Canadians, Canadians living pay cheque to pay cheque, getting by on Old Age Pension and perhaps a Guaranteed Income Supplement. 28% of pensioners had less than $15,000 income which is below the poverty line; employer pensions accounted for just 50% of retirement income for men and women; and that 50% of pensioners filed their tax return on less than $20,000 of income in 1991.

Picture a retired person on a fixed income of $1,000 per month. Assume a 5% inflation rate. Now look down the road 8 years when, due to inflation, the purchasing power of the $1,000 buys only $680 worth of goods.

The 675,000 Canadian pensioners who are living on a fixed income of $20,000 or less, with no ability to accumulate or add to their assets, are inflation's victims. They don't have the ability to save and get ahead. They just continue to go downhill year after year after year, living month-to-month on their next government cheque.

Based on these statistics, I often ask employers: "Do your employees know their other sources of income?" Most people don't even know where they stand with regard to their pension, let alone how to plan. They move through their working years; age 60-65 arrives and they find themselves, quite suddenly, on the "victim" side of the inflation scenario.

The Beneficiaries

On the other side of the coin are inflation's beneficiaries. They may be people like yourself who are gainfully employed. You have income, you're able to save 5%, 10%, 20% of your salary, and you really are starting to work hard to put money aside, especially during the last 7% to 10% years of your career.

Picture yourself with the same $1,000, and put it to work in the various asset classes. Imagine you purchase a GIC with a 5-year term, and a return in the 7% to 8% range; or a new preferred share issue being offered on a quality corporation with an 8% dividend rate. With the dividend tax credit and gross up, the return for someone in the highest tax bracket would exceed 10%. Those who can harness inflation and put it to work through wise investment are inflation's beneficiaries.

Income Lifestyle Requirement with Inflation at 6%

If you earned $20,000 a year in 1975, by 1985 your annual salary would have had to be $35,800 just to maintain the same purchasing power you had in 1975. By

Choice,

not chance,

will determine

your destiny.

Graydon Watters

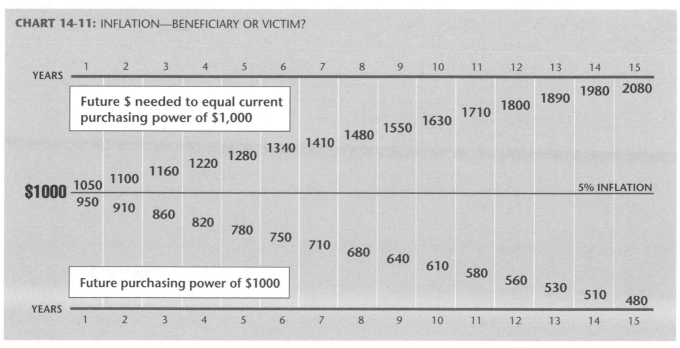

CHART 14-11: INFLATION—BENEFICIARY OR VICTIM?

YEARS	1	2	3	4	5	6	7	8	9	10	11	12	13	14	15

Future $ needed to equal current purchasing power of $1,000

| 1050 | 1100 | 1160 | 1220 | 1280 | 1340 | 1410 | 1480 | 1550 | 1630 | 1710 | 1800 | 1890 | 1980 | 2080 |

$1000 — 5% INFLATION

| 950 | 910 | 860 | 820 | 780 | 750 | 710 | 680 | 640 | 610 | 580 | 560 | 530 | 510 | 480 |

Future purchasing power of $1000

YEARS	1	2	3	4	5	6	7	8	9	10	11	12	13	14	15

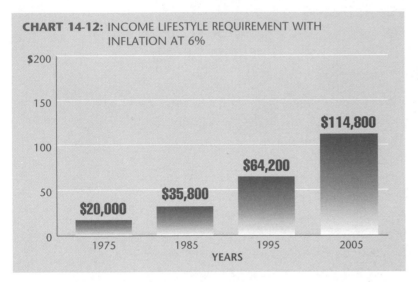

CHART 14-12: INCOME LIFESTYLE REQUIREMENT WITH INFLATION AT 6%

Inflation is not all bad. After all, it has allowed every American to live in a more expensive neighborhood without moving.

Senator Alan Cranston

1995, that $20,000 salary will have to jump to $64,200; and by the year 2005, $114,800.

If you earned $25,000 in 1985, let me assure you that if your salary increases are averaging 6% a year, keeping pace with inflation, you are soon going to be in a very high tax bracket, if you aren't there already. Be prepared by planning.

The Plague of Government Deficits

The government deficit in our country today is over $500 billion. By 2005, I estimate that the government deficit will be in the area of $900 billion. The Minister of Finance, in his most recent budget, has taken measures to cut back the deficit. But, when added to the existing deficit of $511 billion, the deficit will still increase an additional $40 billion this year, and slightly less in the ensuing years.

I dare say that we'll be looking at a figure with a compounded effect of about $900 billion by 2005. Therefore, the time is coming when we will not be able to afford our social programs. The government has only two options to address the deficit—massive cutbacks and cancellation of social programs, and substantial tax increases.

The Demise of Government-Sponsored Social Programs

I project further tax increases in the future and reductions in social programs such as Old Age Security, Guaranteed Income Supplement, and the Canada Pension Plan. You can't get something for nothing. Government deficits can't continue indefinitely.

You must plan for yourselves—now. You cannot rely on the government. There will probably always be social and retirement programs, but these handouts surely will be insufficient for retirement with financial dignity.

In fact, just as the family allowance and old age security programs are now based on need, many of the other social and retirement programs will be subjected to a means test—the beginning of the end of universality in national social programs.

Uncertainty With the Government—What to Do

Uncertainty is the number one enemy of your personal wealth—the uncertainty of Government from budget to budget, of not knowing where you stand, of not knowing what's going to be increased, of what's going to be taken away, of how government will alter tax advantages such as the dividend tax credit or the capital gains tax, and more.

People are being forced to become investors. If you're going to prepare adequately for retirement, you can't afford not to become an investor in your working lifetime. Capturing your cash flow and investing it properly is more important than what you do with the assets you already hold today.

It doesn't matter whether you're reading this book with $1,000 in the bank and another person already has $50,000 in the bank and a head start. What is important is *what you do from this point forward with your cash flow.*

Take the reins. Invest properly, and consider optimum tax planning strategies.

I once heard a story of a Dutchman talking to an American. "My Government's tax system can't provide for my future. I have to save for the future entirely myself. Red, white, and blue. That's the Dutch flag and that's how I feel—red when I calculate my taxes, white when I pay them, and blue when I look at what's left." Said the American, "Me, too. But I'm also seeing stars and stripes."

Inflation Summary

Seriously consider the following investment recommendation I have for you. This investment was selling for $100 in 1951. By 1961, it's value dropped to $88; by 1971, it was worth $63; by 1981, it was worth $28; and by 1991 it was just $18. I project it will be worth about $13 in 2001. Before you say, "You've got to be kidding," you should know that this investment is recommended every day by our government, our banks and trust companies, and our other deposit-taking institutions.

What is this investment? The Canadian dollar. Every time you purchase a savings vehicle, based on the value of the dollar, you risk losing real purchasing power in the long run, due to the ravages of inflation. Still feel like saving your money? Still feel like turning a blind eye to taxes and inflation? Still feel like going broke?

Invest, invest.

Above all, remember that inflation is not an increase in prices, although prices do increase. It is a decrease in the value of your money.

Basic Steps in Retirement Planning

Only one in ten Canadians retires with financial dignity. Taking responsibility for your finances now will ensure your place in the ranks of the dignified.

Looking Ahead

As hard as it seems to believe, the 21st century will be here in less than a decade. In the year 2000, today's 40-year-olds will enter middle age; many of today's 50-year-olds will be leaving their careers. If you are among the latter group, roughly one quarter to one third of your lifetime will lay before you— your so-called "golden years" of retirement living.

Now that you have an understanding of where you stand financially, where you could go if you wanted to, and how you could get there, look ahead 5, 10, 15 years down the line, and think about what you hope to be doing with your life.

- Where will you be living?
- Will your spouse be alive?
- Will you move among the same circle of friends and enjoy the same pastimes?
- Will you still be employed at the same job?
- Will your health be good?
- Will you get up each morning feeling a sense of purpose, looking forward to the new day?

The Future of Retirement in Canada—Not a Pretty Picture

Only one in ten Canadians retires with financial dignity. What do I mean by financial dignity? There are many definitions. The one I like best is to be able to:

1. Do what you want
2. When you want
3. Where you want and
4. With whom you want.

I like this definition of financial dignity because it allows one the flexibility to determine "how much is enough" to accomplish the above. More important, this is not just a retirement lifestyle goal, but one that can be attained much sooner in the working career if the appropriate strategies and objectives are put in place.

By the year 2000, Canadian men will live to an average age of 75 and women to an age of 81. No other group in history will have lived as long or have enjoyed better health and fitness. With such health and longevity, your "golden years" should be the best of your life. But are you financially prepared? For the coming wave of retirement-age individuals, all the key ingredients for a rewarding lifestyle exist; all, that is, but one of the most crucial: financial

> When I was young, I thought that money was the most important thing in life; now that I am old, I know that it is.
>
> **Oscar Wilde**

well-being. If you enter retirement as financially insecure as many of today's seniors, you may find the final years of your life a period of trial and hardship.

Think about the following statistics:

- The 65-plus age group is the fastest growing segment of the Canadian population.

- By the year 2030, the proportion of retirees in Canada will have doubled.

- Early in the 21st century, when the last of the baby boomers (now in their early 30's to late 40's) reach retirement age 65, there will be some 6,000,000 senior citizens in Canada.

- Nearly half of Canada's senior citizens qualify for the Guaranteed Income Supplement (GIS). These people live at the minimum subsistence level defined by North American standards.

- Of 1.35 million pensioners filing tax returns in 1991, 50% showed less than $20,000 of income.

- During the 1980s the cost of living rose 237%; the cost of operating a home was up 226%; mortgage interest was up 293%; utilities increased 344%; home insurance increased 444%.

- An average annual inflation rate of only 5% will strip the purchasing power of a $30,000 pension to $14,400 over the next 15 years.

- By the year 2005, prices for most goods and services will probably be about 50% to 75% higher than they are today.

- In 1993, despite significant tax-saving advantages, only one out of five Canadians owned dividend-paying securities.

> If I'd known I was going to live so long, I'd have taken better care of myself.
>
> **Leon Eldrid**

Disturbing figures. Now consider the disturbing true story of Brent and Mary Forbes in our Case Profile #10.

Can Government Ensure Your Financial Security?

The hard truth is that only a small portion of Canadians will achieve financial dignity and comfort; the government may not be able to support the rest. Although our government's aim is to provide sufficient funding and tax breaks so that we might continue to enjoy our "customary standard of living" well into our retirement years, the reality is that the relatively small work force in the early 21st century will more than likely be unable to support its vast group of retired citizens. There is no agreement on how it can be done or if we can afford it.

Common sense alone suggests that such a system is doomed. Something will have to give. That "something" will most likely be a government-supported retirement income plan—funds which, as discussed in the last chapter, may be seriously depleted or even non-existent in the foreseeable future.

The message is painfully clear—if you are relying solely on your company and/or government pension to see you comfortably through your golden years—don't! You will not make it. The ultimate responsibility for your long-term financial fitness rests not with Government, but with you.

With a little planning you can live the life you want to live and avoid the hardships that appear to be massing in the distance.

Case Profile ⑩ Brent and Mary Forbes

Recently Brent Forbes, a senior manager of a large manufacturing firm, died shortly after retiring. Not only were there no survivor benefits with the company pension he had subscribed to, but he had been talked into rolling all of his RRSPs into a single life annuity which ceased on his death. His wife, Mary, was left with only personal possessions and the family home. She had to sell the house where they had lived for 30 years and go to work on the same assembly line her husband had previously managed! Competent retirement planning advice could have avoided these difficulties.

An Urgent Need for Retirement Planning

If you have had the foresight to anticipate your future needs by establishing a firm financial groundwork and you have good health, retirement can be the best time of your life.

If you decide to take care of your cash flow now; if you understand the difference between saving and investing; if you understand the RRSP maturity options with the cash, annuity, or RRIF alternative; if you can recognize the different types and degrees of risks associated with each and, most importantly; if you are prepared to apply a winning mental attitude to the management of your money, then retirement with the luxury of financial security will be your trophy. It takes time, indeed, but your life is worth it.

Laying the financial groundwork for a secure retirement should begin not at or after age 65, but in your 30s or 40s, or earlier. Nor should the prospect of developing a financial plan for the future be full of unnecessary anxiety. Few people realize how little cash they need to put aside if they start early enough and apply a consistent effort.

For example, consider a 65-year-old professional couple whose family income started at $5,500 forty years ago and increased at a rate of 7.5% compounded annually to nearly $100,000. Inflation averaged about 5% per annum over the same period. (For the sake of simplicity, the effect of taxes has not been taken into account, nor after-tax investment yields used.)

If this couple had consistently saved 10% of their income (a total of $125,000) and invested it to yield 10% per year (5% better than inflation), they would now have $630,000 plus their home, pension plan, and government benefits. If their savings had been 12% instead, they would now have nearly $1,000,000. Had

they put away 15% of their income, those accumulations would amount to $930,000 and $1,440,000. Provocative!

Developing a Rewarding Retirement Lifestyle

Financial security will alleviate many of the hardships and concerns commonly associated with retirement. But don't believe for a minute that money *per se* will ensure a satisfying, challenging, and emotionally rewarding retirement lifestyle. Successful retirement simply doesn't carry a price tag. Nor, as many would believe, does it occur automatically the hour we find ourselves freed from the burdens of the workplace.

True financial planning involves all aspects of finance such as your lifestyle goals and objectives, investments and taxation, income and life protection, wills and estate planning, and pension and retirement planning. Retirement planning involves all of the above as well as the development of meaningful interests. This may take the form of a second career, but more likely it will involve friends and family, hobbies, recreation, travel, further education, a sunbelt home, to mention just a few.

In addition, it is essential to learn how to deal with the psychological roadblocks to a successful retirement that many retirees face such as boredom and loss of identity and self-esteem often associated with a regular job. Boredom can, in fact, be the major reason for dissatisfaction with retirement. Whatever your situation, it is important to start thinking about financial, emotional, social, and psychological changes you and your immediate family may undergo when you retire. There are many exercises in Chapter 20 that will help you through this process.

A satisfying retirement is only possible where there is a meaningful use of your

We must all be concerned with the future because we will spend the rest of our lives there.
Charles Kettering

time. Ideally, you will have an opportunity to find leisure interests without having to earn money. Although some people choose a second income-producing career, retirement will most likely give you a range of leisure interests to pursue such as:

- Hobbies and crafts
- Educational courses
- Socializing and friends
- Travel and vacations
- Reading and artistic pursuits.

Stretch for your true potential. Sift through the possibilities for your future. Allow yourself to find meaning and value. It is important to acquire faith in your future, a zest for living, and an appreciation for all that life has to offer.

Your Income During Retirement

You probably have a fairly clear idea of your cost of living. That is, you know how much money is left over each month after the bills are paid. What you probably don't know as accurately is how your money is actually spent. Food, clothing, mortgage or rent payments, income tax, recreation, and transportation are all necessary expenses, so many people feel, "What's the difference how I spend my money? Bills have to be paid!"

It does matter. How you pattern your spending now dictates how you will spend after you retire. It also gives you the keys to budgeting efficiently and reducing your living expenses. These two factors will be very important during your retirement because although you will become eligible for many financial benefits, the basic financial change will be that you won't be working. And for most people, retirement means a reduction in overall income. You will have to seek out the means to stretch that income.

You will have to assess your projected available assets. (Chapter 16 will give you the format.) And you will have to weigh the advantages and disadvantages of your various retirement goals from an economic and lifestyle point of view. Choices will have to be made and, in most cases, sacrifices as well. But with preparation and determination, you can mold the retirement experience you desire.

Creating Your Retirement Plan

To create a financial plan for your retirement you must follow five steps:

1. Specify your needs.
2. Estimate your income requirements.
3. Analyse your resources.
4. Select your investments and accumulate.
5. Do an annual financial fire drill to make sure you stay on course with the retirement objectives.

Case Profile ⑪ Thomas Kettle

Let me tell you a story about a client of mine when I was in the investment industry. I dealt with this man for 23 years. In his working lifetime, Tom never earned more than $14,400. Yet today he has an investment account worth $300,000 because he and his wife have been investing throughout his 40-year working career.

In the days when Tom was making $3,000 a year, they were saving 10% of their income; 10% on $3,000 is $300 a year. Seems like a pittance, doesn't it? The point is that throughout their working lifetime they consistently paid themselves first. Whether it was 5% or 7% or 10%, they lived frugally and planned wisely.

Today, they have an estate that many people would be proud of: a $400,000 investment account, a house worth $200,000, and other assets worth $125,000. People who have earned 3, 4 or 5 times Tom's income in their latter stages still do not have the kind of assets that these people have.

Specify Your Needs

As we saw in an earlier chapter, budgeting involves a hard look at your income and expenses. Be as specific as possible. Unless you plan to retire within the next few years, there is no way to gauge precisely what your annual cost of living will be. A rule of thumb is to count on needing between 60% and 80% of your last working year's income. The exact amount you will require will depend upon such factors as:

- *Your desired retirement lifestyle*
  Will you be moving permanently to some remote getaway region where living expenses will be far less than they would be in the city? Will you be splurging on extensive, first-class travel? Will your newly acquired hobbies such as golf, tennis, adventure outings, and so on, involve expensive initial costs for equipment, club membership, etc.?

- *Your personal commitments and responsibilities*
  Will you still be providing financial assistance to your children? Will you and your spouse's health care costs be climbing? Will you be divorced or recently remarried? Will you be retiring earlier or later than you planned and how will this affect the amount of your assured yearly income?

- *Your assured sources of income*
  How much money will you be receiving from company and private government pensions? Will you be supplementing this amount through part-time and/or self-employment? (See Chapter 16 for assistance with this exercise.)

Anticipating your eventual retirement income needs doesn't have to mean preparing to scrimp to extremes, any more than it means simply stowing away as much money as you can. For one thing, it would be both unnecessary and foolish to stop having fun due to a constant fear of going broke.

Even with inflation, it is not difficult to live with the 60% to 80% of employment income, given some sensible money management and some established, rewarding investments. Remember, personal income taxes will be low or nil and the cost of things such as public transportation, movies, prescription drugs, and sometimes accommodation costs, are greatly reduced for seniors.

Most retirees do tend to slow their pace of living considerably by the time they reach 70 or so. They drive less, travel less, entertain less, and accordingly, their living costs tend to be reduced considerably. In most cases, retired citizens spend less than they might have thought feasible to maintain a satisfying style of life.

Still, one of the most welcomed rewards of pre-retirement planning is to be able to live out your retirement years free from financial burdens and the shackles of constant penny-pinching and budgeting concerns. If you've set an effective financial plan in motion prior to your retirement, the rewards will be there. In the final analysis, such rewards are measured in terms of peace of mind, never in dollars and cents!

You will have to watch your cash flow carefully, especially during the first two or three years of retirement living. There will have to be some budgetary "policing," some inevitable give and take, and usually some curtailing of pleasures and associated expenses. With restricted opportunities to increase your post-retirement income, spending can easily get out of hand. Some vigilance will be necessary.

On balance, the best time to establish a base for retirement budgeting is three to five years prior to leaving the workforce. By that time, you should count on having eliminated many personal expenses. For example, according to most planning

> The great end of life is not knowledge but action.
>
> **Thomas Henry Huxley**

experts, by the time you leave the work-force you should have:

- Paid for many major personal items (appliances, furniture, equipment, vehicles, etc.)
- Completed major repairs or renovations to your home, if you anticipate remaining there
- Repaid all major outstanding personal debts, with the exception of those that are on excellent terms, e.g., a 9% mortgage; a 6% loan on a life insurance policy, with proceeds invested at 12% or higher; etc.
- Completed and reviewed all legal documents and have arranged for the effective transfer of your estate.

Estimate Your Income Requirements

Your retirement income needs should include the following:

- The four major costs of food, shelter, clothing and, to a lesser extent, transportation
- Insurance and property taxes
- Debt repayment of mortgages or other loans
- Personal expenses
- Recreational expenses
- Discretionary expenses
- Travel expenses
- Estimated income taxes
- Project inflation for the next several years to try to ascertain any vulnerability you may have in becoming a victim of inflation.

It is very important to control your income needs, if you expect to retire with financial dignity. The amount of money you will receive from the government in pensions for OAS, CPP/QPP, and GIS is generally thought to account for only 30% to 40% of your needs.

If your spouse is also participating in this, share your thoughts with each other in order to understand each other's needs and expectations regarding retirement. With all the necessary data gathered, you can now complete the Resource Analysis Worksheet in Worksheet 15-1.

WORKSHEET 15-1: RESOURCE ANALYSIS WORKSHEET

Total all retirement benefits from employer, including
pensions and retiring allowances. _____

Total all personal retirement plans such as RRSPs. _____

Calculate CPP/QPP, OAS, and GIS (if applicable). _____

Project your net worth and the anticipated yield. Be sure to include the
sale of major assets, such as your residence, and the subsequent
reinvestment of those assets, and the anticipated yield they can produce. _____

Project the depletion of net worth, including any one-time expenditures,
and your estimated percentage erosion from inflation,
over the foreseeable future. _____

Summary of your net worth and your income from all sources will create:
  Surplus Projected resources exceed requirements plus a cushion of _____
  Deficit Projected retirement income needs exceed resources, therefore,
         goal is to increase net worth by saving and investing more
         and/or reducing requirements. _____

Analyse Your Resources

In the next step of planning for retirement, you go through what is called resource analysis. Do you know how much your employer's pension plan is worth to you and any other retiring allowance you may be entitled to?

It is time you sat down with them and found out. You should know the answers to these questions by the time you are age 40. It is never too soon to know right where you stand. In fact, as I have said before, you should plan for retirement the day you begin to work.

Let's turn now to the crucial question of your own long-term financial planning. Complete the retirement Planning Questionnaire in Worksheet 15-2.

The purpose of these questions is to start the creative juices moving and to activate the thought processes. By taking the time to think through each question, and committing answers to paper, you commence the personal planning process.

WORKSHEET 15-2: RETIREMENT PLANNING QUESTIONNAIRE

Have you put aside the daily demands of your routine, and begun to face the challenge for your own financial security? _____

Have you organized your own affairs so that it is clear to you what you need and want for the future? _____

Have you sought out the information and the help you need? _____

Have you initiated the necessary steps towards attaining financial fitness, and maintained that level of fitness once it has been reached? _____

What will your personal savings and investments be worth at the time you retire? _____

Are you considering a change of occupation before retirement? _____

Would you consider starting your own business? _____

Are you considering partial retirement? _____

What is your present age? _____

At what age would you like to retire? _____

How many years is that from now? _____

Where would you like to live? _____

Would you like a retirement home in the sunbelt? _____

Would you consider selling your home? _____

Would you like to take major trips and travel extensively? _____

What activities would you like to participate in and what will they cost? _____

Continued on next page

Success is peace of mind in knowing you did your best.
John Wooden

WORKSHEET 15-2: RETIREMENT PLANNING QUESTIONNAIRE (CONTINUED)

Are you in good health?   _____

Is your spouse (if applicable) in good health?   _____

Does your family tend towards longevity?   _____

Does your spouse's family tend towards longevity?   _____

Have you established your income needs?   _____

Do you know what sources of retirement income will be available to you?   _____

Do you understand each of these sources of income?   _____

Do you know what options you will have in each of these income sources,
such as timing, guarantees, investment yields?   _____

Have you adequately divided your assets between you and your spouse
so as to minimize taxes payable at retirement?   _____

Have you arranged your investments for maximum inflation protection?   _____

Will you meet your retirement goals and objectives?   _____

How will you weight your investment goals to achieve financial dignity?

     Reserves (Cash): Liquidity   _____%

     Debt (Bonds): Income   _____%

     Equities (Stocks): Growth   _____%

                                                                           100%

Consumer Price Index

> Keep your face to the sunshine and you cannot see the shadows. I thank God for my handicaps, for through them, I have found myself, my work, and my God.
>
> **Helen Keller**

The very first thing to understand as you approach retirement age is that your personal consumer price index changes, and changes greatly. It is calculated that, for most Canadians, somewhere between 60% and 80% of the income you required before retirement will be necessary after retirement.

The day you leave the workforce to retire, your costs drop to about two-thirds of what they were when you were working. Look at the Consumer Price Index for 1986 in Table 15-3. When you do a summation of the major components in the Index, you will find that the average person's personal index at retirement is 66% of the Consumer Price Index.

Where food costs were 18.1% before, your personal index concerning food at retirement, in many cases, will be half of that if your children are grown or, have moved away from home and you have only two mouths to feed.

Remember that the components in the Consumer Price Index are based on a basket of goods for an average family of four. Your costs in the average family scenario, including only you and your spouse will be half of what it is for the average Canadian family.

I have assumed you own your own home. Most people have their own dwelling by age 65. So you only have taxes, heat, light, and utilities to pay. Your costs are probably 65% of the housing costs of a standard family. Even if you have sold your house, taken a good profit, bought or rented a condominium, a trailer, or something like that in the sunbelt, your costs should be about 65% of the Consumer Price Index for housing at retirement.

You no longer need the same suits, skirts, shirts, and blouses that you needed when you were working. Your clothing costs should drop by 35% at retirement.

Transportation costs will also drop by 40% now that you no longer travel to work each day. Transportation will be one of your biggest sources of savings; in 1986, for example, 18.3% of a family's budget was spent on transportation.

Health and personal care costs will stay at 100% of what they were at preretirement.

Recreation, reading, and education, which is 8.8% of the average family's budget, will also stay at 100%. You will have more free time, and probably participate in more recreational activities than before. You will read as much, and probably more, than before.

Finally, tobacco and alcohol—your costs will almost certainly drop here. Tobacco and alcohol costs averaged out at 5.6%. At retirement, they tend to drop to 70% of that figure once you leave the workforce.

The rule of thumb in terms of your drop in cost of living is that your retirement lifestyle will cost only 60% to 80% of the average Canadian family. So, if you are an average type of person, perhaps 70% of your current income is what you will require at retirement in order to maintain the same lifestyle you now enjoy.

What is your personal inflation index? Every family has its own inflation index that can be substantially different from the stated figures in the economy, at any point in time. The published figures rarely have any direct relation to your personal situation.

TABLE 15-3: CONSUMER PRICE INDEX

Family or Personal Major Components	1986	% at Retirement	Indexed at Retirement
Housing	36.3%	65%	23.6%
Food	18.1%	50%	9.1%
Transportation	18.3%	60%	11.0%
Clothing	8.7%	65%	5.6%
Tobacco & Alcohol	5.6%	70%	3.9%
Health & Personal Care	4.2%	100%	4.2%
Recreation, Reading & Education	8.8%	100%	8.8%
All Items	100.0%		66.2%

If inflation is 5% at a given point in time, and your personal or family costs and expenditures are 70% of the Consumer Price Index, your personal inflation index is 70% x 5%, or 3.5%, which is 1.5% lower than the national average.

Retirement Age Goal

Although the cost of living generally increases in line with the Consumer Price Index during the working years, most families experience three major decreases in their personal cost of living index during this time. These decreases occur:
- When their home is paid for
- When children complete their education and when they leave home
- When they retire and costs drop by 30% to 35%.

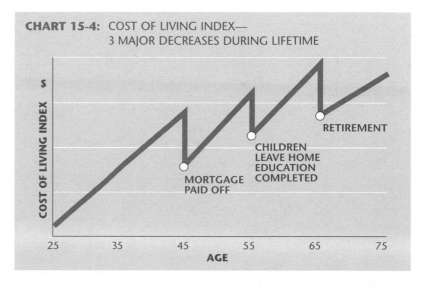

CHART 15-4: COST OF LIVING INDEX— 3 MAJOR DECREASES DURING LIFETIME

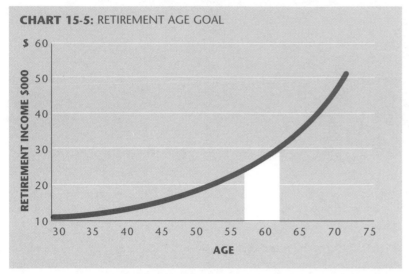

CHART 15-5: RETIREMENT AGE GOAL

- You are contributing for five years less to your pension.
- You have five years additional drawings on your pension.

Three Stages of Retirement Planning

- *Stage One*
  Age 55 to 62. Retirement from workforce on fixed pension.
- *Stage Two*
  Age 60 to 65. OAS and CPP/QPP added to your existing pensions which provide an increase in cash flow.
- *Stage Three*
  Age 71. Convert your RRSP to a RRIF or an annuity to give you a further increase in cash flow. The selection of a RRIF could give you the flexibility of increased cash flow as needed, to offset inflation beyond the age of 71.

  More on these stages later. For now, let's take a closer look at your sources of retirement income.

Your retirement age goal will depend upon when your working career began, when you bought your home, and at what age you raised your family. For example, if you leave your job at age 57, instead of age 62, your income might be $24,000 instead of $32,000. There is a substantial difference in income at retirement if you leave early because:

- You have five years less earnings.

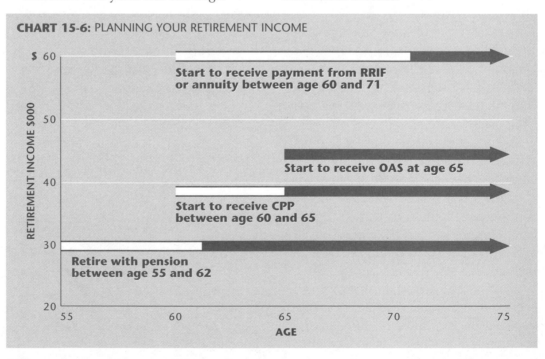

CHART 15-6: PLANNING YOUR RETIREMENT INCOME

Start to receive payment from RRIF or annuity between age 60 and 71

Start to receive OAS at age 65

Start to receive CPP between age 60 and 65

Retire with pension between age 55 and 62

Your Sources of Retirement Income

When we baby-boomers retire during the next two decades, with fewer younger workers to pay for our government pensions, who will support us? Us.

If we took a group of 10 men and women age 40 twenty-five years ago, and projected to age 65 today, the results would be as follows:

- Three would be dead
- Six would be financially dead
- One would be alive, healthy, and financially successful.

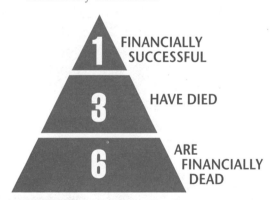

More recent statistics, compiled in 1991, suggest that for every 100 people starting their careers, the following situation will exist at age 65:

- 28 dead
- 21 with annual incomes under $15,000 (below poverty level)
- 27 with annual incomes between $15,000 and $25,000
- 21 with annual income between $25,000 and $50,000

- 3 with annual incomes over $50,000 (financially successful).

Many people are now being asked by their employers to retire early, and this can be more than a little surprising. There is also a parallel trend toward voluntary early retirement by employees who wish to enjoy other interests. Regardless of why you may find yourself leaving the work force early, you should start preparing for your retirement now.

To retire with financial dignity, you should plan for an appropriate mix of pension payments and annuity income, as well as a Registered Retirement Income Fund, supplemented by investment income and perhaps a capital withdrawal plan. Carefully timing the point at which each source of income activates makes a substantial difference to the outcome.

What Is a Pension Plan?

The purpose of a *pension plan* is to deliver a fixed or indexed benefit that will provide a reasonable standard of living for the remainder of your lifetime after you retire. The pension plan is a procedural tool that allows the accumulation of money by an employer, an employee, or

> The less a man knows about the past and the present, the more insecure must be his judgement of the future.
>
> **Sigmund Freud**

both, on a tax-free basis until retirement; at that point it will be taxable as it is withdrawn, but usually, at a lower rate.

The money is held and invested in a pension fund, which traditionally ranks safety and income as primary objectives. After the inflation of the last decade, however, there is increased emphasis on providing a rate of return to match the combined inflation and interest rates in the economy. So, once again, Canadians are being forced into investment positions— the best thing that can happen to us!

Pensions are monitored by actuaries and benefits consultants. When a company sets up a defined benefit plan, the actuary calculates the cost of the ultimate benefits, estimates how much investment income the plan will generate over the long term, and how fast salaries will increase. Actuarial forecasts and studies are compared with actual results, and every three years the plan must file an actuarial valuation with the Federal Government.

Pension plans can experience a surplus or a deficiency, based on the assumptions made by the actuaries. You may recall the controversy generated by corporations dipping into surpluses over the last few years. The theory is that if a corporation is responsible for making up any deficit in the defined benefit pension plan, it should also be allowed to retrieve any surplus that is generated. The regulatory authorities to date have disagreed with this kind of thinking.

Government Sources of Pension Income

Pension reform is urgently needed in Canada. Although the last budget provided a major overhaul of the pension system, there will no doubt be continuing changes to our retirement income system over the next several years. What will become clear to you in this section is that

Old Age Security, Canada/Quebec Pension Plans, and the Guaranteed Income Supplement were designed to provide only a portion, perhaps 30% to 40% of your retirement income needs based on average incomes. Of course, the higher your pre-retirement income level, the less these government plans will provide as a percentage of your retirement income needs. The other 60% to 70% will have to come from your employer's pension plan, or your personal pensions, as well as your personal investment assets.

The two main government plans that provide retirement assistance for those over the age of 65 are the Old Age Security program (OAS), and the Canada Pension Plan (CPP). A similar pension plan for Quebec (QPP) is comparable to the Federal plan. Other financial assistance programs that form a part of these major plans include the Guaranteed Income Supplement (GIS) and the Spouse's Allowance (SPA). In addition, some provinces such as Ontario, have established senior assistance programs that offer funds in addition to the usual government retirement plans. The Guaranteed Annual Income Supplement for Ontario Senior Citizens, or GAINS, is one such plan. The guaranteed individual monthly income July 1, 1994, for Ontario, is:

Guaranteed Individual Monthly Income
July 1, 1994

	Single	Couple (each receives)	Couple (joint)
Gains	$83.00	$83.00	$166.00

Old Age Security (OAS)

If you have lived in Canada for most of your life, you will be eligible for OAS payments when you reach age 65. As of January 1994, OAS pensioners can count on a yearly (taxable) income of $4,630, or $9,260 if you are a couple.

TABLE 16-1: OAS AND GIS MONTHLY BENEFITS

Maximum Monthly OAS Benefits - January 1994

$385.81   OAS

$458.50   GIS - basic

OAS/GIS Combined Maximum Benefit	Marital Status	Maximum Allowable Income For GIS Supplement (combined if married)
$844.31	Single	$11,064
$687.88	Married (both are pensioners)	$14,448
$848.53	Married (one is a pensioner)	$26,784
$687.88	Married pensioner (spouse receives spouse's allowance)	$20,688
$759.42	Widowed spouse's allowance	$15,168

TABLE 16-2: INDEXED OAS PAYMENT PROJECTED FOR 10 YEARS

Year	Monthly Payment, April 1st
1994	$385.81
1995	405.10
1996	425.36
1997	446.63
1998	468.96
1999	492.41
2000	517.03
2001	542.88
2002	570.02
2003	598.52

Though you might be entitled to Old Age Security payments, you still must apply for them through the Federal Department of Health and Welfare. Application forms can be obtained through the post office, or from the Income Security Programs Client Service Centre nearest you. You should apply six months prior to your 65th birthday.

A summary of current monthly benefits for OAS and GIS in January 1994, are listed in Table 16-1.

The OAS is an indexed pension, adjusted quarterly in line with the CPI, to a maximum of 5% per year. The OAS for the first quarter of 1994 is $385.81. Assuming a 5% annual increase, the payment would grow as shown in Table 16-2 over the next 10 years.

The "Clawback" on OAS

Old Age Security (OAS) is one of Canada's oldest forms of social assistance. It began in 1952, to help all Canadians over 65 years of age enjoy financial security. But like other social programs, OAS came under scrutiny in the late 1980s. In 1991, the Mulroney government introduced the *clawback,* effectively taking back some of the OAS benefit from higher-income earners.

The clawback was initially targeted at high-income earners, but it is really an ever widening net designed to capture more taxpayers each year. This results because each year's inflation threshold is set at 3%. Therefore if inflation rises by 5% this year, the clawback income level only increases by 2%.

If your taxable income is $53,215 or less in 1994, you will not be affected by the clawback. However, if your taxable income is more than that amount, you will have to pay an additional 15% tax on your taxable income over $53,215. If that figure is approximately $83,000, you will be clawed back the entire amount. Over time, more and more people will find their OAS benefits taken away. Fortunately, there are several options for you to avoid or minimize the clawback:

- Make sure that you take every possible tax deduction and credit that you are allowed
- Make your maximum RRSP contribution in your first year of retirement based on your prior year earnings
- Maintain your investments in your RRSP as long as you can and when you turn 71, convert it into a RRIF, which will enable you to take lower income in the early years

Politics are almost as exciting as war, and quite as dangerous. In war you can only be killed once, but in politics many times.

Winston Churchill

177

- Split your CPP benefits with your spouse and open a spousal RRSP
- Have the higher-income earner pay all household expenses and allow the lower-income earner to invest the family savings
- A Canadian non-resident living in the U.S. can receive full OAS benefits with no clawback, providing you lived in Canada for 20 years as an adult.

Canada Pension Plan (CPP)/ Quebec Pension Plan (QPP)

These plans came into being on January 1, 1966, and are financed by employers, employees, and self-employed persons. *CPP/QPP* benefits depend on covered earnings. A summary of all of the CPP/QPP benefits for January 1994 is shown in Table 16-3.

Each Canadian must work and contribute to the CPP/QPP in order to be eligible for a pension under these plans. The plans are linked to the number of years you have worked, and to the amount you have contributed to the plan. Since the inception of the plans in 1966, contribution levels have been set at 1.8% of salary by the employee and a matching 1.8% by the employer. Self-employed persons pay both shares.

Due to an anticipated shortfall in the money that will be required to fund future pensions, contribution levels for both employees and employers were increased beginning January, 1987 and will continue each year until January 2011. These increases are subject to a review every five years. Contribution rates for the next three years are as follows:

Contribution rates are expected to be 7.6% by 2011, but this will not be enough to support the vast number of baby boomers who will be retiring. Between 2011 and 2030 joint contributions may have to climb above 13% to support all those retirees.

There is a maximum yearly contribution, based on the difference between your "year's basic exemption" and your year's "maximum pensionable earnings." Currently, earnings under $3,400 a year and any amount over $34,400 a year are exempt from deductions. If you are self-employed, you pay both the employee and employer share, currently 5.2% of contributory earnings in 1994.

One of the options provided by CPP/QPP is a flexible retirement date whereby you can select your pension benefit as early as age 60, or as late as age 70. Normal retirement is considered to be age 65. Should you choose an earlier retirement date, you receive a reduced pension because you contribute for fewer years, and receive the benefit for a longer period of time. Your CPP/QPP is reduced by .5% for each month you are under age 65, or 6% per year. Therefore, if you retire at age 62, for example, you receive a pension of 82% of the normal amount (3 years = 36 months x .5% = 18%). Similarly, if you retire later, your pension will increase .5% for each month above age 65. Therefore, if you retire at age 67, you would receive a pension of 112% of your normal amount (2 years = 24 months x .5% = 12%).

You must meet certain qualifications when applying for CPP/QPP before reaching age 65—you must have wholly or substantially stopped working and you cannot be self-employed at the time your pension payments begin. *Upon reaching age 65*, however, it is not a requirement to have stopped working in order to receive your pension. Finally, you can no longer con-

Year	Employer	Employee	Self-Employed
1994	2.6	2.6	5.2
1995	2.7	2.7	5.4
1996	2.8	2.8	5.6

TABLE 16-3: CANADA/QUEBEC PENSION PLAN — 1994

	CPP	QPP
Annual basic exemption	$ 3,400.00	$ 3,400.00
Annual maximum pensionable earnings	34,400.00	34,400.00
Maximum contribution:		
• employee or employer (2.6% of contributory earnings)	806.00	806.00
• self-employed (5.2% of contributory earnings)	1,612.00	1,612.00
Maximum retirement benefit age 65	694.44	543.06
Death benefit–lump sum:	3,440.00	3,440.00
Maximum monthly spouse's pension:		
• If 45–54	384.59	578.68
• If 55–64	384.59	660.01
• 65 or over	416.66	416.66
Disability benefit:		
• Maximum monthly contributor's pension	839.07	839.09

tribute to the plan after you start receiving payments, nor after you reach age 70.

How Safe is CPP/QPP?

When CPP/QPP was established in 1966 one of its major failings was to invest all of the funds in the plan in fixed income investments. Essentially, the plans were designed to give each of the provinces a source of funds from which they could borrow. if CPP/QPP were managed similarly to corporate pension plans allocated to the three major asset classes of reserves, debt, and equities, there would be no question as to their long-term viability.

Major reform will be necessary soon if CPP/QPP is to survive. What form this will take is anybody's guess. Here are some possible solutions to consider:

- Raise the retirement age by two to five years, but keep flexible early retirement options open with a reduced pension.
- Eliminate basic exemption and base contributions on all earnings up to the year's maximum pensionable earnings (YMPE).
- Eliminate automatic indexing of CPP/QPP benefits received.

- Reduce survivor benefits.
- Increase contribution rates during the next decade and invest these excess funds in equities.

Company Pension Plans— Registered Pension Plans (RPPs)

Most major companies in Canada offer *registered pension plans* (RPPs) for their employees. These plans vary widely according to:

- percentage of income contributed
- retirement age
- indexing of payments (to lighten the burden of inflation, some companies build a full or partial cost-of-living increase into their pension payments)
- payments to spouse in the event of death
- additional benefits of the plan, such as disability, death insurance, etc.
- vesting—the time you have to work before the plan becomes guaranteed
- portability, or the ease with which you can shift your accumulated financial credit from one plan to another.

Check with your company's personnel department about the details of your particular pension plan.

Defined Benefit Plans (DBP)

The majority of private RPPs are of the *defined benefit* type. With these plans, your benefits are calculated on a formula, based on earnings and length of service. A few examples:

* *Flat Benefit Plan*

  Based on a fixed amount per month for each year of service, and is usually offered to unionized employees or groups with similar earning levels. This type of plan usually results in a very low pension income relative to your pre-retirement income.

* *Career Average Plan*

  Based on a formula of, say 2% per year, of your earnings such that you receive a pension of 2% of your career average earnings multiplied by the number of years worked. Like the flat benefit plan, the career average plan often results in a very low pension when compared to pre-retirement income. This happens because, in a period of high inflation, the benefits earned in the past for a long-service employee become nearly worthless.

* *Final Average Plan*

  This type of plan is based on a formula that provides automatic updating; you receive a pension such as 2% of your average earnings multiplied by the number of years worked, and based on your last five or six years of employment. The advantage of this kind of plan is that your pension will be higher because it is calculated on your high income years just prior to retirement. For example, if you belonged to a defined benefit/final average plan and worked for the same company for 35 years, your pension would be similar to the following:

Private Pension Plan Coverage In Canada

1982	1992
46.5%	47.5%

Earnings During the Last Five Years	1990	$34,000
	1991	36,000
	1992	39,000
	1993	41,000
	1994	44,000
		$194,000

Pension

$194,000 ÷ 5
= $38,800
x 2% x 35 years
= **$27,160**

Contribution Levels

The maximum employee contribution to an RPP (defined benefit plan) is limited to $3,500 per year. The maximum employer contribution is not restricted to $3,500, but is the amount in addition to the employee's contribution, required to fund the pension benefit that has been promised under the company's defined benefit program.

The maximum pension benefit allowable by Revenue Canada is $60,278 per year for a defined benefit plan, calculated by a formula as the lesser of two amounts:

* $1,722 per year of service to a maximum of 35 years
* 2% of the average of the best three consecutive years of remuneration times the number of years of pensionable service to a maximum of 35 years

It is important, however, to note that an employer is under no obligation to provide the maximum benefit under a defined benefit RPP.

Defined Contribution Plans (DCP)

An increasingly popular alternative to the defined benefit plan is the *defined contribution plan,* or money purchase plan. These plans provide a pension based on the amount of accumulated funds available at the time the pension is to commence.

Used mainly by smaller and medium size employers, these plans do not guarantee a specific benefit level. Contributions by the employer and employee accumulate in a fund and whatever the fund is worth at retirement, purchases an annuity, a life income fund (LIF), a locked-in RRSP, a *locked-in retirement account* (LIRA) or similar plan. We will provide a complete discussion on these last two options in the next chapter. Your pension annuity will be based on a number of factors:

* how well the money was invested through the years

- the total amount of money accumulated in your DCP
- the type of annuity you select
- the level of interest rates at the time you purchase the annuity
- your age when the annuity payments begin

Deferred Profit Sharing Plan (DPSP)

This pension plan is very similar to a defined contribution plan, however, employer contributions vary according to

the company's profitability. The plan is designed to encourage employee interest and loyalty in the company's growth prospects and future potential. In theory this type of plan creates a win-win situation, whereby if the company is successful, the employee will be rewarded as well.

Independent Pension Plan (IPP)

If you've always wanted to have your own pension plan, then an *Independent Pension Plan* (IPP) could be for you.

WORKSHEET 16-4: YOUR EMPLOYER'S PENSION PLAN

How knowledgeable are you about your corporate pension plan? Now's the time to gather all the information you'll need to know for your future.

1. What will my future pension benefit be in today's dollars at retirement age? (This will be a general projection if your plan is a defined benefit plan, and a less accurate estimate if it is a money purchase plan.) $_____

2. What is the youngest age at which I can receive retirement income?   _____

3. What is the oldest age at which I can elect to receive retirement income?   _____

4. What is the formula used to reduce my pension income if I retire early?   _____

5. Is my employer pension plan indexed?   Yes ☐   No ☐

6. If yes, what is the formula that is used to determine the amount of indexing?
   Consumer Price Index
   Other (specify) _____
   _____

7. How much will my spouse receive in the event of my death? $_____

8. What provisions in the plan protect my retirement income should a disability force me to retire early?   _____

9. Is my pension fully vested? If not, how much longer must I wait before my pension is fully vested?
   _____
   _____

10. What provisions apply to my pension plan if I change employers before retirement?
    _____
    _____

11. What special benefits are applicable on retirement?
    Medical coverage in retirement   Yes ☐   No ☐
    Dental coverage in retirement   Yes ☐   No ☐
    Other _____   Yes ☐   No ☐

12. Are their special exclusions from the above? (Specify)
    _____
    _____

That is if you're age 40 or older and consistently earning more than $100,000 a year.

An IPP is a defined pension benefit plan that allows the owner of a business or a high-earning executive or professional to contribute more than the maximum under an RRSP. The rationale for an IPP is that it allows a person to accumulate more retirement savings than are possible with an RRSP. In order for there to be enough time to allow the additional contributions to compound and grow, the person should be further from, rather than closer to, retirement.

Your estate will also benefit if you have an IPP. If you belong to a company-sponsored pension plan, any surplus after you die goes into a pool. The surplus in an IPP, however, goes to the deceased's estate. Another advantage is that unlike most RRSPs, an IPP is creditor proof. And if you have long years of service with a company, you can roll them into an IPP.

But before you look into an IPP, consider these facts. Start up and administrative costs are high; you may have to pay as much as $5,000 to set one up, and $1,500 to administer it each year. You also won't be able to convert your IPP into a RRIF; a life annuity will be your only option. Finally, you won't be able to split your income with your spouse. These disadvantages may make what appears to be right for you—an IPP—less appealing. In any case, you should ask lots of questions before you decide.

Corporate Pension Plans Are Under Review

80% of the population simply cannot afford to retire because they are not prepared. They face a potentially bleak existence. The need for adequate retirement income is one of the largest compensation issues today. Why?

- OAS and CPP/QPP will only supply 30% to 40% of what you will need to live in comfort.
- Life expectancy rates are climbing. If you are a male, age 65, you can expect to live another 15 to 16 years. If you are a female, age 65, you can expect to live another 18 to 19 years.
- Income taxes and the ravages of inflation are particularly cruel, especially for the elderly and for those on fixed income.
- Most employees of small business, and many larger retail stores and service industries do not have pension plans, and these employees are skewed heavily towards females.
- Vesting and portability rules historically have proven grossly inadequate, due to age restrictions and the limitations on transferability.

The question is: Who is responsible? Government? Your Employer? You? Historically, all three have contributed to the dilemma. But let me assure you, if you are relying on the government or your employer to bail you out, you have been misguided.

The ultimate responsibility for your retirement belongs only to you.

That being said, there is a trend today among employers to review, restructure, and upgrade their existing pension plans, often with the addition of a money purchase plan or Group RSP. Corporations are also taking steps to provide financial education and pre-retirement planning for employees. Education and counselling on financial services will be a major growth area for the next 25 years.

The Federal Government is doing its part as well. In 1986 they estimated that the combined annual contributions of the employee and employer required to fund the maximum pension benefit of $60,025 over a 35-year period, would be $15,500. This resulted in the establishment of new RPP/RRSP contribution limits subject to a limit of 18% of earned income. A major question that arises is: "Should a company even continue to structure their RPP on a defined benefit basis?" For many younger employees, the opportunity for tax deferral under a money purchase plan or an RRSP may be greater than that available under a defined benefit plan. For older employees, the defined benefit plan may still offer the more attractive alternative.

For the employer, there is no question that the excessive regulation and administration costs of the defined benefit plan make the money purchase plan or group RSP a more attractive alternative. What we are already seeing and will likely continue to see develop over the next several years are hybrid plans that combine the best features of each type of benefit.

Major Pension Reforms

The government has introduced a number of major pension reforms during the last several years. These reforms go a long way towards addressing the imbalances and weaknesses in the system, but they by no means alleviate all of the problems. Always remember that you are ultimately responsible for yourself.

- *Transfer of periodic benefits from an RPP/DPSP*
  For the 1990—1994 taxation years, a limited rollover of up to $6,000 a year to a spousal RRSP is available with respect to periodic amounts received out of, or under, an RPP.
- *Vesting and portability*
  An individual is vested after two years of service, and should he/she leave the company, there are three alternatives:
  1. Leave their pension credit in that employer's plan until age 65

  2. Transfer the funds to the new employer's plan
  3. Transfer the funds to a portable plan such as an RRSP.
- *Part-time workers*
  This group includes a high percentage of females who work in retail store occupations. They have the right to join their employer's pension plan after two years of service if they have earned in excess of 35% of the average industrial wage during those two years.
- *Divorce*
  Pension credits, earned during a marriage, can be divided between a couple at the time of a divorce, providing one of the spouses applies for the division. This is a major benefit for women who have never worked outside of the home and who can now receive a CPP/QPP pension, as well as a split of the spouse's employer's pension or any other personal pensions the spouse may have.
- *Survivor benefits*
  All RPPs must provide a survivor benefit to the pensioner's spouse that is at least 60% of a full pension.
- *Age discrimination*
  All RPPs, under Federal jurisdiction, will require that men and women who retire at the same age, and who have made equal contributions, must receive equal benefits.
- *Factor of 9*
  The maximum defined benefit per year of pensionable service in a DBP is:
  - flat dollar maximum of $1,722.22 per year
  - percentage maximum of 2% per year times maximum 35 years of service.

DBP Limits		DCP Limits
2% of earnings	x 9	= 18% of earnings
$1,722.22 per year	x 9	= $15,500 per year

- *Pension adjustment (PA)*
  If you belong to your employer's registered pension or deferred profit sharing

plan (DPSP), you will want to know something about a *pension adjustment* (PA). It is the amount of your employer's contribution to your plan for the year, subtracted from the maximum contribution you can make to your RRSP. The resulting figure, the amount you actually can contribute to your RRSP, is your PA. That amount is indicated on your T4 slip. The higher that amount, the lower your RRSP contribution.

The amount of your PA will depend on whether you are a member of a *defined benefit plan* (DBP) or a *defined contribution plan* (DCP). You are a member of the former if you know the exact amount of the pension benefit you will receive when you retire. The amount of your benefit from a DCP will not be known until you retire. That's because the contributions your employer makes will vary over the years; those contributions are invested, and the interest earned will also vary.

If you belong to a DPSP or a DCP and want to know your PA, your task is easy. Your DPSP PA is simply the amount your employer contributed during the past year. The amount of your PA under a DCP is also the amount your employer contributed or the total of your own and your employer's contributions.

Your PA for a DBP plan is different and more difficult to calculate. That's because it is based on a formula that sometimes challenges even accountants; it is also not based on your employer's contribution. It will help you to know that your PA will generally be higher than the value of the benefit you earn early in your career and lower than the benefit you earn later.

- *Past Service Pension Adjustment (PSPA)* These evolve whenever additional or increased past service benefits are

provided to members of a DBP for service in 1990 or later years. The calculations for this adjustment can be very complex and unique pertaining to a specific corporate employer's pension plan, therefore, should you receive a PSPA and desire more information, contact your human resource department.

Now calculate your sources of retirement income in Worksheet 16-5.

Begin Your Retirement Plan Today

All of the exercises you have completed in Chapters 15 and 16 will enable you to complete this final Worksheet to determine your retirement income in Table 16-6. This Worksheet will provide the answer to the question all future retirees ask—"Am I saving and investing enough?"

This Worksheet is designed for people of any age. When you complete the following 10 steps, you will have the numbers you need to start working toward a comfortable retirement today.

Don't be concerned that you're using 1994 dollars; the calculations are valid no matter what future inflation rates may be—although they do make the assumption that your savings and investments will give you a real rate of return of 3% (i.e., if inflation is running at 4%, you must make 7%). If you and your spouse are both earning, you should complete separate worksheets, although you'll probably want to pool the bottom lines to come up with your joint savings goal. Whatever your circumstances, it would also be a good idea to keep the Worksheet and go through the exercise again a year or three hence, both to adjust the calculations to your current income level and to monitor your progress.

Assume you can increase your RRSP contributions by 4% per year and aver-

WORKSHEET 16-5: YOUR RETIREMENT INCOME GOALS AND STRATEGIES

Source	Asset Value	INCOME Self	Spouse	Joint
Canada/Quebec Pension Plan (CPP/QPP)		$_____	$_____	$_____
Old Age Security (OAS)		_____	_____	_____
Guaranteed Income Supplement (GIS)		_____	_____	_____
Registered Pension Plan (RPP)		_____	_____	_____
Retiring Allowance		_____	_____	_____
Deferred Profit Sharing Plan (DPSP)	$_____	_____	_____	_____
Registered Retirement Savings Plan (RRSP)	_____	_____	_____	_____
Locked-In Retirement Account (LIRA)	_____	_____	_____	_____
Life Income Fund (LIF)	_____	_____	_____	_____
Annuities	_____	_____	_____	_____
Registered Retirement Income Fund (RRIF)	_____	_____	_____	_____
Personal Savings	_____	_____	_____	_____
Stocks and Bonds	_____	_____	_____	_____
Mutual Fund (withdrawal plans)	_____	_____	_____	_____
Real Estate	_____	_____	_____	_____
Life Insurance	_____	_____	_____	_____
Business Ownership	_____	_____	_____	_____
Other Investments	_____	_____	_____	_____
Total Asset Value	$_____			
Total Income		$_____	$_____	$_____
Less Estimated Taxes		$_____	$_____	$_____
Net Income After Tax		$_____	$_____	$_____

age 10% growth over 20 years prior to retirement. The multiplier to do this calculation is in Reference Table B. Find the multiplier under 4% inflation, 20 years, and at a 10% annual growth rate = .0117. Multiply this figure by your shortfall to find the annual contribution required this year and increasing by 4% each year in the future to offset inflation. Take a look at Worksheet 16-6 to follow these calculations and then look at the case profile for Maria Fernandez to see her retirement income requirements put into practice.

WORKSHEET 16-6: RETIREMENT INCOME REQUIREMENTS

Step 1	Estimate your current annual income before taxes.	$_____
Step 2	Estimate growth rate of your annual income to retirement.	$_____
Step 3	Estimate annual income you would like at retirement in today's terms (present value). *(Most retirees need 60% to 80% of final years' earnings before taxes.)*	$_____
Step 4	What are your future pension benefits?	

a) OAS *(current maximum benefit $4,630 at January 1, 1994).* $_____

b) CPP *(current maximum benefit $8,333 at January 1, 1994).* $_____

c) GIS *(current maximum benefit $5,502 at January 1, 1994).* $_____

d) Company Pension Plan (RPP/DPSP). *Ask your employer for an estimate in 1994 dollars.* $_____

e) Severance or retiring allowance. $_____

	Total Pension Benefits:	$_____
Step 5	Retirement income surplus or shortfall to be provided by RRSPs, savings, and investments. *(Subtract total of Step 4 from Step 3.)*	$_____
Step 6	Amount needed to save by retirement. *(Step 5 x multiplier in Table A)*	$_____
Step 7	Current value of savings, investments, and RRSPs.	$_____
Step 8	Future value of savings, investments, and RRSPs at retirement. *(Step 7 x multiplier in Table 1-3)*	$_____
Step 9	Surplus or shortfall. *(Step 6 minus Step 8)*	$_____
Step 10	Amount I need to save each year. *(Step 9 times multiplier from Table B)*	$_____

REFERENCE TABLE A

Age at which you plan to retire	MULTIPLIER A	
	Female	Male
55	27.4	22.3
56	26.6	21.5
57	25.7	20.7
58	24.9	19.9
59	24.0	19.2
60	23.2	18.4
61	22.3	17.7
62	21.5	17.0
63	20.7	16.3
64	19.9	15.6
65	19.1	14.9
66	18.3	14.2
67	17.6	13.6
68	16.8	13.0
69	16.1	12.4
70	15.3	11.8

REFERENCE TABLE B

		SAVINGS MULTIPLIER YEARLY GROWTH RATE		
Index	Years	8%	10%	12%
3%	5	.1273	.1212	.1154
	10	.0528	.0477	.0430
	15	.0275	.0234	.0199
	20	.0158	.0126	.0101
	25	.0095	.0072	.0053
	30	.0060	.0042	.0029
	35	.0038	.0025	.0016
4%	5	.1244	.1185	.1129
	10	.0505	.0457	.0413
	15	.0258	.0220	.0188
	20	.0145	.0117	.0094
	25	.0087	.0066	.0049
	30	.0053	.0038	.0027
	35	.0034	.0022	.0015
5%	5	.1216	.1159	.1105
	10	.0483	.0438	.0396
	15	.0241	.0207	.0177
	20	.0133	.0108	.0087
	25	.0078	.0060	.0045
	30	.0047	.0034	.0024
	35	.0029	.0020	.0013

Case Profile ⓬ **Maria Fernandez**

Name: Maria Fernandez   Current Age: 43   Retirement Age Goal: 60

Current Income: $42,000   Projected Annual Income Increases: 4%

Step 1	Estimate your current annual income before taxes.	$42,000
Step 2	Estimate growth rate of your annual income to retirement. *(Maria is currently age 43: Assume retirement at age 60. From Table 1-3 find factor where year 17 and 4% intersect—([1.95 x $42,000]).*	$81,900
Step 3	Estimate annual income you would like at retirement in today's terms (present value). *(Most retirees need 60% to 80% of final years' earnings before taxes. Maria projected her future income needs will be 70% of final years' earnings.) (.70 x $81,900)*	$57,330
Step 4	What are your future pension benefits?	
	a) OAS *($4,630 benefit will not be available to Maria due to clawback).* $0	
	b) CPP *($8,333 benefit indexed to offset inflation at 3% and CPP taken at age 65. From Table 1-3 find factor where year 22 and 3% intersect—[1.92 x $8,333]).* $15,999	
	c) GIS *($5,502 not applicable due to other income).* $0	
	d) Company Pension Plan (RPP/DPSP). *(Maria's company has estimated her pension at age 60 to be approximately 25% of final years' average)* $16,250	
	e) Severance or retiring allowance. $0	
	Total Pension Benefits:	$32,249
Step 5	Retirement income surplus or shortfall to be provided by RRSPs, savings, and investments. *(Subtract total of Step 4 from Step 3.)*	$25,081
Step 6	Amount needed to save by retirement. *(Step 5 x multiplier in Table A—[$25,081 x 23.2])*	$581,879
Step 7	Current value of savings, investments, and RRSPs.	$32,000
Step 8	Future value of savings, investments, and RRSPs at retirement. *(Step 7 x 22 years. From Table 1-3 find where 22 years and 10% intersect—[$32,000 x 8.14])*	$260,480
Step 9	Surplus or shortfall. *(Step 6 minus Step 8)*	– $321,399
Step 10	Amount I need to save each year. *(Step 9 times multiplier from Table B. Assume 4% inflation, 20 years, and 10% annual growth rate —[$321,399 x .0117])*	$3,767

Registered Retirement Savings Plans

Registered Retirement Savings Plans are an effective way to save while enjoying the benefits of tax-sheltered compounding. But they are savings plans. To accumulate significant wealth, you must invest.

Registered Retirement Savings Plans

In 1957, the Federal Government created an ideal savings shelter for Canadian taxpayers called a *Registered Retirement Savings Plan* (RRSP). The objective of the RRSP legislation is to help retired Canadians live comfortably by allowing them to supplement their income by using savings that have accumulated in a tax-sheltered plan prior to retirement.

The RRSP is a procedural investment tool that allows Canadians the opportunity to enjoy tax-sheltered compounding in order to amass a substantial pool of retirement capital. The income earned inside an RRSP is tax-deferred until removed at retirement by way of a cash withdrawal or payments from a Registered Retirement Income Fund (RRIF), Life Income Fund (LIF), or annuity. These maturity options are designed to allow a systematic flow of taxable income over the remainder of your lifetime.

The cornerstone of most successful retirement plans is an RRSP, or a company pension plan supplemented with an RRSP. RRSPs are easily the most widely-used procedural tool for funding your retirement beyond company and government pensions. Many types of RRSPs exist, but common to all is the fact that contributions are sheltered from current taxation.

For example, assume $1,000 is contributed to RRSPs by individuals with marginal tax rates of 30%, 40%, and 45%. The tax savings are:

	30%	40%	45%
Contribution	$1,000	$1,000	$1,000
Tax savings	300	400	450
After-tax cost	$700	$600	$550

RRSP funds are managed by banks, trust companies, life insurance companies, mutual fund companies, and investment

There is a tide in the affairs of men, which, taken at the flood, leads on to fortune...

William Shakespeare

The Major Benefits of RRSPs

Reap big rewards with years of *Tax-Free Compounding*

Reduce your *Taxable Income* and *Defer Income Tax*

Shelter your Retirement *Savings Growth*

Prepare yourself for a Financially *Secure Retirement*

dealers, and the funds are administered by a trustee licensed to issue these plans. Interest, dividends, and capital gains are added to the original contribution without current personal income tax being deducted.

Earnings on the money are not taxed while they are in the particular plan and, therefore, an RRSP can grow much more rapidly than a taxable savings program. When you do eventually draw from such funds, the amount will be taxable, but since you will have reached retirement age, you will most likely be in a lower tax bracket than when you were working and so the overall tax you will pay at that time will be reduced.

If you are a Canadian taxpayer with an earned income, you can open an RRSP up to and including December 31st of the year in which you are to turn age 71. You may contribute to more than one RRSP so long as your total investment does not exceed your annual contribution limit. Contributions can be made for 60 days beyond year-end. Thus contributions made in January and February can be applied to the current year or the previous year.

There are a number of important guidelines for you to consider when establishing an RRSP.

Contribution Limits for 1994
For individuals who are not members of a Registered Pension Plan (RPP) or Deferred Profit Sharing Plan (DPSP) the limits, subject to 18% of earned income for the preceding year, are $13,500.

For individuals who are members of an RPP or DPSP the limits are based on earned income for the preceding year and is decreased by your pension adjustment (PA) for the same year. The PA is obtained from your employer and reflects the benefit accruing to you based on contributions to your employer's plan. PAs are reported in Box 52 on the employee's T4 slip.

Earned Income
Contribution limits are subject to an *earned income test*. The main components of earned income are:
- net salary or wages
- disability pension benefits, CPP/QPP
- supplementary unemployment benefit plan receipts (but not UIC benefits)
- net income from a business carried on by a self-employed individual or by an active partner of a partnership, less losses
- net rental income from real property (less rental losses)
- alimony or maintenance received (subtract alimony or maintenance paid)
- certain royalties, supplementary unemployment benefits, net research grants.

Excluded from earned income calculations are:
- dividends
- interest
- capital gains
- other investment income
- superannuation or pension benefits
- family allowances
- unemployment insurance benefits
- retiring allowance
- death benefits
- amounts received from an RRSP
- taxable amounts from a DPSP

Excess Contributions
Excess contributions are subject to a penalty of 1% per month on the amount that exceeds the greater of $8,000 and your annual contribution limit.

Excess contributions can be removed with Revenue Canada approval in the year that the Notice of Assessment is received, or in the following year.

For Some, An RRSP Over-contribution Can Pay
If you're like many Canadians, you used to participate in one of the rites of winter—contributing more to your RRSP

I've been poor and I've been rich. Rich is better!

Sophie Tucker

WORKSHEET 17-1: 1994 RRSP CONTRIBUTION WORKSHEET

Step 1   Calculate 1993 Unused Contribution Limit

Your 1993 RRSP contribution limit $_____

    MINUS: Your RRSP contribution in 1993 $_____

    EQUALS: Your 1993 unused RRSP contribution limit $_____

Step 2   Your 1994 Contribution Limit Calculation

Your 1993 unused RRSP contribution limit $_____

    PLUS:

        ❶ *18% of 1993 earned income* $_____

        ❷ *1994 RRSP dollar limit* $_____

        ❸ *lessor of* ❶ *and* ❷ $_____

    MINUS:

        ❹ *1993 pension adjustment (PA)* $_____

        ❺ *1993 past service pension adjustment (PSPA)* $_____

    EQUALS: 1994 RRSP Contributions ❸ – ❹ – ❺ $_____

than you were allowed. The reason? Calculations so challenging that it was hard to figure out your limit. Moreover, you paid a price—a penalty for over-contributing. Revenue Canada officially recognized the problem in 1991, when it said taxpayers could contribute $8,000 more to their RRSPs than allowed during their lifetime. Contributions over $8,000 will be penalized 1% per month until withdrawn.

An over-contribution is appealing. The interest you can earn compounds and accumulates tax free, like the money already in your RRSP. Though you can't deduct your over-contribution when you make it, you can carry it forward seven years and deduct it during that time. If you can't carry it forward, you'll end up paying a double tax—there is no upfront deduction when you put the money into the RRSP (it's after-tax money) and you'll be taxed again when you withdraw it. You can neutralize the second tax by leaving your over-contribution in until the interest earned starts to exceed the tax payable. That will depend on the prevailing interest rates and your marginal tax rate. The higher your marginal tax rate, the less time you'll need for tax-free compounding to work. As a guideline, you'll need to leave your contribution in for a period of 10 to 14 years.

Two of the more favourable situations for making an over-contribution occur at different times: When you're relatively young and have at least 15 years of compounding ahead of you; or when you're about to retire you can make a contribution based on your income in your last year of work by using the over-contribution room instead of drawing on your cash resources.

Two final points to consider: If you're considering splitting your income, you may over-contribute to your own plan and another $8,000 to a spousal plan and an additional $8,000 to each of your children who are over age 18. Revenue Canada introduced this age requirement to prevent parents and grandparents from giving money to minors who would simply put the fund in a tax-sheltered RRSP. The attribution rules should not apply if you lend money to your spouse or children because there would be no taxable income generated by the gift.

TABLE 17-2: CONTRIBUTION LIMITS 1994 AND FUTURE YEARS

RRSP contribution limits are subject to 18% of prior year's earned income. The unused portion of contribution limits can be carried forward for up to 7 years. Beginning in 1994 the proposed changes to contribution levels are:

Year	No RPP	Defined Benefit RPP	Money Purchase RPP
1994	$13,500	Limits will be calculated for you based on the terms of the plan.	RRSP limits will reflect employer and employee contributions to the RPP.
1995	$14,500		
1996	$15,500		
1997	INDEXED TO GROWTH IN THE AVERAGE INDUSTRIAL WAGE.		

Qualified Investments

This includes all government bonds, corporate bonds, banker's acceptance, warrants for property investments, listed limited partnership units, listed common and convertible and preferred shares, Canadian covered call options, and qualified mutual funds.

Foreign content can be 20% based on book value. Book value is the sum of the cost price of securities held plus cash. It is not the market value of the plan.

Non-Qualified Investments

Examples of non-qualified investments are precious metals, certain installment receipts, unlisted stocks, foreign stocks not listed in the U.S., U.K., or France, and foreign bonds.

On Death of the RRSP Holder

If the annuitant dies prior to maturity, the RRSP can be transferred to the surviving spouse's RRSP. A surviving spouse can use any of the retirement options that were available to the deceased.

If there is no spouse, but there are dependant children or grandchildren, the proceeds can be taxed in their hands subject to a maximum of $5,000 x 26 less the age of the dependant.

If there is no spouse or dependants, the market value of the RRSP must be included as taxable income in the last return of the deceased. The proceeds then form part of the estate.

Special Rollovers of Retirement Income

There are several types of income sources eligible for rollover to an RRSP on a tax-free basis in addition to the regular contributions allowed by RRSP legislation:

- Direct transfer between RRSPs (use form T2033)
- Direct transfer of lump sum RPP/DPSP benefits to RRSP/LIRA (use form T2151)
- Rollover of an RRSP refund of premiums at death to RRSP of a surviving spouse
- Direct transfer of an RRSP/RRIF to RRSP of an ex-spouse on marriage breakdown (use form T2220)
- Direct transfer of a commuted amount from a RRIF to an RRSP (or annuity if over age 71)
- Rollover of a retiring allowance to an RRSP (maximum $2,000 per year or part year of service with an employer; plus $1,500 for each year or part year of service prior to 1989 if employee was not covered by benefits from RPP/DPSP

Tax Shelters Provide an Extra Edge

Assume you are an investor in a 50% tax bracket and that you have $1,000 of income available for an investment offering a 12% return.

	Investment (Unsheltered)	RRSP (Sheltered)
Earned Income $1000	$1,000	$1,000
Income Taxes (50%)	500	
Available for Investment	500	1,000
Compound @ 6% for 30 years	$41,900	$270,290

As you can see, the $1,000 investment in the RRSP is compounding at 12%, and provides a six times greater return than

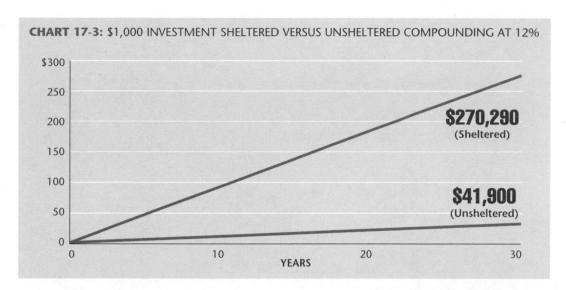

CHART 17-3: $1,000 INVESTMENT SHELTERED VERSUS UNSHELTERED COMPOUNDING AT 12%

$270,290
(Sheltered)

$41,900
(Unsheltered)

YEARS

the unsheltered investment after 30 years. The unsheltered funds available for investment each year are $500 after-tax and at 12% would produce $60 income the first year. However, the income would also be taxable each year and assuming a 50% tax rate, the net effective compound rate of return would be 6% for the 30 years, or $41,900. Of course, the funds accumulated in the RRSP will become taxable as they are taken out at maturity. Even so, your investment will be worth over three times more, even after taxes, than the same investment outside an RRSP. And that is all due to years of tax-sheltered compounding.

Are You Getting Enough from Your RRSP?

Assume an annual contribution of $1,000 in each of the following savings and investment vehicles. Chart 17-4 suggests what a typical experience during the last thirty years might have been like, using various types of securities.

The performance of your RRSP is very important to your financial success. For many Canadians, their RRSP is the only major tool they use to accumulate wealth, outside of owning their home.

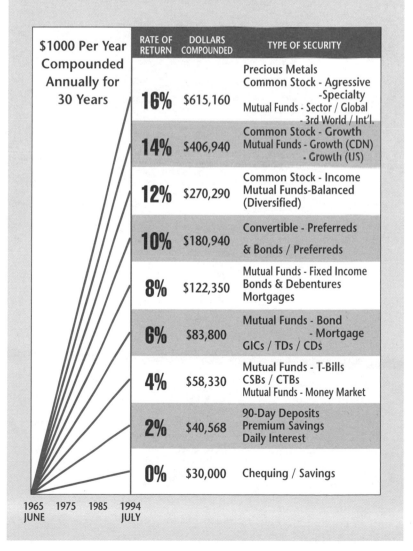

CHART 17-4: SAVINGS AND INVESTMENT RETURNS—30 YEARS
$1000 PER YEAR COMPOUNDED ANNUALLY

$1000 Per Year Compounded Annually for 30 Years	RATE OF RETURN	DOLLARS COMPOUNDED	TYPE OF SECURITY
	16%	$615,160	Precious Metals Common Stock - Agressive -Specialty Mutual Funds - Sector / Global - 3rd World / Int'l.
	14%	$406,940	Common Stock - Growth Mutual Funds - Growth (CDN) - Growth (US)
	12%	$270,290	Common Stock - Income Mutual Funds-Balanced (Diversified)
	10%	$180,940	Convertible - Preferreds & Bonds / Preferreds
	8%	$122,350	Mutual Funds - Fixed Income Bonds & Debentures Mortgages
	6%	$83,800	Mutual Funds - Bond - Mortgage GICs / TDs / CDs
	4%	$58,330	Mutual Funds - T-Bills CSBs / CTBs Mutual Funds - Money Market
	2%	$40,568	90-Day Deposits Premium Savings Daily Interest
	0%	$30,000	Chequing / Savings

1965 1975 1985 1994
JUNE JULY

TABLE 17-5: HOW MUCH COULD YOU EARN IN YOUR RRSP WITH EQUAL ANNUAL DEPOSITS CALCULATED AT VARIOUS RATES?

Future Worth of $1,000 Invested Each Year at Varying Rates, Annual Compounding

End of Year	4%	6%	8%	10%	12%	14%	16%
5	5,630	5,980	6,340	6,720	7,120	7,540	7,980
10	12,490	13,970	15,650	17,530	19,650	22,040	24,730
15	20,820	24,670	29,320	34,950	41,750	49,980	59,930
20	30,970	38,990	49,420	63,000	80,700	103,770	133,840
25	43,310	58,160	78,950	108,180	149,330	207,330	289,090
30	58,330	83,800	122,350	180,940	270,290	406,740	615,160
35	76,600	118,120	186,100	298,130	483,460	790,670	1,300,030
40	98,830	164,050	279,780	486,850	859,140	1,529,910	2,738,480

Future Worth of $4,000 Invested Each Year at Varying Rates, Annual Compounding

End of Year	4%	6%	8%	10%	12%	14%	16%
5	22,520	23,920	25,360	26,880	28,480	30,160	31,920
10	49,960	55,880	62,600	70,120	78,600	88,160	98,920
15	83,280	98,680	117,280	139,800	167,000	199,920	239,720
20	123,880	155,960	197,680	252,000	322,800	415,080	535,360
25	173,240	232,640	315,800	432,720	597,320	829,320	1,156,360
30	233,320	335,200	489,400	723,760	1,081,160	1,626,960	2,460,640
35	306,400	472,480	744,400	1,192,520	1,933,840	3,162,680	5,200,120
40	395,320	656,200	1,119,120	1,947,400	3,436,560	6,119,640	10,953,920

Future Worth of $7,500 Invested Each Year at Varying Rates, Annual Compounding

End of Year	4%	6%	8%	10%	12%	14%	16%
5	42,225	44,850	47,550	50,400	53,400	56,550	59,850
10	93,675	104,775	117,375	131,475	147,375	165,300	185,475
15	156,150	185,025	219,900	262,125	313,125	374,850	449,475
20	232,275	292,425	370,650	472,500	605,250	778,275	1,003,800
25	324,825	436,200	592,125	811,350	1,119,975	1,554,975	2,168,175
30	437,475	628,500	917,625	1,357,050	2,027,175	3,050,550	4,613,700
35	574,500	885,900	1,395,750	2,235,975	3,625,950	5,930,025	9,750,225
40	741,225	1,230,375	2,098,350	3,651,375	6,443,550	11,474,325	20,538,600

The RRSP Calculator

Contributions to your RRSP should be made as soon as possible within the current tax year. You must not procrastinate or delay—you want time working for you immediately.

The exercise I illustrate in my seminars uses rates of return of 9%, 10%, and 11%. Why? Because I know that, if you allocate assets in a balanced approach to each of the major categories of reserves, fixed income, and growth, these returns are attainable.

I use the example of $1,000 as an annual contribution earning a rate of return of 10% to illustrate the lost opportunity of accumulating an extra $4,200 by starting at age 51 instead of age 50.

Using this same exercise and delaying your $1,000 contribution from age 30 to 31, the lost opportunity amounts to $28,000, based on a $1,000 contribution for the year at a rate of 10% if compounded for 35 years from age 30 to age 65. Can you imagine what the lost opportunities will amount to, considering that RRSP annual contribution levels will be increasing to $15,500 over the next few years!

Building Capital for Your Future

What rate of return have you been getting in your RRSP? Is it enough? An RRSP is the ideal procedural tool to complement your other pension plans for your retirement, so work it for all it's worth. Assess your expected income needs in terms of today's dollars and remember to build inflation into your calculations. Strive for a rate of growth in excess of what you anticipate inflation will be.

Can you reposition your investment to improve your return? Consider the difference an additional 5% return can mean over time when you restructure your investment to earn a 15% return instead of 10%. See Table 17-7.

TABLE 17-7: $3,000 RRSP CONTRIBUTIONS COMPOUNDED ANNUALLY AT 10% AND 15%

Years	10%	15%
10	$47,820	$60,900
20	111,810	307,820
30	493,470	1,304,250
40	1,327,770	5,337,270

Table Guide

Assume you were making $4,000 contributions each year to your RRSP from age 45 to age 65 at the end of each year compounding at 12%. If you were to make your RRSP contribution at the beginning of each year instead of the end, you would accumulate an additional $38,600. Under Contribution level of $4,000 find 20 year line at 12% = $38,600. This figure is the opportunity cost of delaying contributions to the end of each year instead of making them at the beginning of each year.

TABLE 17-6: COST OF PROCRASTINATING BY CONTRIBUTING TO YOUR RRSP AT THE END OF THE YEAR VERSUS BEGINNING OF THE YEAR

Contribution	Compounded Years	8%	10%	12%	15%
$1,000	10	$2,160	$2,590	$3,100	$4,050
	20	4,670	6,730	9,650	16,370
	30	10,060	17,450	29,960	66,210
$4,000	10	8,640	10,360	12,400	16,200
	20	18,680	26,920	38,600	65,480
	30	40,240	69,800	119,840	264,840
$7,500	10	16,200	19,425	23,250	30,375
	20	35,025	50,475	72,375	122,775
	30	75,450	130,875	224,700	496,575

TABLE 17-8: HOW TO HAVE A $1 MILLION RRSP

Current Age	CURRENT RRSP AMOUNT PLUS ANNUAL CONTRIBUTIONS OF				
	$3,500	$4,500	$5,500	$6,500	$7,500
26	$2000				
27	6000				
28	11000				
29	16000	$5000			
30	21000	11000			
31	27000	17000	$6000		
32	34000	23000	13000	$3000	
33	41000	31000	20000	10000	
34	49000	39000	28000	18000	$8000
35	57000	47000	37000	27000	17000
36	67000	57000	47000	37000	27000
37	77000	68000	58000	48000	38000
38	89000	79000	70000	60000	50000
39	102000	92000	83000	73000	64000
40	116000	107000	97000	88000	78000
41	131000	122000	113000	104000	94000
42	148000	139000	130000	121000	112000
43	167000	158000	149000	140000	132000
44	188000	179000	170000	162000	153000
45	210000	202000	193000	185000	177000
46	235000	227000	219000	211000	203000
47	262000	255000	247000	239000	231000
48	292000	285000	277000	270000	262000
49	325000	318000	311000	304000	297000
50	362000	355000	348000	342000	335000

Table Guide

As an example, a person 45 years of age with approximately $202,000 in an RRSP would be able to accumulate $1 million by age 60 with annual contributions of $4,500.

How to Have a $1 Million RRSP

How much do you need in your RRSP now along with annual contributions to accumulate $1 million by age 60?

This is shown in Table 17-8 for ages 26 to 50. The amounts given are what you currently should have, along with the necessary annual contributions each year to age 60, invested at 10%, to reach $1 million.

Home Sweet Home—Should You Raid Your RRSP?

The government's last budget has extended the RRSP assisted Home Buyer's Plan indefinitely. The Home Buyer's Plan is restricted to first time buyers and allows you to borrow $20,000 per individual ($40,000 per

couple). The loan must be repaid interest free over a period not exceeding 15 years. Loan payments not made as required are included in the taxpayer's income.

A downside of this plan is that a taxpayer taking advantage of its provisions is not permitted to deduct contributions to an RRSP in the year that the funds are withdrawn.

Both newly built and existing homes qualify. The home cannot be previously owned by you or your spouse and you cannot have owned any other principal residence within five years of making an RRSP withdrawal.

Your RRSP is paid back the funds you borrow based on $1/15$ each year.

Amount Borrowed	Annual Payback	Monthly Payback
$5,000	$333.33	$27.78
$10,000	$666.67	$55.56
$15,000	$1,000.00	$83.33
$20,000	$1,333.33	$111.11

The opportunity cost of removing funds from the RRSP can be substantial. If you removed $20,000 from your RRSP that otherwise would have remained intact earning at a rate of 10% compounding tax free, it would have grown to $83,600. The $20,000 borrowed and paid back over 15 years would grow to $48,587 a difference of $35,014. Of course in a hot real estate market it could also become a profitable venture. I personally would have a rough time raiding my future retirement funds. If at all possible you should leave your RRSP intact. Most analysts would agree with this statement. In the final analysis it is a lifestyle decision.

Should I Pay Down My Mortgage or Buy a RRSP?

In a word—both! This is probably the question most often asked in our semi-

Case Profile ⓭ Kristine Wozniak

Kristine Wozniak, age 37, has $45,000 invested in her RRSP currently growing at a rate of 12% per year. What would be the real cost of borrowing $20,000 interest free from her RRSP to make a downpayment on a home?

Answer: $50,213

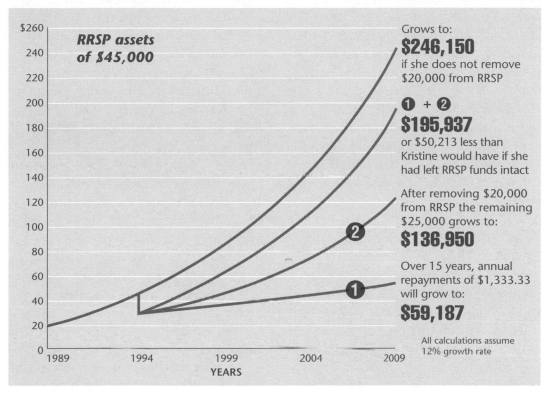

RRSP assets of $45,000

Grows to:
$246,150
if she does not remove $20,000 from RRSP

❶ + ❷
$195,937
or $50,213 less than Kristine would have if she had left RRSP funds intact

After removing $20,000 from RRSP the remaining $25,000 grows to:
$136,950

Over 15 years, annual repayments of $1,333.33 will grow to:
$59,187

All calculations assume 12% growth rate

YEARS

nars. And the ideal answer is to do both if possible. The solution to the question is twofold because it is both a financial and a lifestyle decision.

Let's start with the financial decision. As a generalization when interest rates are high, the stock market is lower. Similarly, bond prices move in an inverse relationship to interest rates (see Chart 6-2 in Chapter six).

Scenario 1: Assume you have a mortgage at 12% on your home, you're in a 40% tax bracket, and you only have $1,000 of disposable income: "What should you do?" We'll further assume that guaranteed investment certificates are yielding 10.5% for a 5-year term. I would probably pay down my mortgage in this scenario because in order to make a 12% mortgage payment with after-tax dollars I would have to earn 20% pre-tax.

Scenario 2: Imagine you have a mortgage at 7%, you're in a 40% tax bracket, interest rates have been declining and look as if they are headed even lower, and you have only $1,000 disposable income: "What should you do?" We'll further assume that guaranteed investment certificates are yielding 6% for a 5-year term. If this were my only choice, I might still pay down the mortgage. However, if I were intending to purchase an equity based product for my RRSP, I would more likely make the RRSP deposit. When interest rates have been low, historically, the stock market has produced double digit returns. As well, I would receive a tax reduction reflecting my 40% tax bracket, years of tax-free compounding, and tax deferral until the funds were withdrawn long into the future.

The lifestyle decision is based on age and your investment personality. If you are under age 40, put the maximum into your RRSP and if you are over age 40, pay down the mortgage first. In the latter case try to make up the RRSP payments within the seven year carry-forward period. The Investment Personality Questionnaire you answered in Chapter seven will give you a further hint about the lifestyle decision. If you were a risk-avoider personality you would automatically pay down the mortgage; whereas a risk-minimizer or risk-blender might lean more to a pure financial decision.

Why You Should Consider a Spousal RRSP

The monies put into the plan for your spouse in a spousal RRSP enable your spouse to have a pension at retirement and enables him/her to participate in the $1,000 pension credit at age 65. Spousal RRSPs provide many very important benefits:

- At retirement, the money in the RRSP belongs to your spouse, and therefore will create a second taxable income. This means two lower tax brackets instead of a single higher one
- By income splitting with your spouse using an RRSP, your high income may drop into a lower tax bracket
- You obtain the tax credit regardless of whose name the contribution is made in

- The spousal option can also be used, as a means of balancing the family income at retirement, when both spouses are working
- When you reach the age of 71, you can contribute to your spousal RRSP until your spouse also reaches 71, providing you have earned income
- If the spousal plan is deregistered within three years of the last contribution to any spousal plan, the income is attributed to the contributing spouse.

RRSPs — A Formula For Financial Independence

Perhaps the greatest opportunity Canadians have is the ability to ensure their financial independence. Yet statistics have shown that less than 50% of Canadians participate in the annual rites of winter.

Our seminars and workshops are mainly sponsored by companies that have a higher end range of benefits including a corporate pension plan (RPP) for their employees.

We have solicited information in our seminars showing that over 80% of the participants have made RRSP contributions within the last few years. Therefore, the same people who are covered by a (RPP) are also topping up their RRSPs when they have additional contribution room.

Conclusion
In the future there will be an even greater disparity between those who "have" and "have not".

RRSP Maturity Options

*Registered Retirement Income Funds can offset the
double wallop inflation delivers at retirement.*

Your Options When Your RRSP Matures

When you use an RRSP as a procedural tool to obtain the benefits of tax-sheltered compounding, you will accumulate a substantial pool of capital at retirement. Unlike an RPP with your employer, your RRSP has greater flexibility. It provides three options at retirement, often called your *maturity options:*

- Withdraw the funds and pay tax
- Purchase an annuity
- Set up a Registered Retirement Income Fund (RRIF).

The timing of this decision can be at any age prior to age 71. When you are making this decision, ask yourself these questions:

- What is my life expectancy?
- What is my present age and how is my health?
- What resources do I have in addition to my pension plans?
- Am I going to plan an estate for my beneficiaries?
- What are the income tax implications of each of my options?
- What are the effects of inflation on each of those options?

It is imperative that you weigh your RRSP maturity options carefully. The wrong decision can result in substantial losses in income and higher taxes throughout your lifetime. It can adversely affect the financial security of your surviving spouse and dependants and deny beneficiaries the opportunity to inherit any funds remaining in your estate.

The timing of your RRSP maturity decisions can also have a tremendous bearing on your financial security; the overall economic and market conditions when you make your selection will have a significant impact on the amount of income you receive.

Interest rates and inflation can have an effect on your maturity selection for the rest of your life. Once you have made your decision with regard to your maturing RRSP, it is irrevocable. All the more reason to give careful consideration to the selection of the appropriate option for your circumstances. There is an increasing trend today towards a combination of maturity options, with regard to annuities and RRIFs, taken at different times over a few years on either side of your official retirement date.

> Life shrinks or expands in proportion to one's courage.
>
> **Anaïs Nin**

Cash Withdrawal

First, let's look at cashing in your RRSP. The cash alternative for your RRSP makes sense only if you have a very small amount of money built up in the plan, and you drop from a very high bracket to a lower income bracket at retirement. It may be prudent for you to take out the money in a lump sum, or spread it out over four or five years, taking it out a little at a time.

The *cash withdrawal* option is available at any age. However, the entire amount of cash withdrawal is subject to tax in the year that the money is withdrawn, and will be taxed at your top tax marginal rate. In addition, you will not receive the full amount when withdrawn, because a certain percentage of tax must be withheld by the trustee for remittance to Revenue Canada.

Should you fail to select a retirement income option by the end of the year in which you reach age 71, the entire amount of your RRSP will be taxed as income in the following year.

TABLE 18-1: WITHHOLDING TAX

The provincial and federal governments require tax to be deducted from all lump sum withdrawals at source. The withholding tax rates are:

Lump Sum Withdrawal	QUEBEC		ALL OTHER PROVINCES
	Federal	Provincial	Federal & Provincial
$0 – $5,000	5%	16%	10%
$5,001 – $15,000	10%	20%	20%
$15,001 & over	15%	20%	30%

Annuity Alternatives

By far the most popular maturity alternative since the inception of the RRSP in 1957 has been the annuity. Why do most investors choose the *annuity alternative?* The vast majority of RRSPs are invested in fixed-income securities. If you do that throughout your working years, it is a natural transition to look at a fixed income return in an annuity—even though the interest rate may be lower than is available with other investments.

Annuity Defined

An *annuity* is a contract that provides periodic payments to the purchaser for life or for a specified period of time. The financial institution selling the contract reinvests the funds and provides the purchaser with periodic payments. These are normally paid monthly, but can be quarterly, annually, or at whatever intervals are agreed upon by the purchaser and issuer.

Each payment consists of an interest portion and a principal portion, the latter being a return of part of the funds used to purchase the annuity. This is very similar to the mortgage on a house that combines interest and principal payments over a long amortization period.

All payments received from annuities purchased with registered money from an RRSP are fully taxable. No tax is paid when you purchase the annuity. Moving funds from an RRSP into an annuity is treated as a "tax-free rollover" by Revenue Canada.

Annuity Choices

The selection of an annuity involves many complex choices. The major alternatives are as follows:

- Single or Joint Annuity
- Life or Term Certain Annuity to age 90
- No Guarantee Period / Guaranteed Period 5–, 10–, 15 years
- Annuity increased by 4% to offset inflation
- Joint Annuity which decreases when one spouse passes away
- Increased annuity payment if in bad health

Single or Joint Annuity

A contract to purchase a *single annuity* is based on your age. Payments of interest and principal are calculated on your projected life expectancy defined by mortality statistics. The monthly, quarterly, or annual income stream is guaranteed for the lifetime of the annuitant. The payments cease at death whether you live one year or 30 years from the day you sign the contract. The insurance company simply pools the rest of the money to fund other annuities for people who live longer. For this reason, single annuities are rarely purchased.

A *joint and last survivor annuity* is purchased in the name of two people, usually the annuitant and her/his spouse. Income from the annuity is paid as long as either spouse lives, and ceases when the second person dies. The income generally is reduced after the death of the first annuitant. Joint annuities are very popular for couples, because of the lifetime guarantee factor. They do not, however, leave estate benefits.

Life or Term-Certain Annuity to Age 90

Since annuities are structured on a payment system based on life expectancy, only life insurance companies may issue life annuities. Payments on a *life annuity* are guaranteed for the lifetime of the annuitant.

Term-certain annuities, on the other hand, may be issued by life insurance companies or trust companies. This type of annuity distributes the interest and principal evenly over a specified number of years to age 90. Payments are reduced due to the long guarantee period. At the annuitant's death, the balance of interest and principal payments are "commuted," or valued in terms of the worth of a dollar at the time of death, and become part of the annuitant's estate.

No Guarantee Period/Guarantee Period

If an annuitant has no family or ultimate beneficiaries to consider, then a *no-guarantee life annuity* is attractive because it produces the largest amount of monthly income of all forms of annuities. In most cases, however, you have a spouse and dependants whom you want to consider in your estate planning, so an annuity with a guarantee period is the best choice.

The longer the *guarantee period* chosen, the less income the annuity will pay. 5–, 10–, and 15–year guarantee periods are most common, but 20 years or to age 90 can also be selected. If you choose a 15-year guarantee period with monthly payments, the annuity will make those payments until your death, then commute the value of the remaining payments for the guaranteed period to a specified beneficiary or the estate. This option is attractive for annuitants who have a lesser need for cash flow, and who prefer to leave a larger estate for their ultimate beneficiaries.

Annuity Increased by 4% to Offset Inflation

Indexed annuities provide lower income in the early years and larger payments in the later years, increasing to a maximum of 4% per year to help offset inflation. This is a popular inflation hedge technique that can be combined with the other annuity choices we have discussed so far.

Joint Annuity Which Decreases When One Spouse Passes Away

A *joint life-and-last-survivor annuity* pays income for the lifetime of two people. Instead of receiving equal payments until the death of the second person, you can receive larger payments until the death of the first spouse and reduced payments for the lifetime of the second spouse. The reasoning behind this choice is that because one person can live more cheaply than two, less money will be required when one spouse dies. A common selection is to reduce payments by 50% after the death of the first spouse.

Increased Annuity Payment if in Bad Health

Most life insurance companies will offer a substandard health life annuity with higher payments to an applicant in poor health. Be sure you make full disclosure of your health to your insurance agent or annuity broker when you apply for this type of annuity.

When you reach age 65, your annuity might increase if you are considered to be in bad health. Insurance companies do this because you are a poor health risk on their books according to mortality tables. They respond by increasing your annuity payments based upon a "set back" in age.

Substandard payments only apply to life annuities. Be aware that the increases may not even be worth consideration on some annuities. Normally, this option is most appealing for straight life annuities.

Life Annuity Comparisons

To summarize the complexity of annuity options, let's look at a series of comparisons for a male age 65, based on a $50,000 lump sum maturing in an RRSP. Each of these options is illustrated in Table 18-9.

Life Annuity—No Guarantee

For a male age 65, an annuity of $50,000 with *no guaranteed term* provides $5,486 annually, based on current annuity rates. It is a lifetime annuity only and stops at death.

Assume a man starts receiving his annuity at age 65 and passes away at age 68. He has received three years of payments at $5,486 a year or just under $16,500 of his $50,000 original principal. The life insurance company pockets the remainder.

The life annuity with no guaranteed payment is based on life expectancy tables for men and women over the age of 65. Whatever the magic number, the insurance company relates it to the interest rates at the time the annuity is purchased, to arrive at the payment. The man who dies three years into his contract ends up "losing" so to speak. Live to be 100 and you "win."

Life Annuity—10–Year Guarantee

For a male age 65, an annuity of $50,000 with a *10–year guarantee* will provide a payment of $4,970 annually. The guarantee period is 10 years. Payments stop at death. He must accept a smaller annuity payment because of the guaranteed term.

In this example, the man buys an annuity providing $4,970 annually. As in the last example, he dies at age 68, having received about $15,000. The life insurance company commutes the remaining payments for the next seven years of the guarantee period to age 75 and calculates their present value back to the date of death. The commuted value then becomes part of his estate.

Term Certain Annuity—Age 90

A trust company's *Term Certain Annuity* to age 90 for $50,000 delivers a payment of $4,348 annually to a male age 65. This figure is significantly less than the previous example but does guarantee payment to age 90. If he dies at age 68 and has had only three years of payments, or about $13,000, all remaining payments are commuted back to the date of death and form part of his estate.

Joint Life Annuity— 15–Year Guarantee

One of the most popular choices of annuities is a *Joint Life Annuity*. A Joint Annuity is a lifetime annuity that stops only after

is a lifetime annuity that stops only after both partners have passed away.

Let's look again at an annuity of $50,000, guaranteed for a term of 15 years, on a 65-year old male and his spouse. This annuity pays $4,033 annually and the guaranteed payment period runs for 15 years. If the husband dies at age 68, the $4,033 keeps coming to his wife each year as long as she lives. If she dies at age 76, the last four years of that guarantee to age 80 are commuted back to her date of death and form part of her estate.

Annuity Comparison Summary

By comparing various annuity alternatives and options, we saw annual annuity payments for the same individual ranging from $5,486 to $4,033. The ultimate annuity payment depends upon the "bells and whistles" included in the annuity contract. Two other annuity options that are often considered are a life annuity guaranteed to age 90, and a joint life annuity with no guarantee.

The most common selection is a joint-life annuity with a 15-year guarantee period. While there are many other options

for consideration, the 15–year guaranteed annuity ensures that:

- Either spouse will receive the annuity income for as long as either one is alive
- Should both spouses die before the 15-year guarantee period expires, the remaining commuted value is paid to the estate of the last survivor.

It is important to note that the annuity alternative can limit many of the benefits you may have had during the years you accumulated funds in your RRSP. Inflation protection and the lack of growth and flexibility are the major deterrents to the annuity alternative.

The RRIF Opportunity

A *Registered Retirement Income Fund* (RRIF) is a contract that provides periodic payments from the commencement date until death or until the funds are depleted. Historically, RRIFs were fixed on a formula basis that provided very little flexibility. Recently, the government has provided a great many new options:

- All RRIFs are created by the transfer of assets from RRSPs or other RRIFs and a person can own more than one RRIF

Good instincts usually tell you what to do long before your head has figured it out.
Michael Burke

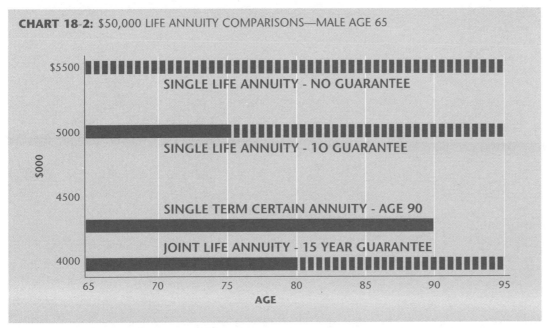

CHART 18-2: $50,000 LIFE ANNUITY COMPARISONS—MALE AGE 65

SINGLE LIFE ANNUITY - NO GUARANTEE

SINGLE LIFE ANNUITY - 10 GUARANTEE

SINGLE TERM CERTAIN ANNUITY - AGE 90

JOINT LIFE ANNUITY - 15 YEAR GUARANTEE

$000

AGE

- There is no limit on the RRIF payment each year, subject to a minimum withdrawal that is based on the person's age subtracted from age 90 until the RRIF holder reaches age 71 at which time a minimum formula, as established by the government, kicks in (see Table 18-3)
- A RRIF continues to allow the tax-free accumulation of funds until withdrawn which means the tax-shelter features of your RRSP continues for many years
- You get to choose how your retirement funds are invested
- You may start your RRIF payments immediately rather than waiting until the next calendar year after purchase
- There is no more minimum RRIF age stipulation. Previously, you had to make this decision between age 60 and 71.

One of the major benefits of a RRIF selection is that you retain flexibility in your investment decisions. A RRIF is similar to an RRSP; in fact, most of the rules are the same in terms of the investments that can be held in the plan. The major difference is that the RRSP is a procedural tool for accumulating and investing assets tax-free, whereas the RRIF is a procedural tool that may also invest assets tax-free until withdrawn. The RRIF may include growth investments unlike the annuity, which is based on fixed income returns.

Historically, RRIFs have been more suitable for individuals with larger RRSP assets, or who have reasonably high income at retirement. This is no longer the case now that RRIFs have an unlimited withdrawal allowance.

The process of transferring from an RRSP to a RRIF is simple, involving only the completion of a government transfer form. In addition, there are often minimal or no costs or fees required to establish a RRIF unlike an annuity which often costs up to 3% of the asset value purchased.

Now...A Newer, Longer-Lasting RRIF
It used to be that a RRIF provided a nice, steady income for most Canadians until they died, usually in their late 70s or early 80s. But, as the song says, "used to be's" don't count anymore. What happened is that many people started to live longer, well into their 80s. However, that also meant that they had less and less of their RRIFs left to live on. Those who lived to be 90 years of age got a double wallop; all RRIF funds had to be withdrawn by that time. In a major and welcome move several years ago, the government changed those regulations.

The new rules allow you to maintain your RRIF for as long as you live or at least as long as there is money in the fund. But if you're between 71 and 78 years of age, you now have to withdraw a higher annual

TABLE 18-3: MINIMUM RRIF PAYMENT SCHEDULE

Age at Jan. 1st	Old Rules % To Be Withdrawn Each Year. (RRIFs set up prior to 1993)	New Rules % To Be Withdrawn Each Year. (RRIFs set up in 1993 or later)
71	5.26	7.38
72	5.56	7.48
73	5.88	7.59
74	6.25	7.71
75	6.67	7.85
76	7.14	7.99
77	7.69	8.15
78	8.33	8.33
79	9.09	8.53
80	10.00	8.75
81	11.11	8.99
82	12.50	9.27
83	14.29	9.58
84	16.67	9.93
85	20.00	10.33
86	25.00	10.79
87	33.33	11.33
88	50.00	11.96
89	100.00	12.71
90	0	13.62
91	0	14.73
92	0	16.12
93	0	17.92
94+	0	20.00

minimum amount during those years than before. While that means more tax payable in the first few years of a RRIF, it also means a longer-lasting RRIF, and one with a smoother flow of cash out of the fund.

How much more do you have to withdraw? If you're 71, you must now withdraw at least 7.38% of your RRIF, more than the 5.26% you had to take out under the old rules. At 75, you will have to withdraw 7.85% instead of the previous 6.67%. But if you're 78, you'll find that the amount is the same. In fact after that, from 79 on, you'll actually be able to withdraw less from your RRIF than before. The long-term effect means more capital in your RRIF for your later years.

While the new schedules will apply to all RRIFs bought after 1992, the old schedule still applies if you owned a RRIF before 1992, and are still between 71 and 78 years of age. As well, keep in mind that though the new rules mean your RRIF will last longer, they do not mean it will last forever. While a RRIF is more flexible than, say, a life annuity, you should consider using some of your retirement savings to buy an annuity or any other instruments that provide a guaranteed lifetime income.

RRIF Payouts

To understand a *RRIF minimum payout*, work from age 90 and, depending on the year when you begin your RRIF, the payment structure is based on that year subtracted from age 90. If you start your RRIF at age 65, the first year is $1/25$ of the pool of money in the RRIF. If you start at age 66, it is $1/24$; age 67–$1/23$, and so on until you reach age 71 when the minimum payment schedule is set. (see Chart 18-4). Remember you must select your RRSP maturity by the year you attain age 71.

Throughout your retirement, payments are lower in the early years, and increase each year as you move closer to age 94 at which point your payments remain at 20% of the balance of your RRIF until death.

RRIF Payout Examples

Sandor Toth, age 63, matures his RRSP into a RRIF with a value of $105,000. His first minimum payout would be age 90 less age 63 = 27.

$105,000 ÷ 27 = $3,888

Anita Yaneff, age 76, has had an established RRIF for several years with a value of $160,000. Her minimum payout is subject to the old rules based on her age subtracted from age 90.

$160,000 ÷ 14 = $11,429

Yvonne Dupuis, age 71, established a RRIF this year with a value of $210,000. Her minimum payout based on the new rules is 7.38%.

$210,000 x 7.38% = $15,498

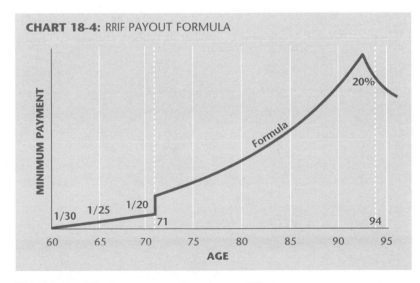

CHART 18-4: RRIF PAYOUT FORMULA

There are three common income withdrawal methods for a RRIF.

- *Minimum Withdrawal Method*
  All of the examples above were based on this method. The future value of your RRIF will be dependent on your rate of return. If your rate of return exceeds your minimum withdrawals,

your RRIF value will grow, otherwise the value of your RRIF will be eroded. Investors who want their RRIF to be tax-sheltered as long as possible, and wish to maintain their RRIF value for estate purposes or higher income in later years choose this option.

- *Level Income Withdrawal Method*
Similar to a level income annuity this method blends investment returns with encroachments on the RRIF principal. The higher the income level selected, the faster the value of the RRIF will erode.

- *Level Adjustable Withdrawal Method*
If you want the flexibility to adjust your income, such as increasing the income each year to offset inflation this method may appeal to you. Of course the higher the indexing rate is set, the faster you will erode the value of your RRIF.

RRIF Comparisons at 10%— Old Versus New Rules

Under the old RRIF rules all of the funds in the RRIF had to be withdrawn by age 90. Table 18-5 shows a $100,000 RRIF commencing at age 71, with a return of 10% per year. Over 19 years the RRIF would pay out $296,189 based on minimum withdrawals. Note that the RRIF was growing at a faster rate than the withdrawals in the earlier years. Assuming the RRIF holder had died at age 80, his RRIF value for estate purposes would have been worth $122,871 in addition to the $92,262 he had received in RRIF payments since inception.

The dollars remaining in the RRIF holder's plan grow to a peak of $124,112 at age 79 as shown in Table 18-5 and illustrated on Chart 18-7. It is very obvious how beneficial the RRIF alternative is

TABLE 18-5: RRIF PAYOUT—OLD RULES

Age	Interest Principal	@10%	Total	Withdrawal Percent	Amount	New Principal
71	$100,000	$10,000	$110,000	5.26%	$5,786	$104,214
72	104,214	10,421	114,635	5.56	6,374	108,261
73	108,261	10,826	119,087	5.88	7,002	112,085
74	112,085	11,209	123,294	6.25	7,706	115,588
75	115,588	11,559	127,147	6.67	8,481	118,666
76	118,666	11,867	130,533	7.14	9,320	121,213
77	121,213	12,121	133,334	7.69	10,253	123,081
78	123,081	12,308	135,389	8.33	11,278	124,111
79	124,111	12,411	136,522	9.09	12,410	124,112
80	124,112	12,411	136,523	10.00	13,652	122,871
81	122,871	12,287	135,158	11.11	15,016	120,142
82	120,142	12,014	132,156	12.50	16,520	115,636
83	115,636	11,564	127,200	14.29	18,177	109,023
84	109,023	10,902	119,925	16.67	19,991	99,934
85	99,934	9,993	109,927	20.00	21,985	87,942
86	87,942	8,794	96,736	25.00	24,184	72,552
87	72,552	7,255	79,807	33.33	26,600	53,207
88	53,207	5,321	58,528	50.00	29,264	29,264
89	29,264	2,926	32,190	100.00	32,190	0
					$296,189	

compared to an annuity for estate planning purposes when you analyse these numbers.

The new RRIF rules ensure that the RRIF holder receives a higher payout in the earlier years, but unlike the old RRIF rules, the new RRIF continues for life. Table 18-6 shows a RRIF starting at age 71 and continuing to receive a payout of 20% per year on the remaining funds in the plan from age 94 to age 99. In this example the RRIF has returned $340,241 by age 99 using a 10% return. Of course the RRIF will continue to payout 20% of whatever remains in the RRIF until the RRIF holder is deceased.

Finally, in Chart 18-8 we graph a comparison of annual withdrawals from a RRIF under both the old and new scenarios. As shown, the new RRIF rules allow you to plan much further into the future.

TABLE 18-6: RRIF PAYOUT—NEW RULES

Age	Principal	Interest @10%	Total	Withdrawal Percent	Amount	New Principal
71	$100,000	$10,000	$110,000	7.38%	$8,118	$101,882
72	101,882	10,188	112,070	7.48	8,383	103,687
73	103,687	10,369	114,056	7.59	8,657	105,399
74	105,399	10,540	115,939	7.71	8,939	107,000
75	107,000	10,700	117,700	7.85	9,239	108,461
76	108,461	10,846	119,307	7.99	9,533	109,774
77	109,774	10,977	120,751	8.15	9,841	110,910
78	110,910	11,091	122,001	8.33	10,163	111,838
79	111,838	11,184	123,022	8.53	10,494	112,528
80	112,528	11,253	123,781	8.75	10,831	112,950
81	112,950	11,295	124,245	8.99	11,170	113,075
82	113,075	11,308	124,383	9.27	11,530	112,853
83	112,853	11,285	124,138	9.58	11,892	112,246
84	112,246	11,225	123,471	9.93	12,261	111,210
85	111,210	11,121	122,331	10.33	12,637	109,694
86	109,694	10,969	120,663	10.79	13,020	107,643
87	107,643	10,764	118,407	11.33	13,416	104,991
88	104,991	10,499	115,490	11.96	13,813	101,677
89	101,677	10,168	111,845	12.71	14,215	97,630
90	97,630	9,763	107,393	13.62	14,627	92,766
91	92,766	9,277	102,043	14.73	15,031	87,012
92	87,012	8,701	95,713	16.12	15,429	80,284
93	80,284	8,028	88,312	17.92	15,826	72,486
94	72,486	7,249	79,735	20.00	15,947	63,788
95	63,788	6,379	70,167	20.00	14,033	56,134
96	56,134	5,613	61,747	20.00	12,349	49,398
97	49,398	4,940	54,338	20.00	10,868	43,470
98	43,470	4,347	47,817	20.00	9,563	38,254
99	38,254	3,825	42,079	20.00	8,416	33,663
					$340,241	

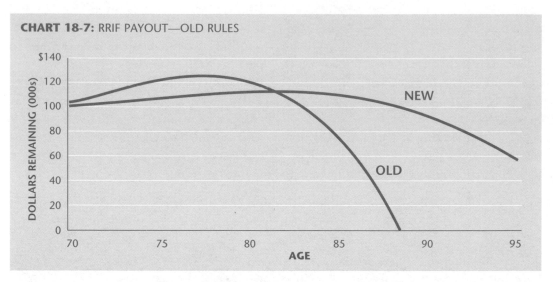

CHART 18-7: RRIF PAYOUT—OLD RULES

(Y-axis: DOLLARS REMAINING (000s); X-axis: AGE)

NEW

OLD

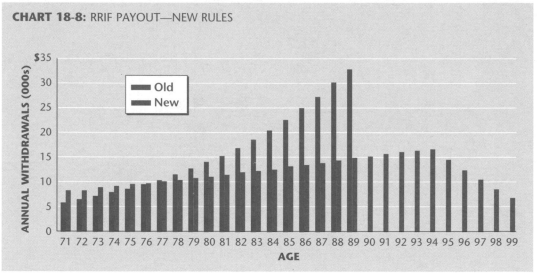

CHART 18-8: RRIF PAYOUT—NEW RULES

(Y-axis: ANNUAL WITHDRAWALS (000s); X-axis: AGE)

Legend: Old, New

What Happens if the RRIF Planholder Dies?

- With a RRIF, one spouse can name the other spouse as annuitant of the payments under the plan.

- When the planholder dies, the RRIF continues and payments are made to the surviving spouse. The surviving spouse is taxed on these payments.

- Alternatively, one spouse can name the other as beneficiary. In this case, the RRIF is collapsed and the amount passing to the surviving spouse is included in that spouse's income.

- If any other beneficiary is named, the value of the RRIF must be included as income in the deceased's date-of-death tax return; it is then taxed, with one exception.

- The exception is: funds (within certain limits) passing to a dependant child or grandchild of the planholder are included in that child's or grandchild's income, not in the income of the deceased planholder.

RRIF at 11% Versus Annuity at 9%

Let's look at a comparison of a RRIF and an annuity in Table 18-9 and Chart 18-10. The annuity example is based on a $100,000 principal amount at a 9% interest rate, joint annuity with a 15–year

TABLE 18-9: $100,000 JOINT ANNUITY AT 9% PAYOUT VERSUS RRIF AT 11%

Age	Joint Annuity Based on Interest at 9%	Annuity Purchasing Power in Current Dollars	RRIF Principal Based on Return at 11%	RRIF Payout at Minimum Allowed	RRIF Purchasing Power in Current Dollars
65	$9,600	$9,600	$100,000	$0	$0
66	9,600	9,143	111,572	4,649	4,427
67	9,600	8,707	119,592	5,200	4,716
68	9,600	8,293	127,961	5,816	5,024
69	9,600	7,898	136,650	6,507	5,353
70	9,600	7,522	145,618	7,281	5,705
71	9,600	7,164	154,809	11,425	8,525
72	9,600	6,823	160,704	12,021	8,543
73	9,600	6,498	166,655	12,649	8,561
74	9,600	6,188	172,634	13,310	8,580
75	9,600	5,894	178,609	14,021	8,608
76	9,600	5,613	184,527	14,744	8,620
77	9,600	5,346	190,370	15,515	8,639
78	9,600	5,091	196,078	16,333	8,662
79	9,600	4,849	201,585	17,195	8,685
80	9,600	4,618	206,823	18,097	8,705
81	9,600	4,398	211,719	19,034	8,719
82	9,600	4,188	216,196	20,041	8,744
83	9,600	3,989	220,130	21,088	8,763
84	9,600	3,799	223,419	22,185	8,780
85	9,600	3,618	225,934	23,339	8,796
86	9,600	3,446	227,526	24,550	8,812
87	9,600	3,282	228,029	25,836	8,832
88	9,600	3,125	227,237	27,178	8,848
89	9,600	2,977	224,942	28,590	8,865
90	9,600	2,835	220,896	30,086	8,884
91	9,600	2,700	214,807	31,641	8,899
92	9,600	2,571	206,378	33,268	8,911
93	9,600	2,449	195,263	34,991	8,926
94	9,600	2,332	181,048	36,210	8,797
95	9,600	2,221	163,906	32,781	7,585
	$297,600	**$157,176**		**$585,581**	**$242,516**

Purchasing power calculations assume an inflation rate of 5%.

guarantee, for a couple aged 65, to provide income of $9,600 a year for each year for life.

I start the comparison for the RRIF at age 66 when it provides a minimum payment of $4,649. At age 70, it provides $7,281. By age 75, it pays $14,021. In fact, it overtakes the fixed-term annuity in the 71st year. By age 80, you receive $18,097 in the RRIF; by age 85, you receive $23,339; by age 90, your payout is $30,086, and by age 95, your payout is $32,781. During the 30 years you have received $585,581, and you still have $163,906 principal in your RRIF growing at 11% per year that will continue to be paid out at the minimum withdrawal level of 20% per year.

In this example, the annuity had a 9% return and the RRIF had an 11% rate of return. Over the 30-year period, the annuity brings in a total of $297,600 while the

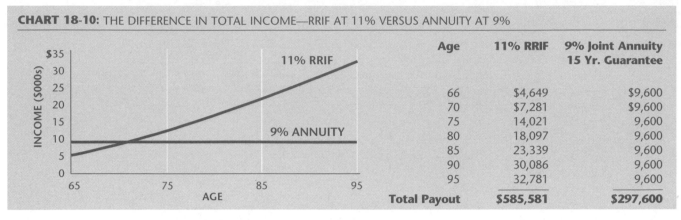

CHART 18-10: THE DIFFERENCE IN TOTAL INCOME—RRIF AT 11% VERSUS ANNUITY AT 9%

Age	11% RRIF	9% Joint Annuity 15 Yr. Guarantee
66	$4,649	$9,600
70	$7,281	$9,600
75	14,021	9,600
80	18,097	9,600
85	23,339	9,600
90	30,086	9,600
95	32,781	9,600
Total Payout	**$585,581**	**$297,600**

RRIF brings in a total of $585,581—nearly two times greater for the same $100,000 principal we began with in each example!

When you consider Chart 18-10, you can see the annuity as a fixed line providing $9,600 each and every year. The RRIF payments start lower, then overtake the annuity payments in the 71st year, growing annually until age 95. Because less money is taken out of the RRIF in the early years, more money is left in the fund to accumulate and compound over the years, providing you with a much greater return over the 30-year period.

RRIF Versus Annuity—Inflation

Do you remember earlier when we were looking at the inflation/beneficiary or inflation/victim concept? We had 5% inflation and we examined the effect of inflation on $1,000. Purchasing power weakened and weakened. By the seventh year, the $1,000 was worth $710. By the fifteenth year, it was down to $480. With inflation at 5%, it took just 15 years to reduce the purchasing power of $1000 to a mere $480.

We can apply the same inflation concept in the annuity example. 15 years from now, if inflation averages 5%, the purchasing power of that $9,600 will be $4,618. As we move through a total of 30 years, the purchasing power will become less and less. In fact, by the 30th year, it will be only $2,221. (see Chart 18-11)

The RRIF, on the other hand, starts off with a much lower payment of $4,649. The payment increases gradually, year by year. It provides a real hedge against inflation. Over the period of 30 years, the result is a much larger sum of money for the holder of the RRIF.

Inflation Packs a Double Wallop at Retirement

Inflation impacts greatly those people who are on a fixed-income or pension and no longer have the opportunity of increasing their income from employment. The only option is to consider diversifying their investments to include equities and mutual funds to obtain the

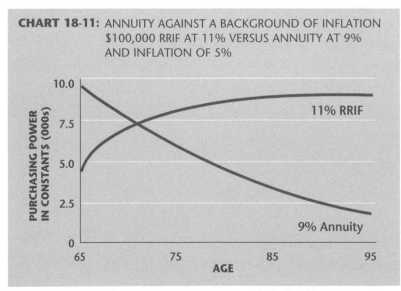

CHART 18-11: ANNUITY AGAINST A BACKGROUND OF INFLATION $100,000 RRIF AT 11% VERSUS ANNUITY AT 9% AND INFLATION OF 5%

benefits of the dividend tax credit and long-term capital gains.

Most people who amass substantial assets by retirement usually do so by investing in all three asset classes with a large percentage weighted to equities. Sophisticated investors know that they must continue to overweight the equity portion of their portfolios in order to offset the ravages of inflation especially if they're fortunate to enjoy longevity in their retirement.

Table 18-12 clearly illustrates what happens to your purchasing power over the years. The only way to survive this loss of purchasing power is to reinvest your original capital as well as a part of your earnings—an amount equal to the rate of inflation times your capital. Therefore, if inflation was 5% this year, you need to reinvest 105% of your original capital for next year.

Many people thought investing in the 1980s was easy—pick a GIC or Term Deposit, throw a dart, and obtain a double digit return. Both inflation and interest rates have declined substantially during the last few years. If you had invested in fixed income GICs then, the absolute dollars generated by your invested capital have also declined. As you can see in Table 18-13, your income has declined from $50,000 to $30,000 and after expenses you have a shortfall of $900.

Not only has your capital generated less income, but your expenses increase each year with inflation. The overall inflation rate declines but actual prices do not. The only way to hedge the double wallop that inflation packs is to include growth in your portfolio. One of the major advantages of a self-directed RRIF versus an annuity is the opportunity the RRIF provides to offset the impact of inflation.

TABLE 18-12: INFLATION PACKS A DOUBLE WALLOP AT RETIREMENT

	VALUE OF CAPITAL	INCOME
Year	5% Inflation	10% Return
1994	$500,000	$50,000
2004	305,000	30,500
2014	190,000	19,000
2024	115,000	11,500

Retirement Income Options

Now that we have compared the various maturity options for annuities and RRIFs, it would appear that, for most people, RRIFs have some very definite advantages over annuities. Table 18-14 clearly outlines the retirement income options for your maturing RRSP.

The major advantages of RRIFs over annuities include:
* Growth opportunities as a hedge against inflation

> There came a time when the risk to remain tight in a bud was more painful than the risk it took to blossom.
>
> **Anaïs Nin**

TABLE 18-13: THE FIXED-INCOME DILEMMA

Investment: $500,000

Annual expenses: $30,000

	Year 1	Year 2
GIC rates	10%	6%
Inflation	5%	3%
"Real" rate of return	5%	3%
Income:	$500,000 x 10% = $50,000	$500,000 x 6% = $30,000
Expenses:	$30,000 + ($30,000 x 5%) = $31,500	$30,000 + ($30,000 x 3%) = $30,900
Balance *(Income minus expenses)*:	**$18,500**	**($900)**

TABLE 18-14: RETIREMENT INCOME OPTIONS — RRSP/RRIF/ANNUITIES

	RRSP	RRIF	Straight Life	Joint & Last Survivor	Fixed Term
			ANNUITIES		
Minimizing Taxes	Yes	Yes	Yes	Yes	Yes
Protection From Inflation	Yes	Yes	No*	No*	No*
Growth Potential	Yes	Yes	No	No	No
Flexibility					
Control Over Assets	Yes	Yes	No	No	No
Spousal Protection	Yes	Yes	No	Yes	Yes
Men & Women Equally	Yes	Yes	No	No	No
Flexibility in Payments	Yes	Yes	No*	No*	No*
Estate Planning	Yes	Yes	No	No	Yes

* Indexed payments provide some protection.

- Estate planning features, whereby assets pass to your spouse or beneficiaries
- Transferability allows you to manage your assets
- Rate of payout flexible to suit your needs

Often there is no choice but to be conservative and choose an annuity, particularly when income during retirement is limited. In other cases, it is possible to use a combination of an annuity and a RRIF. The challenge is to be able to take a look at all retirement options and match them to your total resources in order to come up with what is suitable for your needs and objectives.

Until recently, most people cashed their RRSPs or chose an annuity. But life does not stop at age 65. With your newly acquired investment knowledge, you can select investment products in a well-balanced RRIF, using a combination of professionally managed mutual funds so you can enjoy the benefit of higher returns far beyond the age of 65.

Annuitize Your RRIF

People very often leave their RRSP conversion option until age 71. Should they decide on an annuity at a low point in the interest rate cycle, they must accept a low rate of return on the annuity they choose. The way to avoid this situation is to start a RRIF when interest rates are high, and then purchase some long-term, high-yield bonds and debentures for the RRIF. You can place all of your funds in these high-yield securities, or you can diversify your RRIF with good quality, balanced mutual funds.

The process of purchasing high-yield, fixed-income investments for your RRIF allows you the flexibility of seeking investments at the appropriate time in the economic cycle. I refer to this process as "annuitizing your RRIF"—

Chart Guide

The graph below is based on the values in Table 18-17. It shows vividly the difference in inflation-adjusted performance over the long term between the RRIF and the annuity.

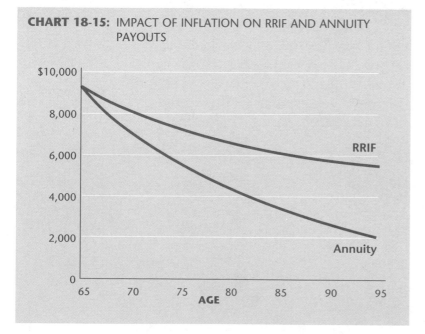

CHART 18-15: IMPACT OF INFLATION ON RRIF AND ANNUITY PAYOUTS

locking-in some high-yield securities to allow you a much greater return on your investments.

For example, in a time of falling interest rates (and typically, rising stock markets), RRIF funds could be kept in dividend-yielding, blue chip stocks and short-term, interest-bearing deposits such as T-Bills. As interest rates rise later in the economic cycle, you could shift all assets to short-term notes—a wise decision either inside or outside a RRIF. If and when rates get to the 13% to 14% range, you should consider purchasing long-term government bonds with a portion of your RRIF assets. If rates continue to rise, buy more, and so on. Don't forget to leave some cash in the RRIF for emergencies and special buying opportunities.

And Now For Something Just a Little Different— a LIF

If you understand a RRIF you're more than half-way to understanding a *Life Income Fund* (LIF). In fact, think of a RRIF with not only a minimum, but also a maximum annual payout that cannot be cashed in, and you've just defined a LIF.

If you left your company two years ago, and your pension funds were vested, one of the options for your pension was to transfer it into a *Locked-In RRSP* or *Locked-In Retirement Account* (LIRA). Locked-In means that you would not have been able to withdraw the benefits until retirement; and legislation stated that you would be guided by the rules of your previous employer's pension plan. Even when you did retire you had only one option—to purchase an annuity. Sure, that annuity guaranteed you an income for life, but it also guaranteed the same rate of interest for life. If rates went up or down, as in the last two years, you could not renegoti-

ate to take advantage of those higher or lower rates.

Then along came LIFs, which are regulated either provincially or federally. What this gives you is flexibility and what this allows you to do is to convert your Locked-in RRSP or pension at an earlier age to permit a limited payout, while allowing for the potential growth of locked-in retirement assets. In most provinces you can buy a LIF as early as age 55. More important, you can treat your LIF like a RRIF by investing in instruments as diverse as GICs and mutual funds. While GIC interest rates are fixed, they remain the same only for 1–, 3–, 5–years, or the period that you determine. You choose the term and consequently the interest rate.

LIFs are designed to act as a bridge between a Locked-in RRSP and an annuity. If rates are low upon retirement you have the benefit of delaying the purchase of a life annuity until rates improve. In the interim you must receive a minimum LIF payout (like a RRIF) and you won't be able to receive more than a pre-set maximum amount. The maximum annual payout is set so you won't use up all of the funds and it is based on your life expectancy. Your LIF payments will continue until you become 80 years old, when you will have only one option—to buy a lifetime annuity. Then again, maybe you will decide to convert your locked-in pension at a time when rates are high long before you turn age 80.

General Guidelines for LIFs
- LIFs are regulated by provincial and federal governments and are usually purchased between ages 55 and 71 using assets from:
  - Locked-in RRSP
  - Locked-In Retirement Account (LIRA)
  - Registered Pension Plan (RPP) (* must be transferred to a Locked-in RRSP

first although, some RPPs have received approval to transfer directly to a LIF)

– Deferred Profit Sharing Plan (DPSP)

- Minimum and maximum annual payouts are calculated based on the net asset value of the LIF at December 31st each year. No payout is required in the year the LIF is established.

- If a payout is required for the year the LIF is set up, the maximum payout will be determined on a proportionate basis to the time the LIF was established.

  Example: Wolfgang Winkler established a LIF in June. His maximum payout is calculated to be $1,350 based on the value of his plan and his current age. Therefore his payout is:

  $$\$1,350 \div 12 \times 7 = \$787.50.$$

- LIFs can be transferred to other LIFs, annuities, or prior to age 71, Locked-In RSPs or LIRAs.

- Upon the death of the annuitant the balance of the funds in the LIF are transferable to a spouse, a named beneficiary, or an estate. A spouse may arrange to have the LIF converted to an annuity or may waive survivor's benefits to receive the balance of the LIF. In the latter case, the remaining assets in the LIF must be included in the annuitant's final tax return; and then the after-tax proceeds are paid to his/her beneficiary. Now it's time to add additional options and a new column for LIFs to the retirement income table we looked at earlier in this chapter and summarized here in Table 18-16.

TABLE 18-16: RETIREMENT INCOME OPTIONS — RRSP/RRIF/LIF/ANNUITY

Investment Options	RRSP	RRIF	LIF	ANNUITY
Choice of Investments	Yes	Yes	Yes	No
Minimize Taxes	Yes	Yes	Yes	Yes
Maximize Tax Deferral	Yes	Yes	No	No
Protection From Inflation	Yes	Yes	Yes	No
Pension Tax Credit at Age 65	No	Yes	Yes	Yes
Growth Potential	Yes	Yes	Yes	No
Income Flexibility Options	Maximum	Maximum	Some	None
Number of Payments	Yes	Yes	Yes	No
Variable Amount of Payments	Yes	Yes	Yes	No
Lump Sum Withdrawal	Yes	Yes	No	No
Men and Women Treated Equally	Yes	Yes	No	No
Estate Planning Options	Yes	Yes	Yes	Some
Spousal Protection	Yes	Yes	Yes	Some
Term Based on Spouse's Age	Yes	Yes	No	No
Control Over Assets	Yes	Yes	Yes	No
Builds Estate Value	Yes	Yes	Yes	No

Case Profile ⓮ The Smiths and the Johansons

To illustrate the tremendous differences between an annuity and a RRIF in a real-life situation, let's look at two fictional couples—the Smiths and the Johansons.

In 1994 both couples at age 65 had accumulated $100,000 in their RRSPs towards their retirements and each couple had to make a very serious decision on how to employ funds from their RRSPs for the future.

The Smiths

The Smiths were very conservative with their selection of a 15-year guaranteed joint annuity, which offered a return of 8%. They were pleased to find a safe dependable fixed-income vehicle that would provide a consistent return of 8%. The Smiths were delighted to receive $8,883 per year on their $100,000 investment and they felt very safe and secure. With a guaranteed income of $8,883 per year, yielding 8%, they felt they had no worries about inflation. In fact they believed they would be set for the rest of their lives.

But are they really safe and secure? Let's assume the Smiths both live to age 95. Now let's look at what will happen to their purchasing power over the next 30 years with inflation averaging 5% (see Table 1-2).

1994	2004	2014	2024
1.00	0.61	0.38	0.23

Each dollar they receive each year is worth less and less in real purchasing power. They will receive $8,883 times 31 years or $275,366 in total, but the real purchasing power of that sum in 1994 adjusted dollars is only $145,433 over the same time frame. Furthermore, if they die beyond age 80 after the 15-year guaranteed period has expired, the annuity will have no value left for their beneficiaries. The Smiths do not understand how the ravages of inflation will diminish their purchasing power. Their safe investment will turn out to be not so safe after all.

The Johansons

The Johansons understood that the only "safe" investment was one that would protect their purchasing power. They realized that they would need more and more income in future years and therefore their investment would have to grow to offset inflation.

The solution for the Johansons was the selection of a self-directed RRIF invested in both fixed-income vehicles and mutual funds. They recognized there would be times when their investments would fluctuate, but they also knew that a rising income would be the best hedge against inflation.

The actual investment funds they chose have averaged an 11% return for the last 30 years, and while there is no guarantee that the funds will continue to offer this high return, we will assume the Johansons will enjoy longevity, live to age 95, and enjoy an 11% return on their capital of $100,000. They decided they would take a RRIF payout at the same level as the annuity amount for the first 7 years or $8,883 per year; thereafter the minimum as required by RRIF legislation and let the additional income and growth accumulate to meet their estate planning goals. Table 18-17 will give you an idea of what happened. After the first 7 years, the Johansons will receive more income which will help to offset inflation. By age 75, they will receive $10,659; by age 85, they will receive $17,744; and by age 95, they will receive $24,922. Compare their results to the Smiths who will receive just $8,883 per year, or a total of $145,433 inflation-adjusted for the 31 years. But even more important than current income, the Johansons will create a substantial estate through the use of a RRIF. If they should pass away prior to age 95, the remaining assets in the RRIF will pass to their beneficiaries. For example, if they were to pass away at age 85, the value of the RRIF would be $171,768 for their beneficiaries, whereas the Smiths estate would have no value left from their annuity at the same age. Of course, if the Johansons live to age 95, or beyond, they will be removing substantial sums from their RRIF until their deaths. During the 31-year period they will enjoy inflation-adjusted income of $212,684 compared to the Smiths who will have inflation-adjusted income of only $145,433. During the 31-year period, the actual dollars paid out from the annuity are $275,366 versus the RRIF payout of $476,296; clearly a $200,930 greater benefit from the RRIF.

Think about the Smiths and Johansons as you plan your retirement in financial dignity. Always remember that a fixed return is never "safe" as long as there is inflation to contend with. Where should you invest your retirement dollar—in an annuity or a RRIF?

TABLE 18-17: $100,000 ANNUITY AT 8% VERSUS RRIF AT 11%

	THE SMITHS			THE JOHANSONS	
Age	Joint Annuity Based on Interest at 8%	Annuity Purchasing Power in Current Dollars	RRIF Principal Based on Return at 11%	RRIF Payout at Annuity Amount or Minimum Allowed	RRIF Purchasing Power in Current Dollars
65	$8,883	$8,883	$100,000	$8,883	$8,883
66	8,883	8,460	102,227	8,883	8,460
67	8,883	8,057	104,712	8,883	8,057
68	8,883	7,673	107,485	8,883	7,673
69	8,883	7,308	110,578	8,883	7,308
70	8,883	6,960	114,030	8,883	6,960
71	8,883	6,628	117,881	8,883	6,628
72	8,883	6,313	122,177	9,139	6,495
73	8,883	6,012	126,701	9,617	6,509
74	8,883	5,726	131,247	10,119	6,523
75	8,883	5,453	135,789	10,659	6,544
76	8,883	5,194	140,289	11,209	6,554
77	8,883	4,946	144,731	11,796	6,568
78	8,883	4,711	149,070	12,418	6,585
79	8,883	4,486	153,257	13,073	6,603
80	8,883	4,273	157,240	13,758	6,618
81	8,883	4,069	160,961	14,470	6,629
82	8,883	3,876	164,365	15,237	6,648
83	8,883	3,691	167,356	16,033	6,662
84	8,883	3,515	169,856	16,867	6,675
85	8,883	3,348	171,768	17,744	6,687
86	8,883	3,188	172,979	18,664	6,699
87	8,883	3,037	173,361	19,642	6,715
88	8,883	2,892	172,759	20,662	6,727
89	8,883	2,754	171,015	21,736	6,740
90	8,883	2,623	167,938	22,873	6,755
91	8,883	2,498	163,309	24,055	6,765
92	8,883	2,379	156,901	25,292	6,775
93	8,883	2,266	148,450	26,602	6,786
94	8,883	2,158	137,644	27,529	6,688
95	8,883	2,055	124,612	24,922	5,766
	$275,366	**$145,433**		**$476,296**	**$212,684**

**Purchasing power calculations assume an inflation rate of 5%.

Chart Guide

For consistency we have used a male age 65 to compare the various annuity alternatives. A woman age 65 would generally receive a lower annuity payment each year in each of the annuity alternatives due to longer life expectancy. The lower payment is a result of the annuity issuer generally having to make payments for a longer period of time.

Giving it Away — Estate Planning

The cornerstone of your estate plan is your will, which distributes your assets when you die. But effective estate planning can provide significant benefits today.

The Need for Estate Planning— a Case in Point

Financial planning, as we have seen, has three stages: accumulation, conservation, and distribution. The purpose of estate planning, or distribution, is to ensure that your assets are transferred as you wish and that minimum income tax is paid at the time of transfer.

Estate planning is one of the greatest opportunities you will ever have to provide special benefits for your family and friends, not only after your death, but also while you're alive. It is one of the most challenging projects you'll ever tackle, yet it can be one of the most rewarding. You make the decisions that determine your future. Without an estate plan, you invite hardship for those you love.

Consider the following true story: *"In 1987, a very close friend of a friend of mine (I will call him Doug) visited Kitchener, Ontario with three friends to partake in the Oktoberfest festivities. After a drinkfest, Doug stepped out of the tents in search of the washroom. He found himself out in an open field by a rain gutter, fell in, suffered a concussion, and subsequently died. He was just 44."*

Doug had made a will nine years earlier to provide for his family. However, over those nine years, Doug divorced his first wife and had two children by his new common-law wife. Doug's outdated will left all his assets to his former wife and nothing to his common-law wife and two children. Nothing could be done to rectify the matter.

I share this personal disaster with you to impress upon you the urgency you should feel about your estate and your responsibility to those who depend on you. You can't take it with you, but you can determine where you want it left behind.

Guidelines for Estate Planning

As the example of Doug forcefully illustrates, estate planning is not a one-time endeavour. Over the course of your lifetime, goals change, your family grows, your career develops, and your financial circumstances expand. Each of these changes provides an excellent opportunity to make new decisions about your estate.

Regardless of what stage you have reached in life, now is the time to seriously plan your estate, if you haven't already.

> The power of perpetuating our property in our families is one of the most valuable and interesting circumstances belonging to it.
> **Edmund Burke**

There are three keys to successful estate planning:

1. *Charting your course*

   Before setting sail, all good sailors spend hours studying charts, determining prevailing winds, noting the tides and hidden shoals, and looking for the markers that will provide safe passage. Effective estate planning requires the same intensity of preparation and the careful study of legislation governing all areas of estate planning.

2. *Assembling an effective support team*

   You make the crucial decisions in your estate plan and, although you may choose to coordinate and implement those plans and decisions on your own, there are professional advisors who can help you—your lawyer, accountant, insurance agent, stockbroker, and, of course, your financial advisor.

   Most people prefer the assistance of a financial planner. Your planner will orchestrate your estate planning needs and objectives and utilize the services of each of your professionals to help you attain your goals.

3. *Starting immediately*

   The sooner you begin, the stronger the plan, and the greater opportunity you have to accomplish your personal objectives.

The Components of Your Estate Plan

A thorough *estate plan* has several components:

- A Will
- Trusts
- Gifts
- Power of Attorney

These instruments enable you to implement your decisions with precision, and prepare you for the challenges each stage of life brings.

He spent his health to get his wealth .... he spent his wealth to get back his health.

Lloyd Percival

The Will

The *Will* is a written instrument, a piece of paper telling the world how it must deal with your estate after you die. You, and only you, have the opportunity to determine how your estate will be divided, and when.

Although the form of your Will may vary depending on where you live, the subject matter will probably include:

- The "domicile of the Testator" (where you live), listing your street address, city, country, borough, and province
- The designation of someone to manage and distribute your estate; your trustee or executor/executrix
- A sentence revoking any wills you have made before, ensuring that your executor has only one set of instructions to follow
- Guidelines regarding the payment of funeral expenses, debts, and taxes
- A guardian for your children if they are still quite young
- Bequests—special gifts and sums of money for specific people
- Financial support for your children and grandchildren
- What to do with the residue of your estate—what is left over after your expenses, bequests, and family have been taken care of.

What Happens If You Die Without A Will?

I constantly meet people 45 to 50 years old who have never drafted a Will. And I am constantly amazed. Here are mature adults with a spouse, two or three children, a home, a cottage, assets to be looked after, and they have not set up a plan for the way they wish their possessions and responsibilities to be handled after they die.

Consider this: if you and your spouse perish in a car accident, having made no formal declarations concerning the guardianship of your children, they may become wards of the province. Where they are sent to live may not be what you would wish. Are you really so unconcerned about your family's future that you would not spend the $150 to $250 it takes to get a Will completed? I'm sure this is not so.

Why, then, do you procrastinate about something so important and so inexpensive? Is it because estate planning is really an aspect of death planning, not only agitating to consider, but also something that is so far down the road that you don't really need to deal with it for decades?

This is not planning—it is avoidance— the ostrich syndrome. Act now. Draw up a Will immediately, or update your existing one and review it as often as necessary.

What happens to your estate if you die without a Will, or if the one you made 30 years ago isn't valid or appropriate? If most people were fully aware of the consequences of not making a Will, they would run, not walk, to their lawyer's office to have their Will drafted. The *laws of intestacy* (dying without a Will) are inflexible. Table 19-1 outlines how your estate will be divided in the province of Ontario if you die without a Will. There are slight variations from province to province.

It's your choice whether you want to let the government make critical decisions for you, but it is easy to avoid this situation. Take control of the estate planning process yourself and prepare a Will that properly reflects your wishes. You must set the objectives and develop a plan on your own. Your lawyer can help you by:

TABLE 19-1: LAWS OF INTESTACY

If You Die and Leave:	The Distribution of Your Estate Will Be:
Wife or husband and no children or grandchildren	Everything goes to your spouse.
Wife or husband and child	The first $75,000 plus one-half of the remainder will go to your spouse. One-half of the balance will go to your child. If the child is under age, the Official Guardian will administer the funds. (Wouldn't you prefer to have someone you selected administer these funds?)
Wife or husband and two or more children	The first $75,000 plus one-third of the remainder will go to your spouse. Two-thirds of the balance will be shared equally by your children. The Official Guardian will administer these funds so this raises questions similar to the above.
Wife or husband and parent (no brother or sister)	All to spouse.
Wife or husband and brother and sister	All to spouse.
Wife or husband, mother and brother or sister	All to spouse.
Brothers and sisters only	Equally among all, with representation in favour of issue.
No wife / husband children	Everything will go to parents. (Would you prefer that your no brothers or sisters or others benefit?)

CHART 19-2: FLOW CHART OF EXECUTOR'S DUTIES AND RESPONSIBILITIES

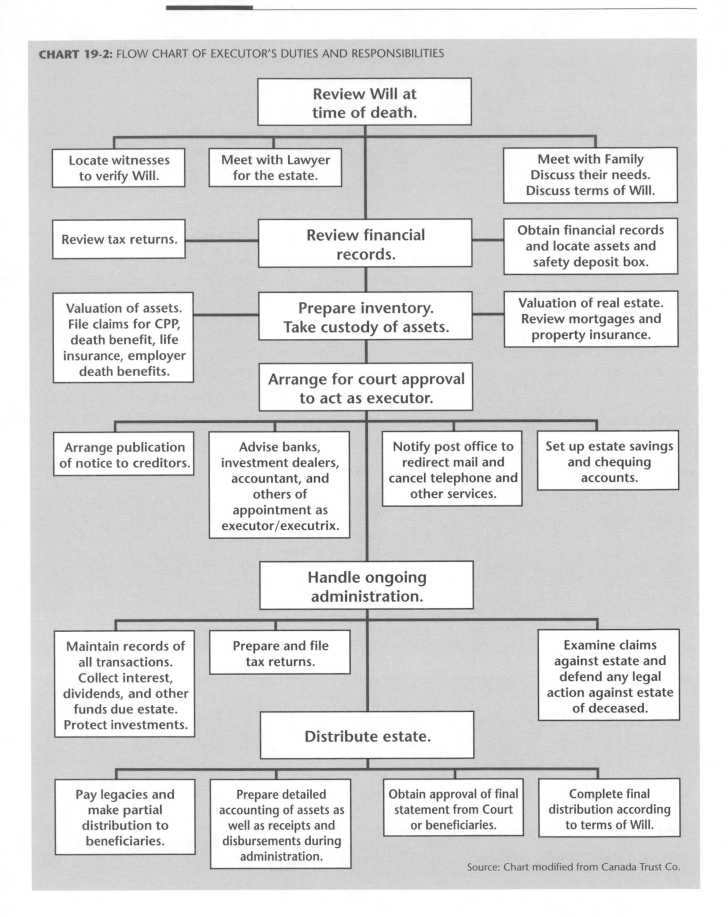

Review Will at time of death.

Locate witnesses to verify Will.

Meet with Lawyer for the estate.

Meet with Family Discuss their needs. Discuss terms of Will.

Review tax returns.

Review financial records.

Obtain financial records and locate assets and safety deposit box.

Valuation of assets. File claims for CPP, death benefit, life insurance, employer death benefits.

Prepare inventory. Take custody of assets.

Valuation of real estate. Review mortgages and property insurance.

Arrange for court approval to act as executor.

Arrange publication of notice to creditors.

Advise banks, investment dealers, accountant, and others of appointment as executor/executrix.

Notify post office to redirect mail and cancel telephone and other services.

Set up estate savings and chequing accounts.

Handle ongoing administration.

Maintain records of all transactions. Collect interest, dividends, and other funds due estate. Protect investments.

Prepare and file tax returns.

Examine claims against estate and defend any legal action against estate of deceased.

Distribute estate.

Pay legacies and make partial distribution to beneficiaries.

Prepare detailed accounting of assets as well as receipts and disbursements during administration.

Obtain approval of final statement from Court or beneficiaries.

Complete final distribution according to terms of Will.

Source: Chart modified from Canada Trust Co.

- Advising the best way to distribute your assets
- Helping you choose a Trustee
- Ensuring that monies left for children are invested wisely and are protected until your children grow up
- Showing you how to provide ongoing financial security for your spouse.

In addition, your lawyer can explain the difference between a formally executed Will and a Holograph Will. A Holograph Will is prepared in your own handwriting and signed by you. While there is no witness to the document, a Holograph Will may be valid depending on where you live. Finally, your lawyer can help you review your Will each year and make the changes that reflect your current wishes.

The Executor or Executrix

The *Executor* or *Executrix* is the person you designate to manage and distribute your estate after your death. Choosing an executor is one of the most important decisions you'll make as part of the estate planning process. As you consider candidates for the position, ask yourself these questions:

- How old are they? Are they likely to survive you?
- Would they be willing to handle your business affairs, and assuming they are willing, are they capable?
- How much do they know about your personal circumstances and your family relationships? Should you consider a relative or close family friend?
- If your estate is sizeable and complex, should you perhaps choose a trust company as executor?
- Would the combination of a trust company and a relative as co-executors be the best plan?

An executor's responsibilities are many. Your selection deserves a great deal of thought and careful consideration. Chart 19-2, a condensed version of a brochure published by Canada Trust entitled Your Executor and Your Estate, outlines the executor's duties and responsibilities.

Choosing a guardian for your children is another important decision in your overall estate plan. Your children could become wards of the province if both parents die without formally choosing a guardian.

Trusts

For any one of a number of reasons, you may want to transfer ownership of some of your assets to your children or your spouse while maintaining control over how the assets are managed. This is done with a *trust* (see Chart 19-3).

- A trust allows one person (you) to hold property for the benefit of another person.
- A trust is created when the Settlor (you) transfers specific property to a Trustee.
- The Trustee holds the property for the benefit of the person you have chosen (the beneficiary).

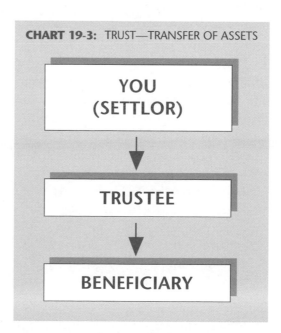

CHART 19-3: TRUST—TRANSFER OF ASSETS

YOU (SETTLOR)

TRUSTEE

BENEFICIARY

Trusts are a simple and flexible way to transfer ownership of assets to your intended heirs while the Trustee, with your guidance, continues to control the assets. The rules have changed, but trusts still present opportunities that might be attractive to you. For example, you could establish a trust for a child and deposit their monthly child tax benefit. Or, you might consider establishing a Registered Education Savings Plan to help with the costs of a post-secondary education.

Testamentary Trusts and Inter-Vivos Trusts

A testamentary trust is created when you die. You can establish this type of trust in your will. An *inter-vivos* trust is a trust you create during your lifetime. It is often referred to as a "living trust" and can provide such benefits as:

- Minimizing probate expenses
- Passing assets directly to your beneficiaries
- Taking precedence over your will
- Avoiding a successful contesting of key provisions in your will
- Saving money through ease of drafting.

Gifts

Sooner or later, most of us feel the urge to give some of our assets to our spouse or children while we are still alive. It's a natural instinct and a normal part of estate planning. And it's as easy as transferring the ownership of the asset to the person you've chosen. However, while giving away property may accomplish specific estate planning goals, you should be aware of some of the drawbacks.

- When you give away an asset while you are still alive, the law says you receive an amount equal to the value of the gift on the open market. This amount is called the "Fair Market Value." Since you have just received

this sum of "money," it may be taxable. Also, depending on where you live or where the property is located, there may be a special gift tax to pay.

- Once you give away an asset, you have lost control over it and any future income it may produce.
- If you plan to give assets to your spouse or a child under 18, a special set of rules called the "Attribution Rules" must be considered.

In spite of these drawbacks, giving gifts is a great way to accomplish certain estate planning objectives. And you don't have to wait 'til Christmas.

One excellent strategy to consider is to give money to an adult child, age 18 or over. There is no attribution back to the donor on this gift. If the adult child were to deposit this gift in an RRSP subject to his/her allowable contribution room plus the $8,000 permitted by the over-contribution rule, you would help your child establish a substantial retirement nest-egg. Assume your adult child could invest $4,000 in an RRSP plus an $8,000 over-contribution at 12% for 40 years in a mutual fund. This $12,000 contribution would grow to $1,116,600 by the time he/she reaches age 58.

Charitable Giving Can Help You Now— and Later

When it comes to tax savings, charitable giving offers the best of both worlds: an opportunity to support your favourite cause or charity, and a way to reduce your taxes payable. Yet according to a recent survey, 47% of Canadians are unaware that they could claim charitable donations on their income tax and save tax as well.

Many people equate charitable giving with a cash donation to a charity. However, there is another, lesser-known form of giving that is growing in popularity. This is called deferred, or planned giving—charitable gifts

---

HOW TO LEAVE A MILLION DOLLAR ESTATE TO YOUR CHILD

Gift of $12,000 to your child at age 18. Have your child deposit it in an RRSP.

Assume mutual fund purchase returns of 12% for 40 years

= **$1,116,600.**

that a charity cannot use until you have died. However, you begin and continue to realize the tax advantages the moment you make the gift.

Charitable Contributions provide a significant tax break.

For example annual contributions over $250 would receive approximately a 40% tax credit.* i.e. every $1 you give over $250 saves 40 cents of tax.

The Federal Tax Credit is 17% on the first $250; 29% on donations over $250; plus tax savings on the federal surtax and provincial income tax.

*tax credit varies according to province.

Gift Annuity

One type of planned giving is a gift annuity. Essentially, you give a cash sum to an institution, which in turn buys an annuity for you. There are several types—gift, gift plus annuity, and a prescribed annuity. In principle, each type provides you with a guaranteed, fixed income for life. All or part of both the principal and monthly payments will be tax free; the portion that will be tax free will depend on your age and life expectancy. Though you may be taxed on the payments you receive, the rate of tax will generally be lower than the rate for more traditional instruments like GICs or other income securities. When you die, the principal remaining in the annuity passes to the institution, which must use it for the purpose that you specified.

Gifts of Property

Life annuities, gifts, or property such as real estate, securities, or personal possessions allow you to make a gift to your charity—either cash or a work of art or property—while you continue to enjoy the use of that gift (or receive an income, if cash) while you are still alive. For example, say you wanted to leave your house to

Charitable Giving — Bequests

Specific Bequest: designates a specific piece of property.

General Bequest: designates a specific amount of a certain kind of property. This gift is usually a sum of cash.

Residual Bequest: designates all or a portion of the remainder of an estate after all other debts, taxes, expenses, and other bequests have been paid.

Restricted Bequest: designates a specific purpose for the gift such as a named fund, scholarship, program, or event that the money is to support.

a university, you would continue to live there and receive a tax receipt equal to the charities residual interest in the house. This could be accomplished by transferring the property to an irrevocable trust managed by a trustee. The trustee would provide you with a charitable donation receipt each year based on the residual interest that belongs to the charity.

Gifts of Life Insurance

A life insurance policy—either one that is paid up or a new one that is taken out—is another charitable gift that provides a major infusion of capital to the charity and offers you significant tax advantages as well. The premiums can be deducted by you and they entitle you to a tax credit that can be used in the current tax year or carried forward for a maximum of five years.

Gift Bequest

Still another planned gift is a bequest, a gift of cash or property that you designate in your Will. While there are several types of bequests any one entitles your estate to a gift receipt for the full value of the bequest, and a significant reduction in the tax payable when your final return is filed.

You only live once. But if you work it right, once is enough.
Fred Allen

House-Rich, But Cash Poor? A Reverse Mortgage May Help

What do you do if you don't have enough cash flow to fund your retirement needs? Perhaps a *reverse mortgage* will provide the answer.

If you have spent most of your good wage-earning years paying off your mortgage you may find yourself in retirement like thousands of Canadians, house-rich, but cash poor. This is hardly the ideal circumstance to find oneself in to pay for an unexpected expense or to satisfy your urge to spend more freely than a fixed income allows. But if selling your home was once the only solution to obtaining a sizable amount of cash in your retirement, now there is another. It is called a reverse mortgage.

A reverse mortgage allows you to convert the equity in your paid-up home into cash by using the home as collateral for a loan which is then used to buy an annuity. You'll receive a cash amount of up to 35 % of the value of your home, and must repay it, along with the accumulated interest, when you sell the house or move. To appreciate how a reverse mortgage works, imagine if your banker or mortgagor made monthly payments to you instead of you to them. And unlike a conventional mortgage, which allows you to build equity, a reverse mortgage means that you are building debt.

You can obtain a reverse mortgage as a cash lump sum, or as a combination of cash and a monthly annuity paid to you for a fixed period or life. The amount is based on the value and location of your house, and the prevailing interest rate. If you choose to receive an annuity, the amount is based on your life expectancy; the older you are, the higher the payments.

The main advantage of a reverse mortgage is that it gives you an immediate income. As well, the cash and annuity payments are non-taxable, as long as you live in your home. However, a reverse mortgage also reduces your equity in your home. It may consume your entire equity, if you outlive the term of the mortgage. Even if you don't, the effect of compounding interest may erode all your equity after a short time. Therefore, this concept is best suited to those people who plan to live in the house for the rest of their lives. Moreover, the term and the rates for a reverse mortgage are fixed; you can't re-negotiate if interest

---

Case Profile ⓯ Grace and Marc Tessier

Purchase a Reverse Mortgage

- Grace and Marc Tessier age 70 and 71 respectively

- House valued at $250,000

- Obtain reverse mortgage $87,500 based on their age and 35% value of the home

- Mortgage rate of 10% provides monthly income of $621.43 or $7,457.16 annually

- The Tessiers debt will grow to:

  $138,283 in 5 years
  $221,803 in 10 years
  $359,238 in 15 years
  $585,340 in 20 years

- If their house appreciates at 4% per year it will be worth:

  $305,000 in 5 years
  $370,000 in 10 years
  $450,000 in 15 years
  $547,500 in 20 years

- Subtracting the debt from the property value at five year intervals leaves this residual value for their estate:

Years	House Value Increase at 4%	Debt	Residual Value
5	$305,000	$138,283	$166,717
10	370,000	221,803	148,197
15	450,000	359,238	90,762
20	547,500	585,340	(37,840)*

* The value for estate purposes is NIL. Most reverse mortgage contracts allow the homeowner to make no payments until death, a preset date, or when the property is sold. In this example the homeowners would have remained in the house until death at which point the mortgagor would probably sell the property and there would be no money left for the homeowner's estate.

rates decline or annuity rates rise. Finally, a reverse mortgage may also reduce the size of your estate, and even remove from it, a significant (and sentimental) family asset.

Given those disadvantages, you should consider a reverse mortgage only if you haven't any other options. These include a conventional bank loan, cashing in a bond or savings certificate, or selling other assets like stocks or collectibles. If you do need cash until your pension benefits begin or until you move into a retirement home, or even to treat yourself a little lavishly, any of these options is preferable to a reverse mortgage. Besides, you'll still have the peace of mind to enjoy your most important asset—and all of it.

Caveat Emptor!

None of the larger financial institutions issue reverse mortgages; in fact it goes against their wisdom of saving to build assets rather than depleting assets.

Most companies that do sell reverse mortgages require the client to seek independent legal advice to avoid any possible future repercussion.

Power of Attorney

The fourth element of estate planning is a *power of attorney*. It is quite common to give power of attorney to your spouse or other trusted advisor so they can manage your affairs while you are still alive. Of course, the power of attorney would only be used in cases of temporary infirmity and you can restrict the actions your attorney can take by simply having your lawyer draft the appropriate limiting clauses.

A power of attorney is good protection against accidents and other circumstances that leave you unable to manage your affairs. It's a good way to avoid the lengthy legal and other delays that could occur if you have not made the proper provisions.

However, be careful in your selection of the person who will manage your affairs. This person will have full control over your affairs and there have been abuses in the past. Some provinces such as Alberta require you to consult a lawyer before granting a power of attorney to ensure that you understand the significance of the document you will be signing.

Ontario has introduced new legislation "The Substitute Decisions Act" to take force in 1995 governing power of attorney in two areas property (finances) and personal care.

My recommendation is that, as part of your estate plan, you execute a power of attorney and leave it with your lawyer along with instructions as to the circumstances under which it should be used.

WORKSHEET 19-4: ESTATE PLANNING CHECKLIST

	Date last reviewed	To be reviewed
Will	_____	_____
Trusts	_____	_____
Gifts	_____	_____
Power of Attorney	_____	_____

Are you satisfied with your selection of executor/executrix?	_____
Are you happy with your choice of guardian?	_____
Do you plan to leave an estate for your children?	_____
Do you plan to leave an estate for your grandchildren?	_____
Have you thought about what bequests you would like to make?	_____
Are you planning to leave any money to specific charities?	_____

A Word to the Wise

Do not assume that understanding the terminology surrounding estate planning makes you an expert. To effectively achieve the specific objectives you have in your estate plan, you will need the help of your team of professionals. With the right help, you can rest in the satisfaction of knowing that your spouse, your children, and even your grandchildren can enjoy the benefits of your assets both while you're still alive and when they may need them most, after your death.

Planning for the Opportunity of a Lifetime

Retirement liberates you from the pressures and demands of the working world. Bind yourself to meaningful endeavours and keep that freedom alive.

Dreams and Nightmares

Every day 500 Canadians enter retirement. Then what? With up to 2500 hours a year of free time that used to be work time, you can do anything you want. In a recent national magazine poll of senior citizens, the majority placed adventure travel at the top their list of preferred retirement activities—visions of steamy hikes through tropical forests, or trekking along cobblestone streets in a quaint foreign village. But, the poll also revealed that study participants spent most of their time slouched in front of a television.

People who adopt a naive, passive, dreamlike attitude toward retirement invariably find themselves disillusioned and miserable in their work-free years. You have probably heard the story about poor old "Wally Workaholic"—great guy, solid, productive employee, who retired at 65 and died a year later. Could it be that unrealistic expectations, plus a lack of solid retirement planning lead to such tragedies?

Get up from the TV and do what you want. Start by watching out for the three Rs: Uncertainty, Fear, and Procrastination. (Three Rs because they Really Ruin Retirement.)

Uncertainty: "I can't ever see myself slowing down; besides, I don't know where my life will be that far ahead."

Fear: "Deep down I dread the thought of not having my work to fall back on. What am I going to do with myself?"

Procrastination: "I haven't given much thought to my future but I will."

Determining Your Personal Life Goals

Setting strategic goals, establishing objectives, and developing your own plan are essential. Retirement is not unlike any other of life's major turning points. It is fraught with intense emotional upheaval. Planning for momentous events can remove unnecessary and unforeseen sources of stress.

Retirement should be a natural extension of those activities that you like doing now. You must learn to savour your newfound freedom. This extra, unscheduled time has the biggest impact on your retirement.

> Increased means and increased leisure are the two civilizers of man.
>
> **Benjamin Disraeli**

WORKSHEET 20-1: PRELIMINARY RETIREMENT LIFESTYLE CONSIDERATIONS

Do you plan to maintain your present standard of living? _____

Do you plan to upgrade your present standard of living? _____

Do you plan to choose a simpler, less costly lifestyle? _____

Do you honestly feel you will be able to afford your ideal retirement lifestyle, or is it merely a pipe dream? _____

Are you willing to reduce your lifestyle expenses when you retire? _____

Do you feel you could live on your financial reserves if you were disabled tomorrow? _____

Where would you like to live? Will you retain your current home? _____

Would you consider selling your existing home? _____

Will you buy a new home or condominium? _____

Would you consider selling other assets? _____

Are your children's educations provided for in case of early death? _____

Will your estate adequately provide for your spouse if you should die first? _____

Will you leave an estate for the next generation of our family? _____

Would you like to take major trips or travel on vacations? _____

Would you consider involvement in charitable or volunteer work? _____

Would you consider enrolling in educational courses? _____

What types of retirement sports and recreation would you like to explore?

_____

_____

What types of hobbies and crafts would you like to explore?

_____

_____

Other

_____

_____

Which of these activities could you share with your spouse?

_____

_____

What other areas can you begin to consider now?

_____

_____

Other

_____

_____

Take the time to complete Worksheet 20-1, letting your considerations and ambitions soar if you are inclined. If you can include your spouse in the process, do so.

Congratulations! It may not seem like much, but by taking the time to think through the Worksheet, and committing your responses to paper, you initiate the retirement planning process.

Put a ✓ next to each item you would like to realize prior to retirement. If providing for your children's education is high on your list of future objectives, and if you have already invested in an education trust fund, or are soon likely to, note whether that investment will reach maturity prior to your retirement. If buying a vacation property is a major consideration, note the approximate year by which you would like to realize that particular objective, and so on.

Highlight those goals you have rated as being high-priority considerations, and note these in the space provided below.

You can and do have the power to create and shape your future. With this exercise, you have already started to shake your dreams from dreamland and given them the dimension you need in order to realistically translate them into specific goals.

> **Three Types of People**
> ❶ People who make things happen
> ❷ People who watch things happen
> ❸ People who get knocked over the head and they say, "what happened?"

Retirement Goals and Options

Successful retirement is not a finite achievement, but an active ongoing process of choosing retirement goals and activities that can be realistically attained. Planning isn't creating some far-fetched fantasy; it's the groundwork for consistent fulfillment.

If becoming physically fit is one of your retirement objectives, don't dash out from your retirement party and cash in your gold watch for a hang-glider. Rigorous sports later in life often lead to discouragement, lowered self-esteem, if not serious injury. Walking and swimming can be safer and more rewarding, especially if you've already established a taste for them.

Perhaps you long to travel extensively, but never have had the time. Now you do. That doesn't mean selling off all your liquid assets, buying a 12-metre racing yacht and heading off to circumnavigate the globe.

It is seldom that one retires from business to enjoy his fortune in comfort... He works because he has always worked, and knows no other way.
Thomas Nichols

Additional Notes on Life Goals

_____

_____

_____

_____

_____

_____

_____

_____

Test the waters, so to speak. Experiment freely among your various lifestyle options before committing to any one activity. Find activities that suit your needs, inclinations, and available income.

Matching Your Retirement to Your Personality

The most rewarding retirement lifestyle you can choose will be one that matches your habits, interests, preferences, capabilities, and limitations as well as your disposition and temperament. Your retirement lifestyle should more or less reflect the person you are, not someone you would like to become.

Research has shown that the patterns of living we exhibit in our 40s, 50s, and 60s tend to predict the mental and physical condition we will experience in our 70s, 80s, and beyond. Examining your

TABLE 20-2: COMMON HUMAN NEEDS FOR MIDDLE-AGED CANADIANS

Needs	Comments	Specific Suggestions
Relationships—Spouse, Family, and Friends: To share life's joys and sorrows.	Rich is not a dollar amount; it is the individual with many friends. To have a few meaningful friendships in your lifetime is to arrive.	Choose your friends from all age groups; younger, your own age, and older.
Leisure Interests: Should be a balance of both physically and mentally stimulating activities.	Leisure interests are activities that are both absorbing and interesting. They bring refreshment and add a zest to living. Never short change yourself on developing new and old interests.	Leisure interest may include hobbies, crafts, collections, entertainment, sporting, cultural events, art, music, reading, and travel, etc.
Rest, Relaxation, and Recreation: To combat the tension and stress of daily life.	These 3Rs are the key to a happy life with longevity. Too much stress can greatly reduce your lifespan.	Work at obtaining a balanced lifestyle and adopt a healthy approach to stress management.
Intellectual and Artistic Pursuits: Take advantage of your mental and artistic endowment to reach the highest level of self-actualization.	We are free people, in a free country, with a smorgasbord of choices to design the lifestyle pursuit of our dreams. Your brain is a muscle that, without exercise, will wither up and die.	Read the world's greatest authors or biographers. Enjoy books on art, travel, history, science, astrology, and geography. Pursue painting, music, or an educational course.
Social Service and Volunteerism: Really happy and contented people are absorbed in a world larger than themselves.	Health and happiness is found through giving to others. Selflessness rather than selfishness promotes goodwill in the service of others.	Service clubs, church groups, men's and women's clubs, and health and welfare organizations would really appreciate you volunteering your services.
Looking Forward to the Future with a Spirit of Adventure and Optimism:	Start to capitalize on the wisdom of your years by taking advantage of your accumulated experience. Choose the things you want to do, and tackle everything you do with a positive mental attitude.	It's never too late! Some of life's greatest accomplishments develop after age 65.

current patterns of needs and goals will not only produce insights into your inner makeup, but provide a "window on the future"—a view of what is likely to be the most appropriate life pattern your retirement years should follow.

Table 20-2, provides an excellent portrayal of the common needs of middle-aged Canadians.

Maintaining a Winning Attitude

Approach retirement as you would a new "job," especially while you are getting the knack of it. The ground rules of this new job are radically different from what you have learned to expect from a conventional job. No one monitors your progress and no one accounts for your mistakes. You write your own pay cheque.

Most of us are educated to regard as rewarding and worthwhile only those activities that lead to monetary gain. There is more. To retire means to have earned the privilege and opportunity to discover rewards that simply cannot be measured in dollars and cents. Your new mandate is personal growth, self-expression, adventure, and the opportunity to "stop and smell the roses."

Greatest Accomplishments After Age 65

Picasso, Renoir, Goethe, Mother Teresa, Golda Meir, Ronald Reagan, George Bernard Shaw, Buckminister Fuller, Grandma Moses, Mahatma Gandhi, Norman Vincent Peale, Churchill, Colonel Sanders

Retirement Activities

Typically, people who derive the most enjoyment from retirement develop a broad-ranging inventory of stimulating activities. Any activity that proves consistently stimulating, that doesn't exceed your capabilities, and that is not so demanding that it threatens your sense of esteem and accomplishment, should be incorporated into your repertoire of leisure pursuits, hobbies, and pastimes. The notion that lawn bowling, bingo, shuffleboard, and similar activities are lacklustre, unfulfilling activities is a gross distortion of reality! The trick is to find a balance between activities that are long-range and activities that are short-range.

Long-Range

These are projects that require some serious investment of time and effort. They are pleasure-giving activities that give you something to continually look forward to. Long-range activities include events such as planning vacations, renovating or building an addition to your house, scouting for a vacation property, going on weekend trips and outings, and attending daylong or weekend "how-to" seminars. These and similar long-range projects often entail considerable preparation and planning, giving your days a constant momentum. In addition to combatting the dangers of boredom, they also offer opportunities to acquire knowledge, new skills, and the chance to make new social contacts.

Short-Range

Many seniors carry with them a calendar or notebook containing a list of various "rainy day" sorts of activities which, while they may not be as challenging or rewarding as large scale projects, do serve as excellent ways to spend time productively. Small household or car repairs, visiting friends or relatives, browsing in bookstores, visiting the gym or the local library, and collecting new recipes are all activities that can be taken up on any day when you might be at a loss for something to do. By getting into the habit of jotting down tasks or interests as they

All of my possessions

for a moment

of time.

Queen Elizabeth I 1603

spring to mind, you will gradually develop a varied base of interests and will become a more well-rounded person in the process. Remember, it's always better to have too much to do than too little. You can always cut back on your schedule to suit your time and your real interests.

Turn your attention now to Worksheet 20-3 to discover which leisure activities such as sports, hobbies and crafts, social and entertainment, interest you. Indicate in each column those activities that hold no interest for you, that you have tried, or that you would like to try. For those activities that interest you, jot down a few notes in the "comments" column as to your preference for the activity.

WORKSHEET 20-3: LEISURE ACTIVITIES

Leisure Activity	Have no Interest	Have Tried	Would Like to Try	Comments
Sports				
Golf	☐	☐	☐	_____
Tennis	☐	☐	☐	_____
Curling	☐	☐	☐	_____
Bowling	☐	☐	☐	_____
Hiking	☐	☐	☐	_____
Lawn Bowling	☐	☐	☐	_____
Shuffleboard	☐	☐	☐	_____
Walking	☐	☐	☐	_____
Jogging	☐	☐	☐	_____
Bicycling	☐	☐	☐	_____
Swimming	☐	☐	☐	_____
Sailing	☐	☐	☐	_____
Camping	☐	☐	☐	_____
Fishing	☐	☐	☐	_____
Canoeing	☐	☐	☐	_____
Skiing	☐	☐	☐	_____
Hunting	☐	☐	☐	_____
Aerobics	☐	☐	☐	_____
Weight Training	☐	☐	☐	_____
Skating	☐	☐	☐	_____
Snowmobiling	☐	☐	☐	_____
Windsurfing	☐	☐	☐	_____
Billiards	☐	☐	☐	_____
Other	☐	☐	☐	_____

Leisure Activity	Have no Interest	Have Tried	Would Like to Try	Comments
Hobbies and Crafts				
Gardening	☐	☐	☐	_____
Painting	☐	☐	☐	_____
Crocheting	☐	☐	☐	_____
Sewing	☐	☐	☐	_____
Basket Weaving	☐	☐	☐	_____
Auto Mechanics	☐	☐	☐	_____
Woodworking	☐	☐	☐	_____
Metalworking	☐	☐	☐	_____
Photography	☐	☐	☐	_____
Music	☐	☐	☐	_____
Educational Courses	☐	☐	☐	_____
Financial Planning	☐	☐	☐	_____
Writing	☐	☐	☐	_____
Reading	☐	☐	☐	_____
Crossword Puzzles	☐	☐	☐	_____
Jigsaw Puzzles	☐	☐	☐	_____
Electronics	☐	☐	☐	_____
Inventing	☐	☐	☐	_____
Ballroom Dancing	☐	☐	☐	_____
Square Dancing	☐	☐	☐	_____
Round Dancing	☐	☐	☐	_____
Stamp Collecting	☐	☐	☐	_____
Coin Collecting	☐	☐	☐	_____
Stained Glass	☐	☐	☐	_____
Other	☐	☐	☐	_____
Collecting Books				
Geography	☐	☐	☐	_____
History	☐	☐	☐	_____
Limited Editions	☐	☐	☐	_____
Biographies	☐	☐	☐	_____
Other	☐	☐	☐	_____
Social				
Cards	☐	☐	☐	_____
Bridge	☐	☐	☐	_____
Cribbage	☐	☐	☐	_____

Leisure Activity	Have no Interest	Have Tried	Would Like to Try	Comments
Euchre	☐	☐	☐	_____
Coffee Klatsch	☐	☐	☐	_____
Politics	☐	☐	☐	_____
Volunteer Work	☐	☐	☐	_____
Church Work	☐	☐	☐	_____
Teaching	☐	☐	☐	_____
Group Leader	☐	☐	☐	_____
Cubs	☐	☐	☐	_____
Beavers	☐	☐	☐	_____
Scouts	☐	☐	☐	_____
Brownies	☐	☐	☐	_____
Girl Guides	☐	☐	☐	_____
Investment Club	☐	☐	☐	_____
Kinsmen	☐	☐	☐	_____
Masons	☐	☐	☐	_____
Canadian Progress Club	☐	☐	☐	_____
Elks	☐	☐	☐	_____
Visiting Friends	☐	☐	☐	_____
Family Activities	☐	☐	☐	_____
Other	☐	☐	☐	_____

Entertainment

	Have no Interest	Have Tried	Would Like to Try	Comments
Television	☐	☐	☐	_____
Radio	☐	☐	☐	_____
Movies	☐	☐	☐	_____
Videotaping	☐	☐	☐	_____
Taping Music	☐	☐	☐	_____
Musical Instrument	☐	☐	☐	_____
Acting (Community Theatre)	☐	☐	☐	_____
Other	☐	☐	☐	_____

Cultural Events

	Have no Interest	Have Tried	Would Like to Try	Comments
Museums	☐	☐	☐	_____
Art Galleries	☐	☐	☐	_____
Exhibits	☐	☐	☐	_____
Concerts	☐	☐	☐	_____

Leisure Activity	Have no Interest	Have Tried	Would Like to Try	Comments
Ballet	☐	☐	☐	_____
Jazz	☐	☐	☐	_____
Classical	☐	☐	☐	_____
Dining Out	☐	☐	☐	_____
Opera	☐	☐	☐	_____
Other	☐	☐	☐	_____
Attending Sports Events				
Baseball	☐	☐	☐	_____
Hockey	☐	☐	☐	_____
Soccer	☐	☐	☐	_____
Football	☐	☐	☐	_____
Other	☐	☐	☐	_____
Travel				
Auto Trips	☐	☐	☐	_____
Cruises	☐	☐	☐	_____
Group Tours	☐	☐	☐	_____
Other	☐	☐	☐	_____

Money Makes Retirement Go Around

Money, to be sure, is an essential pre-condition for securing a satisfying life as a retiree. You will have to earn enough to support your lifestyle expectations. Whether or not the world will, in fact, become your oyster will depend on the strength of the financial plan you set in motion during your productive middle years.

As C. Colburn Hardy, an authority on the subject of retirement planning, notes:

"To achieve any goal you must set a target. For retirement, that means financial security: enough assets to meet the lifelong needs of you and your spouse... Success requires constant savings, rewarding investments, and the use of all your resources. If you play while you work and fail to set aside reserves for the future, you will have trouble. But if you set up and adhere to a plan, your future will be safe and sure. What you do or do not do while working, will determine what you can or cannot do after you retire."

Most retirees face an ironic dilemma. They don't want to oversave and eventually realize that they squirrelled away too much money and therefore lived their lives less abundantly than they could have. On the other hand, they are reluctant to live beyond their means for fear of squandering their financial resources and being forced to live below accustomed standards. Worse, they may feel the teeth of poverty nipping at their heels.

The way around this dilemma is to clearly establish your present cash flow situation, understanding where your money is coming from, where it is going, and what you can do with it.

Your Personal Retirement Objectives Profile

Taking the time to put your goals in writing makes them clear in your mind and helps you to keep your pledge to realize these goals. Like any good navigator, you must plot your course if you are to reach your destination. As you jot down your objectives, give some thought to the sacrifice and risks you are willing to accept in order to realize your stated objectives.

WORKSHEET 20-4: YOUR PERSONAL RETIREMENT OBJECTIVES PROFILE

Examples

Written Objectives

Short-Term, 1-2 years
Reduce credit card balances; buy home furnishings; buy a boat, car, other assets; save for a holiday; make maximum RRSP contribution; establish a savings plan or investment program; draft Will; begin estate planning and retirement planning strategies; review insurances, etc.

_____
_____
_____
_____
_____
_____
_____
_____
_____

Medium-Term, 3-5 Years
Buy a new home; build addition to current home; finance children's education; travel; buy a business; make a major investment; adopt multi-year estate plans; commit to guardian, executor, and power of attorney considerations; maximize RRSP or other pension plans, etc.

_____
_____
_____
_____
_____
_____
_____
_____
_____

Long-Term, 6-15 Years
Invest for a major trip, for home in sunbelt; make charitable donations and other estate plans; assist children or grandchildren; partial or full retirement; review all retirement strategies, and determine approximate retirement date, etc.

_____
_____
_____
_____
_____
_____
_____
_____
_____

A Final Word

The credit belongs to the one who strives valiantly; who comes up short again and again; who knows great enthusiasm and great devotion; who spends himself in a worthy cause; and who, at the best, knows in the end the triumph of high achievement; and who, at the worst, if he fails at least fails while daring greatly, so that his place shall never be with those timid souls who know neither victory nor defeat.

—Theodore Roosevelt

In the summer of 1994, on the occasion of the 10th anniversary of the incorporation of FKI Financial Knowledge Inc., we know that financial planning, counselling, and pre-retirement education will evolve as one of the greatest growth industries during the next 25 years. You and I are fortunate to be in at the ground stage of this growth. We will have more tools and opportunities to accumulate wealth and achieve a financially-dignified retirement than anyone in history. It can be done, and it can be enjoyable.

Your positive winning mental attitude will play a major role in your success. You have an incredible journey ahead of you, and I am delighted to have shared some of that journey with you.

May you have financial success, and a happy, fulfilling retirement.

Personal Record and Family Data

Name: _____ Date of Birth: _____

Address: _____ Place of Birth: _____

_____ Soc. Ins. No.: _____

_____ Prov. Health Ins. No.: _____

Occupation: _____ Drivers Lic. No.: _____

Employer's Name: _____

Address: _____

Business Phone: _____ Home Phone: _____

Spouse Name: _____ Maiden Name: _____

Address: _____ Date of Birth: _____

_____ Place of Birth: _____

_____ Soc. Ins. No.: _____

Occupation: _____ Prov. Health Ins. No.: _____

Driver's Lic. No.: _____

Employer's Name: _____

Address: _____

Business Phone: _____ Home Phone: _____

CHILDREN'S NAMES	Married Name	Date of Birth	Soc. Ins. No.

GRANDCHILDREN'S NAMES   Married Name   Date of Birth   Soc. Ins. No.

_____

_____

_____

_____

_____

MY PARENTS	Name	Date of Birth	Place of Birth	Date of Death
Father:				
Mother:				
Grandfather:				
Grandmother:				
Grandfather:				
Grandmother:				

SPOUSE'S PARENTS	Name	Date of Birth	Place of Birth	Date of Death
Father:				
Mother:				
Grandfather:				
Grandmother:				
Grandfather:				
Grandmother:				

BROTHERS AND SISTERS

Name	Date of Birth	Date of Death	Married to	Address

IN CASE OF EMERGENCY CONTACT

Family Name	Address	Phone

CLOSE FRIENDS' NAMES   Address   Phone

Lawyer:

Banker:

Accountant:

Broker:

Insurance Agent:

Investment Advisor:

Clergyman:

Doctor:

Dentist:

Employer:

Others:

University or College:

Clubs & Associations:

Union:

Lodges:

Professional Associations:

Community Organizations:

Other:

LOCATION OF DOCUMENTS	Date	Description	Location

Will: _____

Spouse's Will: _____

Funeral Arrangments: _____

Bank Accounts _____

Chequing: _____

Savings: _____

Current Account: _____

Trust Accounts _____

Chequing: _____

Savings: _____

Current Account: _____

Mortgages: _____

Property Deeds: _____

Insurance Policies _____

Whole Life: _____

Universal Life: _____

Term: _____

Disability: _____

Group: _____

Accident and Health: _____

Automobile: _____

General: _____

Investment Certificates _____

Stocks: _____

Bonds: _____

Warrants: _____

Options: _____

	Date	Description	Location

CSB's: _____

Term Deposits: _____

Mutual Funds: _____

Real Estate Contracts: _____

Business Documents: _____

Employment Contracts: _____

RRSPs: _____

RESPs: _____

RPPs/DPSPs: _____

RRIFs: _____

LIRAs/LIFs: _____

Annuities: _____

Birth Certificates: _____

Baptismal Certificates: _____

Passports and Visas: _____

Marriage Contracts: _____

Marriage Licenses: _____

Separation Papers: _____

Divorce Documents: _____

Notes Receivable: _____

Notes Payable: _____

Income Tax Returns: _____

Safety Deposit Box: _____

Safety Deposit Keys: _____

Other Records: _____

Other Valuables: _____

Fundamentals of Sound Investing and My Personal Investment Philosophy

- The tape never lies—the best test of truth can be found in the stock market—it tells all in the end. Collectively, buyers' and sellers' actions will cause the tape to reflect the truth.
- The stock market is a mechanism by which buyers and sellers can reach differing conclusions, the end result rewarding one person and punishing the other.
- 30% of your portfolio selections will account for 70% of your results; 70% of your portfolio selections will account for 30% of your results, due to mediocre performance, stocks marking time, and small losses.
- Invest for long-term gains rather than short-term, get-rich-quick, in-and-out trading, and speculative schemes.
- Investment performance should be measured over the long-term, in years, rather than the short-term, over weeks. Too many investors want it all right now and become dissatisfied in the short-term rather than allowing their investment selection the time to mature over the longer term. Patience is a virtue!
- Search for value in companies with strong balance sheets, that trade at low multiples of prices related to earnings, and that have a potential for consistent and stable future earnings growth.
- Diversification by asset allocation and investment selection are of paramount importance to the success of most wealth accumulation programs.

- Beware of the herd instinct to follow the leader in the latest fad or glamour stock. Choose a stock based on value rather than it being "the talk of the town." Popular opinions are invariably wrong.
- Cut your losses and let your profits run. Don't be caught selling your performance stocks too soon. You will never get hurt taking a profit, but you can lose precious performance points. Many people sell their winners and hang on to their losers to avoid taking a loss and, over time, end up with a portfolio of non-performing stocks.
- Beware of downgrading quality for the lure of a higher yield. The reason a company trades for a higher yield generally means the issue is of a lesser quality or a higher risk and at some point in the economic cycle, this type of stock could cause you a lot of aggravation.
- Beware of over-staying a winner. Prices are often driven to extreme levels. Good stocks in good industries, in a healthy market and economy, eventually complete a cycle. There can be a tendency to lose sight of the fundamentals and over-stay your time. For every stock there is a season!
- You must have an understanding of psychology to become a successful investor.
- More often than not, "New Issues" are priced to sell and, generally, they increase your odds of investment success.
- The law of demand and supply always works in the market. When everyone is

bullish, a market must go down because there are no buyers left. Conversely, when everyone is bearish, a market must go up because there are no sellers left.

- Always buy on rumor and sell on news. Oil and gas, metals and minerals, and precious metals are the best examples that speculative markets generally sell off on the news.
- Prior to making any investment, consider the possibility of being wrong and what those consequences would mean to you.
- Currencies are nothing but common shares, and their earnings per share (EPS) are expressed as balance of payments. Dividends on currencies are interest on the currency, and its ability to repay debt near-term versus long-term. The international level of inflation on currencies is a barometer for investors.
- There is no time for FEAR in a bear market. FAITH, ENTHUSIASM, AMBITION, and RESOURCEFULNESS are the traits you require for investment success. The best values in the market are born in a bear market.
- The history of the markets is to overdiscount both ways; the market is a series of extremes, often becoming overbought or over-sold. A professional investor, using market timing skills, can be very successful catching the mood of the market.
- The stock market is always more concerned with the future than the present. Therefore, the market behaviour today is a reflection of what is anticipated in the future, usually six to nine months in advance.
- Never buy the stock market. Rather, buy individually selected stocks. More money is lost trying to guess where the market is going when the concentration should be applied to specific companies.

- Information about a company's product or service, such as up-to-date research, is vital to your investment success. But businesses are run by management, and this ingredient is by far the most important factor to analyze in terms of the company's future performance possibilities. Management's ownership in the company is important.
- It is better to own the wrong stock at the right time than the right stock at the wrong time.
- Bull markets follow bear markets follow bull markets follow bear markets because they always have. It is the nature of cycles. Generally, bull markets average three to four years and bear markets about one year in a typical cycle.
- If a stock has had a long and rapid rise, and then seems to stay level in the face of continuing good news, SELL! The theory would suggest that supply has caught up with demand, and the supplier is probably better informed.
- Buy and sell stocks on a scale. If the direction is working for you, it tends to confirm your original position and opinion.
- That which is hardest to do is probably correct.
- If you ever find yourself hoping instead of believing, sell your position immediately.
- When a stock fails to respond as well as it should on good news, it is a danger sign. Be sure that there has been time for the news to become generally known.
- When a stock tops out or bottoms out at a steady price for about three days, the next trend is usually opposite to the first.
- In all of your strategies, encompass the power of positive thinking. You become like that which you associate yourself with. "As a man thinketh, so is he." Recognize the miracle you truly are!

Important Market Factors

A Short Course on Technical Analysis

by Leon Tuey, Technical Research Consultant

The five most important factors are:

> Monetary
>
> Supply/Demand
>
> Psychological
>
> Internal
>
> Fundamental

Monetary Factors

The most important influence on stock prices is monetary policy. The monetary policy variables—bank reserve requirement, discount rate, and margin requirement—are the tools with which the Federal Government effects its monetary policy. Consecutive increases or reductions in monetary policy variables signal a change in monetary policy.

What to follow:

- Treasury Bond Futures and Treasury Bill Futures.
- Dow Jones 20-Bond Average and the Dow Jones Utility Average. Watch for divergence.
- Federal Funds rate and Treasury Bill rate.
- The yield curve—spread between the Treasury Bills and long-term yield.

Supply/Demand Factors

Stock prices are affected by supply/demand. Hence, one must monitor the cash levels of institutions and individual investors.

What to follow:

- Institutional cash reserves reported by *Indata* and other services
- Mutual Fund Liquid Asset Ratio as reported by the *Investment Funds Institute of Canada*
- Individuals' percentage of financial assets in equities
- Customers' margin debt

Psychological Factors (Market Sentiment)

Psychology affects supply/demand. Typically, major market tops are marked by over-confidence and euphoria and major market bottoms are marked by excessive pessimism and panic. Sentiment always moves from one extreme to another.

What to follow:

- *Market Vane's* survey of market sentiment
- *Investors Intelligence* survey of advisory service sentiment
- Put/Call Options Ratio
- Public short-selling versus specialist short-selling

Internal Factors

Market averages do not provide an accurate picture of the real market. The Dow Jones Industrial Average, for example, only represents 30 blue chip stocks. Moreover, it is dominated by cyclical stocks. Hence, it is important to look under the market to find out what the real market is doing.

What to follow:

- All market averages and divergence
- The Advance-Decline line
- The High-Low Differential Indicator
- The Advance-Decline ratio

Fundamental Factors

These are poor tools for market timing. Nevertheless, they do provide an understanding and appreciation of the market's valuation level from a historical standpoint.

What to follow:

- Yield—the most important and useful
- Price/Earnings ratio
- Book Value
- Replacement Cost
- Earnings Momentum. More important and more valuable than P/E ratios

In Addition

Watch key commodities such as crude oil, copper, gold, lumber, and aluminum. And because the world economies are so inter-linked, watch other markets.

Compounding Statistics

HOW MUCH HAVE YOU EARNED IN YOUR LIFETIME SO FAR? *(Based on starting work at age 25 and working to age 65)*

Age	Years of Work	MONTHLY INCOME				Monthly Cheques Spent	Monthly Cheques Left
		$2,000	$2,500	$3,000	$4,000		
26	1	$24,000	$30,000	$36,000	$48,000	12	480
27	2	48,000	60,000	72,000	96,000	24	468
28	3	72,000	90,000	108,000	144,000	36	456
29	4	96,000	120,000	144,000	192,000	48	444
30	5	120,000	150,000	180,000	240,000	60	432
31	6	144,000	180,000	216,000	288,000	72	420
32	7	168,000	210,000	252,000	336,000	84	408
33	8	192,000	240,000	288,000	384,000	96	396
34	9	216,000	270,000	324,000	432,000	108	384
35	10	240,000	300,000	360,000	480,000	120	372
36	11	264,000	330,000	396,000	528,000	132	360
37	12	288,000	360,000	432,000	576,000	144	348
38	13	312,000	390,000	468,000	624,000	156	336
39	14	336,000	420,000	504,000	672,000	168	324
40	15	360,000	450,000	540,000	720,000	180	312
41	16	384,000	480,000	576,000	768,000	192	300
42	17	408,000	510,000	612,000	816,000	204	288
43	18	432,000	540,000	648,000	864,000	216	276
44	19	456,000	570,000	684,000	912,000	228	264
45	20	480,000	600,000	720,000	960,000	240	252
46	21	504,000	630,000	756,000	1,008,000	252	240
47	22	528,000	660,000	792,000	1,056,000	264	228
48	23	552,000	690,000	828,000	1,104,000	276	216
49	24	576,000	720,000	864,000	1,152,000	288	204
50	25	600,000	750,000	900,000	1,200,000	300	192
51	26	624,000	780,000	936,000	1,248,000	312	180
52	27	648,000	810,000	972,000	1,296,000	324	168
53	28	672,000	840,000	1,008,000	1,344,000	336	156
54	29	696,000	870,000	1,044,000	1,392,000	348	144
55	30	720,000	900,000	1,080,000	1,440,000	360	132
56	31	744,000	930,000	1,116,000	1,488,000	372	120
57	32	768,000	960,000	1,152,000	1,536,000	384	108
58	33	792,000	990,000	1,188,000	1,584,000	396	96
59	34	816,000	1,020,000	1,224,000	1,632,000	408	84
60	35	840,000	1,050,000	1,260,000	1,680,000	420	72
61	36	864,000	1,080,000	1,296,000	1,728,000	432	60
62	37	888,000	1,110,000	1,332,000	1,776,000	444	48
63	38	912,000	1,140,000	1,368,000	1,824,000	456	36
64	39	936,000	1,170,000	1,404,000	1,872,000	468	24
65	40	960,000	1,200,000	1,440,000	1,920,000	480	12

HOW MUCH WILL YOU EARN BETWEEN NOW AND AGE 65?

MONTHLY INCOME

Years	$1,000	$2,000	$3,000	$4,000	$5,000
21	$540,000	$1,080,000	$1,620,000	$2,160,000	$2,700,000
22	528,000	1,056,000	1,584,000	2,112,000	2,640,000
23	516,000	1,032,000	1,548,000	2,064,000	2,580,000
24	504,000	1,008,000	1,512,000	2,016,000	2,520,000
25	492,000	984,000	1,476,000	1,968,000	2,460,000
26	480,000	960,000	1,440,000	1,920,000	2,400,000
27	468,000	936,000	1,404,000	1,872,000	2,340,000
28	456,000	912,000	1,368,000	1,824,000	2,280,000
29	444,000	888,000	1,332,000	1,776,000	2,220,000
30	432,000	864,000	1,296,000	1,728,000	2,160,000
31	420,000	840,000	1,260,000	1,680,000	2,100,000
32	408,000	816,000	1,224,000	1,632,000	2,040,000
33	396,000	792,000	1,188,000	1,584,000	1,980,000
34	384,000	768,000	1,152,000	1,536,000	1,920,000
35	372,000	744,000	1,116,000	1,488,000	1,860,000
36	360,000	720,000	1,080,000	1,440,000	1,800,000
37	348,000	696,000	1,044,000	1,392,000	1,740,000
38	336,000	672,000	1,008,000	1,344,000	1,680,000
39	324,000	648,000	972,000	1,296,000	1,620,000
40	312,000	624,000	936,000	1,248,000	1,560,000
41	300,000	600,000	900,000	1,200,000	1,500,000
42	288,000	576,000	864,000	1,152,000	1,440,000
43	276,000	552,000	828,000	1,104,000	1,380,000
44	264,000	528,000	792,000	1,056,000	1,320,000
45	252,000	504,000	756,000	1,008,000	1,260,000
46	240,000	480,000	720,000	960,000	1,200,000
47	228,000	456,000	684,000	912,000	1,140,000
48	216,000	432,000	648,000	864,000	1,080,000
49	204,000	408,000	612,000	816,000	1,020,000
50	192,000	384,000	576,000	768,000	960,000
51	180,000	360,000	540,000	720,000	900,000
52	168,000	336,000	504,000	672,000	840,000
53	156,000	312,000	468,000	624,000	780,000
54	144,000	288,000	432,000	576,000	720,000
55	132,000	264,000	396,000	528,000	660,000
56	120,000	240,000	360,000	480,000	600,000
57	108,000	216,000	324,000	432,000	540,000
58	96,000	192,000	288,000	384,000	480,000
59	84,000	168,000	252,000	336,000	420,000
60	72,000	144,000	216,000	288,000	360,000
61	60,000	120,000	180,000	240,000	300,000
62	48,000	96,000	144,000	192,000	240,000
63	36,000	72,000	108,000	144,000	180,000
64	24,000	48,000	72,000	96,000	120,000
65	12,000	24,000	36,000	48,000	60,000

FUTURE WORTH OF $1,200 INVESTED EACH YEAR WITH ANNUAL COMPOUNDING

Rate of Return	END OF YEAR							
	5	10	15	20	25	30	35	40
5%	$6,631	$15,093	$25,894	$39,679	$57,273	$79,727	$108,384	$144,960
6%	6,765	15,817	27,931	44,143	65,837	94,870	133,722	185,714
7%	6,901	16,580	30,155	49,195	75,899	113,353	165,884	239,562
8%	7,040	17,384	32,583	54,914	87,727	135,940	206,780	310,868
9%	7,182	18,232	35,233	61,392	101,641	163,569	258,853	405,459
10%	7,326	19,125	38,127	68,730	118,016	197,393	325,229	531,111
11%	7,473	20,066	41,286	77,043	137,296	238,825	409,907	698,191
12%	7,623	21,058	44,736	86,463	160,001	289,599	517,996	920,510
13%	7,776	22,104	48,501	97,136	186,743	351,839	656,017	1,216,445
14%	7,932	23,205	52,611	109,230	218,245	428,144	832,287	1,610,430
15%	8,091	24,364	57,096	122,932	255,352	521,694	1,057,404	2,134,908

RATES OF RETURN AND THE LUMP SUM INVESTMENT REQUIRED TO HAVE $100,000 AVAILABLE AT THE END OF SPECIFIED PERIOD

Rate of Return	END OF YEAR							
	5	10	15	20	25	30	35	40
5%	$78,353	$61,391	$48,102	$37,689	$29,530	$23,138	$18,129	$14,205
6%	74,726	55,839	41,727	31,180	23,300	17,411	13,011	9,722
7%	71,299	50,835	36,245	25,842	18,425	13,137	9,366	6,678
8%	68,058	46,319	31,524	21,455	14,602	9,938	6,763	4,603
9%	64,993	42,241	27,454	17,843	11,597	7,537	4,899	3,184
10%	62,092	38,554	23,939	14,864	9,230	5,731	3,558	2,209
11%	59,345	35,218	20,900	12,403	7,361	4,368	2,592	1,538
12%	56,743	32,197	18,270	10,367	5,882	3,338	1,894	1,075
13%	54,276	29,459	15,989	8,678	4,710	2,557	1,388	753
14%	51,937	26,974	14,010	7,276	3,779	1,963	1,019	529
15%	49,718	24,718	12,289	6,110	3,038	1,510	751	373

APPROXIMATE ANNUAL INVESTMENT REQUIRED TO EQUAL $100,000 AT VARYING RATES

Rate of Return	END OF YEAR							
	5	10	15	20	25	30	35	40
5%	$18,097	$7,950	$4,634	$3,024	$2,095	$1,505	$1,107	$828
6%	17,740	7,587	4,296	2,718	1,823	1,265	897	$646
7%	17,389	7,238	3,979	2,439	1,581	1,059	723	$501
8%	17,046	6,903	3,683	2,185	1,368	883	580	$386
9%	16,709	6,582	3,406	1,955	1,181	734	464	$296
10%	16,380	6,275	3,147	1,746	1,017	608	369	$226
11%	16,057	5,980	2,907	1,558	874	502	293	$172
12%	15,741	5,698	2,682	1,388	750	414	232	$130
13%	15,431	5,429	2,474	1,235	643	341	183	$99
14%	15,128	5,171	2,281	1,099	550	280	144	$75
15%	14,832	4,925	2,102	976	470	230	113	$56

How to Read Newspaper Listings—Stocks

$	17	$14-3/4	Acme T. & D.	$ .72	$16-3/4	$16-1/8	$16-1/8	400
	29-3/8	26	Comput Co.	2.28	29-1/4	29-1/4	29-1/4	100
	15	7-7/8	O & G Expl. A		9	8-3/4	8-7/8	14400
	8	490	Ven Mining		5-1/2	5-1/2	5-1/2	z 20
	3/4	26-1/2	Sec. Bank	2.00	27	26-1/2	27	19626
	345	270	Alpha Oil		280	270	280	30500
	15-1/4	10-1/2	Imp Trust	1.20	13-1/2	12-7/1	13-1/4	64353
	5-1/4	350	West Ont. Pr.		400	40	400	205
	24-1/4	15-1/2	UNI C	.90	21-3/4	17-1/8	21-3/4	24300
	2-5/8	39-1/8	C Farm Ent.	2.05	42-3/4	41-1/2	42-5/8	90874
	31	24	Korea Iron	1.70	27	26-3/4	27	908
	23-1/2	19-1/4	Silv Tel	1.45	22-1/4	21-1/8	21-3/4	17038
	10-1/4	8-1/2	Plywood Pkg		9-1/2	9-3/8	9-1/2	1600
	11-1/2	7-3/4	Gamma Res.		9-5/8	9-1/8	9-3/8	9724
	175	75	SYNBLEND Pr.		140	108	132	76200
	310	202	IBL br		275	220	265	27600
	150	146-1/2	Lon Util	3.15	149-1/4	147-3/4	149-1/4	344

Highest and lowest price paid for the stock to date this year. Venture Mining stock has traded as high as $8.00, and as low as $4.90 during the year. Shares traded under $5.00 are quoted in cents.

Abbreviated name of the company issuing the stock. This listing refers to Oil and Gas Exploration Limited's Class 'A' stock.

Number of shares traded during the trading session. The symbol **z** indicates that less than a board lot traded.

Price paid for the last board lot traded was $27.00. This was up 1/4 or 25 cents from the closing price in the previous session.

Annual dividend paid by the company. This is a projected annual rate based on dividend payments over the last twelve months.

Highest price paid for the stock during this trading session was $16-3/4, and the lowest was $16-1/8.

Source: The Toronto Stock Exchange

How to Read Newspaper Listings— Mutual Funds

Vol	Cde	Assets	NAVPS	Fund Name	1Yr	Rnk of 167	3Yr	Rnk of 140	5Yr	Rnk of 128	10Yr	Rnk of 72
2	FD	146	16.47	20/20 Canadian Growth	37.3	66	13.0	96	-	-	-	-
10	N	29	10.02	ABC Fundamental-Value	143.8	1	45.3	4	-	-	-	-
7	FD	799	11.93	AGF Canadian Equity	36.2	74	14.9	74	5.1	112	8.8	53
9	FD	403	21.28	AGF Growth Equity	62.6	11	33.9	9	17.0	9	12.5	8
10	FD	144	25.15	AIC Advantage	71.0	7	35.2	8	19.2	8	-	-
2	FR	11	6.46	Admax Cdn Performance	31.8	103	12.9	98	-	-	-	-
1	XF	15	17.23	All-Canadian Compound	43.0	41	14.0	81	9.3	48	8.6	55
-	N	133	17.20	Alta Fund Investment	41.3	51	-	-	-	-	-	-
3	N	83	13.83	Altamira Capital Growth	42.1	47	21.5	27	14.4	13	10.0	38
9	N	1699	29.58	Altimira Equity	51.8	24	39.5	5	29.5	1	-	-

CANADIAN EQUITY FUNDS:

VOL — VOLATILITY: The historical variability in a fund's monthly rate of return compared with other funds in the same group. Lower number means more stable; higher means more volatile.

CDE — CODE: N= no load; F= front end fee; D= deferred declining redemption on original capital invested; R= deferred declining redemption on current market value; FD or FR= at buyer's option; X= not available to general public.

ASSETS: Total net assets in millions.

NAVPS: Net asset value per share.

NAME OF FUNDS: May or may not be abbreviated.

RETURN: 1,3,5, and 10 years, average annual compound rates of return assuming reinvestment of dividends and net of all management fees or expenses.

RNK — RANK: Measurement of fund's performance relative to all other funds in the same group.

Commissions; Management Fees; Service, Administration, and Trustee Fees

Mutual Fund Purchase

- Front-end Load: generally 2% – 9%
- Back-end Load: generally 4% – 5% declining 1/2% annually
- No-Load

Stock Purchase

Based on price and volume on both buy and sell; generally 1% – 3%

GICs, TDs, CDs

No costs, built-in

Bonds and Debentures

Quoted on net basis

Trustee Fees

Generally fixed dollar amounts. e.g. $125 RRSP Self-directed plan

Management Fees/Administration Fees/Service Fees

Cash Reserves (Money Market)	1/2% – 1%
Fixed Income	1% – 2%
Equities	2% – 2 3/4%

Financial Planners — fee structure

- Hourly based
- Flat fee
- Fee based on % of assets

You Can Participate in Business Expansion

1. ABC Inc. needs money to expand.

2. The company decides to go public and raise money by selling its shares to investors.

3. The shares are purchased by an Investment firm, or group of firms, who then sell them to the public.

4. Through the sale of its shares to investors, ABC Inc. has raised the money it needs to complete its expansion.

5. The newly issued publicly owned shares can now be traded on the stock exchange.

6. ABC Inc. shares will be owned by many different investors, including individuals, pension funds, and institutions. They all participate in our free enterprise system.

Source: Modified after chart by The Toronto Stock Exchange

Financial Planning—Year-End Checklist

☐ Collect Personal Data

☐ Organize Financial Statements and Documents

☐ Review Budgeted Statements to Actual Results

☐ Review Goals and Strategies

☐ Needs Analysis—Identification of Issues and Problems

☐ Establish Priorities

☐ Establish Assumptions

☐ Construct Balance Sheet / Net Worth Statement

☐ Construct Cash Flow Statement

☐ Income Tax Planning
  • Pension and RRSP Maximum Contribution
  • Tax Shelters
  • Income Splitting and Trusts
  • Minimize Non-deductable Costs
  • Charitable and Medical Deductions

☐ Asset Allocation

☐ Investment Planning
  • Portfolio Mix
  • Dividend Income
  • Interest Income
  • Capital Gains

☐ Risk Management Insurance

☐ Wills and Estate Planning

☐ Retirement Planning—Retirement Income Statement

☐ Recommendations

☐ Implementation

A Glossary of Terms

Actuaries: Professional "odds-makers" who study life expectancy or mortality rates for insurance purposes.

After-tax cost: The final cost of an investment to an investor in a particular tax bracket, after calculating the effect of income tax.

Agent: One who acts on behalf of another person or company, called a principal, usually for a fee or commission.

Amortization: The process of gradual liquidation of a future obligation or capital outlay, such as paying off a mortgage with periodic payments.

Annual report: A statement of results issued by a company to its shareholders at the end of the fiscal year (the company's year-end) containing reports on company operations and formal audited financial statements.

Annuity: An agreement under which assets are turned over to an institution on the condition that the donor (or other designated person) receive regular payments for a specified period. Most often used as a retirement vehicle to provide the annuitant with a guaranteed income. A type of contract that entitles the buyer to a series of payments. Annuitants (the beneficiaries of the plan) pay a fixed sum when purchasing an annuity. Life annuities pay for the lifetime of the annuitant and fixed-term annuities until the annuitant reaches age 90.

Arbitrage: The simultaneous purchase and sale of securities or options on two separate markets at prices that yield a profit to the arbitrage trader.

Ask (Offer): The price at which a seller offers his/her security or property for sale.

Asset: What a firm or individual owns. On a balance sheet, that which is owned or receivable.

Asset allocation: The planned percentage distributions of your investment assets into various categories such as reserves, bonds and debentures, preferred shares, common shares, precious metals, and real estate.

Asset value: The monetary value of holdings; sometimes expressed as asset value per share by dividing a total asset figure by the number of shares outstanding.

Average or Index: For stocks, indicators of broad market performance. The Dow Jones industrial average includes the shares of 30 large companies; the Toronto Stock Exchange's composite index includes 300 companies. Derived from statistical tolls that measure the state of the stock market or the economy, based on the performance of stocks or other meaningful components, such as the Consumer Price Index.

Averaging down: Buying more of a security at a lower price than the original investment. Aim: to reduce the average cost per unit.

Back-end redemption charge: Many mutual funds apply a back-end redemption charge on the sale of units, which usually begins at $4^1/2$% to 6% in the first year and declines by $^1/2$% to 1% per year, eventually reaching 0% several years into the future. This charge may apply to the original purchase value or the market value when units are redeemed.

Bear market: A stock market whose index of representative stocks, such as the Toronto Stock Exchange 300 Composite Index, is declining in value. A "bearish" investor believes share prices will fall.

Bid: The price at which a buyer offers to pay for a security or property.

Blue chip stocks: Stocks with good investment qualities. They are usually common shares of well-established companies with good earnings records and regular dividend payments that are known nationally for the quality and wide acceptance of their products and services.

Bond: A debt instrument issued by governments and corporations. A bond is a promise by the issuer to pay the full amount on maturity plus interest payments at regular intervals.

Broker: An agent who handles the public's orders to buy and sell securities, commodities, or other property. A commission is charged for this service.

Bull market: A stock market whose index has been rising in value. A "bullish" investor believes share prices will rise.

Callable: This is a feature of a bond or preferred stock that allows the issuing company the right to redeem the issue prior to the maturity date at a previously specified price.

Canadian Bond Rating Service (CBRS): An independent evaluation of credit worthiness whereby the quality of an issuing company is measured and rated on a system of P1 (highest) to P5 (lowest).

Capital gain: A profit made on the sale of an asset when the market price rises above the purchase price. Profit that is made from the sale of real estate, stocks, bonds, or other capital assets.

Capital loss: Loss that is incurred from the sale of capital assets at a price below the purchase price.

Capital property: Securities or physical property such as real estate, that may increase or decrease in value and on which a gain or loss may be realized on deposition.

Carry-forward: The difference between a person's RRSP contribution limit and the amount actually contributed. Unused contributions may be carried forward for up to seven years.

Cash flow: Income from all sources. Net income for a stated period plus all deductions that are not paid out in actual cash such as depreciation, deferred income taxes, and amortization.

Caveat emptor: A Latin credo that means "Let the buyer beware."

Certificate of deposit (CD): A time deposit with a specified maturity date.

Collateral: Property or securities pledged by a borrower as backing for a loan.

Commercial paper: Short-term, unsecured promissory notes issued by corporations to finance their short-term needs. Commercial paper is usually sold on a discount basis and has a maturity at the time of issuance not exceeding twelve months.

Commission: The broker's or agent's fee for buying or selling securities for a client.

Common share: A class of stock that represents ownership or equity in a company. Common shares sometimes carry a voting privilege and entitle the holder to a share in the company's profits, usually issued in the form of dividends.

Compounding: Reinvesting interest as capital to earn additional interest.

Compound interest: Interest earned on the initial investment as well as on interest previously earned. Interest may be compounded daily, weekly, monthly, quarterly, semi-annually, or annually for compounding purposes.

Consumer price index: A statistical device that measures the increase in the cost of living for consumers.

It is sometimes used to illustrate the extent that prices in general have risen, or the amount of inflation that has taken place.

Convertible: A condition attached to a security, such as a bond, debenture, or preferred share which may be exchanged by the owner, usually for the common stock of the same company, in accordance with the terms of the conversion privilege.

Convertible term: Term life insurance which can be converted to any permanent or whole life policy without evidence of insurability subject to time limitations.

Cum-dividend: ("With Dividend.") The purchaser of shares trading cum-dividend will receive the declared dividend.

Cyclical stock: A stock within a particular industry sector that is particularly sensitive to swings in economic conditions.

Debenture: An unsecured bond. A certificate of indebtedness of a government or company backed only by the general credit of the issuer and unsecured by mortgage or lien on any specific asset.

Decreasing term: Insurance benefits reduced monthly or yearly with the premium remaining constant.

Deferred annuity: An annuity under which payments begin some time after the annuity is purchased. Benefits begin after a given number of years or at optional ages specified in a contract purchased with a single premium or annual premiums.

Deferred Profit Sharing Plan (DPSP): A plan that enables a company to share profits on a tax assisted basis with non-shareholder employees. Contributions to a DPSP are tax-deductible for the company and tax-sheltered for the employee until withdrawn from the plan.

Defined benefit plan: A company-sponsored pension plan in which retirement benefits are usually determined by a formula based on salary and years of service. In most cases, these plans are "contributory" because employees must make regular contributions. The alternative, in which the company pays the total bill, is "non-contributory."

Discount: The amount by which a bond or note sells below par value.

Diversification: Spreading investment risk by buying different issues in different companies in different industries and/or in different countries.

Dividend: A portion of a company's profit paid out to common and preferred shareholders, the amount having been decided on by the company's board of directors. A dividend may be in the form of cash or in additional stock. A preferred dividend is usually a fixed amount, while a common dividend fluctuates according to the earnings of the company.

Dividend reinvestment: Some stocks and virtually all mutual fund companies allow dividends to be reinvested to purchase additional shares or units.

Dollar cost averaging: Buying securities at regular intervals with specific and equal dollar amounts. This results in lowering the average price of securities because more are purchased when the prices are depressed than when then they are high.

Earned income: For tax purposes, loosely defined as the total of income from employment, self-employment, pensions and alimony. Losses from rentals and losses incurred in self-employment are deducted from these amounts.

Earnings per share: A company's net earnings less preferred share dividends, divided by the number of common shares outstanding.

Equities: Those shares issued by a company that represent ownership in the company. Common and preferred shares are usually called equity stock.

Equity funds: Mutual funds that invest in common and preferred shares.

Estate: All assets owned by an individual at the time of death. The estate includes all funds, personal effects, interests in business enterprises, titles to property, real estate and chattels, and evidence of ownership, such as stocks, bonds, and mortgages owned, and notes receivable.

Excess contributions: RRSP contributions that exceed your annual limit and that connot be claimed as a tax deduction.

Ex-dividend: (Without Dividend) The purchaser of shares quoted ex-dividend is not entitled to receive an already-declared dividend.

Face value: The value of a bond or debenture that appears on its face. Usually this is the amount that is due on maturity.

Fixed-income funds: Mutual funds that invest in mortgages, bonds, or a combination of both. Mortgages and bonds are issued at a fixed rate of interest and are known as fixed-income securities.

Fixed term: A stipulated term of a contract. In the case of annuities, fixed terms are generally from the date of purchase to age 90.

Floor-trader: A brokerage firm employee who works on the stock exchange floor and is responsible for executing buy and sell orders on behalf of the firm's clients.

Front-end load: The sales commission or acquisition fees charged by the salesperson on the initial purchase are based on the total value of the units purchased. The fees range from 2% to 9% but most often average 4% to 5% on most purchases.

Future value: The amount that an investment will be worth at some future time if invested at a constant rate of interest.

Futures: Exchange-traded contracts that give the holder the right to buy or sell a certain commodity, currency, or financial instrument at a specified price at a specified period of time.

GIC: Guaranteed investment certificate, a deposit certificate usually issued by a trust company or other financial institution and covering a specific period. An interest-paying investment in which the investor commits for a specified term for a specified rate of interest, usually anywhere from 30 days to 5 years.

Growth stock: A company whose earnings are expected to grow faster than the average rise in similar businesses and prosperity as a whole.

Guaranteed income funds: Mutual funds that invest in and earn interest on term deposits and guaranteed investment certificates.

Guaranteed term: The length of time for which annuity payments are guaranteed. If the annuitant dies before the specified term, payments will continue to the beneficiary until the term ends.

Hedge: A position taken in commodities or securities dealings to assure a sale or purchase at a future date at a specific price, or to counterbalance the sale or purchase of one commodity or security by buying or selling another. The implementation of these strategies, often involving options and futures, is designed to reduce or eliminate the risk of certain investments.

Holograph will: Prepared in your own handwriting and signed by you. Not valid in all areas. Consult your lawyer.

Income splitting: The process of diverting taxable income from an individual in a high tax bracket to one in a lower tax bracket.

Institutional investors: Large investors such as insurance companies, pension funds, trust companies, mutual funds, etc.

Interest: The payments that a borrower is obligated to pay to the lender for the use of a fixed sum of money.

Inter-vivos trust: Created during your lifetime to provide benefits to minimize probate expenses and passing assets directly to your beneficiaries. Often referred to as a living trust.

Intestate: Someone who dies without leaving a valid and operative will.

Investment: The use of money for the purpose of making more money to gain income or increase capital, or both.

Issuer: A corporation or municipality that raises cash through the public sale of bonds or stock.

Joint and last survivor: A type of annuity which pays benefits until both the annuitant and the annuitant's spouse die.

Leverage: Increasing the return on an investment through borrowing or special contract terms. Using borrowed funds to maximize the rate of return on investment. Keep in mind, however, that losses can mount very quickly if your investment starts losing money.

Life income fund (LIF): A non-annuity investment vehicle created specifically to access locked-in RRSP and pension plan savings to provide retirement income.

Limit order: An order to buy or sell securities at a price stipulated by the client, whereby the order can only be executed at the specified price or a better one.

Listed stock: The stock of a company that is traded on a stock exchange.

Liquidity: The ease with which an asset can be sold and converted to the most liquid of assets—cash—without a substantial change in price. It is one of the most important characteristics of a good market.

Load: A sales charge on each share or unit of a mutual fund. It covers the sales commissions paid to the broker or distribution company plus other administration and selling expenses. The load may range from 1% to 9%. There are also "no-load" funds.

Locked-in retirement account (LIRA): An account set up to receive locked-in funds from a registered pension plan. Funds in locked-in RRSPs or LIRAs can be transferred to a LIF at or prior to age 71.

Management company: The business entity that establishes and manages the mutual fund(s); each a separate entity with its own board of directors or trustee(s).

Management expense ratio: An accounting of all costs of operating a fund, expressed as a percentage of the net assets of the fund.

Management fee: The sum paid to the investment company for investment management and administrative services; typically expressed as a percentage of assets.

Margin: The percent of a portfolio that is owned. When trading on margin, investors must borrow to finance the leveraged part of their portfolios. When you borrow money from your broker to invest in stocks or bonds, "margin" is the percentage of the market value of the security you must provide.

Margin account: A special type of brokerage account that allows the client to pay a portion of the price of the securities and borrow the balance from the broker. The word "margin" refers to the difference between the market value of the stock and the loan which the broker makes against it.

Marginal tax rate: The amount of tax imposed on the next dollar of income earned by the taxpayer. In Canada's progressive system of combined federal and provincial taxes the rate increases as earnings rise.

Market order: An order to buy or sell securities immediately at the best possible price.

Maturity: The date on which a loan or a bond or debenture comes due and is to be paid off.

Money market: Part of the capital market established for short-term borrowing and lending of funds. Money market dealers conduct business over the telephone and trade securities such as short-term (three years or less) government bonds, government treasury bills and commercial paper.

Money market fund: Fixed-income mutual funds that invest in short-term securities (maturing within one year).

Money purchase plan: A pension plan in which employees purchase their future retirement benefits. A company may also contribute to the plan, but the benefits that each employee receives are related to the contributions, not to a formula. Also called a "defined-contribution plan."

Monthly income receipts (MIR): designed to provide monthly income, liquidity, and attractive interest.

Mortgage: A legal instrument given by a borrower to the lender entitling the lender to take over pledged property if conditions of the loan are not met.

Mortgage backed securities (MBS): provide higher yields than other savings options by investing in first mortgages on residential properties.

Mutual fund: A pooled group of investment assets that provides diversified holdings and professional management to investors. The total value of the investment is subdivided in equal shares and distributed among fund holders in proportion to their dollar investment. An open-ended investment company, which combines the money of many people whose investment goals are similar and invests this money in a wide variety of securities.

Mutual fund switching privileges: Allow an investor to switch out of and into a different fund(s) within the same family of funds at very low or no commission.

Net asset value per share (NAVPS): Used in reference to mutual fund shares, net asset value is the total market value of all securities owned by the fund less its liabilities divided by the number of units outstanding.

Net cash flow: Your overall direction of cash flow or money flow.

Net earnings: The profits after all expenses and taxes are deducted.

New issue: A stock or bond sold by a corporation for the first time. Proceeds may be used to retire outstanding securities of the company, for new plant or equipment, or for additional working capital. New debt issues are also offered by government bodies.

No-load fund: A mutual fund where no sales or redemption charges are levied for buying or selling its units.

No par value: A description of a company's stock. Prior to 1917, the capital stocks of all companies in Canada had a par value. In that year the Dominion Companies Act permitted the issuance of stock without par value. The par value of a share of stock is usually of little significance compared to the book value and the market value.

Open order: An order to buy or sell a security at a specific price which is valid until filled by the trader or cancelled by the client.

Option: A device used to speculate or hedge in securities markets. Buying a "call" option gives an investor the right to buy 100 shares of a stock at a certain price within a specified time; buying a "put" option allows an investor to sell a stock under the same conditions.

Over-the-counter: This is the market for securities not listed on one of the exchanges.

Par (or face) value: The amount returned to bondholders at maturity — $5000 for most municipal bonds and $1000 for most government and corporate bonds. The stated face value of a bond or stock as assigned by the company's charter and expressed as dollars and cents per share. Par value of a common stock usually has little relationship to the current market value and so "no par value" stock is now the norm. Par value of a preferred stock is significant as it indicates the dollar amount of assets each preferred share would be entitled to in the event of winding up the company.

Penny stock: Low-priced, often speculative issues selling at less than $1 per share.

Pension adjustment (PA): The total value of contributions made by you or your employer to an employer sponsored pension plan. The difference between your PA and the allowable RRSP limit is your contribution room.

Personal net worth: The difference between your assets versus your liabilities.

Portability: The ability to take the benefits promised by one company's pension plan and switch them to a second company's plan, or another approved plan such as an RRSP, when changing jobs.

Portfolio: A group of securities held or owned for investment purposes by an individual or institutional investor. An investor's portfolio may contain common and preferred shares, bonds, options, and other types of securities.

Portfolio manager: A financial specialist hired by the management company to invest money in various securities.

Power of attorney: Give signing authority for your affairs to spouse or other trusted person in case of accident or other circumstances that leave you unable to manage your own affairs.

Preferred share: A class of share capital that entitles its owners to certain preferences over common shareholders such as a fixed rate of prior dividend and return of the stock's par value in a liquidation. Preferred shares usually only have voting rights when their dividends are not being paid.

Premium: The amount paid to the option seller or writer for assuming the risk that he or she may have to buy (for puts) an underlying security for more than the market price or sell (for calls) at less than the market price. The amount by which a preferred stock or bond may sell above its par value. In the case of a new issue of bonds or stocks, premium is the amount the market price rises over the original selling price. May also refer to that part of redemption price of a bond or preferred stock in excess of par.

Prescribed annuity: Provides regular payments of principal and interest to provide the annuitant with a guaranteed income and purchased from non-registered funds.

Present value: The current worth of an amount to be received in the future.

Price-earnings ratio: The price of a stock divided by annual share profit, used to indicate whether a stock is relatively expensive or inexpensive. The market price of a common stock divided by annual earnings per share. Also called P/E ratio or P/E multiple. For instance, if a company's net earnings amount to $1 million and it has one million shares outstanding, its earnings per share are one $1; if its shares are trading at $10, then its P/E ratio is 10 to 1. It indicates what investors are willing to pay for one year of a company's earnings per share.

Principal: The amount of money lent or borrowed.

Prospectus: A legal document describing a new issue of securities for sale to the public which is prepared in accordance with provincial securities commission regulations. A mutual fund prospectus contains information regarding the fund's investment objectives and restrictions, management fees, tax considerations, and all other details pertinent to the fund.

Purchase fund: A method whereby the company purchases a stated number of shares each year, but only below par value. This helps to support the market price of the shares.

Purchase plan: An arrangement that allows an investor to purchase mutual fund units on a regular basis.

Rate of Growth of Investable Capital (ROGI):—a financial concept designed to make savings and investment strategies easier.

Real rate of return: The stated rate of return less both the inflation rate tax considerations and the risk premium.

Record date: The date on which you must be registered on the books of the company as a shareholder, in order to receive a declared dividend or to participate in voting, etc., as a shareholder.

Redemption: The right of a unit holder to sell some or all of his/her units back to the investment fund at the current net asset value per unit.

Redemption price: The price at which bonds or preferred shares may be redeemed. The price is fixed at the time the securities are issued.

Registered Education Savings Plan (RESP): A savings program for post-secondary education that earns tax-sheltered income. It is taxable when taken out by the beneficiary of the plan who is generally in a lower tax bracket, if in a tax bracket at all, at the time of applying the funds for further education.

Registered Pension Plan (RPP): A private pension plan usually established by an employer on behalf of its employees to provide for their retirement years. There are two basic types of private pension plans, defined benefit plans and money purchase plans (also referred to as deferred contribution plans).

Registered Retirement Income Fund (RRIF): A non-annuity investment vehicle for maturing RRSPs. One of the options available to RRSP holders upon cashing in their retirement funds at age 71 or sooner. RRIFs generally provide for a series of payments which increase each year until the holder reaches age 90.

Registered Retirement Savings Plan (RRSP):. A savings program approved by Revenue Canada that permits tax-deferred saving for retirement purposes. Contributions to an RRSP are tax-deductible. Earnings on contributions are sheltered from tax while they remain in the plan.

Renewable term: Term life insurance policies which may be renewed at the rate for the attained age without evidence of insurability.

Retractable shares: Usually applies to preferred shares of a company whereby the company can buy back the shares at a stated price on a certain date.

Return: The amount of income, in dollars, you receive from an investment.

Reverse mortgage: A loan against the equity in your home used to purchase an annuity to provide you with regular monthly income.

Right: Issued by a company to existing shareholders. A right entitles you to buy additional shares at a specified price over a specified period in proportion to the number of shares you already own.

Risk: The possibility that your investment will not achieve its expected return. The higher the potential reward, the greater the risk that is involved.

Self-directed RRSP: An RRSP whose investments are controlled by the plan holder. A self-directed RRSP may include stocks, bonds, home mortgages, or a number of other types of investments approved by Revenue Canada.

Sinking fund: A method whereby the company purchases a given percentage of its bonds or shares as per agreement in the trust indenture or prospectus. This provides the investor with some degree of liquidity, knowing that the company must purchase shares each year.

Speculative stocks: High risk area of the market that provides only a handful of winners, but many losers.

Spousal RRSP contribution: A contribution by a taxpayer to an RRSP held by his or her spouse. The amount is considered a portion of the contributor's yearly RRSP limit and is subject to a tax deduction on the contributor's tax return but remains part of the spouse's plan.

Stock yield: The percentage of the dividend paid in relation to the price of the stock. For example, a stock selling at $40 a share with an annual dividend of $2 a share, yields 5%.

Strip bonds: Bonds from which the interest coupon has been detached and sold separately. The two units, the interest-bearing coupon and the underlying principal, are sold with significant discounts to face value.

Tax deferral: The postponing of income taxes until a later date through various legal methods.

Tax shelter: An investment that, by government regulation, can be made with untaxed or partly taxed dollars. The creation of tax losses in order to offset an individual's taxable income from other sources thereby reduces tax liability.

Taxable income: The amount of your annual income that is used to calculate how much income tax must be paid; your total earnings for the year minus deductions.

Term deposit: Similar to a guaranteed investment certificate. An interest-paying investment under which the investor commits funds for a specified term at a specified rate of interest.

Term insurance: A form of life insurance issued for the period of years specified in the contract.

Term to redemption: The number of years until the company can pay off your security at a stipulated price and exercisable at the company's option.

Term to retraction: The number of years until the company must return your principal investment at a stipulated price and exercisable at the investor's option.

Testamentary trust: A trust that is established by a will. The will may state that particular assets on property are to be held in trust for some person or persons. Most often you would choose a trustee to manage this trust and you would state your desires in your will.

Transfer fees: Most mutual funds charge fees for transfers between funds and for RESPs, RRIFs, RRSPs, and regular investment or withdrawal programs.

Treasury bills: Short-term debt securities sold by governments for usually three months to one year. They carry no stated interest rate, but trade at a discount to the face value of the T-bill. The discount represents the return.

Trust: An instrument placing ownership of property in the name of one person, called a trustee, to be held by the trustee for the use and benefit of some other person.

Unit: In mutual funds, a unit represents a portion, or share, of the total value of the fund. Investors purchase a number of units and the unit value fluctuates with the net asset value of the fund.

Universal life: An interest-sensitive form of life insurance indexed to money market yields, offering variable cash values and mobility between permanent and term life insurance plans.

Warrant: Gives the holder the right to buy a security at a specified price within a specified period of time. Warrants often are "attached" to new securities issues of a company as an added inducement for prospective investors.

Whole life: Life insurance policies that provide both life insurance and cash value. The cash value results from a deliberate premium overcharge in the early years of the policy.

Yield: The amount of interest or dividend paid on a loan or an investment, expressed as a percentage. The yield on a stock is calculated by dividing the dividend by the current market price. This is also called "rate of return."

Index

FKI

Specialists in Financial and Pre-retirement Education

SEMINARS ◆ WORKSHOPS ◆ TRAINING

Distributors of the Andex Chart for Canadian Investors

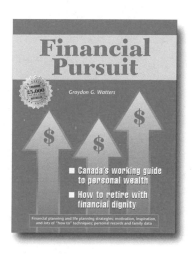

TOPICS

Financial Planning	Tax Planning	Housing and Real Estate
Setting Goals	Asset Allocation Strategies	Maximizing Use of Leisure Time
Designing Action Plans	Mutual Funds	Second Careers
Developing a Positive Attitude	Selecting a Financial Planner	Volunteerism
Handling Procrastination	Employer Pension Plans	Travel
Power of Compounding	Social Security Plans	Wellness Issues
Paying Yourself First	RRSPs	Relationships
Cash Management	Annuities, RRIFs, and LIFs	Creating a Vital Retirement Lifestyle
Designing Statements	Wills and Estate Planning	Retiring With Financial Dignity

Financial Knowledge Inc.
70 Nably Court, Scarborough, Ontario M1B 2K9
Tel. (416) 292-7020 Fax (416) 292-2064

FKI Financial Knowledge Inc.

Corporate Objectives

FKI is committed to becoming the leading firm in financial planning and pre-retirement education in Canada. We are achieving our goal through the design, development, and delivery of high quality educational programs and services that help individuals prepare for a retirement in which their lifestyle and financial goals will be achieved.

Seminars and Workshops

Our goals are to educate participants in the lifetime skills of financial self-management; to motivate the individual to take action to secure a rewarding future; and to provide the tools and strategies needed to achieve financial independence and a fulfilling retirement.

Our two major programs include:

1-Day Financial Planning Workshop to address the following type of needs:
- financial self-management skills and techniques
- investment and asset allocation strategies
- pre-retirement preparation and planning
- creating a happy, healthy, lifestyle.

2-Day Financial & Lifestyle Planning Workshop in addition to the topics covered in the 1-Day Financial Planning Workshop covers many other topics such as:
- lifestyle and wellness issues
- attitudes towards retirement
- utilization of time
- human support systems
- personal fulfillment
- six powers of success.

Presentations are sponsored by employers for groups of employees, by professional advisors for their clients, and by professional associations for their members.

For more information on our corporate seminars and workshops please contact:

FKI Financial Knowledge Inc.
70 Nably Court
Scarborough, Ontario
M1B 2K9

Telephone: (416) 292-7020
Fax: (416) 292-2064

Financial Pursuit

Perhaps the greatest gift that you could give to someone else
is their own personal copy of Financial Pursuit.
The book makes a great gift for those significant others in your
life: son, daughter, niece, nephew, friend, or business associate.

Financial Pursuit is the perfect resource for all Canadians
from the time they begin their working careers until they retire.

Please send me _____ copies of *Financial Pursuit* at the special price of $29.95 each.
(price includes GST and shipping)

Method of Payment

I have enclosed a cheque made payable to Financial Knowledge Inc. in the amount of $_____.

OR

Please debit my visa credit card in the amount $_____

Visa #:_____ Card Expiry Date: _____

Name of Cardholder: _____

Signature of Cardholder: _____

Shipping Instructions

Full Name: _____

Address: _____

_____

City: _____ Province: _____ Postal Code: _____

Telephone: (   ) Fax: (   )

We offer a discount for orders of 10 or more books. Please write, call, or fax us for details.

Distributed in Western Canada by:

Todd & Associates Financial Knowledge Inc.
305, 4625 Varsity Place N.W., Suite 364, Calgary
AB T3A 5A4 Tel: (403) 547-0328 Fax (403) 547-7828